The Ministers Manual for 1982

Holy Holy Land
The Treasure Chest
Words of Life
Our American Heritage
1010 Sermon Illustrations from the Bible
Worship Resources for the Christian Year
Stories on Stone: A Book of American Epitaphs
American Epitaphs: Grave and Humorous
The Funeral Encyclopedia
A Treasury of Story-Sermons for Children
Treasury of Sermon Illustrations
Selected Poems of John Oxenham
Poems of Edwin Markham
Notable Sermons from Protestant Pulpits
Treasury of Poems for Worship and Devotion
88 Evangelistic Sermons
Speaker's Resources from Contemporary Literature
Christmas in Our Hearts (with Charles L. Allen)
Candle, Star, and Christmas Tree (with Charles L. Allen)
When Christmas Came to Bethlehem (with Charles L. Allen)
The Charles L. Allen Treasury
Lenten-Easter Sourcebook
365 Table Graces for the Christian Home
Speaker's Illustrations for Special Days
Table of the Lord
The Eternal Light
Twentieth Century Bible Commentary (co-editor)
Prayers for Public Worship (co-editor)
Christmas (with Charles L. Allen)
A Complete Sourcebook for the Lord's Supper

FIFTY-SEVENTH ANNUAL ISSUE

MINISTERS
MANUAL
(Doran's)

1982 EDITION

Edited by
CHARLES L. WALLIS

1817

HARPER & ROW, PUBLISHERS, SAN FRANCISCO

Cambridge, Hagerstown, New York, Philadelphia
London, Mexico City, São Paulo, Sydney

Editors of THE MINISTERS MANUAL

G.B.F. Hallock, D.D., 1926–1958
M.K.W. Heicher, Ph.D., 1943–1968
Charles L. Wallis, M.A., M.Div., 1969–

THE MINISTERS MANUAL FOR 1982
Copyright © 1981 by Charles L. Wallis. All rights reserved.
Printed in the United States of America. For information
address Harper & Row, Publishers, Inc., 10 East 53rd Street,
New York, N.Y. 10022. Published simultaneously in Canada
by Fitzhenry & Whiteside Limited, Toronto.

FIRST EDITION

The Library of Congress has cataloged the first printing of
this serial as follows:

The ministers manual: a study and pulpit guide. 1926–
New York, Harper.

V. 21–23 cm. annual.
Title varies: 1926–46, Doran's ministers manual (cover
title, 1947: The Doran's ministers manual)
Editor: 1926– G. B. F. Hallock (with M. K. W. Heicher,
1942–

1. Sermons—Outlines. 2. Homiletical illustrations.
I. Hallock, Gerard Benjamin Fleet, 1856– ed.
    BV4223.M5   251.058   25–21658 rev*
                        [r48n2]

ISBN 0–06–069238–3

81 82 83 84 85 10 9 8 7 6 5 4 3 2 1

PREFACE

The publication of the 1982 edition of *The Ministers Manual* marks the fifty-seventh milestone in the publishing of this worship and homiletic resource series.

Like the earlier volumes in this annual series, the 1982 edition represents something old and something new.

A number of the preaching and parish features in this edition were included in the earliest editions, and the format has remained relatively the same. Then as now *The Ministers Manual* centered in the redemptive life, teaching, death, and resurrection of the Lord Jesus.

But there is that which is new. The content of each successive volume is new, containing materials not previously included. Many of the writers have not contributed before. The preaching emphases reflect the changes in a dynamic and always relevant gospel.

Introduced fifty-seven years ago as a sourcebook for pastors, *The Ministers Manual* today is used not only by church professionals but also by church laity workers, Sunday school teachers, seminary students, missionaries, youth leaders, chaplains, and others.

Letters from readers indicate the book's usefulness in a variety of ways.

A senior in a private religious school writes that as chairman of the daily chapel program he has had little difficulty in soliciting student leaders when they know of the resources available in *The Ministers Manual.*

A superintendent of a home for the elderly says that the residents asked for a morning devotional period, adding: "The task fell to me, although I'd never before preached or prayed in public. I couldn't carry on this helpful work without *The Ministers Manual.*"

A native preacher in an African village uses *The Ministers Manual* in his Bible study group and then dispatches his students to other villages on preaching missions.

A woman asked that a copy be sent to her husband for Christmas. The package was addressed to the Rev. So-and-So. The recipient replied that he was not a minister but a businessman who began each day by using *The Ministers Manual* for his private devotions.

The editor is appreciative of writers who have contributed manuscripts or permitted reprinting of extracts from their sermons and other writings, to the editorial staff at Harper & Row for experienced counsel, and to those who assisted in the arduous chores of preparing the manuscript for publication. The editor is fortunate to be a member of a college faculty, because always nearby are students and secretaries who are willing to type and file.

Rev. Charles L. Wallis

Keuka College
Keuka Park, NY 14478

CONTENTS

SECTION I. General Aids and Resources

Civil Year Calendars

1982

```
        JANUARY                  FEBRUARY                  MARCH                   APRIL
 S  M  T  W  T  F  S      S  M  T  W  T  F  S      S  M  T  W  T  F  S      S  M  T  W  T  F  S
             1  2                 1  2  3  4  5  6             1  2  3  4  5  6             1  2  3
 3  4  5  6  7  8  9      7  8  9 10 11 12 13      7  8  9 10 11 12 13      4  5  6  7  8  9 10
10 11 12 13 14 15 16     14 15 16 17 18 19 20     14 15 16 17 18 19 20     11 12 13 14 15 16 17
17 18 19 20 21 22 23     21 22 23 24 25 26 27     21 22 23 24 25 26 27     18 19 20 21 22 23 24
24 25 26 27 28 29 30     28                       28 29 30 31              25 26 27 28 29 30
31

          MAY                      JUNE                     JULY                    AUGUST
 S  M  T  W  T  F  S      S  M  T  W  T  F  S      S  M  T  W  T  F  S      S  M  T  W  T  F  S
                   1                 1  2  3  4  5                1  2  3      1  2  3  4  5  6  7
 2  3  4  5  6  7  8      6  7  8  9 10 11 12      4  5  6  7  8  9 10      8  9 10 11 12 13 14
 9 10 11 12 13 14 15     13 14 15 16 17 18 19     11 12 13 14 15 16 17     15 16 17 18 19 20 21
16 17 18 19 20 21 22     20 21 22 23 24 25 26     18 19 20 21 22 23 24     22 23 24 25 26 27 28
23 24 25 26 27 28 29     27 28 29 30              25 26 27 28 29 30 31     29 30 31
30 31

       SEPTEMBER                  OCTOBER                 NOVEMBER                 DECEMBER
 S  M  T  W  T  F  S      S  M  T  W  T  F  S      S  M  T  W  T  F  S      S  M  T  W  T  F  S
          1  2  3  4                    1  2                1  2  3  4  5  6                1  2  3  4
 5  6  7  8  9 10 11      3  4  5  6  7  8  9      7  8  9 10 11 12 13      5  6  7  8  9 10 11
12 13 14 15 16 17 18     10 11 12 13 14 15 16     14 15 16 17 18 19 20     12 13 14 15 16 17 18
19 20 21 22 23 24 25     17 18 19 20 21 22 23     21 22 23 24 25 26 27     19 20 21 22 23 24 25
26 27 28 29 30           24 25 26 27 28 29 30     28 29 30                 26 27 28 29 30 31
                         31
```

1983

```
        JANUARY                  FEBRUARY                  MARCH                   APRIL
 S  M  T  W  T  F  S      S  M  T  W  T  F  S      S  M  T  W  T  F  S      S  M  T  W  T  F  S
                   1                 1  2  3  4  5                1  2  3  4  5                   1  2
 2  3  4  5  6  7  8      6  7  8  9 10 11 12      6  7  8  9 10 11 12      3  4  5  6  7  8  9
 9 10 11 12 13 14 15     13 14 15 16 17 18 19     13 14 15 16 17 18 19     10 11 12 13 14 15 16
16 17 18 19 20 21 22     20 21 22 23 24 25 26     20 21 22 23 24 25 26     17 18 19 20 21 22 23
23 24 25 26 27 28 29     27 28                    27 28 29 30 31           28 29 30
30 31

          MAY                      JUNE                     JULY                    AUGUST
 S  M  T  W  T  F  S      S  M  T  W  T  F  S      S  M  T  W  T  F  S      S  M  T  W  T  F  S
 1  2  3  4  5  6  7                 1  2  3  4                1  2      1  2  3  4  5  6
 8  9 10 11 12 13 14      5  6  7  8  9 10 11      3  4  5  6  7  8  9      7  8  9 10 11 12 13
15 16 17 18 19 20 21     12 13 14 15 16 17 18     10 11 12 13 14 15 16     14 15 16 17 18 19 20
22 23 24 25 26 27 28     19 20 21 22 23 24 25     17 18 19 20 21 22 23     21 22 23 24 25 26 27
29 30 31                 26 27 28 29 30           24 25 26 27 28 29 30     28 29 30 31
                                                  31

       SEPTEMBER                  OCTOBER                 NOVEMBER                 DECEMBER
 S  M  T  W  T  F  S      S  M  T  W  T  F  S      S  M  T  W  T  F  S      S  M  T  W  T  F  S
             1  2  3                       1                1  2  3  4  5                1  2  3
 4  5  6  7  8  9 10      2  3  4  5  6  7  8      6  7  8  9 10 11 12      4  5  6  7  8  9 10
11 12 13 14 15 16 17      9 10 11 12 13 14 15     13 14 15 16 17 18 19     11 12 13 14 15 16 17
18 19 20 21 22 23 24     16 17 18 19 20 21 22     20 21 22 23 24 25 26     18 19 20 21 22 23 24
25 26 27 28 29 30        23 24 25 26 27 28 29     27 28 29 30              25 26 27 28 29 30 31
                         30 31
```

1

Church and Civil Calendar for 1982

JANUARY

1   New Year's Day
    The Name of Jesus
5   Twelfth Night
6   Epiphany
13 The Baptism of Jesus
15 Martin Luther King, Jr.'s, Birthday
17 Missionary Day
18 Confession of St. Peter
18–29 Week of Prayer for Christian Unity
19 Robert E. Lee's Birthday
25 Conversion of St. Paul

FEBRUARY

1   National Freedom Day
2   Presentation of Jesus in the Temple
    Groundhog Day
3   Four Chaplains Memorial Day
7   Race Relations Sunday
12 Abraham Lincoln's Birthday
14 St. Valentine's Day
14–21 Brotherhood Week
15 Susan B. Anthony Day
18 Presidents' Day
21 The Transfiguration
22 George Washington's Birthday
23 Shrove Tuesday
24 Ash Wednesday
28 First Sunday in Lent

MARCH

5   World Day of Prayer
7   Second Sunday in Lent
9   Purim
14 Third Sunday in Lent
17 St. Patrick's Day
21 Fourth Sunday in Lent
    Passion Sunday
25 The Annunciation

APRIL

4   Palm Sunday
    Passion Sunday (alternate)
4–10 Holy Week
8   Maundy Thursday
    Passover

9   Good Friday
11 Easter
14 Pan American Day
18 Easter (Orthodox)
    Low Sunday
25 St. Mark, Evangelist
30 Arbor Day

MAY

1   Law Day
    Loyalty Day
    May Day
    St. Philip and St. James, Apostles
2–9 National Family Week
9   Festival of the Christian Home
    Mother's Day
15 Armed Forces Day
16 Rural Life Sunday
20 Ascension Day
22 National Maritime Day
24 Victoria Day (Canada)
28 Shabuoth
30 Pentecost (Whitsunday)
31 Memorial Day

JUNE

6   Trinity Sunday
10 Corpus Christi
11 St. Barnabas, Apostle
13 Children's Day
14 Flag Day
20 Father's Day
24 Nativity of St. John the Baptist
29 St. Peter and St. Paul, Apostles

JULY

4   Independence Day
7   Dominion Day (Canada)
22 St. Mary Magdalene
25 St. James the Elder, Apostle

AUGUST

2   Civic Holiday (Canada)
6   The Transfiguration (alternate)
15 Mary, the Mother of Jesus
19 National Aviation Day
24 St. Bartholomew, Apostle

SEPTEMBER

5 Labor Sunday
6 Labor Day
12 Rally Day
17 Citizenship Day
   General von Steuben Memorial Day
18 Rosh Hashana
21 St. Matthew, Apostle and Evangelist
24 American Indian Day
26 Senior Citizens Day
27 Yom Kippur
28 Francis Willard Day
29 St. Michael and All Angels

OCTOBER

2 Sukkoth
3 World Communion Sunday
4 Child Health Day
10 Laity Sunday
   Sinhath Torah
11 Columbus Day
   Thanksgiving Day (Canada)
15 World Poetry Day
18 St. Luke, Evangelist
24 United Nations Day
29 St. Simon and St. Jude, Apostles
31 Reformation Day
   Halloween
   National UNICEF Day

NOVEMBER

1 All Saints' Day
2 All Souls' Day
5 World Community Day
11 Armistice Day
   Remembrance Day (Canada)
   Veterans Day
12 Elizabeth Cady Stanton Day
14 Stewardship Day
21 Bible Sunday
   Thanksgiving Sunday
24 Thanksgiving Day
28 First Sunday in Advent
30 St. Andrew, Apostle

DECEMBER

5 Second Sunday in Advent
10 Human Rights Day
11 Hanukkah
12 Third Sunday in Advent
15 Bill of Rights Day
17 Wright Brothers Day
19 Fourth Sunday in Advent
21 St. Thomas, Apostle
25 Christmas
26 Boxing Day (Canada)
   St. Stephen, Deacon and Martyr
27 St. John, Apostle and Evangelist
28 The Holy Innocents, Martyrs
31 New Year's Eve
   Watch Night

Lectionary for 1982

The following scripture lessons, with occasional alterations according to denominational preferences, are commended for use in public worship by various Protestant churches and the Roman Catholic church and include first, second, and gospel readings according to Cycle B from January 1 to November 25 and according to Cycle C from November 28 to December 31.

CHRISTMASTIDE

January 1 (New Year's Day): Eccl. 3:1–13; Col. 2:1–7; Matt. 9:14–17.
January 3: Isa. 60:1–5; Rev. 21:22–22:2; Luke 2:21–24.

EPIPHANY

January 6 (Epiphany): Isa. 60:1–6; Eph. 3: 1–6; Matt. 2:1–12.
January 10: Isa. 61:1–4; Acts 11:4–18; Mark 1:4–11.
January 17: I Sam. 3:1–10; I Cor. 6:12–20; John 1:35–42.
January 18–25 (Week of Prayer for Christian Unity): Isa. 35:3–10; I Cor. 3:1–11; Matt. 28:16–20.
January 24: Jonah 3:1–5, 10; I Cor. 7:29–31; Mark 1:14–22.
January 31: Deut. 18:15–22; I Cor. 7:32–35; Mark 1:21–28.
February 7: Job 7:1–7; I Cor. 9:16–19, 22–23; Mark 1:29–39.

February 14: Lev. 13:1-2, 44-46; I Cor.
10:31 to 11:1; Mark 1:40-45.
February 21: Isa. 43:18-25; II Cor. 1:18-
22; Mark 2:1-12.

LENT

February 24 (Ash Wednesday): Isa. 58:
3-12; James 1:12-18; Mark 2:15-20.
February 28: Gen. 9:8-15; I Pet. 3:18-22;
Mark 1:12-15.
March 7: Gen. 22:1-2, 9-13; Rom. 8:31-
39; Mark 9:1-9.
March 14: Exod. 20:1-3, 7-8, 12-17; I
Cor. 1:22-25; John 4:19-26.
March 21: II Chron. 36:14-21; Eph. 2:
1-10; John 3:14-21.
March 28: Jer. 31:31-34; Heb. 5:7-10;
John 12:20-33.

HOLY WEEK

April 4 (Palm Sunday): Zech. 9:9-12; Heb.
12:1-6; Mark 11:1-11.
April 5 (Monday): Isa. 50:4-10; Heb. 9:
11-15; Luke 19:41-48.
April 6 (Tuesday): Isa. 42:1-9; I Tim. 6:
11-16; John 12:37-50.
April 7 (Wednesday): Isa. 52:13 to 53:12;
Rom. 5:6-11; Luke 22:1-16.
April 8 (Maundy Thursday): Deut. 16:1-8;
Rev. 1:4-8; Matt. 26:17-30.
April 9 (Good Friday): Lam. 1:7-12; Heb.
10:4-18; Luke 23:33-46.

EASTERTIDE

April 11: Isa. 25:6-9; I Pet. 1:3-9; Mark
16:1-8.
April 18: Acts 4:32-35; I John 5:1-6;
Matt. 28:11-20.
April 25: Acts 3:13-15, 17-19; I John 2:
1-6; Luke 24:36-49.
May 2: Acts 4:8-12; I John 3:1-3; John
10:11-18.
May 9: Acts 9:26-31; I John 3:18-24;
John 15:1-8.
May 16: Acts 10:34-48; I John 4:1-7;
John 15:9-17.
May 20 (Ascension Day): Acts 1:1-11;
Eph. 1:16-23; Luke 24:44-53.
May 23: Acts 1:15-17, 21-26; I John 4:
11-16; John 17:11-19.

PENTECOST

May 30: Joel 2:28-32; Acts 2:1-13; John
16:5-15.
June 6: Isa. 6:1-8; Rom. 8:12-17; John 3:
1-8.
June 13: Deut. 5:12-15; II Cor. 4:6-11;
Mark 2:23 to 3:6.
June 20: Gen. 3:9-15; II Cor. 4:13-5:1;
Mark 3:20-35.
June 27: Ezek. 17:22-24; II Cor. 5:6-10;
Mark 4:26-34.
July 4: Job 38:1-11; II Cor. 5:16-21; Mark
4:35-41; (Independence Day) Isa. 26:
1-8; I Thess. 5:12-23; Mark 12:13-17.
July 11: Gen. 4:3-10; II Cor. 8:7-15;
Mark 5:21-43.
July 18: Ezek. 2:1-5; II Cor. 12:7-10;
Mark 6:1-6.
July 25: Amos 7:12-17; Eph. 1:3-10;
Mark 6:7-13.
August 1: Jer. 23:1-6; Eph. 2:11-18;
Mark 6:30-34.
August 8: II Kings 4:42-44; Eph. 4:1-6,
11-16; John 6:1-15.
August 15: Exod. 16:2-4, 12-15; Eph. 4:
17-24; John 6:24-35.
August 22: I Kings 19:4-8; Eph. 4:30-5:2;
John 6:41-51.
August 29: Prov. 9:1-6; Eph. 5:15-20;
John 6:51-59.
September 5: Josh. 24:14-18; Eph. 5:21-
33; John 6:60-69.
September 12: Deut. 4:1-8; Jas. 1:19-25;
Mark 7:1-8, 14-15, 21-23.
September 19: Isa. 35:4-7; Jas. 2:1-5;
Mark 7:31-37.
September 26: Isa. 50:4-9; Jas. 2:14-18;
Mark 8:27-35.
October 3: Jer. 11:18-20; Jas. 3:13-4:3;
Mark 9:30-37; (World Communion
Sunday) Isa. 25:6-9; Rev. 7:9-17; Luke
24:13-35.
October 10: Num. 11:24-30; Jas. 5:1-6;
Mark 9:38-48.
October 17: Gen. 2:18-24; Heb. 2:9-13;
Mark 10:2-16.
October 24: Prov. 3:13-18; Heb. 4:12-
16; Mark 10:17-27.
October 31: Isa. 53:10-12; Heb. 5:1-10;
Mark 10:46-52; (Reformation Sunday)
Gen. 12:1-4; II Cor. 5:16-21; Matt. 21:
17-22.

November 7: Jer. 31:7-9; Heb. 5:1-6; Mark 10:46-52.

November 14: Deut. 6:1-9; Heb. 7:23-28; Mark 12:28-34.

November 21: I Kings 17:8-16; Heb. 9: 24-28; Mark 12:38-44.

November 25 (Thanksgiving Day): Deut. 26:1-11; Gal. 6:6-10; Luke 17:11-19.

ADVENT

November 28: Jer. 33:14-16; I Thess. 5: 1-6; Luke 21:25-36.

December 5: Isa. 9:2, 6-7; Phil. 1:3-11; Luke 3:1-6.

December 12: Zeph. 3:14-18; Phil. 4:4-9; Luke 3:10-18.

December 19: Micah 5:1-4; Heb. 10:5-10; Luke 1:39-47.

December 24 (Christmas Eve): Zech. 2: 10-13; Phil. 4:4-7; Luke 2:15-20.

CHRISTMASTIDE

December 25: Isa. 52:6-10; Eph. 1:3-10; John 1:1-14.

December 26: Isa. 45:18-22; Rom. 11:33 -12:2; Luke 2:41-52.

Four-Year Church Calendar

	1982	1983	1984	1985
Ash Wednesday	February 24	February 16	March 7	February 20
Palm Sunday	April 4	March 27	April 15	March 31
Good Friday	April 9	April 3	April 20	April 5
Easter	April 11	May 12	April 22	April 7
Ascension Day	May 20	May 22	May 31	May 16
Pentecost	May 30	May 29	June 10	May 26
Trinity Sunday	June 6	June 5	June 17	June 2
Thanksgiving	November 25	November 24	November 23	November 22
Advent Sunday	November 28	November 27	December 2	December 1

Forty-Year Easter Calendar

1982 April 11	1992 April 19	2002 March 31	2012 April 8
1983 April 3	1993 April 11	2003 April 20	2013 March 31
1984 April 22	1994 April 3	2004 April 11	2014 April 20
1985 April 7	1995 April 16	2005 March 27	2015 April 5
1986 March 30	1996 April 7	2006 April 16	2016 March 27
1987 April 19	1997 March 30	2007 April 8	2017 April 16
1988 April 3	1998 April 12	2008 March 23	2018 April 1
1989 March 26	1999 April 4	2009 April 12	2019 April 21
1990 April 15	2000 April 23	2010 April 4	2020 April 12
1991 March 31	2001 April 14	2011 April 24	2021 April 4

Traditional Wedding Anniversary Identifications

1 Paper	7 Wool	13 Lace	35 Coral
2 Cotton	8 Bronze	14 Ivory	40 Ruby
3 Leather	9 Pottery	15 Crystal	45 Sapphire
4 Linen	10 Tin	20 China	50 Gold
5 Wood	11 Steel	25 Silver	55 Emerald
6 Iron	12 Silk	30 Pearl	60 Diamond

Colors Appropriate for Days and Seasons

White. Symbolizes purity, perfection, and joy and identifies festivals marking events, except Good Friday, in the life of Jesus: Christmas, Easter, Eastertide, Ascension Day, Trinity Sunday, All Saints' Day, weddings, funerals.

Red. Symbolizes the Holy Spirit, martyrdom, and the love of God: Pentecost and Sundays following.

Violet. Symbolizes penitence: Advent, Lent.

Green. Symbolizes mission to the world, hope, regeneration, nurture, and growth: Epiphany season, Kingdomtide, Rural Life Sunday, Labor Sunday, Thanksgiving Sunday.

Black. Symbolizes mourning: Good Friday.

Flowers in Season Appropriate for Church Use

January.	Carnation or snowdrop.	**August.**	Gladiolus or poppy.
February.	Violet or primrose.	**September.**	Aster or morning glory.
March.	Jonquil or daffodil.	**October.**	Calendula or cosmos.
April.	Lily, sweet pea, or daisy.	**November.**	Chrysanthemum.
May.	Lily of the valley or hawthorn.	**December.**	Narcissus, holly, or poinsettia.
June.	Rose or honeysuckle.		
July.	Larkspur or water lily.		

Historical, Cultural, and Religious Anniversaries in 1982

10 years (1972). *February 17:* Nixon leaves for China in a "journey for peace" that alters American China policy. *March 22:* Senate approves constitutional amendment banning discrimination against women on the basis of their sex. *March 24:* Britain takes over direct rule in Northern Ireland in bid for peace. *May 14:* Okinawa returned to Japan after American rule for twenty-seven years. *May 22:* Nixon in first visit to Russia by an American president signs strategic arms pact that Senate ratifies on August 3. *June 17:* five apprehended in Watergate break-in. *September 5:* Israeli athletes killed by Arab commandos at Olympic Games in Munich.

25 years (1957). *April 29:* first civil rights legislation since the Reconstruction protects voting rights of blacks. *September 24:* Eisenhower sends federal troops to Little Rock to quell mob and protect school integration. *October 4:* Sputnik I in first orbit by a man-made satellite.

50 years (1932). *January 7:* Stimson Doctrine stipulates that the United States will not recognize gains achieved by armed aggression. *May 29:* Bonus march by World War I veterans on Washington, D.C. Amelia Earhart makes first solo flight across the Atlantic by a woman.

75 years (1907). *March 13:* stock market crash results in financial panic and depression. *November 16:* Oklahoma becomes forty-sixth state. Gandhi leads his first civil disobedience campaign in Africa. Second Hague Peace Conference establishes rules of war.

100 years (1882). Persecution of Jews in Russia forces many to flee to other countries. John D. Rockefeller forms Standard Oil Trust.

150 years (1832). *April 6–August 2:* Black Hawk War pushes Sauk and Fox Indians west of the Mississippi River. Chinese Exclusion Act bans immigration of Chinese laborers.

200 years (1782). *November 30:* Britain recognizes American independence in peace treaty negotiated in Paris.

250 years (1732). *June 9:* royal charter for Georgia granted to James Oglethorpe. Benjamin Franklin publishes his first *Poor Richard's Almanac.*

300 years (1682). *April 9:* LaSalle claims Louisiana for France. William Penn founds Philadelphia for Quakers.

350 years (1632). Maryland is founded as a Roman Catholic colony. Galileo confirms Copernican theory of astronomy. Shah Jahan begins construction of the Taj Mahal.

400 years (1582). Douay version of the New Testament completed. Gregorian calendar introduced.

500 years (1482). Portuguese explorer Diego Cao discovers mouth of the Congo River.

550 years (1432). Jan van Eyck completes altarpiece with panels portraying the Annunciation and the Adoration of the Lamb.

600 years (1382). John Wycliffe directs translation of the Vulgate Bible into English.

1250 years (732). The Venerable Bede writes *The Ecclesiastical History of the English Nation.*

1450 years (532). Construction of the Cathedral of Hagia Sophia in Constantinople begun.

1550 years (432). St. Patrick begins missionary effort in Ireland.

1850 years (132). Revolt by Jews in Jerusalem leads to the final Diaspora or dispersion of Jews.

Anniversaries of Hymns, Hymn Writers, and Composers in 1982

50 years (1932). Writing of "And have the bright immensities" by Howard C. Robbins. Death of Edmond L. Budry (b. 1854), author of "Thine is the glory"; Charles H. Gabriel (b. 1856), author and composer of "He lifted me," "More like the Master," "O that will be glory," "Oh, it is wonderful," and "Pentecostal power" and composer of "I'll go where you want me to go," "Higher ground," "Just when I need him most," and "Since Jesus came into my heart"; Dorothy F. Gurney (b. 1858), author of "O perfect love, all human thought transcending"; John Hughes (b. 1873), composer of hymn-tune RHONDDA ("God of grace and God of glory," "Guide me, O thou great Jehovah," and "Look, ye saints, the sight is glorious"); Somerset C. Lowry (b. 1855), author of "Son of God, eternal Saviour"; Walter J. Mathams (b. 1851), author of "Christ of the upward way" and "Now in the days of youth."

75 years (1907). Composing of hymn-tune RHONDDA ("Guide me, O thou great Jehovah," etc.) by John Hughes. Writing of "Joyful, joyful, we adore thee" by Henry van Dyke; "Lord God of hosts whose purpose, never swerving" by Shepherd Knapp. Birth of Carlton C. Buck, author of "O Lord, may church and home combine"; Gerald Kennedy (d. 1979), author of "God of love and power." Death of James McGranahan (b. 1840), author and composer of "Go ye into all the world" and composer of "The banner of the cross," "Christ receiveth sinful men," "Christ returneth," "I know whom I have believed," "Revive thy work," "There shall be showers of blessings," etc.; John S. Norris (b. 1844), composer of "Where he leads me"; Horatio R. Palmer (b. 1834), author and composer of "Yield not to temptation" and composer of "Lord, for tomorrow and its needs"; David C.

Roberts (b. 1841), author of "God of our fathers, whose almighty hand."

100 years (1882). Composing of hymn-tune MATERNA ("Eternal God, whose power upholds," "O beautiful for spacious skies," and "O master workman of the race") by Samuel A. Ward. Writing of "O love that wilt not let me go" by George Matheson; "When on my day the light of night is falling" by John Greenleaf Whittier. Birth of Walter Russell Bowie (d. 1969), author of "God of the nations," "Lord Christ, when first thou cam'st," and "O holy city seen of John"; Edward A. Burroughs, author of "Lord God, from whom all life"; Julia Bulkley Cady Cory, author of "We praise thee, O God, our redeemer"; Kenneth G. Finlay, composer of hymn-tune AYRSHIRE ("As pants the hart for cooling streams" and "Immortal love, forever full"; J. Donald Hughes, author of "Creator of the universe." Death of Dora Greenwell (b. 1821), author of "I am not skilled to understand"; Samuel Johnson (b. 1822), author of "City of God, how broad and far," "Father, in thy mysterious presence kneeling," and "Life of ages, richly poured"; Henry Wadsworth Longfellow (b. 1807), author of "Ah! what a sound" and "I heard the bells on Christmas day"; Samuel Longfellow (b. 1819), author of "God of the earth, the sky, the sea"; Mary B. C. Slade (b. 1826), author of "Footprints of Jesus"; John Zundel (b. 1815), composer of hymn-tune BEECHER ("Lord, whose love through humble service" and "Love divine, all loves excelling").

150 years (1832). Composing of hymn-tunes BOYLSTON ("A parting hymn we sing"), DORT ("Thou whose almighty hand"), and OLIVET ("My faith looks up to thee") by Lowell Mason; FEDERAL STREET ("Behold, a stranger at the door" and "My dear Redeemer and my Lord") by Henry

K. Oliver; STRACATHRO ("The Lord is in his holy place") by Charles Hutcheson. Birth of Charles C. Converse (d. 1918), composer of hymn-tune ERIE ("What a friend we have in Jesus"); William H. Doane (d. 1915), composer of "Ancient of days," "Draw me nearer," "More love to thee, O Christ," "Near the cross," "Pass me not," "Rescue the perishing," "Saviour, more than life to me," "Take the name of Jesus with you," "Tell me the old, old story," etc.; Robert Murray (d. 1910), author of "From ocean unto ocean"; Francis Pott (d. 1900), author of "Angel voices, ever singing"; Caroline V. Sandell-Berg (d. 1903), author of "Children of the heavenly father."
200 years (1782). Composing of hymn-tune MELCOMBE ("O Spirit of the living God") by Samuel Webbe. Writing of "Blest be the ties that bind" by John Fawcett; "We plough the fields and scatter" by Matthias Claudius. Birth of Charles Meineke (d. 1850), composer of hymn-tune GLORIA PATRI ("Glory be to the Father").

Death of Samuel Howard (b. 1710), composer of hymn-tune ST. BRIDE ("Father, in whom we live," "Give to the winds thy fears," and "Lord of the harvest, hear").
250 years (1732). Birth of Franz Joseph Haydn (d. 1809), composer of hymn-tunes AUSTRIA ("Glorious things of thee are spoken" and "We are living, we are dwelling"), CREATION ("The spacious firmament on high"), HAYDN ("Come, my soul, thou must be waking"), and ST. ANTHONY'S CHORALE ("We, thy people, praise thee"). Death of Simon Browne (b. 1680), author of "Come, gracious Spirit, heavenly dove."
350 years (1632). Death of George Herbert (b. 1593), author of "Let all the world in every corner sing" and "Teach me, my God and King."
800 years (1182). Birth of St. Francis of Assisi (d. 1226), author of "All creatures of our God and King."
1250 years (732). Death of Andrew of Crete (b. 660), author of "Christian, dost thou see them."

Quotable Quotations

1. I believe in Christianity as I believe that the sun has risen not because I see it but because I see everything by it.—John Busby.
2. The crosses we make for ourselves by a restless anxiety as to the future are not crosses which come from God.—Fenelon.
3. Man and the devil use all good for evil; God uses all evil for good.—Martin Luther.
4. It is not easy to love God while looking in the mirror.—John Leinbach.
5. Leave tomorrow's troubles to tomorrow's strength, tomorrow's work to tomorrow's time, tomorrow's sorrows to tomorrow's grace, and all of it to tomorrow's God.—Jack Key.
6. A Christian is a mind through which Christ thinks, a voice through which Christ speaks, a heart through which Christ loves, and a hand through which Christ helps.—James R. Webb.
7. Some prayers have a longer voyage than others, but they return with the richer lading at last, so that the praying

soul is a gainer by waiting for an answer.—William Gurnall.
8. One of the most exciting things about being a Christian is that you can have a certain freedom that other people don't enjoy—the freedom to risk, to dare, to do.—Betsy Ancker-Johnson.
9. We shall have to repent in this generation not so much for the evil deeds of the wicked people but for the appalling silence of the good people.—Martin Luther King, Jr.
10. Every step in the progress of missions is directly traceable to prayer.—A. T. Pierson.
11. There is a sufficiency in the world for man's need but not for man's greed.—Gandhi.
12. The opposite of love is not hate—it's apathy.—Hoover Rupert.
13. If you preach the gospel in all aspects with the exception of the issues which deal specifically with your time, you are not preaching the gospel at all.—Martin Luther.

14. Love of mankind is an empty phrase unless we can first learn to love our neighbor.

15. Who travels for love finds a thousand miles only one mile.—Japanese proverb.

16. Satan trembles when he sees the weakest saint upon his knees.—William Cowper.

17. There is no Christianity without repentance of some kind.—Addison H. Leitch.

18. We hate some persons because we do not know them, and we will not know them because we hate them.—Charles C. Colton.

19. Hope is the flame of the Christian religion.—Graham Greene.

20. God writes with a pen that never blots, speaks with a tongue that never slips, and acts with a hand that never fails.

21. Worry happens when we assume responsibility God never intended us to have.

22. We never know how much one loves till we know how much he is willing to endure and suffer for us; and it is the suffering element that measures love.—Henry Ward Beecher.

23. He who begins by loving Christianity better than Christ will proceed by loving his own sect or church better than Christianity and end loving himself better than all.—Samuel Taylor Coleridge.

24. There is more to life than increasing its speed.—Gandhi.

25. He who would do good to another must do it in minute particulars.—William Blake.

26. The two most beautiful things in the universe are the starry heavens above our heads and the feeling of duty in our hearts.—Jacques B. Bossuet.

27. I am only slowly coming to experience things that I have all along accepted.—Flannery O'Connor.

28. Prayer is our whole service to God.—John Donne.

29. Christians are people who hope in the midst of the most hopeless situations.—Howard L. Rice.

30. Our Lord has written the promise of the resurrection not in books alone but in every leaf in springtime.—Martin Luther.

31. Easter is not a passport to another world. It is a quality of perception for this one.—W. P. Lemon.

32. It is hard to look up to a leader who keeps his ear to the ground.—James H. Boren.

33. We have tried to practice the Christian faith as if it were a home correspondence course in self-improvement.—William H. Willimon.

34. All things come to him who waits, provided he knows what he is waiting for.—Woodrow Wilson.

35. The wages of sin have never been reduced.

36. On the basis of the eternal will of God we have to think of every human being, even the oddest, most villainous or miserable, as one to whom Jesus Christ is brother and God is father, and we have to deal with him on that assumption.—Karl Barth.

37. What greater rebellion, impiety, or insult to God can there be than not to believe his promises?—Martin Luther.

38. Where there is no love, put love and you will find love.—St. John of the Cross.

39. Those who have not often felt the joy of doing a kind act have neglected much and, most of all, themselves.—Andries Nielsen.

40. When you flee temptation don't leave a forwarding address.—*Christian Herald.*

41. If God's main purpose is to cure our sick souls, then it doesn't make sense for him to coddle and baby us for the sake of sparing us unhappiness.—Betty Garton Ulrich.

42. Never take your eye from the goal nor disturb the calmness with which you pursue it.—Pablo Casals.

43. No one can know the height of heaven without climbing mountains.

44. The teaching of Jesus provides a source of profound social revolution at the same time that his healing deeds are the most forceful word that the saving power of God has broken forth in our world.—Bernard Cooke.

45. The spinal cord of redemption is the nerve to submit all my images of the self

to Christ and his people for correction.—Carlyle Marney.

46. It is not how much we have but how much we enjoy that makes happiness.— *Michigan Christian Advocate.*

47. The difference between a good man and a bad one is the choice of the cause. —William James.

48. The light that shows us our sins is the light which heals.—George Fox.

49. The prayer that we find hardest to comprehend, namely, the intercessory, Jesus took most easily and naturally for granted.—Francis J. McConnell.

50. The few little years we spend on earth are only the first scene in a divine drama that extends on into eternity.—Edwin Markham.

51. Christ was crucified, was buried, and was raised from the dead—and he spoke to me this morning.—Gerard Manley Hopkins.

52. If you wish your neighbors to see what God is like, let them see what he can make you like.—Charles Kingsley.

53. We need a value system that will allow us to fulfill our essential human and humane task to be producers, to be providers, and to be protectors.—Jesse Jackson.

54. Prayer is and remains always a native and deepest impulse of the soul of man.—Thomas Carlyle.

55. Some open minds should be closed for repairs.—*The Anglican Digest.*

56. Mankind was never so happily inspired as when it made a cathedral.—Robert Louis Stevenson.

57. Cooperation is doing with a smile what you have to do anyway.—Marvin Gregory.

58. Some folk go to church just three times in their lives—to be hatched, matched, and dispatched—and they get sprinkled three times—with water, rice, and dust.

59. If you expect to succeed at anything without failing at it and failing pretty badly too at least a hundred times, you must think success a cheaper commodity than it actually is.—George Bernard Shaw.

60. The only thing that will take the place of preaching is better preaching.—Paul Scherer.

61. The forgiveness of God is the foundation of every bridge from a hopeless past to a courageous present.—George Adam Smith.

62. The peace we need is an inside job. —Denise Turner.

63. What God does he may do by public evangelism, but he may also do it through private evangelism.—Erik Routley.

64. Let us be the first to give a friendly sign, to nod first, to smile first, to speak first, and—if such a thing is necessary—to forgive first.—*The Anglican Digest.*

65. Worship is man's acknowledgement of God. Its language is the language of response.—Robert E. Cushman.

66. Don't play it safe since to be inoffensive sometimes is offensive to God.—H. Ellis Finger.

67. Religion must come down from the altar and mingle with the world. It must worry less about salvation in the hereafter and more about salvation in the here-and-now.—W. Gunther Plaut.

68. Loneliness rarely comes to people who are interested in others.—Gary R. Collins.

69. Sad will be the day for any man when he becomes contented with the thoughts he is thinking and the deeds he is doing and when there is not forever beating at his soul some great desire to do something larger which he knows that he was meant and made to do.—Phillips Brooks.

70. Nothing would ever be attempted if all objections must first be overcome.—Samuel Johnson.

71. On the basis of the New Testament in the Christian vocabulary there is simply no place for despair.—Richard Smith.

72. We must live more simply in order that others may simply live.—Albert C. Winn.

73. The great leaps are still the surest way to higher ground.—Norman Cousins.

74. The prayers of joy are among man's most beautiful creations.—C. L. Sulzberger.

75. In actual life every great enterprise begins with and takes its first forward step in faith.—August Schlegel.

76. Without God, we cannot; without us, God will not.—St. Augustine.

77. Old age is when you know all the answers but nobody asks you the questions.—Laurence J. Peter.

78. The saddest failures in life are those that come from not putting forth the power and the will to succeed.

79. The good that comes from working together toward common goals must be a product of the spirit, the thinking of men and women, the unselfish demonstration that good will prevail.—James Hilton.

80. Sick or well, blind or seeing, bond or free, we are here for a purpose and, however we are situated, we please God better with useful deeds than with many prayers or pious resignation.—Helen Keller.

81. The word of God will stand a thousand readings, and he who has gone over it most frequently is the surest of finding new wonders there.—James Hamilton.

82. It is so hard to believe because it is so hard to obey.—Søren Kierkegaard.

83. There are a thousand hacking at the branches of evil to one who is striking at its root.—Henry David Thoreau.

84. To be a Christian in a world such as ours is to trust God when there is no evidence, to hope in God's mercy when we know we do not deserve it, to rely on God's leading when the clues are most difficult to discern.—Howard L. Rice.

85. We do not fall in love; we grow in love, and love grows in us.—Karl Menninger.

86. Old age is fifteen years older than I am.—Bernard M. Baruch.

87. The way to the soul's final greatness lies through its misery rather than through its success.—P. T. Forsyth.

88. We are not forced to accept God's generous gifts, but what a terrible sin it is to refuse them or to treat them lightly.—*The Anglican Digest.*

89. If you cannot think of anything to be thankful for, you have a poor memory.

90. Christian spirituality is the art of being Christianly human.—*The Living Church.*

91. Real joy comes not from ease or riches or from the praise of men but from doing something worthwhile.

92. Christ's radical diminishments—his birth as a helpless baby and his death as a common criminal—accomplished our salvation.—Elisabeth Elliot.

93. The Bible was written for men with a head upon their shoulders.—Martin Luther.

94. Judge a man's courage by the hope that is in him.—Ralph Waldo Emerson.

95. There are two ways of spreading light—to be the candle or the mirror that reflects it.—Edith Wharton.

96. God remains present to you when you have been sent forth; he who goes forth on a mission has always God before him—the truer the fulfillment the stronger and more constant his nearness.—Martin Buber.

97. We all live under the same sky, but we don't all have the same horizon.

98. Those who know the path of God can find it in the dark.—*The War Cry.*

99. Trust in what God has already done in the past makes it possible to trust in what he will do in the future.—Robert McAfee Brown.

100. I've made it a habit all through to close gates behind me.—William Gladstone.

Questions of Life and Religion

RAISING QUESTIONS. Honest questions, candid expressions of ignorance, often bring light. The unquestioning spirit is sometimes only the result of superficiality. The faith which does not pretend to believe things it does not believe but which, with incisive mind, probes down to the deep things of God is the faith which honors Christianity. Jesus said many things which they did not understand, and the candid question of Thomas brought to them all an answer of illumination. Confession of faith is a duty, but there are times when it helps to raise questions. And if we ask our questions honestly, desiring an answer, they will lead us into a fuller knowledge of the truth.—Edward A. George.

LIVING THE QUESTIONS.   Be patient toward all that is unsolved in your heart and try to love the questions themselves. Do not seek the answers that cannot be given you because you would not be able to live them. And the point is to live everything. Live the questions now. Perhaps you will then gradually, without noticing it, live along some distant day into the answer.— Rainer Maria Rilke.

JOURNEYS AND QUESTIONS.   While we all long for the certainty and security that come with absolute and pat answers and while we all want to feel that God is in our corner, the reality is that we live by faith and not by certainty or security or even knowledge. Faith implies questioning, searching, wondering, and hoping. Faith understands life as a journey that never ends. Such a quest is not a matter of just having questions but living the questions we have and even loving the questions. Somehow we want to live with our fears and hopes and wonderings in the confidence that, trusting the process in this fashion, we shall live our way into the purpose of God and our own fulfillment.— Robert Raines.

These questions may be useful to prime homiletic pumps, as discussion starters, or for study groups.

1. When Christ said that knowing the truth would bring freedom, what did he mean by truth and freedom?

2. How can an individual be a Christian in an unchristian society?

3. What is a Spirit-controlled life?

4. Is there a biblical teaching concerning abortion?

5. How can we worship the Lord in the beauty of holiness?

6. Where can Christian parents get help in their parental role?

7. What are the characteristics of growing Sunday schools?

8. Explain the inspiration of the Bible.

9. How should we interpret the hosannas of Palm Sunday in terms of the crucifixion a few days later?

10. Relate Christian stewardship and ecology.

11. What is grace?

12. How can I know God accepts me?

13. Can a person be too ambitious?

14. Has the church lost the battle against social drinking?

15. What do the words, "Make me a captive, Lord, and then I shall be free," mean?

16. What is the reign of God?

17. When, where, and why were bells first placed in church steeples?

18. Should religious teaching be excluded from public schools?

19. What proofs do the gospels offer for Christ's resurrection?

20. What are the bases of Christian hope?

21. What are the various churches doing to relieve world hunger?

22. What were Christ's last words to his disciples?

23. How should Christian convictions determine the decisions of public officials who are professing Christians?

24. Did Christ offer the Lord's Prayer as a model for all Christian prayer?

25. How can Christmas become a holy day and not merely a holiday?

26. In what ways can the church attract more young people?

27. Which books in the Bible are most persuasive in Christian evangelism?

28. What specific training is usually needed for those wishing to be missionaries?

29. What minimal requirements should churches expect of persons wishing to have their names kept on membership roles?

30. What can one person do about global problems?

31. How can I know God?

32. What biblical promises have Christians found most helpful.

33. For whom should we pray?

34. Explain the incarnation.

35. Is the final victory of Christ inevitable?

36. What must I do to be saved?

37. Should church property be taxed?

38. How can a Christian be cheerful in a world filled with suffering and sin?

39. Why does God seem so far away?

40. Should local and state governments sponsor gambling?

41. Why can't we learn from the lessons of history?

42. How can I express criticism without sounding censorious?

43. In what ways do the prophets speak to our day?

44. Is one religion as good as another?

45. Why did Jesus use parables in his teaching?

46. Do the four gospels differ in their basic emphases?

47. What is Christian holiness?

48. What can Protestants learn from Catholics and Jews?

49. How can Christian missionary work be made more real to local church members?

50. What is the work of the Holy Spirit?

51. What are humanity's most baffling problems?

52. How would you explain the sinfulness of sin?

53. What can we know about the afterlife?

54. Are there sins which God will not forgive?

55. Is baptism necessary for church membership?

56. Why is Christ said to have come in the fullness of time?

57. Why do we pray if God already knows our needs?

58. Is violent protest ever justified?

59. How can I learn to be patient?

60. How can you know that a person is a Christian?

61. Is the language of the Bible too sexist?

62. Should the church participate in the political arena?

63. Will Jesus come again?

64. How does Christian education differ from public education?

65. How should we pray for the incurably ill?

66. Are there circumstances in which the church should condone divorce?

67. How can I keep my balance in the midst of confusing situations?

68. What should Christians do when there is evidence of police brutality?

69. How may young people be given a significant role in church leadership?

70. What can I learn from failure?

71. Why do we say that Jesus was human and divine?

72. Explain the compelling power of Christ in the lives of multitudes of people?

73. What are the purposes of the sermon?

74. Was Jesus an idealist or a realist?

75. What are the hallmarks of mature Christian behavior?

76. Will we know one another in heaven?

77. What should be a Christian's priorities?

78. How should I determine what portion of my income belongs to God?

79. Can the church rescue Sunday from commercial exploitation?

80. Am I responsible for another person's sins?

81. How can I obey God when there are so many interpretations of God's requirements?

82. Must I be born again to be a Christian?

83. Why are there so many joyless Christians?

84. Does Christ's commandment to love supersede the ten commandments?

85. Why is hymn singing a part of worship services?

86. Am I personally accountable to God?

87. If Christians are pilgrims, toward what goal does their pilgrimage lead?

88. Is salvation personal or social?

89. What does redemption mean?

90. Why is so much of the New Testament given to the writings of the apostle Paul?

91. Does the Old Testament anticipate Christ's atonement?

92. Do all things work together for good?

93. Why does God tolerate human sinfulness?

94. How do you explain the continued strength of the church during the past twenty centuries?

95. How does the Holy Spirit guide my life?

96. How can we be laborers together with God?

97. Explain eternal life.

98. Can you give me some guidelines for a systematic reading of the Bible?

99. Does Christianity represent an impossible dream?

100. What is the biblical answer to human suffering?

Biblical Benedictions and Blessings

The Lord watch between me and thee, when we are absent one from another.—Gen. 31:49.

The Lord bless thee, and keep thee; the Lord make his face shine upon thee, and be gracious unto thee; the Lord lift up his countenance upon thee, and give thee peace.—Num. 6:24–26.

The Lord our God be with us, as he was with our fathers: let him not leave us, nor forsake us: that he may incline our hearts unto him, to walk in all his ways, and to keep his commandments, and his statutes, and his judgments, which he commanded our fathers.—I Kings 8:57–58.

Let the words of my mouth, and the meditation of my heart, be acceptable in thy sight, O Lord, my strength, and my redeemer.—Ps. 19:14.

Now the God of patience and consolation grant you to be likeminded one toward another according to Christ Jesus: that ye may with one mind and one mouth glorify God, even the Father of our Lord Jesus Christ. Now the God of hope fill you with all joy and peace in believing, that ye may abound in hope, through the power of the Holy Ghost. Now the God of peace be with you all.—Rom. 15:5–6, 13, 33.

Now to him that is of power to establish you according to my gospel, and the preaching of Jesus Christ, according to the revelation of the mystery, which was kept secret since the world began, but now is manifest, and by the scriptures of the prophets, according to the commandment of the everlasting God, made known to all nations for the obedience of faith: to God only wise, be glory through Jesus Christ for ever.—Rom. 16:25–27.

Grace be unto you, and peace, from God our Father, and from the Lord Jesus Christ.—I Cor. 1:3.

The grace of the Lord Jesus Christ and the love of God, and the communion of the Holy Ghost, be with you all.—II Cor. 13:14.

Peace be to the brethren, and love with faith, from God the Father and the Lord Jesus Christ. Grace be with all them that love our Lord Jesus Christ in sincerity.—Eph. 6:23–24.

And the peace of God, which passeth all understanding, shall keep your hearts and minds through Christ Jesus. Finally, brethren, whatsoever things are true, whatsoever things are honest, whatsoever things are just, whatsoever things are pure, whatsoever things are lovely, whatsoever things are of good report; if there be any virtue, and if there be any praise, think on these things. Those things, which ye have both learned, and received, and heard, and seen in me, do: and the God of peace shall be with you.—Phil. 4:7–9.

Wherefore also we pray always for you, that our God would count you worthy of this calling, and fulfill all the good pleasure of his goodness, and the work of faith with power: that the name of our Lord Jesus Christ may be glorified in you, and ye in him, according to the grace of our God and the Lord Jesus Christ.—II Thess. 1:11–12.

Now the Lord of peace himself give you peace always by all means. The Lord be with you all. The grace of our Lord Jesus Christ be with you all.—II Thess. 3:16, 18.

Grace, mercy, and peace, from God our Father and Jesus Christ our Lord.—I Tim. 1:2.

Now the God of peace, that brought again from the dead our Lord Jesus, that great shepherd of the sheep, through the blood of the everlasting covenant, make you perfect in every good work to do his will, working in you that which is well-pleasing in his sight, through Jesus Christ, to whom be glory for ever and ever.—Heb. 13:20–21.

The God of all grace, who hath called us unto his eternal glory by Christ Jesus, after that ye have suffered a while, make you perfect, stablish, strengthen, settle you. To him be glory and dominion for ever and ever. Greet ye one another with a kiss of charity. Peace be with you all that are in Christ Jesus.—I Pet. 5:10–11, 14.

Grace be with you, mercy, and peace, from God the Father, and from the Lord Jesus Christ, the Son of the Father, in truth and love.—II John 3.

Now unto him that is able to keep you from falling, and to present you faultless before the presence of his glory with exceeding joy, to the only wise God our Savior, be glory and majesty, dominion and power, both now and ever.—Jude 2:24–25.

Grace be unto you, and peace, from him which was, and which is to come; and from the seven Spirits which are before his throne; and from Jesus Christ, who is the faithful witness, and the first begotten of the dead, and the prince of the kings of the earth. Unto him that loved us, and washed us from our sins in his own blood, and hath made us kings and priests unto God and his Father; to him be glory and dominion for ever and ever.—Rev. 1:4–6.

SECTION II. *Vital Themes for Vital Preaching*

January 3. The Second Touch

SCRIPTURE: Mark 8:22–25.

Nineteen centuries ago Jesus healed a blind man at Bethsaida. At our Lord's first touch the man opened his eyes. When asked, "Do you see anything?" he replied, "I see men but they look like trees walking." His vision was dim and confused. Then Christ laid his hand a second time on the man's eyes. The record is that "he looked intently and was restored and saw all things clearly."

I. We need the second touch of Christ to transform the seekers into servants of Christ. Jesus drew great multitudes at the beginning of his ministry. Some came to be healed, some came to be fed, and some came out of mere curiosity. But Christ did not start his church with the five thousand whom he fed with the loaves and fishes. He had to develop a small hard core of trained disciples to carry on his work. Today Christ must count on consecrated disciples rather than on crowds of the curious and self-seeking.

II. We need Christ's second touch to advance us from servants to friends. As he came to the close of his earthly ministry, Jesus said to his disciples: "No longer do I call you servants, for the servant does not know what his master is doing; but I have called you friends, for all that I have heard from my Father I have made known to you." It is not enough to say, "Come to Jesus" or even "Follow Jesus." We must learn what it means to follow him. We must study and teach Christ until we enter understanding friendship with him.

III. We need Christ's second touch to advance from friend to witness. Luke closes his gospel by recording the risen Christ as saying, "You are witness of these things." The word "witness" may be used with two obviously different meanings. If you were to go to a courtroom tomorrow where a trial was in progress, you could take your seat in the spectators' section and thereby become a witness of the trial. But up near the judge's bench and the jury box is a seat reserved for those who give testimony. It is called the witness chair. Those who take that seat are not mere witnesses of the trial. They are witnesses at the trial. The word "witnesses" as used by the risen Christ means those who testify. That is the word our Lord would say to us.—Ralph W. Sockman.

January 10. He Went to the Mountain (Martin Luther King's Birthday)

TEXT: Deut. 34:1.

The day before his assassination, Martin Luther King, Jr., said: "We've got some difficult days ahead. But it really doesn't matter with me now. Because I've been to the mountaintop." He drew on his life-long familiarity with the Bible to recall Moses' journey up the mountain of Nebo to the top of Pisgah where the Lord showed him all the land of Judah.

I. The man who went to the mountain couldn't be intimidated. King said: "Like anybody, I would like to live a long life. But I'm not concerned about that now. I just want to do God's will. And he's allowed me to go up to the mountain. And

I've looked over, and I've seen the promised land. I may not get there with you, but I want you to know tonight that we as a people will get to the promised land. 'Mine eyes have seen the glory of the coming of the Lord!' "

II. The man who went to the mountain couldn't be inferior. He said of his people: "Before the Pilgrims landed at Plymouth, we were here. Before the pen of Jefferson etched across the pages the majestic words of the Declaration of Independence, we were here. We will win our freedom because the sacred heritage of our nation and the eternal will of God are embodied in our echoing demands."

III. The man who went to the mountain couldn't be intolerant. He expressed it this way: "We will match your capacity to inflict suffering with our capacity to endure suffering. We will meet your physical force with soul force. And in winning our freedom we will so appeal to your heart and conscience that we will win you in the process."—Bramwell Tripp.

January 17. When God Calls

SCRIPTURE: Isa. 6:1–8.

The scripture is a brief, vivid description in the life of Isaiah when he responded to the call of God, a perfect example of a beautiful worship experience.

I. A person finds himself in crisis, "In the year that King Uzziah died." You and I are in crisis. We live in crisis. The tragedy is that we do not recognize our crisis, or more truthfully, we refuse to recognize our crisis.

II. In crisis we are really seeking and begin with adoration of the greatness of God. "I saw also the Lord." Then follows a beautiful and symbolic experience or vision of "how great thou art."

III. He sees himself and his life silhouetted versus this great God. He understands, feels his own unworthiness, and confesses (repents) to God. "Woe is me. I am a man of unclean lips and I dwell among a people of unclean lips."

IV. As follows the day the night, God forgives, cleanses, and accepts us. "A coal from the altar, touched to our lips. Our guilt is taken away." And here unfortu-

nately is where most of us brag about what the Lord has done for us—our great charismatic experience. Not so Isaiah.

V. In any legitimate worship experience we pray, "Lord, what will you have me do?" He responds, if we listen, "Who will go?"

VI. The great human response, validating any worship experience, is "Here am I, send me."

VII. God says: "Go! Get Going!" Isaiah, at the risk of his own life, went out and spoke to his people. "Thus saith the Lord!"—Wilmer A. Blankenbaker.

January 24. The Blessing of Not Knowing It All

TEXT: I Cor. 13:9.

"For we know in part." When you and I realize the truth of this statement, it will bring some very practical benefits to our lives.

I. It will keep us humble, and humility is an important factor in a happy, holy life. The person who admits his ignorance is the one who learns the most. Paul's pride of learning kept him ignorant of God's simple plan of salvation. God literally had to knock Paul down. He had to humble him before he could teach Paul the truth. Then, after Paul experienced many wonderful blessings including being taken into the third heaven, God had to give Paul a thorn in the flesh to keep him humble. Humility is the secret of wisdom, and humility comes when you and I realize that we know in part.

II. The blessing of kindness toward others. The next time you are tempted to judge someone severely remember what Paul wrote: "For we know in part." More than once I have wrongfully passed judgment on another Christian without really knowing all the facts, and more than once I have had to confess it to God and to those involved. We know perfectly well that "man looks on the outward appearance but God looks on the heart," yet we jump to conclusions and pass judgment anyway. The French have a proverb, "If we knew all, we would forgive all." That may not be totally true, but it does remind us to be slow to judge because we know in part.

III. When you realize that you know in part, you are better able to accept the burden and disappointments of life. Many a person has wrecked his life on the rocks of disappointments only to discover later that those same rocks could have been used as steppingstones to greater things. Never doubt in the darkness what God has told you in the light. Rest on his promises, and all will be well.—Donald O'Quin.

January 31. Churches That Attract People

TEXT: I John 1:3.

I. They are people willing to put time and effort to a cause they consider important.

II. They are people with a conviction of rightness, and they want to be on the side of God.

III. They are people who can be linked together in a supportive movement who will re-enforce one another in times of weakness, in trouble, and in doubt.

IV. They are people who will subordinate their own personal desires and interests to the support of the group.—*The Cumberland Presbyterian.*

February 7. We Know

One of Paul's favorite expressions was "we know," and he repeated it many times in his letters.

I. "We know that God is on our side" (Rom. 8:28).

II. "We know that God's creation suffers because of sin" (Rom. 8:22).

III. "We know that idol worship is idle worship" (I Cor. 8:4).

IV. "We know that our performance is limited because our knowledge is limited" (I Cor. 13:9).

V. "We know that God has provided for the life beyond" (II Cor. 5:1).

VI. "We know that God's law is for man's good" (I Tim. 1:8).

VII. "We know that every man needs a savior" (Rom. 3:19).—Fred M. Wood.

February 14. Bridging the Gap (Brotherhood Week)

TEXT: Rom. 10:12.

Bridging the gap between the church and the people remains a challenge and a charge for all who would serve the present age.

I. Bridging the gap between believers and unbelievers.

II. Bridging the gap between fear and faith.

III. Bridging the gap between one nationality and another.

IV. Bridging the gap between ethnic groups.

V. Bridging the gap between those who love and those who hate.

VI. Bridging the gap between ideologies.

VII. Bridging the gap between generations.

VIII. Bridging the gap between feuding family members.

IX. Bridging the gap between neighbor and neighbor.

X. There are many other widening gaps in our society, in our relationships, in our homes, and in our hearts. Bridging those gaps calls for a ministry of understanding, patience, grace, empathy, and love. Whatever the gap may be in your situation or experience, take the first step over the bridge of faith that has been provided through the grace and guidance of God.—*The War Cry.*

February 21. Relating to Those Who Suffer

TEXT: John 16:33.

I. Our Christian experience equips us to relate to persons in the midst of pain and suffering. It gives us the knowledge of a caring and involved God, one who hears and answers prayer in ways best for our unique situations. It gives us a knowledge of a comforting God who always recognizes our personhood.

II. Our Christian experience equips us because of the incarnation of God's love in Jesus Christ and our awareness of the time he spent with persons who suffered and of the times he wept and prayed.

III. Christians need to know that God works through them. God is able to multiply the effect of the efforts we make to express his concern and love. So our words and actions may seem awkward to us, but God may use them in the healing he gives.—Jim Beaumont.

February 28. Christ and the Daily Routine (Lent)

TEXT: Phil. 1:27.

If Christ is to fill our daily lives with meaning, there are several essential ingredients that must go into the mix of the daily routine.

I. We must take time to seek his presence and await his presence in some quiet time of prayer. If we miss him in the quiet hour, we will lose him in the rush hour.

II. Throughout the day there must be a conscious effort to see God at work in our lives, in the lives of others, and in the events that transpire. Here is where God gives life's eternal meanings.

III. As one weaves the strands of Christian fellowship and friendship, reaching out to others with Christ, caring and being open to the Christian caring of others, life will be flooded with the meaning that Christ gives.

IV. The daily reading and searching for the meaning from God's word in the scriptures is an immeasurable source for the meaning that Christ gives.

V. Christ gives meaning to life because through faith in him we can know the forgiveness of sins and reach out to others with a forgiving spirit.

VI. Christ gives meaning to life because he sets us free in the power of his love and grace. In the freedom of Christ we are not striving to do enough good deeds to cancel out our sins. He has forgiven our sins and remembered them no more against us. We now look forward to living daily by his presence and doing his will.

VII. The meaning which Christ gives to life transcends death. It is the risen Christ who has broken the powers of death and gives to those who believe in him assurance of the victory over death.—W. Aubrey Alsobrook.

March 7. Passion (Lent)

TEXT: I Cor. 1:27.

"I am the way," Jesus said. I am the road. And in some fashion or another we are all on the road that is his or that is he, or such at least is our hope and prayer. One way or another the road starts off from a passion for what is holy and hidden, a passion for Christ.

I. Passion must be related not just to the world inside your skin where it is born but to the world outside your skin where it has to learn to walk and talk and act in terms of social injustice and human need and politics and nuclear power and God knows what.

II. Passion must be harnessed and put to work, and the power that first stirs the heart must become the power that also stirs the hands and feet because it is the places your feet take you to and the work you find for your hands that finally proclaim who you are and who Christ is.

III. Passion without wisdom to give it shape and direction is as empty as wisdom without passion to give it power and purpose. You learn as much from the wise as you can until finally, if you do it right and things break your way, you are wise enough to be yourself, brave enough to speak with your own voice, and foolish enough for Christ's sake to live and serve out of the uniqueness of your own vision of him and out of your own passion.—Frederick Buechner.

March 14. To Live Is to Suffer (Lent)

TEXT: II Cor. 4:17.

I. To live is to suffer. If life is to be meaningful, we need desperately to find a place for suffering in it and to discover how to cope with it.

(a) Victor Frankl tells us that "to live is to suffer and to survive is to find meaning in suffering." He says that of great significance is the attitude we take toward suffering—"the attitude in which we take our suffering upon ourselves." He discovered that "suffering ceases to be suffering in some way at the moment it finds a meaning, such as the meaning of a sacrifice."

(b) A mother will go through untold hardship for the sake of her child. A father will do without so that his family may have the necessities of life. An unhappy workman will continue on his unimaginative job so that his son might get an education. Men and women will leave home and much of what they hold dear to go on perilous journeys to far-off lands as missionaries if they see some meaning in life and some purpose in what they are doing.

II. Deprivation and suffering lose some of their sting if there is some reason for them and if some meaning can be seen.

(a) I wonder if the agony of the cross was withstood by Jesus partially because he saw some meaning in it. He said, "And I, if I be lifted up, will draw all men unto me." His suffering was not wasted. God used it even for his purposes.

(b) Perhaps in our suffering, even when we can see no good in it and it is void of apparent meaning, the cross of Christ and all the suffering it represented can help us bear our own. Jesus prayed in the garden, "Father all things are possible unto thee; take away this cup from me: nevertheless not what I will, but what thou wilt." But there seemed to be no other way but suffering for him, and then with confidence he prayed on the cross, "Father, into thy hands I commend my spirit." In our suffering Christ is very near to us in compassion and in understanding. He can help us bear our own.

(c) Frankl tells us that "man is not fully conditioned and determined but rather determines himself whether he gives in to conditions or stands up to them. One of the main features of human existence is the capacity to rise above such conditions and transcend them." It is God who gives us this power to overcome.—W. Wallace Fridy.

March 21. Man's Best Friend (Lent)

TEXT: John 15:13–14 (NASV).

Man's best friend is Jesus.

I. The first characteristic of Jesus' friendship is sacrificial self-giving. Jesus made the highest expression of love for his friends. He laid down his life for everyone. He gave up his life in order that we might have life. Some of us would give up life for a loved one, but few would give up life for just a friend. Jesus did.

II. Another characteristic of Jesus' friendship is unselfish guidance. He is seeking man's best interest. I read a slogan recently which said, "A friend is a gift you

give yourself." We human beings tend to cultivate the friendship of a person for what we can give ourselves or for what we can get out of the relationship. Jesus didn't die for us so we would owe him a favor. He died for our own good. He requires that we keep his law for our own good. When we live in his will, we can have abundant life. When we rebel, we break ourselves on his law.

III. A third characteristic of Jesus' friendship is the marvelous family. Being a friend of Jesus is being a friend of the Father. Being a friend of the Father is being a friend of all his children. Wherever one goes he is able to have good friends among God's people. The family of God is a large, loving, and caring family. It is joyous to be related to so many fine folks in God's family.—James D. McLemore.

March 28. Tragic Necessity (Passion Sunday)

TEXT: II Cor. 5:15.

The crucifixion of our Lord was inevitable. This is not to excuse those who, moved by hatred or fear, took part in the death of an innocent man. But it was necessary that our Lord be crucified. The Bible records that Jesus, some time before his death, "began to teach them that the Son of Man must suffer many things . . . and be killed" (Mark 8:31).

I. It was necessary because Jesus shared humanity's lot. Suffering and death are unavoidable. We shrink from them, but pain and dying are part of life. It is futile to speculate on the reason, but we do not need to speculate on the cause. Sin and all its attendant evils have been manifested throughout human history. The corruption and defilement of sin bring inescapable penalties.

II. It was necessary because Jesus must fulfill prophecy. God's revelation of his just and benevolent purposes were given through special chosen messengers. Hundreds of years before Jesus came, Isaiah wrote, "He is despised and rejected of men; a man of sorrows . . . he was wounded for our transgressions, he was bruised for our iniquities" (Isa. 53:3, 5).

To sorrowing disciples on the way to Emmaus, Jesus said, "O fools, and slow of heart to believe all that the prophets have spoken: ought not Christ to have suffered these things?" (Luke 24:25-27).

III. It was necessary because God could not compromise with evil. God's new answer to the problem of man's sin was to establish a new covenant or relationship. Under the old covenant, sin was cleansed by blood sacrifices. Now a new relationship with God was made possible by the shedding of Christ's blood. "God commendeth his love toward us, in that, while we were yet sinners, Christ died for us" (Rom. 5:8).—Bramwell Tripp.

April 4. A Tale of Two Cities (Palm Sunday)

SCRIPTURE: Luke 19:41-48.

I. The terms "Holy City" and "Secular City" can be taken as representing biblical notions.

(a) Holy City designates that whole way and pattern of life, both individual and in community, which is established in commitment to God and which is sustained by worship of God and in service of his purposes for mankind.

(b) Secular City refers to that approach to life which assumes that God—when it assumes that there is a God—really has nothing to do with ordinary life and that God has no practical significance for human existence.

II. We yearn, sometimes desperately, for the Holy City, but we often feel that we are trapped in the Secular City. And Jesus' words come down the long years to challenge us, to warn us, and to judge us: "If only you had known the way that leads to peace!"

III. After his lamentation, Jesus went into the center of Jerusalem on that first Palm Sunday. He continued his preaching and teaching. On the Thursday night, after his last supper with his disciples, he was arrested and quickly tried on trumped-up charges. On Friday he was nailed to a cross and left to die. So much for Jesus. The Secular City triumphed after all.

IV. Did it, really? On the third day, the Sunday following Palm Sunday, Jesus' followers came to the overwhelming awareness that God had raised him from the tomb and that he was not dead but alive. They became aware of him as the living Lord, the Lord of the Holy City, the Lord who could bring peace into the life of mankind. The great struggle was not over; the great struggle was just beginning. We now know that the way that leads to peace is not hidden from our sight. We know now that the Secular City cannot destroy the Holy City.—J. A. Davidson.

April 11. The Gospel of Easter (Easter)

TEXT: I Cor. 15:54-57.

I. Alleluia! Christ is risen from the dead! (a) The early Christians lived in the complete assurance that Jesus was alive forevermore. The apostles claimed to be witnesses of the resurrection. They testified that it was fact, not fiction. The New Testament church was the church of the risen Christ.

(b) The heart of the doctrines of the New Testament church was the resurrection of Jesus Christ. The resurrection theme was so tremendous that the apostles found themselves literally compelled to develop it along many lines. To them the deity of Christ was ratified in the resurrection. To them the powers of evil were overthrown once for all in the resurrection. There was no aspect of the resurrection which inspired them with more joy than the fact that death was vanquished and they could sing, "Death is swallowed up in victory."

(c) Those then who had spent their lifetime in bondage to the fear of death were delivered from that dread servitude and could in one great chorus lift their voices to declare with Paul: "O death, where is thy sting? O grave, where is thy victory? Thanks be to God which giveth us the victory through our Lord Jesus Christ."

II. What is this victory over death? (a) We have to die just as surely as did any from Adam to the second man Adam, even Jesus. We must all tread the path of dusty death. The angel of death is no less constant in his labors now than in the days of the dawn of history. What then is this victory over death?

(b) The victory over death is the removal of the sting of death. The sting of death is sin. What makes us fearful of death is our sin. When in our sin, we think of departing and shrink from that unimaginable light of God's own glory. We fear death because we cannot bear the scrutiny of those all-seeing eyes. That is death's sting, but it has been drawn. We have Christ's promise that those who confess his name before men he will present to his Father perfect. He will present us faultless before the presence of God's glory.

(c) "Yea, though I walk through the valley of the shadow of death, I will fear no evil, for thou art with me." This is wonderful! That is only a part of our faith. The rest is that when we emerge from that valley of the shadow we shall see Jesus and find him greater than all our dreams. The hand that leads us through the darkness belongs to the one whose face will be our joy throughout eternity.

III. The gospel of Easter is that Jesus Christ died our death and that he tasted death for every man. All the terrors of death fell upon him, but God raised him from the dead, bringing him from the death of hell into his own eternal glory. He whose love is greater than our sins and who calleth his own sheep by name will greet us and take us with his nail-pierced hand and welcome us as those for whom he died and rose again. Then to the question, "O death, where is now thy sting?" we shall triumphantly reply, "Thanks be to God, which giveth us victory through our Lord Jesus Christ."—Ernest Edward Smith.

April 18. Walking and Talking with Jesus

Text: Luke 24:32.

Easter, as an annual event, is past. But Easter as an enduring, vibrant truth is not of passing significance. Think of the meaning and hope of Easter as we review one of the events of that first Easter, the walk to Emmaus. Walking can be just a means of getting from here to there. But walking and talking with Jesus can do more than change our location. For the two disciples, it was a walk that began in gloom and ended in joy. The talk was more important than the walk. We too can say, "He talked with us by the way."

I. He talks with us to dispel our despair. Luke tells of two men who were depressed and dejected. But as they walked and talked with Jesus, he gave them new hope and joy until, looking back on it, they said, "Did not our hearts burn?" or as Phillips put it, "Weren't our hearts glowing?" This can be our experience.

II. He talks with us to open the scriptures. "He expounded unto them in all the scriptures the things concerning himself" (v. 27). There are many conflicting voices. Some whisper doubts and some shout derision. But in the midst of the uncertainties and cynicism, remember the Father's words: "This is my beloved Son . . . hear ye him" (Matt. 17:5).

III. He talks with us to reveal himself. That is what he did for those disciples on the Emmaus road. "Their eyes were opened, and they knew him" (v. 31). It was at an ordinary meal in an ordinary house when ordinary bread was broken that they saw him. He can and will reveal himself to us in the usual or the unusual. He may come to us in the person of someone in need, in a scene of beauty, or in a moment of quietness. More important than what comes is that he comes. We can experience a lift to our hearts and new light on scripture, but best of all we can look at him.

IV. Much was revealed as they walked and talked on the road to Emmaus, but greater revelations came after the travelers said, "Abide with us" and "he went in to tarry with them" (v. 29). If you will invite him in, he will tarry with you.—Bramwell Tripp.

April 25. Revealing Our Identity

Scripture: John 10:22–30.

I. The Jews gather round and ask, "Are you the Christ?" (a) This was the question they were wondering, it is the question John hopes his readers are thinking, and it is a question many may ask today. We have the same need to identify Jesus as they did.

(b) Before Easter he is called many things—a prophet, Elijah, John the Baptist, the suffering servant, the son of man, Moses. After Easter his true identity is revealed. He is the Christ. His life, words, and work all testify to that fact.

(c) Jesus mentions two ways he has already answered the question. He says his words should have told them, but they didn't believe it. He says his works have shown it, but they didn't see.

II. Many today may be asking the same type of question about the church. (a) They are saying: "We know what you say you are, but what are you really? Are you really concerned about people? Are you really a servant church? Are you really for this or opposed to that?" I wonder in how many areas of our ministry we can say, "We not only told you what we stood for, but we have also shown you."

(b) Maybe they have questions about us because we have told them, but we haven't shown them. The Easter message reminds us God has both told us he loves us and has shown us that love in Christ. It is time for us to spread the message not only with words but also with deeds.—Robert H. Herzig in *The Circuit Rider*.

May 2. Does Prayer Work?

TEXT: Jas. 5:16.

To say that prayer works seems to suggest that a person gets what he asks for, but isn't there a different test of what "works" when we pray?

I. Prayer works when it gives us a greater sense of the majesty and glory of God.

II. Prayer works when it leads us to true repentance after a confession of sin.

III. Prayer works when it arouses in us an awesome sense of the forgiving grace of God.

IV. Prayer works when it engenders profound thanks for every day that we live and makes us realize that life is a gift to be received with gratitude and a task to be pursued with courage.

V. Prayer works when it leads us to pray for others.

VI. Prayer works when it impels us to action on behalf of our brothers and sisters in this world.

VII. Prayer works when it leads to new commitments in our Christian pilgrimage.

VIII. Prayer works when along with our asking it leads to our giving.—George Laird Hunt in *The Presbyterian Outlook*.

May 9. Job Description for Family Builders (Mother's Day)

TEXT: Ps. 133:1.

I. Establish clear time commitments for the family. Your professional task gets done because it has time assigned to it. Specific blocks of time are essential for being a family.

II. Establish rituals and patterns for your family life. As human beings we need ritual forms. The family meal is most likely to be the best context for this. Unfortunately the daily meal together seems to be eroding in many homes. Food is more than food when it is shared. Create a pattern of reading scripture, of celebrating achievements, and of praying together. You may find a children's Bible helpful to you. You have to fight to build your family culture; everyone else is trying to do it for you.

III. Do more things together as a family unit. It may seem like swimming upstream to reverse the intense individualism of our time, but everyone in your family needs to know how to be a corporate unit—a body that acts together.

IV. Seek and welcome the support of other families. Families are not meant to be isolated. We all have similar needs and problems. Create events which your family will share with one or more other families.—Robert B. Wallace.

May 16. Habakkuk Speaks to Our Day

SCRIPTURE: Hab. 1:1–4; 2:1–4; 3:17–18.

I. God is the moral governor of the universe. The prophecy stresses the universality of the divine government. The prophet accepts a special divine providence over Israel, but he insists with equal emphasis that the destinies of all nations are in God's hands.

II. His judgment against the unrighteous will come, even though it is delayed.

III. The righteous shall live by his faithfulness. In the New Testament, justification (righteousness) by faith, taken by Martin Luther from this text and from Rom. 1:17 and interpreted in a theological sense, became the heart of the gospel.

IV. We must be patient and trust God. The secret of patience in perplexity is an indomitable faith in the purpose of God and in the ultimate defeat of evil and triumph of God. "If it seems slow, wait for it; it will surely come, it will not delay."—Ernest Trice Thompson.

May 23. At Ease in Zion

TEXT: Amos 6:1.

When is the church at ease?

I. When it sees spiritual, physical, and social needs, and even discusses such in depth, yet does little or nothing superficially or sacrificially to relieve them.

II. When it is annoyed by those who stir its conscience.

III. When current giving is approximately the same as last year.

IV. When prayers are said without feeling or fervency or love.

V. When tears are absent in service after service.

VI. When members think of the pastor as the one who is supposed to do the praying, preaching, and Bible study.

VII. When working for the church replaces working as the church.

VIII. When there is resistance to those who speak against the sins in the church or in the community.

IX. When it has an inner fear of a new work of God through the Spirit.

X. When it can allow any sin among its members without fasting and prayer.

XI. When it cannot point specifically to a miracle of God among its members in the last month.—John M. Drescher.

May 30. Guided by the Spirit (Pentecost)

SCRIPTURE: Rom. 8:1–27.

As our comforter, counselor, or teacher, the Holy Spirit is also our guide (John 16:13), directing us into all truth and helping us to understand things to come. The apostle Paul describes in some detail the benefits of the Spirit-filled life.

I. The Holy Spirit makes known to the Christian that he is now "in Christ" and free from condemnation (v. 1).

II. The Holy Spirit gives us new freedom as we actually become aware of a new rule for living called the "law of the Spirit of life" (v. 2).

III. The Holy Spirit brings to the Christian a new mind, enabling him to rise above the low level of fleshly or carnal living and thinking (vv. 5–8).

IV. The Holy Spirit comes to indwell the believer, causing him to be aware of past deliverance, present experience of growing in Christ, and future hope of being quickened or made alive by the Spirit in the resurrection (vv. 9–11).

V. The Holy Spirit ministers to the Christian by leading him (v. 14). This assures the believer of avoiding sin and coming to the knowledge of God's perfect will.

VI. The Holy Spirit bears witness to the individual Christian that he is a child of God (v. 16). With this knowledge of sonship, the Spirit also gives the believer a great assurance of an inheritance as a "joint-heir" of Christ. The gift of the Holy Spirit is the guarantee of the inheritance to come.

VII. The Holy Spirit ministers to the Christian through intercession (v. 26). This means that the Holy Spirit helps us to pray effectively, that he prays for us and through us, according to the will of God.—F. J. May.

June 6. Love and Justice

SCRIPTURE: Luke 11:1–13.

God gave Jesus to show us that his love exceeds his justice.

I. *Our lives.* When we find ourselves doing or saying things we should not do or say, we like to have love applied to us. We must apply love and not justice to others who do and say things they should not do or say.

II. *Marriage.* We do not like for our partners to get even with us when we are unfair to them, so we must not try to get even with them when they are unfair to us.

III. *Family.* If we want the boy down the street who breaks the law to receive justice, we must not expect our children when they break the law to receive love instead of justice.

IV. *Friends.* If we expect our friends to forgive us when we hurt them, we must forgive them when they hurt us.

V. *Church.* When we get our feelings hurt in church, we like for people to humor us. We must be aware of other people who would like for us to humor them.

VII. *Christ.* The unjust death of Christ on the cross shows us that God's love exceeds justice.

VIII. *The next life.* When we die, we shall all be glad that we face a loving God rather than a just God.—Holland R. Vaughan in *The Circuit Rider.*

June 13. True Spiritual Worship

SCRIPTURE: Rom. 12:1–5.

I. Such worship is possible only by the mercies of God (vv. 1,3). (a) A person who senses no need of God's mercy cannot worship God properly. People naturally think too highly of themselves.

(b) When God's mercy covers our sin, our worship is acceptable to God.

(1) God has revealed his mercy in Christ.

(2) Faith, which grasps Christ, is a work of God's mercy.

(3) Connected to Christ by faith, we Christians are able to carry out true spiritual worship.

II. Such worship is practiced by living according to God's will (vv. 2, 4–5).

(a) We are to live as transformed people, not living as the world lives but understanding and doing that which is good and acceptable and perfect in God's sight.

(b) We are to live like Christ, not lording it over one another, but serving one another according to the will of God.

(c) We are to live so as to perform a unique function in the whole body of Christians.—Robert C. Zick.

June 20. Christ Blesses Our Daily Lives

TEXT: John 2:1–11.

I. He blesses us with his presence. (a) He came to Cana as an invited guest. Clearly a human being—true man—but also as a personal friend.

(b) The presence of Christ today is where his word is received. As the Cana wedding was the stage for Jesus' activity, so Christian worship, Christian meditation, and Christian homes become that stage.

II. He blesses us with his power. (a) At Cana, the wine failed.

(1) Man's efforts to bring joy to himself ran out.

(2) Our use of the creative gifts of God will fail before we are satisfied.

(b) Jesus gives new wine. (1) He shows the creative power of the Father.

(2) He shows a love and concern for man's happiness—first for those at the feast but chiefly for all mankind through the continuing creation.

(c) Christ has the power to bring life's best and to give us good things from his hands and to give us the relationship with God so necessary for true happiness in this world.

III. He blesses us with his purpose. (a) His purpose was not fully seen at Cana.

(1) His hour had not yet come.

(2) His hour arrived on Calvary.

(b) His purpose is to perfect purification from the old rites of Jewish purification to the new wine of the atonement.

(c) His purpose is to reveal his identity seen in a sign of his glory but pointing forward to his greater glory on Calvary.—Robert W. Schaibley.

June 27. The God We Worship

TEXT: Deut. 33:27.

When Jesus said, "I and the Father are one," he gave me a photograph of God that I had never seen before. There were some pictures of God that we had from history, but Jesus gave them sharpness. He focused them better. What kind of God is he?

I. A God who cares for the one. One person was important to Jesus. It mattered not who that one person was, what he had done, or where he was in his life. Jesus cared about the one. In three stories he told about one lost sheep, one lost coin, and one lost son. In each story he spoke about a celebration when the one was found.

II. A God who cares about the human situation and circumstance. He moved Israel out of Egypt. He moved Jesus out of a grave. He moved Paul and Silas out of prison. Throughout history he has been busy changing situations and circumstances. He cares about our living conditions. He cares about our famines and earthquakes. He cares about the here and now.

III. A God who makes things happen now. Because of Christ, people have said: "I can take this situation and make something good out of it. I can take this sin, this failure, or this frustration, and through the help of God something beautiful can emerge." If God can make a butterfly out of a caterpillar—something that flies out of something that crawls—then surely God can make something out of me too.

IV. A God who has never surrendered to any power in the universe. He is a God in control, and he wants to burn a few bushes for us right now.—Jerry Hayner.

July 4. Rebirth of Patriotism (Independence Day)

SCRIPTURE: Josh. 24:14–28.

The word "patriotism" comes from the Greek word *pater*, which means father. Thus patriotism means love for the fatherland. If America is to experience a rebirth of patriotism, we must be committed to the following principles:

I. Patriotism results when we give our allegiance to God and family.

(a) As the Hebrews took possession of a new land, Joshua realized that their patriotism was closely related to their allegiance to God (vv. 14–15).

(b) Past experience seems to indicate that true patriotism is linked to love of God and neighbor.

II. Patriotism results when we appreciate our history. (a) As the Hebrews took possession of the new land, they reflected on the past (vv. 16–18).

(b) America's great moments far outweigh the bad. The birth of our national anthem and of our flag are inspiring events in our history.

III. Patriotism results when we take advantage of our opportunities.

(a) With obstacles before them, the Hebrews went forth to develop the new land (v. 28).

(b) Our nation's problems are really opportunities for advancement. President Kennedy said, "We shall pay any price, bear any burden, meet any hardship, support any friend . . . to assure the survival and success of liberty."—Larry W. Kennedy.

July 11. Levels of Giving

TEXT: Luke 16:2.

What will be your level of giving?

I. Will it be the tip level? Small change for God?

II. Will it be the entertainment level? Pay when you go, a kind of a la carte commitment? Only pay for what you get?

III. Will it be the emotional level? Give when you feel like it? When you feel guilty or are in need, you remember the church. When things are going well in your life, you just forget it.

IV. Will it be the good intention level? You'll do better when you've got more to spare. Or you'll do better when it won't interfere with anything else.

V. Will it be the Christian level? You will give systematically and sacrificially, doing great things as a servant of God.—Craig Biddle III.

July 18. On Eagles' Wings

TEXT: Isa. 40:31.

I. Whatever the circumstances, God will supply our needs. There will be times of great emergencies, and God will give us of his grace so that we can mount up with the wings of eagles. An eagle soars high. He lives in lofty places.

II. There will be those days of crises. When those days come, God will provide the necessary strength that makes it possible for us to carry on. I have watched God's people find physical and spiritual strength to meet grave crises over a lengthy period of time.

III. Walking and not fainting speaks of the routine tasks. A person in Isaiah's day, following a plow from sunrise to sunset, could easily grow weary to the point of being bone tired. We need a portion of God's strength as we meet the challenge of the everyday task.—Tom J. Madden.

July 25. Questions for Christians Watching TV

Text: Eccl. 1:8.

I. *Before viewing a program.* (a) Will watching this program represent responsible Christian stewardship?

(b) Why am I considering watching this?

(c) What has this show been like in the past?

(d) Is this a good way to be informed or entertained?

(e) Would watching this program together help or hurt my family?

II. *During a program.* (a) What moral values are promoted or undermined?

(b) Is God's name profaned or is vulgar language used?

(c) Is violence glorified or sex exploited?

(d) Are alcohol and other drugs glamorized or taken for granted?

(e) Does the program make me more trusting or more suspicious of others?

III. *After a program.* (a) Am I a better person for having watched this program?

(b) Was this a program that encouraged morality or immorality?

(c) Should I consider watching this program again? Why or why not?

(d) How can I use this experience to honor God and help others?

(e) Should I communicate my convictions about this program to advertisers and television people?—Robert Chitwood.

August 1. Why I Am a Christian

Scripture: Eph. 2:4–10.

I. I am a Christian because of Jesus Christ.

II. I am a Christian because of the grace of God.

III. I am a Christian because I am a sinner, always standing in the need of God's grace and forgiveness.

IV. I am a Christian because Christ leads me to the greatest relationship of life—to know God as father.—John Thompson.

August 8. What It Means to Be Christian

Text: Jas. 2:7.

I. Christian does not mean everything that is true, good, beautiful, and human. Who could deny that truth, goodness, beauty, and humanity exist also outside Christianity? But everything can be called Christian which in theory and practice has an explicit, positive reference to Jesus Christ.

II. A Christian is not just any human being with genuine conviction, sincere faith, and goodwill. No one can fail to see that genuine conviction, sincere faith, and goodwill exist also outside Christianity. But all those can be called Christians for whom life and death in Jesus Christ is ultimately decisive.

III. Christian church does not mean just any meditation or action group or any community of committed human beings who try to lead a decent life in order to gain salvation. It could never be disputed that commitment, action, meditation, a decent life, and salvation can exist in other groups outside the church. But any community, great or small, for whom Jesus Christ is ultimately decisive can be called a Christian church.

IV. Christianity does not exist wherever inhumanity is opposed and humanity realized. It is a simple truth that inhumanity is opposed and humanity realized also outside Christianity—among Jews, Muslims, Hindus, and Buddhists, among post-Christian humanists and outspoken atheists. But Christianity exists only where the memory of Jesus Christ is activated in theory and practice.—Hans Küng in *On Being a Christian.*

August 15. The Double-Edged Sword

Text: Heb. 4:12 (gnb).

I. The double edges of the sword are grace and judgment. Grace makes ordinary persons realize they are really quite extraordinary, while judgment informs extraordinary persons that they are really quite ordinary. Grace finds the divine spark in the heart of a thief. Judgment exposes the demonic in the heart of a bishop.

II. The word of God cuts through "to

where soul and spirit meet, to where joints and marrow come together." Yet through all the cutting, the author of Hebrews invites us to approach boldly the throne of grace. J. K. Stuart prayed: "Our Father, we are aware that we have been invited to come boldly unto the throne of grace that we may ask what we wish and that we can consider ourselves a chosen priesthood, elite, all sons and daughters of God. Yet with all this assurance, Lord, we do not feel worthy to come boldly before our maker, so we tiptoe into thy presence in confession and contrition."

III. There is the paradox of the double-edged sword. When we look honestly at ourselves, we see our prejudices, our greed, our educated ignorances, and our brokenness. We see the chains which have bound us and the walls that have blocked us from fulfilling all that we are called to be. Yet we are invited to accept grace and identify ourselves with the carpenter's son to become whole and complete.—Mary Ann Swenson in *The Circuit Rider*.

August 22. Three Types of Persons
Text: I Pet. 4:2.

I. The first is the tradition-directed type of individual who does things because they have always been done that way.

II. The second is the inner-directed type of person who has a set of goals or principles for which he drives. Such a man has a built-in gyroscope—a psychological instrumentality keeping him on course. He stays in line with his own deepest principles, within his own goals, and with the deepest inner laws of his being.

III. A third type is called the other-directed person who operates with a built-in radar apparatus. He keeps lined up not with what is immutable within him but with what is happening around him. His signals come from outside, keeping him in line with what others are doing—especially those others he'd like to be like, his peer group. This man is more concerned about adjustment than about achievement, about personality than about character, and about morale than about morality.—Adapted from David Riesman.

August 29. Why We Don't Learn
Text: II Tim. 2:7.

I. We receive the wrong information. Either learning from those who haven't learned themselves or from those who would deliberately mislead us is probably one of the most prevalent problems surrounding the lack of spiritual maturity. In our day we yearn for the whole truth and nothing but the truth. (See I John 4:1–6.)

II. We are too often satisfied with our present condition. Many times because almost everyone around us is in the same condition, we come to the conclusion, "There is nothing better, so why keep searching?" One of the great faults of our society is the lack of courage to move out from our present condition in search for something more that can be ours for the taking. (See Phil. 3:13–14.)

III. We are basically selfish people. We take the attitude of the priest and Levite in the story of the good Samaritan. What is ours we are going to keep to ourselves and not share. God's word tells us in numerous places that in order to receive we must give. (See Luke 10:30–37.)

IV. We are not willing to pay the price. Jesus told several who hinted at receiving the more abundant life from him that they would have to give up what they had to receive what he had. When we are told the price we have to pay for what we really want, we do not look at the reward to be received but at what is involved in obtaining. The price overshadows the outcome. (See Matt. 16:24–28.)

V. Even though these are only four reasons among many why we fail to learn and receive, there is no excuse or reason worth missing what God has in store for those whom he loves. Let us break away from old traditions and move forward with God.—John G. Brock.

September 5. On Being Saved
Text: II Pet. 1:11.

When H. Richard Niebuhr was asked whether he was saved, he replied: "I was saved by what Christ did; I am being saved right now; I shall be saved when the kingdom comes." Salvation is past, present, and future. In its biblical meaning it is both a deliverance from something and a healing or being made whole for something. We are saved from and saved for three major things according to the biblical witness.

I. We are saved from sin—any form of idolatry and every form of ego which separates us from God—and saved for a new singleness and focus to our life.

II. We are saved from evil—those powers and principalities which tend to control us and make us powerless—and saved for a new partnership with God and participation in the life of the Spirit.

III. We are saved from death—the fear of death and a sense of our aloneness in the universe—and saved for a life of obedience, for the most profound obedience is that which has no fear of death.—Robert B. Wallace.

September 12. The Church and the School (Rally Day)

TEXT: Eph. 4:14–15.

I. The Sunday school is a great source of evangelistic outreach to friends and relatives of existing members.

II. The Sunday school provides the opportunity for establishing and developing personal relationships which, in turn, greatly support the incorporation of new members into the life of the church.

III. The Sunday school provides a unique opportunity to teach Bible knowledge and to study the implications of the Christian life in today's world.

IV. The Sunday school is a natural structure to create new classes that appeal to a wide spectrum of new people.

V. The Sunday school provides a system for the church to minister to the entire family and to include every age group in this ministry.

VI. The Sunday school is the most natural organization within the church for training and equipping large numbers of Christians for the work to which Christ has called his church.—Charles and Win Arn.

September 19. Why Attend Church?

TEXT: Ps. 55:14.

I. It honors God. When God is being praised in worship, you should desire to be there to pay him homage. You cannot honor him just as well somewhere else when the saints are gathered.

II. You need it. We've all heard such statements as "I can worship God just as well in the privacy of my own home" or "I can commune with him in the beauty of his creation on the bank of a gentle stream or on a beautiful golf course." I won't argue against God's presence in nature, but I've yet to see a person who forsakes the assembly in favor of recreation on fire for the Lord. God has designed certain worship activities to enlighten and strengthen us. If something else would work as well, he would have said so.

III. Others need you. The proof text so often used for attendance gives good reasons. "Let us consider how to stir up one another to love and good works, not neglecting to meet together . . . but encouraging one another" (Heb. 10:25). You can't encourage your brothers and sisters by your absence. I've seen hundreds of Christians who were terribly discouraged by low attendance. Those who neglect the assembly not only damage their own spiritual health but also violate the rule of brotherly love and concern.—Joe E. Barnett.

September 26. On Doing What We're Saying

TEXT: Jas. 2:14.

I. Our preaching about peace yet refusing to take the initiative to be reconciled to a fellow believer, fellow worker, or neighbor.

II. Our preaching that Christ breaks down all walls yet our allowing all kinds of barriers to exist in feelings toward certain persons.

III. Our preaching about loving our enemies yet our inability to even meet in close sharing together with certain fellow Christians.

IV. Our preaching on forgiveness yet our holding grudges and ill-feelings toward others.

V. Our preaching on putting God first yet spending more time on worldly attractions than in Bible study, prayer, witness, and service.—John M. Drescher.

October 3. Accepting One Another

SCRIPTURE: Rom. 15:4–13.

I. Christ gives us the example of acceptance. (a) He did not please himself (v. 3).

(1) Our problem is that we want to go our own way.

(2) Christ sacrificed and suffered for us.

(b) Christ became the servant of all. (1) He brought together the most diverse groups of people in the ancient world— Jews and gentiles.

(2) He takes us from every walk of life and brings us close to God and to one another.

II. God gives us the power to accept one another. (a) It is only through the gift of God that we can be of one mind (v. 5).

(1) We cannot achieve spiritual unity by ourselves.

(2) With Paul we constantly beseech God to grant it.

(b) God's acceptance of us is the key. (1) Paul gives us the motivation and the power: "Accept one another, for Christ has accepted you!"

(2) Servants of God who have experienced his acceptance are able to accept others. (See Matt. 18:23–34.)

III. God's name is glorified when we accept one another. "Let your light so shine before men that they may see your good works, and glorify your Father who is in heaven." Our life together is to be marked by acceptance. We can learn to deal lovingly with one another, bearing with each other's faults and foibles. We have the example of Christ. We have the power from God through Christ. We know the result— God's name is glorified.—Jeffrey A. Gibbs.

October 10. If I Were a Layman (Laity Sunday)

TEXT: II Cor. 3:3.

I. I would be faithful in attendance at worship—not for the church's sake but because I need this regularity of experiencing the presence of God week after week.

II. I would find a responsible job in the work of the church—and stick to it as creatively as I can. This is not nearly so much for the church's sake as it is for mine. I need to be involved if I care. And I do care that the human story comes out right. I do

care that my life's weight is on God's side, not on his opponent's side because of inactivity and carelessness.

III. I would be a regular giver of my resources—not because my little will make a great difference but because my resources need to be spent in caring ways.

IV. I would encourage others—supporting their lives with the good and uplifting word. Life is not easy for anyone and some seem to have more difficulty than others. Often we are unaware of what burdens others carry.

V. I would remember my life has the eternal around and within it—I am related to God's purpose and care. That gives meaning to the above convictions. This remembrance lifts us above fear of failure, fear of death, and feelings of inadequacy and loneliness. "If God is for us, who can be against us?" Life has a new meaning as we remember that God is life's giver, keeper, and empowerer.—Clark Robbins.

October 17. The Glory of God's Children

SCRIPTURE: Rom. 8:12–17.

We sometimes envy people with outstanding musical or athletic ability or gifts of leadership, administration, or teaching. But regardless of our position, occupationally, financially, or otherwise, all of us who are Christians are in a glorious position. Paul reminds us in our text that we are children of God.

I. As God's child you can glory in the victory of your spirit over your flesh.

(a) Note that Paul sees the struggle still going on.

(b) But as God's children, we can gain the victory day after day.

II. As God's child you can glory in the blessings which are yours. (a) The Holy Spirit speaks to us through the word.

(b) The heavenly Father listens when we cry to him.

(c) Our loving God assures us that we will forever enjoy all that Christ earned for us.

(1) Many of these blessings are ours to enjoy day by day, right now.

(2) The best are kept in trust for us as heirs of God.

(d) You and I can glory in what God has done, is doing, and will do for us, his children.—Mark J. Steege.

October 24. Living on Substitutes

Texts: Luke 12:15; Matt. 6:33.

I. There is nothing wrong with enjoying the good things God has given us, provided they do not become substitutes for the best things of life. One of the mistakes of our society is that of living on substitutes. Many people know the price of everything and the value of nothing. They have a false sense of security and a counterfeit feeling of satisfaction. These people are enjoying the taste of life but getting nothing substantial to really live on. Then when the storms of life start to blow, they topple over like trees without roots.

II. Things—the good things that God wants us to enjoy—are not the center of life but rather are the extra benefits we receive when God is given his rightful place in our hearts. The man who lives for things and ignores God will lose both, but the man who puts God first will have God and the good things that God wants him to enjoy. This does not mean that every obedient Christian will be rich, but it does mean that he will receive the things God wants him to have in this life. This is a very fair contract. David wrote centuries ago, "I have been young and now am old; yet have I not seen the righteous forsaken, nor his seed begging bread" (Ps. 37:25).

III. When we allow Jesus Christ to control our lives, we gradually discover a whole new set of values. Things that once were so important become trivial, and things that used to lie on the edges of life suddenly take their rightful place at the very center. We discover that many things are just adult toys to keep us happy until the next novelty comes along. We discover too that when Christ is at the center, he gives us a deep satisfaction that nothing else can give. We stop living on substitutes and start enjoying a daily experience of reality.—Donald O'Quin.

October 31. Christ Our Mediator

Scripture: Heb. 9:11–15.

I. The mediator of a new covenant. (a) The old covenant. (1) The covenant God made with his Old Testament people was acted out and celebrated in the ceremonial sacrifices of the tabernacle and temple worship which reached their climax in the Day of Atonement (Luke 16:14–16).

(2) These sacrifices were types of Christ.

(b) The new covenant. (1) The covenant established by God with his New Testament people reached its climax in the redemptive act of Jesus Christ.

(2) Christ entered into the tabernacle not made with hands (incarnation) and into the very throne room of God (v. 11). Taking with him his own blood (v. 12), he offered the unique sacrifice, once for all (Heb. 10:10–12, 14).

II. The mediator of greater things. (a) Who secured for us an eternal redemption (v. 12).

(1) He "redeemed us from sin, death, and the power of the devil" (Luther).

(2) The forgiveness which he secured for us is perfect and complete (v. 15).

(b) Who urged us from dead works to serve the living God (v. 14). Luther: "To live under him in his kingdom and serve him in everlasting righteousness, innocence, and blessedness."

(c) Who gained for us an eternal inheritance. (1) "He is risen from the dead, lives and reigns to all eternity" (Luther).

(2) The life now begun reaches fulfillment in heaven (v. 15).—Norbert H. Mueller.

November 7. The Three H's in Bible Reading

Text: II Tim. 3:16.

We should read the Bible with three H's —honesty, humility, and humor.

I. Honesty means recognition of the fact that much of the Bible celebrates God's grace working in and through human sin and weakness—the full human condition, which in the Bible is not made palatable to delicate sensibilities but is realistically portrayed. It also means we cannot moralize while first reading most passages or sections of the Bible. To do that is to do what the ancient biblical writers refused to do—clean up the human condition in the Bible so as to make the individuals in it models for us to follow in our lives.

II. Humility means identifying in the stories, reports, and parables with those with whom we might not otherwise identify—even the so-called bad guys in a story, for example with Joseph's brothers instead of with Joseph or with the congregation at Nazareth instead of with Jesus.

III. Humor means taking God a little more seriously and ourselves a little less seriously day by day and on each reading. If we can't laugh at ourselves a little in the realism of life as the Bible portrays it, we'll never get its message.—James A. Sanders.

November 14. When Less Is More (Stewardship Day)

TEXT: Luke 1:53.

I. Isaiah could envision a leveling experience of judgmental proportion as the humble would be exalted and the exalted humbled. Mary declared that the Lord would satisfy the hungry, and the rich would be empty-handed. The Lord was using the simple things and raising them to new heights of exaltation. When the Lord touches a life, a task, or a few loaves and fishes, they become adequate.

II. The manner of our living can be a good Christian witness or it can be detrimental. Christians are to live a responsible life. It's difficult to stand on the mountain and witness to people in the valley. High atop an affluent lifestyle presents problems in witnessing to a world when half the people are hungry or near hungry. Sacrifice to most Americans means a high ball to the outfield that will advance a runner on a baseball field. We've hardened ourselves to those in need. World evangelization is something to be done piece-meal by using whatever left-overs we have. Wealth begets wealth and calls for super houses and splashy cars, and suddenly consumerism becomes our god.

III. It has been observed that lifestyle is nothing less than a struggle with idolatry, where American secularism is the idol. This is not to say all Americans are idolaters. It is saying that we have a difficult task in keeping our sense of values straight. Neither is wealth nor the accumulation of wealth wrong. It's our attitude that spells the difference. Greed for more and more is a direct violation of the words of Christ about laying up treasures on earth.

IV. We can climb higher and higher on the ladder of affluence and continue to gain an advantage on our fellow man. To use this wealth simply to gain more without a sharing thought toward our brother brings us in conflict with Christ who spoke of a cup of water in my name. Or, as Ken Sehested expressed it, we can "live simply, so that others may simply live."—Guy Henderson.

November 21. The Searching of God

TEXT: Ps. 139:1.

I. We are searched and known by the slow passing of the years.

II. God searches all of us by the responsibilities he lays upon us.

III. God has a way of searching us by lifting our eyes from the detail to the whole.

IV. God has a common way of searching us by showing us our own case in another's life.

V. God searches us by bringing new influences into our lives.—George H. Morrison.

November 28. The Ministry of Surprise (Advent)

TEXT: Matt. 5:42.

I. The unexpectedness of Christ's birth. It did not come with the pomp and ceremony which was commonly anticipated by the Jews for the advent of their messiah. Jesus was born of a woman of humble station and born in a stable, not in a palace.

II. The unexpectedness of Christ's speech. There were many surprises in his teaching. He surprised men's attention by the unexpectedness of his words. Men who came to arrest him were themselves arrested by what he had to say. "Never man spake like this man" was their verdict. His words were familiar, but his thought was startling. "All bore him witness and wondered at the gracious words that proceeded out of his mouth."

III. The unexpectedness of his choice of friends. He chose twelve ordinary men to be his apostles. Throughout his ministry he cultivated the friendship of the social outcasts so that he was accused of being a glutton and a drunkard. Is it not a surprise that the sinless Son of Man should have been the friend of publicans and sinners?

IV. The unexpectedness of his death. In the thought of the Jews death was not on the program for the messiah. He was to be a conqueror. Despite his frank warnings, his disciples were not looking for his death on a cross, and when it came they were confused and disillusioned. "We had hoped," said two of them to a stranger on the Emmaus road, "that he would be the redeemer of Israel, but he is dead and that was three days ago." But in that atoning death there was power to convert and redeem mankind.—John Bishop.

December 5. Approaching Christmas from This Side of Bethlehem (Advent)

TEXT: II Cor. 9:15.

I. You cannot really approach the Bethlehem event with the same mind as the prophets, shepherds, and wise men. You live beyond Bethlehem. You know what they could not know. Yours is a different perspective and a different celebration.

II. You know that the world now harbors a conscience about the manner of its life under God because of that birth in Bethlehem. People cannot quite erase their awareness of the man who declared that he had been annointed to proclaim release to the captives, recovery of sight to the blind, and liberation for those who are oppressed.

III. You know now that the ancient philosophers' search for some great truth in a perfect set of ideas is better found in Jesus Christ. That is because he lived out the deepest truth of all in unconditional love and invited others to join him in a servant lifestyle.

IV. You know the humanizing influences of life which have invaded the world at his impulse because he made himself of no reputation in order that others might be taught, encouraged, helped, and healed.

V. Because that child grew to have open association with all sorts and conditions of people, you know that God really cares about you and that you can even love yourself.

VI. Because you know these things, it becomes a joyful pilgrimage from the other side of Bethlehem to return to that manger scene at Christmas time. It can be for you more than merely time off work and oodles of gifts and more even than a family homecoming. It can be a time to celebrate every good thing which has emerged since that ancient evening.—George M. Tuttle in *The United Church Observer.*

December 12. Christmas: Burden or Blessing? (Advent)

TEXT: Rom. 8:28 (PHILLIPS).

I. Every burden is a blessing. (a) There may be some who are saying that Christmas is a burden this year because of the loss of a loved one. Christmas perhaps is a burden with loneliness, sorrow, and anxiety all building up into negative emotions. You can turn your burden into a blessing by reaching out in love and helpfulness to others. Forget about yourself. Visit someone who is old or lonely. Volunteer your service to your church.

(b) A problem is either a guideline to redirect us or, like pain, a warning sign that we need to take care of something. Your problem may be a guideline, a warning signal, a learning experience, a growth process, or a transition phase, but it can be a blessing.

(c) Christmas should be a joyous time for everyone. Every burden is a blessing if you have a relationship with God through Christ.

II. We should recognize that every blessing is a burden. That may sound strange, but it is true. When a new baby comes into a home, it is a blessing but also a burden of responsibility. It is a joy and a blessing to have a new car or home, but you face the cost of upkeep, maintenance, and insurance. We feel we are blessed when given advancement in our work or profession, but every promotion brings greater responsibility. (See Luke 12:48, RSV.)

III. Are you sure you want a merry Christmas? Are you sure you want a blessed Christmas? Because if you are blessed, you will have to be a blessing.

(a) This is true in our relationship with God and Jesus Christ. When you accept him as your lord and savior, you do so through faith. You believe in the name of Jesus. You experience forgiveness of all your sins and are given the promise and hope of eternal life. The greatest of all blessings is salvation.

(b) But every blessing is a burden. You now have the obligation to share with those who do not have this faith and to be a witness of the saving grace of God to your family, neighbors, and business associates. You have the responsibility to let others know what you have experienced in your life and to urge them to seek this same relationship with God.

IV. You turn the blessing which has become a new burden into a new blessing by fulfilling your responsibility.

(a) This gives you a sense of identity. You are somebody worthwhile. You fulfill your own need to be needed, and this adds meaning to life.

(b) If there were no burdens that could become blessings, your life would be empty. God gives us a new burden so we can have a fresh blessing. He gives us a fresh blessing so we can have enough of a burden to make us aware that we are needed in this world.

(c) Jesus Christ came into the world at Christmas to be a blessing. That blessing became a burden on the cross. But the burden of the cross became the blessing of the resurrection on Easter. That is why we celebrate Christmas.—Ernest W. Holz in *The War Cry.*

December 19. The Decisive Babies of the World (Advent)

TEXT: Luke 2:7.

I. When we center our attention on the the decisive babies of the world, a mood of expectancy and hope arises.

II. Look at history in the large and see how often, when the world seemed hope-less and when the limits of man's achievements seemed reached, a baby was born who became the pioneer of a new era.

III. All great ideas are born small, like babies, and if we are to believe in the creative forces to which the future belongs, we must believe in something inconspicuous, newborn, just growing.

IV. Christendom today acclaims one who came to us as a babe. His coming was decisive. He has it in him to be decisive. He waits for the hour when his determining influence can be made decisive. When Christ has become decisive for enough people, one by one, he will become indeed the most decisive baby in the world.— Harry Emerson Fosdick.

December 26. The Future Belongs to God

TEXT: Deut. 29:29.

By "secret things" the ancient writer means the future. No one has foreknowledge of what will happen in the new year, but God has revealed the laws of life, and we are at liberty and are able to live by them.

I. Any apprehension we feel in our approach to the new year, while understandable, is futile and a waste of time.

II. Our first and foremost task in the new year is to live in the light of what God has revealed. His way of life for man is not easy, but the way is clear enough to follow.

III. To do today's duty well, doing what we can where we are and in terms of what we know, is always the best preparation for any unknown tomorrow.

IV. To trust God for the unknown future is the clearest way to live calmly today.

V. To have present experiences of God's grace and guidance is the surest foundation for hope as we face the unknown future. What faith in Christ has done for generations of believing men and women, it will do for us today and tomorrow.—J. Francis F. Peak.

SECTION III. Resources for Communion Services

SERMON SUGGESTIONS

Topic: Come to the Feast
Text: Rev. 3:20.

I. A beautiful and recurring invitation is dramatized today by the table set before us in remembrance of Jesus' last supper with his disciples. How meaningful the words sound as we meet around this table: "Behold, I stand at the door and knock; if any one hears my voice and opens the door, I will come in to him and sup with him and he with me." Artists have pictured it; experience has verified it; Jesus' invitation is set before us all. One communion liturgy initiates this remembrance by saying we come to the Lord's table "not because we must but because we may." The accent is upon the invitation.

II. Because the invitation is gracious and our acceptance is freely offered, there is a strong desire to be good dinner guests. What a contrast these reactions are to those prompted by coercion! If ever we were forced to assemble at the Lord's table, our typical mood would be one of resentment or impatience. Certainly there would be little readiness to evaluate our lives in the light of Christ's life. We definitely would be poor dinner guests.

III. God never forces the issue. "Behold, I stand at the door and knock" forever is his style. Even the proudest and most stubborn sinner among us is a possible host of God. The high calling of God, the great expectations he has for our lives, and the judgment by which we ultimately will be judged in no way are lessened by this invitational approach. The beauty of it

turns upon the eagerness and joyfulness with which the sinner responds. You and I want to fulfill divine commands because we have been asked to do so, not ordered to do so.

IV. The invitation heard at each communion service relates to self-appraisal. "Let a man examine himself [test himself] before eating his share of the bread and drinking from the cup." We are invited to reflect upon our lives in comparison with the life of Christ. The invitation implicit in the words, "If any one hears my voice and opens the door," relates to personal repentance. Here is the invitation to make Christ the center of one's life, renouncing other loyalties and claiming his fellowship supremely.

V. An invitation denied is a grievous thing. The person who rejects what God offers is the loser, and all heaven is saddened besides. Through his gracious invitations God seeks to provide those things which beautify life and belong to our peace. Every spurning of these blessings shortens the time of opportunity—earthly life obviously is limited—and with every refusal the human heart becomes less and less responsive. There is an RSVP on every invitation God sends our way. Procrastination equals not only bad manners but grievous loss.

VI. There is joy in heaven, Jesus said, over one sinner who repents. There is rejoicing within the Christian community as each newcomer takes up the cross. It is a great thing when one steps over from the sidelines of hesitation to the central arena of Christian service.—John H. Townsend.

Topic: Table Talk

SCRIPTURE: Luke 22:14–38.

I. The table talk can be divided into four dialogues. (a) The first dialogue (Luke 22:21–23) opens with Jesus' shocking statement that "one of you will betray me." All of the disciples are uncertain as to who will betray him. Any may fall away. No one is secure in his faith.

(b) Next is the dispute over greatness (Luke 22:24–27). All of the disciples argue about who will be the greatest in the kingdom of God. In the other gospels this argument occurs in other places. But Luke with real genius places it here at this important meal. Here at the very end of Jesus' ministry the disciples show that they have still not understood what Jesus is doing. They think that discipleship has something to do with achieving greatness, not with being called for service. In this argument they all reveal that they are still basically ignorant and unfaithful. Thus, in one sense, all have betrayed him and his mission. But Jesus still eats with them. Even though these sinners at the table happen to be his twelve best friends, they are unfaithful and half-understanding friends. Jesus not only eats with them, but he also serves them as a vivid example of the kind of service to which he is calling them.

(c) In the third dialogue the focus of concern is on Simon Peter (Luke 22:31–32). Yet when Jesus says, Satan demanded to have you, the you is plural. The use of both the singular and the plural you shows that all will face temptation. Jesus prays for all of the disciples in the midst of their temptation.

(d) The table talk comes to a climax with talk of swords and being prepared for the end. They arise from the table and leave the upper room. In the sequel that follows both the disciples and the captors have swords—proof that they both participate in the powers of darkness for they both use the weapons of evil. "No more of this," Jesus says. Even in the midst of their betrayal Jesus concludes the drama with a promise that the disciples will have a place with him in the banquet which is to come (Luke 22:28–30). Jesus now goes to his crucifixion and the disciples scatter.

II. The last supper was not the last supper. This gospel includes another key meal, the Emmaus meal after Jesus' crucifixion and resurrection (Luke 24:13–35).

(a) Here the disciples were despondent, devoid of hope. The whole Jesus story seemed to have ended at Calvary. That is what the disciples thought. Even on the road to Emmaus when they were side by side with Jesus, they were so blinded by their remorse that they did not recognize him. Then at Emmaus, "When he was at table with them, their eyes were opened," and they saw the risen Christ.

(b) Not until Jesus sat down at the table with them, as he had done so many times before, did they realize that he was present in their midst. In the familiar four-fold action that occurred around the table—the prayer of thanksgiving, the taking and breaking of bread, the taking of the cup, and the giving of the bread and cup—their eyes were opened, the scriptures were made plain to them, and they understood. Jesus was known to them most vividly "in the breaking of the bread" (Luke 24:35).

(c) In a way this is what every meal was like with Jesus. For Luke and for the church, every meal which is eaten in Christ's name is an event whereby Christ's presence releases new power in the participants.

(1) At the Emmaus meal the new power is the power to see and understand the risen Christ.

(2) At the Pentecost meal (Acts 2:42) it is the power of the Holy Spirit which enabled the first Christians to love and understand one another even though they came from diverse races and nations.

(3) Such a meal is also an important occasion for "opening up the scriptures"—as Jesus did in the upper room—and revealing himself to his followers. The presence of Christ at the meal brings power, revelation, understanding, judgment, and forgiveness to all who eat and drink with him and in his name.—William H. Willi-

mon in *South Carolina United Methodist Advocate*.

Topic: The Cup and the Covenant

TEXT: I Cor. 11:23–25.

I. The four characteristics or main points of the Lord's Supper are as follows: It was a formal observance. It was a covenant-sacrifice. It's validity rests entirely on the authority of Christ, as we see from his express command that it be continued "in remembrance of me." It was to be a feast of thanksgiving for all that Christ has done in his redemptive work. In the light of these characteristics we realize that in some way the sacrament is a re-presentation of the crucifixion, which assured his fellowship the benefits of his spiritual return and blessing. As a covenant-sacrifice, according to Paul, Jesus had given assurance of this.

II. When in the presence of those whom he had called to be disciples our Lord broke bread from the common loaf and said, "This is my body," he was reminding them of something that he had done for them. When "likewise after supper he took the cup," as St. Paul writes, he invited them to "drink all of it . . . in remembrance of me," these were, to be sure, manifestations of his life and death. But here was more—the promise of life eternal. Through death to life! Just as "the evening and the morning were the first day," so death and life mark the beginning of the institution of the Lord's Supper.

III. In deed and in truth Jesus instituted a new covenant between God and his creatures (mankind). His death was not that of some martyr who died in vain, simply to be seen by his fellow beings. He died with the purpose and the determination to redeem. He died with the knowledge that God was in him and worked through him for the redemption of the human race. Men could find the freedom of acceptance and the fullness of truth in him. For God was in Christ, reconciling the world unto himself. This reconciliation is the basis of the new covenant.

IV. Jesus gave thanks, blessed the bread, and breaking it, handed it to the disciples, saying, "Take; this is my body"

(Mark 14:22). By this act he transformed the Jewish passover into the evidence of vicarious suffering. He took the suffering upon himself in behalf of the whole human race. Jesus suffered for a purpose, and that purpose is redemption through sacrifice.

(a) In line with the Old Testament, yet transcending it, Jesus makes love the source of all sacrifice. The last supper was not only an act of love but also a witness to obedience. For here we see God's will enacted as redeeming love through Christ who takes upon himself the unique and eternal mission of salvation.

(b) In like manner Jesus lifted the cup and said: "This cup is the new covenant in my blood. Do this as often as you drink it, in remembrance of me." (I Cor. 11:25.) In this admonition to the disciples the master is actually telling them to relive the dramatic meaning of his death and passion, for in this fraternity of faith we have access to the power of the Spirit which assures the ongoing life of the church.

(c) The Lord's Supper is thus the expression of sacrificial love in action. It is the unifying experience of fellowship. It is inclusive in its outreach, encircling mankind. Its covenant relationship brings God's Spirit to us in all its sufficiency.—John Lewis Sandlin.

Topic: Self-Examination Before Communion

TEXT: I Cor. 11:28.

Check the following questions, based on the seven capital sins, and do some serious talking with God before making your communion. Each confirmed person should make some sort of self-examination before receiving his communion.

I. *Pride.* Have I failed in humility? Been self-assertive? Self-indulgent? Opinionated? Set myself up against the church? Been scornful or contemptuous?

II. *Anger.* Have I been deficient in patience and long-suffering? Been overbearing, cruel, or sarcastic? Inflicted hurt on others, bodily or spiritually? Given way to vengeful or jealous thoughts—sullenness, hatred, rage, or irritability?

III. *Lust.* Have I transgressed against

purity in thought, word, imagination, act, and reading? Condoned or spoken lightly of such conduct? Immoderate indulgence in sex gratification?

IV. *Sloth.* Am I diligent in my work and worship? Am I addicted to laziness? Indolent in thought? Slack in devotion? Late for church? Careless or casual?

V. *Envy.* Do I entertain thoughts of charity toward all men? Or do I cherish grudges, old scores, and hatreds? Discontent? Grousing? Peevishness? Nagging? Rebellion against my lot? Resentment of all supposed unfairness? Soured disposition? Cynicisms?

VI. *Avarice.* Have I acquired anything, money or goods, by unfair means? Kept anything back that should be paid? Retained any possessions belonging to others? Refused to share with others? Been stingy or rapacious? Not giving to God his due in time, money, and service?

VII. *Gluttony.* Have I been guilty of overindulgence in eating or drinking, luxury, amusements, spent too much on self, avoided self-denial, or neglected fast days and self-discipline?—*The Anglican Digest.*

Topic: Until He Comes

Text: I Cor. 11:26 (rsv).

What was Paul saying beneath the symbolic language of "until he comes"?

I. We are to proclaim with our words and our living that what God has begun he will finish. The meaning of the metaphor "until he comes" is that, until the end of time, all that Christ revealed to us of the love and goodness of God, of the meaning of the cross and resurrection, and of the power of the life lived with God will be vindicated and will be victorious.

II. This is a reaffirmation of the resurrection. If we are to "proclaim the Lord's death until he comes," the resurrection is being expressed, though not in specific words. Paul is affirming the living, victorious Christ who will come to consummate what he has begun.

III. Paul was writing to the fellowship of those who are in Christ—to the Christian church. It is the gathering of the men of faith who "eat this bread and drink the cup" and who are to "proclaim the Lord's death until he comes." There are Christian solidarity, shared mission, and the oneness of those who are in Christ in the mind of Paul. No Christian flies solo and keeps flying. He is part of an organic, dynamic whole. What Paul seems to be saying is this: Partaking the Lord's Supper together is the way to dramatize the fact that only in the fellowship is our faith nurtured.—Bruce W. Neal.

ILLUSTRATIONS

SHARED EXPERIENCE.　Our English word "communion" has come to have a very specific, almost a technical, meaning as associated with this sacrament. It is treated as a proper name for an ecclesiastical rite. And yet this English word has a far more meaningful usage in ordinary conversation as it describes a very intimate personal interchange of thought and affection and common purpose. The Greek word which is most frequently translated by our word "communion," especially in the kjv, is a very common, ordinary expression indicating a fellowship or a sharing of life experience. But whenever it is used in the New Testament in connection with this sacrament, it very definitely points in two directions: vertically, as it indicates fellowship with Christ, and horizontally, as it indicates fellowship with one another. This is the significance of St. Paul's expression, "a participation in the blood [and body] of Christ."—Peter K. Emmons.

FORGIVENESS.　While working on his famous painting, "The Last Supper," Leonardo da Vinci had an argument with a certain man. He lashed out against the fellow with bitter words and threatening gestures. When the argument was over, Leonardo went back to his canvas where he was working on the face of Jesus. He could not make one stroke. At last he realized what the trouble was. He put down his brush, found the man he had offended, and asked his forgiveness. He returned to his studio and calmly continued painting the face of Jesus.—Arthur Tonne.

REMOVING THE LACE.   An anecdote about Leonardo da Vinci tells about when the great artist had completed "The Last Supper." Before it was displayed to the public, he invited his students to view the finished work. They were immediately overwhelmed by its magnificence. Then the students noticed the beautiful table-cloth on the table. They began to comment on the delicate lace work that Leonardo had painted. But Leonardo was anything but pleased at their attention to the tablecloth. He seized a brush and deftly painted out the lace work.—John Wade.

BREAD OF LIFE.   Bread is a gift of God. Without God's gift of grain, sunshine, and rain, there would be no wheat or corn. The loaf is a symbol of our utter dependence upon our maker. Bread or rice is eaten by all in the world. Food was the most primal need of early man. To produce it was the first requirement. To hoard it was the first sign of wealth. To share it was the first expression of human fellowship. The highest expression in religion is to eat bread together. In the sacrament we feed body and soul by faith with thanksgiving for the Bread of Life.—Don Alexander in *The Cumberland Presbyterian*.

VENERABLE SACRAMENT.   After the last supper, as he was to begin his bitter passion and death for our sin, in this sad, last hour of his life, this truthful and almighty Lord, our creator and redeemer Jesus Christ, selected his words with great deliberation and care in ordaining and instituting this most venerable sacrament, which was to be observed with great reverence and obedience until the end of the world and which was to be an abiding memorial of his bitter passion and death and of all his blessings, a seal of the new covenant, a comfort for all sorrowing hearts, and a true bond and union of Christians with Christ their head and with one another.—Martin Luther.

DAILY FOOD.   While it is true that through baptism we are first born anew, our human flesh and blood have not lost their old skin. There are so many hindrances and temptations of the devil and the world that we often grow weary and faint, at times even stumble. The Lord's Supper is given as a daily food and sustenance so that our faith may refresh and strengthen itself and not weaken in the struggle but grow continually stronger. For the new life should be one that continually develops and progresses.—Martin Luther.

THE CHRISTIAN'S TASK.   "Take, eat" we say in the communion service, and we take and we eat, and we take and we drink. It's just a little bit. It has no nurture for our bodies. It's just a morsel, and yet it is a sacrament. It is symbolic that this is the task of the Christian, to take what God has given and hand it to others and say, "Here, take and eat"—a little love, a little kindness, at least a bit of thoughtfulness. —Vernon Bigler.

MIRACLE.   The miracle of the sacrament is that we are met, we are fed, we are filled, and we are enabled to take up the responsibilities of life as those who dare, as those who have hope, and as those who can live patiently, expectantly, even joyfully in a bewildering, frightening world. —Howard L. Rice.

UNION.   There is a strong tie between the Lord's Supper and the resurrection. If Christ is not risen, the sacrament is void of meaning. The resurrection and the Lord's Supper stand or fall together. When we celebrate communion, we celebrate the risen Christ. We are proclaiming that death has been conquered and our evil is no longer in control. Jesus said, "I am the bread of life" and "I am the resurrection and the life."

The ministry to which we have been called is based primarily on the union between the Lord's Supper and the resurrection. The word did not become plant or mineral or vegetable; the word became flesh and blood. This fact places inestimable value upon anthropology, bringing the creation and human life to the highest order. In the sacrament we not only celebrate our humanity, but also we celebrate the stamp of divinity upon us. Anthropology and theology unite. We are cosmic creatures bearing the divine image.—Henry C. Blount, Jr., in *The Circuit Rider.*

SACRAMENT. When Nelson was buried in St. Paul's Cathedral, a party of his sailors bore his coffin to its grave. One who watched the scene wrote: "With reverence and with efficiency, they lowered the body of the world's greatest admiral into its tomb. Then, as though answering to a sharp order from the quarterdeck, they all seized the Union Jack with which the coffin had been covered and tore it to fragments, and each took his souvenir of the illustrious dead." That is a sacrament. These little pieces of colored cloth had acquired a meaning and a value and a significance far beyond themselves.

When Prince Charlie was fleeing from his enemies, he spent one night in the house of Flora Macdonald and her mother. When the prince left in the morning, the two women went up to the bed where he had slept and took the sheets between which the prince's body had lain and folded them up and put them reverently away and swore that they would never be used again, except as their own winding-sheets. That is a sacrament.

These common things had something in them that made them no longer common. In the home of every one of us there is a drawer filled with what anyone else would call rubbish and junk, but we cannot bear to throw away its contents. Why? Because everything in it speaks to us of some person or some occasion, and when we take these old useless things in our hands, a person or a presence of a memory comes back. That is a sacrament.

The things without value are clothed with a value far beyond themselves. We take into our hands the common bread and wine—and common bread and wine they remain to the end of the day, but for him who has a heart to feel and an eye to see and a mind to understand, they have in them all the wonder and the glory of the love of God.—William Barclay.

BASIN AND TABLE. Two things found in every home are a place to wash and a place to eat. A wash basin and a dinner table are basic to our living. And you aren't supposed to eat off the table until you have washed in the basin. Cleansing is preparatory to nourishment. We have a little trouble enforcing that rule in our home—the food on the table is always more attractive to the children than the water in the basin. But even though it is difficult to enforce among children, most of us accept the connection between basin and table as both natural and necessary.

Two things found in every church are a place to wash and a place to eat. A baptismal font and a communion table are basic to our living. And you aren't supposed to eat off the table until you have washed in the font. Cleansing is preparatory to nourishment. Baptism leads to the Lord's Supper.—Eugene H. Peterson.

SECTION IV. *Resources for Funeral Services*

SERMON SUGGESTIONS

Topic: Coming to Terms with Death
TEXT: Job 1:21.

I. "The Lord gave." Acknowledge God's generosity. Begin where we ought to begin. Don't place the primary emphasis on what is taken. God gave life. Job said, "The Spirit of God hath made me, and the breath of the Almighty hath given me life" (Job 33:4). Another has said, "The world very simply is not ours; at best we're guests." The host is God.

II. "The Lord hath taken away." Acknowledge God's control. Certainly he who alone has the power to create life has the right to govern it. If we really call him Lord, we submit to him and to his authority. "Woe to him that striveth with his Maker. Shall the clay say to him that fashioneth it, What makest thou?" (Isa. 45:9). The Lord takes away, and he has the right to do this.

III. "Blessed be the name of the Lord." Acknowledge God's wisdom. Do not rebel at God's authority when he takes what he has given. Bow to his superior wisdom. Jesus did this in Gethsemane when he said, "Not my will, but thine be done." In God's will we find our highest significance here and hereafter. The ultimate meanings of the experiences through which we are passing are beyond us. Only the eternal God is all-knowing.—Bramwell Tripp.

Topic: Questions and Answers
TEXT: I Kings 19:9–12.

I. There are so many questions that we would like to have answered. Why did death come so rudely to shorten the life of that young child? Why must war be so much a part of man's existence? Why must there be so much suffering and loneliness and heartache in the world? The list is endless, but are there answers?

II. We know that the mystery of life is part of God's wise plan, for there are some things it is best that we do not know. The knowledge that all things are under the control of a just and loving God must suffice for many of our questions. But for many of our questions the answers have already been given. We do not need to hear the answer again. Rather we have to rediscover. We have to act upon what we already know.

III. In the midst of struggle we need to draw upon the strength and knowledge God has given us and not resort to asking God for another revelation. He has spoken. Let us find ways of applying his truth. We grow strong and become patient, mature, and increase in wisdom as we struggle with the hard things and the difficult questions.—Richard G. Taylor.

Topic: The Joys of a Christian's Death
TEXT: II Cor. 5:1.

The tears shed at the loss of a loved one may be tears of joy rather than tears of mourning in knowing that this loved one has been promoted to the life of comfort and peace.

I. *A life well-lived.* (a) By faith in Jesus Christ.

(b) By love to all mankind.

(c) By service to God and man.

II. *A race well-run.* (a) Giving to God our best.

(b) Avoiding hindrances to our faith.

(c) Pressing toward the mark for the prize.

III. *A faith well-proven.* (a) Humble in life and accomplishments.

(b) Going the second mile with ease.

(c) Consistency in faith and practice.

IV. *An eternity so welcomed.* (a) We greet death with joy.

(b) It is a great graduation.

(c) We leave the land of the dying to enter the land of the living.—J. Walter Hall, Jr.

Topic: What Is Heaven?

Text: Eph. 1:3.

I. Heaven is relationship. A popular song declares, "I'm in heaven when I'm with you." Though merely metaphorical, the song puts the finger on the pulse. Eve in *Paradise Lost,* being driven out of Paradise, tells Adam, "To go with you is to stay here." Jesus tells disciples he looks forward to drinking the wine "new with you in my Father's kingdom" (Matt. 26:29). Earth is most like heaven when one is in love and charity with his neighbor and secure in God's love.

II. Heaven is an inner condition. It is Hebrew *shalom* and Greek *eirene.* It is the New Testament benediction, "Love, joy, and peace." It is Jesus' words to the faithful: "Enter into the joy of your Lord" (Matt. 25:21). Some have called it peace of mind and others peace of soul. It is having the right answer to the gospel song, "Is thy heart right with God?" It is knowing that one is "running with Jesus."

III. Heaven is the ruled life, joyous under God's control. It is living in the kingdom. It has the stoic sense of life so providentially ruled that no evil can hurt one. It is St. Augustine's mother asking to be buried far from home because "nothing is far from God." It is life reconciled, totally committed, God-permeated, and God-ordered. It is St. Paul's "Christ living in me."—Turner N. Clinard.

Topic: Why Jesus Wept

Text: John 11:35.

Why did Jesus weep beside the grave of one who was so soon to be restored to glorious life?

I. Jesus wept because he was a Jew. The first seven days following a death were to be observed as a period of deep mourning. Much time was spent by family, friends, and neighbors in doing just what Jesus did when he arrived upon the scene. He wept because they wept. He wept because the whole village was weeping, and any good Jew present might be expected to join in.

II. Jesus wept because he was human. Throughout Christian history, persons have often been tempted to make so much of Jesus' divine nature that they lose sight of his human nature. When we forget that Jesus experienced human thought and feeling, even grief, we deny the reality of the incarnation.

III. Jesus wept because a friend had become seriously ill and had suffered and died. He wept with other friends, the sisters of the dead man, Lazarus. Jesus' friends were few, but the hospitality of Mary, Martha, and Lazarus at Bethany was offered, and it was precious to him.

IV. Jesus wept not only because of what had happened to Lazarus but because of what was about to happen to him. John sees the raising of Lazarus as the final happening in a chain of events leading to the cross. Both popular acclaim and official opposition grew rapidly following this fantastic expression of divine power.

V. John not only records that Jesus was deeply moved emotionally, but he also tells us what Jesus had to say to Martha and to Lazarus.

(a) The statement to Martha in John 11:25–26 is followed by the question, "Do you believe this?" Alexander Maclaren insisted that this question is the kernel of the whole story of Lazarus. He sharpened the issue by reversing the verse above, "He that believeth not in Christ, though he were living, yet shall he die, and whosoever liveth and believeth not shall never live." Do we believe this?

(b) His word to Lazarus, "Lazarus, come out," evokes within us all the deep yearning to be freed from the bondage of sin and death. Jesus calls every human being from death to life. Mary is sure of a resurrection at the last day. The master offers resurrection now.—Ronald M. Fassett.

Topic: The Resurrection of the Body
SCRIPTURE: I Cor. 15:20–58.

Our word "resurrection" comes from the Latin *resurrectio* which is the equivalent of the Greek *anastasis* meaning to cause to stand up again. This standing up again is a transformation of the body by the power of God which moves it into a new arena of life which so far exceeds what we experience now that adequate words have never been found to express its full dimensions. When we talk about the resurrection of the body, we are seeking to express the inexpressible and to describe the indescribable. What kind of bodies will we have? There are some hints in our text about what kind of body the resurrection body will be.

I. Paul says it will be a transformed body. It will be different from the body we have right now. This is the point Paul is making in v. 37. As the corn stalk is different from the kernel of corn that was planted, even so shall the resurrection body be different from the physical body which is planted in the grave. (See vv. 42–44.)

II. Paul says it will be a recognizable body. The same imagery of a plant implies continuity as well as difference. Although there is a difference between the kernel of corn planted and the plant which grows, there is also continuity. You don't plant a kernel of corn and get an apple tree. There will be continuity between our physical body and our resurrection body. It will be a recognizable body, maybe more so by what you say and do than by what you look like.

III. Paul says it will be an incorruptible body. These physical bodies are subject to decay. We are in the process of dying every day. But our resurrection bodies will be separated from this realm of decay. Paul emphasizes this in what he says about Jesus. In vv. 4 and 12–13, when Paul says that Jesus was raised from the dead, he uses the perfect tense which is the Greek way of stating a past action that has a continuing impact in the present. When Jesus was raised from the dead, his body was transformed so that it could never die again.

IV. Paul says it will be a glorious body. In v. 43 he says that our physical bodies are sown in dishonor. What he means is that this body of ours has been defiled by the presence of sin. The marks of sin are on all of us. But our resurrection body, Paul says, will be a body which will never again be brought low by sin. We will be freed from the presence, power, and penalty of sin forever.

V. Paul says it will be a powerful body. In v. 43 Paul refers to the weakness of our physical bodies. We are limited in so many ways. But Paul says that our resurrection body will be one that is free from all the limitations and handicaps that we now know. We will be able to measure up to the highest potential of God's plan and purpose for our lives.

VI. Paul says it will be an adequate body. It will be adequate to function in the new realm of existence in which we will live. In both this life and the next Paul says we have a body. He modifies the word "body" with two adjectives, physical and spiritual. Each of these adjectives in the Greek ends with the letters *ikon* which means adequacy for every need indicated in the word to which it is added. Paul is saying that just as God has given us a physical body adequate to live in this life even so God will give us a resurrection body, a spiritual body, adequate to exist in the next life.—Brian L. Harbour.

Topic: Good Grief
TEXT: Matt. 5:4.

I. To say that there is good grief is to suggest that grieving is all right. Do not condemn yourself for deep feelings of grief. Certainly we should not repress these feelings, for pain is often part of the healing process, but having been raised to be brave many of us find it hard to deal with our real feelings. Good grief does not criticize you when you have angry and rebellious feelings in face of a deep loss. It knows that God's love is not afraid of our anger and that it is far more healthy to be honest about our feelings than to deny them.

II. Good grief is not afraid to share its

sorrow. God has given us ears, and one of the most important ministries you have is expressing your care through the listening ear. But also let yourself be helped. Let someone be an ear for you. God created the world in such a way that we all need to give and we all need to receive.

III. Good grief is patient. It knows that it takes time for the deeper parts of life to accept the reality of death and separation. Grief will likely include shock, feelings of depression and isolation, sometimes physical symptoms, often powerlessness and guilt over things done or left undone, and resentment. But at the end of the process there is not only readjustment to reality but also a new sense of hope. Good grief allows God to work in this process and knows the healing power of expressing gratitude for what God can do in the face of death.—Robert B. Wallace.

Topic: From Here to Eternity
TEXT: Phil. 3:20 (MOFFATT).

What grounds do we have for calling ourselves a colony of heaven?

I. We bring with us at birth some possessions which seem to come from a heavenly homeland. Without the values of beauty, truth, and goodness and without the qualities of faith, hope, and love, life on this planet would be meaningless and unlivable. And the roots of these essentials, we believe, were brought from God who is our home.

II. A second reason for this belief is that life is too large for this physical existence. Every seven years, so we are told, our physical bodies experience a complete renovation. Some of us have run through several bodies during our life spans. Yet our personalities persist. Thoughts, memories, hopes, and purposes have continued through all these bodily changes. Having used up several bodies during a lifetime, why is it hard to believe that a personality can go on to a body celestial? In fact, the most real and valued aspects of life cannot be contained in the body nor measured by science. Mother love, noble character, faithful friendship, values such as these are not bound up in our bodies,

yet they are the most precious possessions of personality.

III. A third reason for belief in a heavenly homeland is that a divine ruler was sent to this earthly colony nineteen centuries ago. We have seen how he lived and loved and died. He walked to his death not as one leaving life but as one entering a larger life. He won the victory over the fear of death and over the fact of death. Christ came from God who is our home and is now living in that heavenly homeland, for he said, "I go to my Father."—Ralph W. Sockman.

ILLUSTRATIONS

ASSURANCE. No longer is the future a befogged landscape into which I peer anxiously because all kinds of obscure perils are brewing there for me. No, everything is changed. We do not know what is coming, but we know who is coming. He who possesses the last hour no longer needs to fear the next minute.—Helmut Thielicke.

BEGINNING. An English officer, who was in the same prison with Pastor Bonhoeffer, describes how on a certain Sunday Bonhoeffer conducted a service of worship for his fellow prisoners. He spoke to them in a way that went straight to their hearts. As soon as the final prayer had ended, a door opened and two civilians entered and said, "Prisoner Bonhoeffer, come with us." These words meant only one thing. They were a summons to the gallows. But in the brief moment before he was led away by the guards, Bonhoeffer took the English officer aside and said to him, "This is the end, but for me it is the beginning of life." The next day, as expected, Bonhoeffer was hanged.—Edward C. Dahl.

EXPLAINING HEAVEN. Suppose a child had been born in the depths of Mammoth Cave. Suppose further that the first twenty-one years of his life had been spent within the cave, where his experiences were limited to dimly lighted passages, stalactites, stalagmites, and bats. Now the time has come for him to emerge into the external world. Your job is to prepare him for the things he will experience in the outside world. How would you explain to him the brilliance of the sun or tell him about bright colors? How would you tell him about trees, flowers, and other planets? How would you explain to him about automobiles and airplanes? A hopeless job? Almost! But that's a bit like the task the inspired writers faced when they attempted to explain to us what heaven is like. Their explanation must of necessity be highly figurative and often confusing to us. But one thing we can be sure of is that its glories will surpass anything we can dream of.—John Wade.

COME FORTH.   Robert Ingersoll traveled back and forth across America, attacking all religions, especially Christianity, maintaining we could know nothing about God or a future life. In one of his lectures he tried to show that the story of Lazarus was a fake miracle, planned to build up the popularity of Jesus. Lazarus "made believe" he took sick and "made believe" he died. His sisters "buried" him in a cave and called Jesus. Lazarus was to stay in the tomb until Jesus called out, "Lazarus, come forth."

To strengthen his story Ingersoll then asked, "Can anyone here tell me why Jesus said, 'Lazarus, come forth?' Why didn't he simply say, 'Come forth'?" A little man stood up and gave the answer: "Yes, sir, I can tell you. If my Lord had not said 'Lazarus,' all the people buried in that cemetery would have come forth to meet their savior."

Ingersoll later admitted that the old man's statement really stumped him because it came from a deep faith, which you and I and all Christians share, that Christ died for all men and that all men will rise at the call of Christ.—Arthur Tonne.

THE ANSWER.   The Christian need not fear death. In Jesus Christ is the only answer to the fact of death, its sorrow and parting and mystery. To the Christian, death is the beginning and not the end. He knows that he will walk with Christ through the valley of the shadow of death to take his place with those whom he has loved and lost a while in the house not made with hands, eternal in the heavens. —Theodore F. Adams.

WITHOUT FEAR.   Charles Kingsley was in one room terminally ill, and his wife of many years was in the next room terminally ill. She sent in a note to Charles Kingsley, and she said, "My darling, is it cowardly of me to tremble before the unseen realities of what lies beyond death?" Charles Kingsley reassuringly wrote back a note: "My darling, it is not cowardly, but we do not need to be afraid. It will not be dark because God is light. We shall not be lonely because Jesus Christ is with us."— David L. Larsen.

CREDO.   I have seen enough decency, goodness, and beauty to be ready to affirm that the world and all of us in it, including me, are not flying it blind in meaningless chase, that the universe bespeaks purpose and direction, and that it is born in the mind of God and proceeds to the fulfillment of his ultimate aim. I do affirm and dwell in the hope that there is more ahead. Whatever it may be it will be good, interesting, adventuresome, and challenging us to further growth, for we will be dealing, as always, with the same God whose name is Christlike love.—George H. Orser.

TO BE REMEMBERED.   This is the way to live, that after you are gone people will wish that you were still around to give them comfort and counsel, love and care, understanding and concern. Some of us have had parents like that, whose memory has been a benediction to us and for whose guidance we have longed even after they have passed away. It may be helpful for us too to be such kinds of people, such kinds of Christians, as parents, as brothers and sisters, as friends and neighbors, that when we are gone others will wish we were still present to give them some encouragement, some love, and some guidance.— Louis Benes.

FACE TO FACE.   The Polish astronomer Copernicus by his research and writings changed man's conception of the universe so that our understanding of the solar system has been called the Copernican Theory. On his deathbed his great work, *The Revolution of the Heavenly Bodies,* just off the press, was laid in his arms. But in that moment, as he came face to face with life's ultimate fact, he did not think of himself as a great scientist, mathematician, astronomer, or one of the world's most learned men but only as a sinner in need of the grace and salvation of Christ on the cross. His faith and prayer is expressed in the epitaph he wrote for himself which can be read today on his grave: "Lord, I do not ask the kindness which thou didst show to Peter. I do not dare to ask the grace which thou didst grant to Paul. But, Lord, the mercy thou didst show to the dying robber, that mercy show to me. That earnestly I crave."—Henry Gariepy.

CALL OF THE DEEP.   When John Buchan planned a trip to London, he applied for reservations in the hotel nearest to the Thames. He made a special request for the room closest to the river bank. A friend inquired about the meticulous choice of a room. Buchan replied: "I want to be near the sea gulls. I like to hear the call from the depths of the ocean at nighttime."

Man is made to respond to the depths beyond us. "Deep calleth unto deep," the psalmist said. Deep needs arouse our deep compassion. Deep mysteries invite deep inquiry. A deep and unexplained love possesses the very foundation of our souls and calls forth its own kind in response. So we are lured out of our shells, out of the encrusted habits and the familiar rituals. It is by such paths that we are elevated above environment, and the soul makes its invincible surmise.—Fred G. Shelnutt.

ROAD TO HEAVEN.   Two monks were threatened by Henry VIII if they did not renouce their faith. They were to be tied in a sack and cast into the Thames. Their answer: "The road to heaven lies as near by water as by land; therefore, it is indifferent to us which way we go thither."

FABLE.   A good man died and went to heaven. Upon approaching the Keeper of the Gates, he made a strange request to visit hell a few days before taking up his heavenly residence. Permission was granted, and he was amazed at what he found below. He saw huge banquet tables piled high with delectable foods fit for kings. But all the people were emaciated, lean, and anemic. They were starving to death. Knives and forks, six feet long, were strapped to their hands and fingers so that they could never reach their mouths. Try as they did, they could not get one bite of food. The startled visitor had enough. He hurried back to heaven, and on entering there he saw practically the same scene: the same kind of banquet tables, and the same kind of long knives and forks strapped to the hands and fingers of the people. But there was one big difference. The saints were pictures of health and strength, and they came in to dinner laughing together. As the newcomer stood by breathlessly, they approached the tables and gathered generous helpings of food with their clinking silverware. Then heaven's happy host turned around and began to feed each other! This had never occurred to the people in hell. According to the fable, that's why they were down there in the first place.—Frank J. Pippin.

SECTION V. Resources for Lenten and Easter Preaching

SERMON SUGGESTIONS

Topic: Who Is This?

TEXT: Matt. 21:10.

A proper identification of Jesus is the most important we can make. Think about three men who made up their minds about Jesus on Good Friday.

I. Caiaphas identified Christ on the basis of prejudice. The high priest said, "He hath spoken blasphemy" (Matt. 26:65). That this was prejudice is proven by Caiaphas' action as outlined in Matt. 21:3-4. Caiaphas believed what he wanted to. His mind was made up.

II. Pilate identified Christ on the basis of indifference. The record is that Pilate "washed his hands" and "delivered him to be crucified" (Matt. 27:24, 26). To be indifferent is to lack interest or concern and to be uncaring. Pilate did not want to condemn Jesus. He only wanted to dodge the issue, to avoid responsibility, and to be neutral.

III. The dying thief identified Christ on the basis of need. He identified him as lord. "Lord, remember me when thou comest into thy kingdom" (Luke 23:42). We might ask: "What else could he do, hanging between heaven and earth and only a few breaths from death? He had only one person to appeal to." That's true. And it's just as true for you and me. We have needs which no one but Christ can satisfy.—Bramwell Tripp.

Meditation: The Tag

Barabbas was a criminal. At least that's what the state called him. Barabbas' friends probably referred to him as a patriot. The charges against him were insurrection and murder, and the penalty was crucifixion. Pilate gives the crowd the opportunity to choose between two men, Barabbas and Jesus, in an apparent gesture of Roman magnanimity, a passover amnesty. The crowd chooses Barabbas, and he's freed.

That's recorded not to tell us about the crowd. That's recorded to tell us about God. It's in the Bible to say that the crowd didn't really free Barabbas—God freed Barabbas. Just as pharaoh didn't free the Jews from Egypt—God freed them. Just as Cyrus the Persian didn't really free the Jews from Babylonia—God freed them. Just as Judas Maccabeus didn't really free them from Greek tyranny—God freed them. So Pilate did not free Barabbas nor did the crowd. God freed him. That's why the story is there. So the meaning of the cross would be specific.

The Bible says Jesus died so Barabbas would have a new life. It wasn't a judicial decision. It wasn't an historical accident. It was revelation. The revelation is that Jesus died to give us new life and to reveal that is God's will for all of us. He came into close proximity to our life, to be specific, in one time and in one place. He chose Barabbas to tell you he chooses you.

We don't know what happened to Barabbas after that, though Pär Lagerkvist did write a story called *Barabbas* in which he picks up his life after the cross. He pictures Barabbas suddenly freed and overwhelmed by what all of this meant in his life. He's confused. He seeks out the place the disciples frequent and tries to relate to them, but he's uncomfortable with them. The disciples understandably have ambivalent feelings toward Barabbas. He eventually turns to his old life as an outlaw. Then he is captured again and sold now as a slave to work in the copper mines on the Island of Cyprus. There he is chained to an Armenian slave, and they work side by side.

One day Barabbas notices the dog tag, the identification tag around the Armenian's neck, which all Roman slaves wore identifying them as the property of the Roman government. The Armenian's tag has the symbol of Rome crossed out, and on the other side the symbol of the fish has been scratched in. *Ichtus* in Greek is the word for fish, but the letters that spell fish are the first letters of each word in the phrase "Jesus Christ, Son of God, Savior." It was the first Christian symbol. The Armenian wears it around his neck.

That prompts Barabbas to tell his chained partner who he is and what has happened to him. Then one day, almost in spite of himself, Barabbas gives himself to this mystery that haunts him and becomes a Christian. He marks this commitment on his own tag where he crosses out the symbol of Rome and inscribes on the other side the fish, the symbol of Christ.

But the story does not end there, just as our story does not end when we are confirmed, converted, or say the vows of membership in the church. Barabbas, like us, continues to struggle against the idea that he lives by grace. Like us he still can't believe that he is worthy of such a gift of grace as to be given a new life.

You and I are baffled by the cross because we feel ourselves to be not worthy of it. We feel ourselves to be too insignificant to ever have the attention of divine grace. But it's happened. That's the Christian gospel. No matter what you do, it's happened. And that grace waits there for you to recognize it.

That's the story of Barabbas. It's not Rome now. It's not even Barabbas that owns Barabbas now. It's Christ who owns him. That tag no longer has the face of Rome on it. It now has the fish of Christ. Paul told the Corinthians: "You are not your own. You were bought with a price." —Mark Trotter.

Topic: The Palm Sunday Christ
TEXT: Luke 9:51.

I. The Christ of Palm Sunday is the Christ who would establish the kingdom of service and not of selfishness, the kingdom of God's will and not of man's willfulness.

II. The forces which brought Jesus to a cross are still the forces of evil which defeat the high hopes of man. There were the forces of evil whether they were represented in Pilate's refusing to do his duty and washing his hands or the entrenched evil in the religious and political systems of his time. All of the forces that nailed Christ to the cross confront our own life and confront our day and still hold back the coming of Christ's kingdom of joy and light.

III. In the cross we find the completion and the crowning glory of Christ's life of ministry, service, and love. The things for which Christ died are the eternal spiritual values for which we should live.

IV. In the cross great forces for good were let loose in the world. Helen Keller said: "There is much evil in the world. No one can deny that. But there also is much of God's goodness in the world overcoming it." In the cross are the healing forces of supreme goodness, courage, faith, and the outpouring of love.

V. God is in this great event drawing the world to himself. You can look at the cross from two sides. On one side you see a human life, unfolding as all of life unfolds as Jesus increased in wisdom and stature in favor with God and mankind. Then finally this glorious life dying on a cross. That is the human side of it all. Then look at it from the light of our Christian faith. In his life God came into our world revealing himself through the beauty of a human face, the strength of his words, and the love of his heart. You cannot divide these two lives in Christ. They are perfectly joined in his life—the downreach of God and the upreach of man's journey.—Frank A. Court.

Topic: The Budded Cross
TEXT: Luke 24:5–6.

Our cross is not only an empty cross. It is also a "budded" cross. The swelling ends of its bars remind the viewer not only of the crucifixion but also of the budding branches of springtime when life begins afresh all over the world.

I. Whenever we come into a house of worship, the story of the risen, living Christ is being proclaimed. Our cross speaks to us in the words of the two men in dazzling apparel who said to the women in the garden on Easter morning: "Why do you seek the living among the dead? He is not here, but has risen. Remember how he told you while he was still in Galilee."

II. Our cross proclaims to all who enter this church that life is more than we supposed it to be. The cross, which was originally an instrument of torture and a symbol of shame and humiliation, shines as the sign and symbol of life, light, peace, confidence, and joy.

III. From a secular point of view, our earthly existence often appears to end in crucifixion or something similar. Certainly every one of us will eventually die. Most of the time we act as if the material world around us is all the world there is and as if the life we now experience is all the life we shall ever know. We concentrate on things, on making money, on the pleasures of the moment, and on the security we think we can create for ourselves and our families here and now.

IV. Easter comes to awaken us with a start to other possibilities, directing our attention to the truths contained in this wonderful story of an empty tomb. "Why do you seek the living among the dead?" We are reminded that the world of things which we taste and touch and handle and smell is not the only world. Our horizons must be stretched until they include infinity—the kingdom of God.—Edward C. Dahl.

Topic: Affirmed to Be Alive
TEXT: Acts 25:19.

I. Christians affirm the resurrection by demonstrating their experience of it. When we are born again by the Holy Spirit, we are buried with him in death and we are raised to new life. We died with him and now we live with him.

II. Christians affirm the resurrection by living in its power. New life begins with new birth and deepens as we walk in the Spirit.

III. Christians affirm the resurrection by living in anticipation of its fulfillment. Although we experience the reality of the resurrection and live in the power of the resurrection, we yet have mortal bodies. "It doth not yet appear what we shall be," the scripture says, "but we know that, when he shall appear, we shall be like him" (I John 3:2).—T. L. Lowery.

Topic: The Challenge of the Resurrection
TEXT: Rom. 1:4.

I. The resurrection validates the claims that Jesus made about himself. It proves that Jesus really was who he said he was. (See Rom. 1:4; I Cor. 15:14.) Without the resurrection the Christian faith would be meaningless. The resurrection gives it meaning. It turns the defeat of the cross into victory. It declares loud and clear that Jesus is the Son of God.

II. The resurrection assures Christian people of eternal life. (See John 14:19; II Cor. 4:14.) The resurrection frees us from the deception that this earthly life is all there is. We are free to give and not to grab and to face death and not to run away. Christians don't have to live life like this is all there is.

III. The resurrection confronts us with a living lord. In talking about the resurrection we are not dealing with theories but with a living person—Jesus Christ. This Jesus confronts us—our lifestyles, our standards, and our beliefs—and calls us to turn away from self and sin and to follow him in total commitment. The resurrected Jesus says to us to be completely committed to him or else to completely turn away but not to be half-hearted about following him.—Steve Simms.

ILLUSTRATIONS

IN OUR BROKENNESS.　The cross is a judgment on all our understanding of religion. This is where God became incarnate. Begin at Calvary and then you'll understand Bethlehem. The cross is very, very down to earth. It is not a symbol; the cross is God meaning business.

Only after the relationship between man and God is restored can we remedy the broken relationships of humanity. The only help you can give broken people is the cross standing in the midst of our brokenness. This is the message of hope that saves the broken from despair—the bleeding, vulnerable, bewildered God on the cross, a bleeding God who alone can heal a bleeding heart.

To clothe the naked and to feed the hungry is to be in the incarnation. You too become invaded, vulnerable—the invasion of Calvary—you can never be the same. Christianity at the cross is a dangerous experience. It is the cross that makes humanity human. What do you receive in communion? A God broken, broken for you. And you get healed and sent out to heal broken humanity.—Festo Kivengere.

ADVENT AND LENT.　A woman commented that she enjoyed the Advent celebration so much that she felt we ought to have it twice a year. In one sense Lent fulfills her desire. Lent is to Easter what Advent is to Christmas—a time of preparation. At that point the similarities end. The whole air of Lent is radically different from Advent. Since it is in the death of Jesus that human sin is most clearly revealed, Lent takes on the atmosphere of humility and repentence rather than expectant joy as in Advent. The Lenten color is purple, the color expressive of penitence and mourning. The season begins on Ash Wednesday and culminates in the drama of Holy Week preceding Easter Sunday. In Lent we walk with our Lord the road that led him to the cross. We experience with the disciples the agony of loss and the horror of the cross. We remember that Christ walked that road for our sake and for our salvation, and we humble ourselves before such a sacrifice of love.—Ray Mendenhall in *The Presbyterian Outlook.*

BOUGHT WITH A PRICE.　One of the greatest moments in all of literature occurs in Victor Hugo's *Les Miserables.* Poor Jean Valjean has been in prison for stealing bread to feed his sister's hungry children. Because he has tried to escape, he has had to serve seven additional years. He is a bitter, hardened, and cynical man. No one will help him. Finally a kindly old bishop opens his home to him and gives him food and a place to sleep.

Jean Valjean can't sleep. He paces the floor, walks through the house, and sees the bishop's silver candlesticks. He decides to steal them. He sees the sleeping bishop and even considers bashing in his skull, but he escapes across the garden, climbs the wall, and is gone.

The next day the housekeeper notices the missing candlesticks and says in effect that she had tried to warn the bishop. Just then there is a knock on the door. The bishop opens the door and sees Jean Valjean held by two policemen. They have the stolen silver candlesticks.

"Ah! There you are!" the bishop says. "I told you you could have the silver candlesticks. Why have you returned them?" "Then what he says is true," say the police. They leave. The bishop and the thief stand face to face. The bishop speaks slowly: "Jean Valjean, you belong no longer to evil but to good. I have purchased your soul with these silver candlesticks."—Joe A. Harding.

BEYOND THE DOOR.　The rough, ugly cross supports a body collapsed in death. The rigid limbs are twisted in pain, and the head is sunk deeply upon the chest. It is a picture of unrelieved pain and utter finality.

Actually, it is the front panel and door of a sixteenth-century movable altar now in one of Europe's great cathedrals. The door opens upon scenes of such breathtaking beauty that the heart is almost overwhelmed.

Open the dark, hopeless door and there, bathed in golden afternoon sunshine, is the mother of our Lord with the radiant angel of the annunciation.

The next is a double panel and here is the mother of our Lord again, seated outside in all the glory of a spring morning, playing with her little son while angels of indescribable beauty and grace watch in adoration.

But the third panel is the glory and wonder. To quote Joseph Fort Newton: "It shows the swift, flashing figure of the risen Christ, radiant under a starry sky, triumphant over death and the grave, His fiery mantle fluttering wildly in the wind, a glittering, dazzling vision, overwhelming in its suggestion of life, power, mastery, and victory, opening the door of the cross and the tomb into a world of light and joy." Here is the revealed mystery of the gospel but not the mystery revealed. Here is life out of death; then out of death, life.—Christine McMillan in *The War Cry*.

HINDRANCE.   A community Good Friday service featured seven half-hour segments, one after the other, with a different minister in charge of each segment. The theme was "The Seven Words from the Cross." Since I hosted the service, I placed a large wooden cross on the Lord's Supper table, directly in front of the pulpit. Every singer, preacher, and liturgist was forced to stand behind the cross. After three or four segments progressed without comment, one of the ministers created a parable for the day. When he stood to speak, he reached around for a music stand, carried it to the altar and to the side of the cross. "You must forgive me," he said, "but I have never believed that the cross was meant to come between the shepherd and the

flock." I doubt that many people heard his sermon. The cross got in our way. Some of us it redeems; others it hinders. —W. Wayne Price.

CONFRONTING OURSELVES.   The way begins where for Christ himself its mortal part ended—at the cross. There alone, with all our earthly defenses down and our earthly pretenses relinquished, we can confront the true circumstances of our beings; there alone grasp the triviality of these seemingly so majestic achievements of ours, like going to the moon, unravelling our genes, fitting one another with each other's hearts, livers and kidneys. There, contemplating God in the likeness of man, we may understand how foolish and inept is man when he sees himself in the likeness of God.—Malcolm Muggeridge.

PETITION.   O Christ, the master carpenter who, at the last, through wood and nails, purchased our whole salvation, wield well your tools in the workshop of your world so that we who come as rough wood to your bench may here be made to a truer beauty by your hands.

WHERE JESUS ISN'T.   A Sunday school teacher was trying to help some of her pupils who were afraid, especially of the dark. "You don't ever have to be afraid of the dark. There's always someone with you—Jesus. Wherever you go, he is there. Jesus is everywhere." But one little boy had an objection. "I know one place where he isn't." he said. "Oh, you do," responded the teacher. "Where is that?" "He's not in his grave, ma'am" was his reply.—John Wade.

EASTER FOCUS.   The Christian community is the Easter community. Our preaching is Easter preaching, our hymns are Easter hymns, and our faith is an Easter faith.—Karl Barth.

SECTION VI. Resources for Advent and Christmas Preaching

SERMON SUGGESTIONS

Topic: Streams in the Desert

SCRIPTURE: Isa. 35.

I. When the prophet spoke of streams in the desert, he was talking about the coming of Christ—about Christmas.

(a) Advent is a call to sense anew the miraculous in that earthy event of a woman giving birth to a child in a stable. Despite our progress and civilization, birth is still a miracle, and the birth of God's Son is the miracle of miracles.

(b) Christmas comes again to announce the same glad tidings: "Unto you a Savior is born." Men and events have tried to dim the light of his glory, but John predicted in his gospel: "The light still shines in the darkness and the darkness has never put it out" (John 1:5, PHILLIPS). That too is a miracle. Through the centuries, despite tyrants and despots, commercialism, and unconcern of forces of evil, nothing can change the meaning and message of Christmas.

(c) Christmas tells us that God has invaded planet earth. Isaiah pointed to the event, and every Christmas we are reminded of its continuity. When Isaiah told his people there would be streams in the desert, he was calling on them for a faith in the miraculous and the incredible, in the ability of God to overcome evil in his own unique way, and in the capacity of God to change things.

II. In our world of bigness we need to sense that, despite our progress, gains, and growth, man is not cured of all his heart, soul, and mind needs. Progress, invention, and discovery cannot mend a broken heart or bring peace and comfort to a troubled soul, balance and resource to a distraught mind, and moral character to a weak life or forgiveness of sins to a disturbed conscience. Only God can do that.

III. Our faith calls us to the stability of the stable event where we see the everliving and ever-loving God reveal his true heart. Our faith calls us to see that Christmas is still the incredible miracle of an incredible God who loves us with an everlasting love and treats us with his amazing grace.

IV. Streams do flow in the desert. Roses do bloom in the barren wastelands. Time has not dimmed the miracle of Christmas or the cross. Come and find refreshment for your soul and let God's plenty and power spring up eternally to sustain you in your journey through this life to the next.

—Allan J. Weenink

Topic: Christmas Mission

TEXT: John 3:16.

I. The birth of Jesus was a new approach in missions. It was God sending his own Son to woo an exiled-from-heaven people to the way of life that is eternal.

(a) He came not to make all gentiles Jews nor to gain added territories by brutal conquest. His mission was not geographical expansion. The purpose of his

52

coming was to give life a new meaning and direction. His sphere was the spirit. He was the king of truth. And as the spirit gives guidance to all of life, he came to give the spirit guidance that life may be spiritually led.

(b) When Jesus was born, he became flesh like all men. In this flesh he could be recognized by men who could not recognize him in spirit. Sending Jesus in the flesh was God's way to woo the world to salvation.

(c) We who have discovered Christ to be the direction-giver to life, the purpose-giver for living, and the hope-giver for dying cannot treat lightly the whole matter of missions. If God gave what was dearest to him to win us, ought we not to give that which is dearest to us to win the unwon?

(d) We find it all too easy to remember Christmas without realizing what it means. In our observance we pamper ourselves, oblivious of the pale, haggard faces of the world's hungering, freezing, and naked people staring at us in our holly-bedecked halls of feasting.

II. Christmas was primarily a mission. (a) In being faithful to the mission of God no one can find a valid excuse for not worshiping at Christmas nor can he properly understand the mission of Christmas until he has matched his Christmas spending with the gift to God's undernourished people of the world.

(b) Even as the world could not understand God's love until he sent Jesus in the flesh, so there are many who cannot understand this Christmas gospel except through a warm coat we have discarded, a meal that had the bare minimum caloric content, or through a friend who proved brotherly on the holy day.

(c) We have a story to tell, a gospel to preach, and a savior to proclaim. Missions can never be a maybe, a left-over. It must be the heartbeat of the Christian life. This means witnessing in our neighborhood, whether it is rural, suburban, or downtown. This means providing homes for displaced persons and feeding victims of war.

(d) At Christmas God showed his love of others. Are we in a position to argue with the master who calls us to a renewed sense of mission?—Lloyd L. Burke.

Topic: The Good News of Christmas
TEXT: Luke 2:10.
I. The Christmas news is divine. It is news that God makes—news that the holy God who had promised redemption for sinners has kept his promise, has sent his one and only Son, and has come in Christ for the salvation of all who trust him. The divine news of Christmas is that God for Christ's sake invites us to his Christmas table, invites us miserable sinners to share personally in the privileges and powers of the kingdom of heaven.

II. The good news of Christmas is durable. It is God's good news throughout this age of grace. Take heart, God says. Here is hope, high hope. Christ, the holy savior of sinners, is come. Christ, the crucified one, is risen, the invincible victor over all the powers that aimed to destroy him. Christ lives today, granting forgiveness to penitents and gifting them with new life. Sin, oppression, and injustice are doomed and dated. Christ, the man of God and the God-man, gives new life to fallen mankind in the midst of this shabby world and raises up his new society that has a destiny in eternity.

III. The good news of Christmas is distributable. It is God's good news for beleaguered humanity and for spiritually famished mankind. It girdles the globe and spans the nations. From scores of modern nations pilgrims will gather in Bethlehem on Christmas Day, mindful that the word became flesh in Jesus of Nazareth.

IV. The good news of Christmas is highly dangerous. (a) It bears on human destiny. It is decisive, and it calls each of us to a personal decision. For God or against God, for the Christ of God or against him, for the forgiveness of sins or against it, for fellowship with God or against it, for the commandments of God or against them, and for the word of God or against it—that is the choice we face.

(b) The good news of Christmas can be the best good news of all or the costliest of all. When the news is best, the cost of neglect is always greatest, and news that the promised redeemer has come is the best good news of all.

(1) God's kingdom of righteousness was manifest in Christ the savior who in his own life vanquished all the forces of sin and evil, in his death became our sinless substitute, and in his resurrection triumphed over everything that would have done him to death.

(2) The crucified one is risen. He lives to give life and to make the joys of the kingdom a reality in the hearts of those who open themselves to him.

(3) He is coming soon, the Prince of peace, returning in great power and glory, to judge and to reign over a world that has peace on its lips but not in its heart.—Carl F. H. Henry in *Christian Herald.*

Topic: Christmas in the Christian Home
TEXT: I John 4:11.
I. Christmas in the Christian home should be a combination of joy and worship.
II. Christmas in the Christian home affords an opportunity to decorate the house to honor the Lord.
III. Christmas in the Christian home should be an occasion when ordinary things take on a special meaning.
IV. Christmas in the Christian home should be a time of family togetherness.
V. Christmas in the Christian home can be both a festive and a worshipful occasion.—Homer G. Rhea, Jr.

Topic: A Night to Remember
TEXT: Matt. 4:16.
I. Christmas Eve is a night to remember because it revealed what God is continually trying to do for the world. We are sometimes guilty of talking about Christianity as though it related exclusively to some few things that God had a hand in a long time ago and which have been accomplished once and for all and are now filed under finished business. We would be nearer to the biblical position if we thought rather of the mighty events of old as clear demonstrations of his continuous activity. The God of the Bible is a God of the living (Luke 20:38). He "is working still" (John 5:14). And the mighty acts he wrought through Moses and Isaiah and Jesus are not sudden bursts of divine activity but places where we see more clearly than usual what he is continually doing.

II. Christmas Eve is a night to remember because it exalts kindness over cruelty. The days when decrees went out from Caesar Augustus were crude and cruel days, and human flesh was cheap. For all its engineering skill, legal genius, military prowess, and cosmopolitan sophistication, the civilization of the Roman Empire was short on human kindness. For the most part it looked on kindness as a weakness. The Roman method of criminal execution—crucifixion—was a death by torture that normally took two or three days. Defective or unwanted babies were exposed—left unattended out of doors until they died. Herod the Great was so skillful and successful a ruler that Rome let him keep his kingdom and even made him something of an imperial favorite. But Herod was also so ruthless that he was not only capable of killing in cold blood the children of Bethlehem, as the gospel reports, but he also killed his own sons and finally his favorite wife lest they be threats to his own position. The Emperor Augustus remarked that it was safer to be Herod's pig than his son. The wealth of Rome rested on the backs of millions of slaves treated like mere animals, and its citizenry thronged to see men fight to the death in gladitorial games. But Herod and Rome are now one with Ninevah and Tyre while millions celebrate a baby who made a kingdom of kindness.—Raymond E. Balcomb.

ILLUSTRATIONS

OUR TOO-CROWDED LIVES.   We're a time-oriented people. There's no room in our busy lives for all we want to put into them, much less for what someone else might want to insert. So we drive ourselves forward, brushing others out of the way. Life becomes an exercise in rush-hour traffic tolerance. Where does this leave us? With lives too crowded for Christmas.

A contemporary Christmas cantata by

Lanny Wolfe, Don Marsh, and Bob Benson includes a number called "No Room." It reveals afresh the incongruity of Joseph and Mary finding no room at the inn at Bethlehem. "No room," it says, "for Jesus in the world he made. . . . Room for things that pass away; but for the one who reigns forever there's no room today." That song closes, "He just keeps knockin' but he hears you say, 'No room.'"

We're remarkably like the people in Bethlehem almost 2,000 years ago, although they weren't as busy as we. When their lives were filled, they were filled with the desire for money or power or political revolution. All those people crowded into Bethlehem were there because the Romans wanted more tax money. That's what the enrollment was about. Herod filled his life with his search for power. That's what the killing of the infants was about. Jews filled their lives with hopes and dreams of political revolution and of the lifting of Rome's yoke. That's what crowded a peaceful messiah out of their lives. We knew that Jesus found only a small reception then. The risk is that he may find an equally small reception among us.—John Stapert in *The Church Herald.*

HE COMES.   In Advent we prepare for the celebration of God's coming to us in the past in the holy child of Bethlehem. He has come! In Advent we anticipate the coming of a conquering Christ in the future. He will come! But in Advent we give attention to a God who comes to us and our world in the present. He comes! He comes to us every day in the scriptures but also in all kinds of ways. "How silently, how silently the wonderous gift is given." Or as another hymn writer says, "He speaks to me everywhere." He comes to the world through ordinary people like you and me and in ordinary ways. Luther said, "Let no one give up the faith that God wants to do a deed through him." God did a deed through a human being like us—Mary from Nazareth. He will do a deed through you and me—a Lucy or George or Becki or Eric—an ordinary or extraordinary person like us who live in the present. If we are available to him, he will "be born in us today."—Richard E. Lofgren.

HE COMES IN LOVE.   The incarnation of God in Jesus Christ teaches us that, in Browning's words, the "all-great" is the "all-loving" too. The high and holy God chooses to come to us in love by becoming one of us. This love is not the denial of his holiness but the supreme manifestation of it. It is not the opposite of his justice but the best expression of it. The way he has created us, giving us freedom of choice and setting laws by which the universe moves, reflects his love, not his distant separation from us. All this is made clear in the act of the incarnation for here we see the Son of God in perfect obedience to his Father's will becoming like us in every way, entering into our sorrowing and our suffering, and bearing in his body the iniquity of us all. And with his stripes we are healed. Jesus Christ shows us that the God who created us and made the world to be what it is—the theater of his glory—is the God who has in his being all the grace and truth we see in his Son.—George Laird Hunt in *The Presbyterian Outlook.*

BLAZE OF LIGHT.   The wreath, without beginning and end, stands for eternity. The greens are for life and growth. The four candles, preferably of beeswax and set aside since Candlemas, present the ages "sitting in darkness and the shadow of death." Each candle adds more light until on Christmas the light from the wreath sets off, as it were, the blaze of light on the tree of life, the Christmas tree. Originally the Advent wreath might have been a cart wheel, wound with greens and decorated with lights, strung up in the halls of the sunworshiping tribes of northern Europe. To appease their hidden god during the darkest winter days, they took a wheel from their cart, sacrificing its use, while they pondered about the blessings of light and life and implored the sun god to return to them.—*Sunshine Magazine.*

AT CHRISTMAS.   We must reach out to others as God reaches out to us—gently.

We must offer ourselves to one another as he gave himself for us—humbly. We must be born anew into the world as he was born into it—loving.—Walter A. Kortrey.

HOW SCROOGE SAW IT.   When you get right down to it, the celebrated miser in Charles Dickens' *A Christmas Carol* had nothing against Christmas. His gripe essentially was that people were using the holiday as an excuse for cheating a man of his hard-earned money, getting out of an honest day's work, or engaging in other forms of nonsense—all in the name of goodwill. Or, in Scrooge's words, the fact that it was Christmas was "no excuse to pick a man's pocket every twenty-fifth of December."—John F. Connors in *The Lookout.*

REQUESTS.   A great and mighty king issued a proclamation that on a certain festive day all requests would be granted. Some asked for gold, others for land, still others for weapons of war. Each wish was fulfilled. But there was one man wiser than the others. His request, he said, was only that he be permitted to enter the palace each day and speak in person with his royal highness, the king. His request found more favor in the eyes of the king than did the requests of all the others.

UNDERSTANDING.   For a Christian there is nothing peculiarly difficult about Christmas in a prison cell. I dare say it will have more meaning and will be observed with greater sincerity here in this prison than in places where all that survives of the feast is its name. That misery, suffering, poverty, loneliness, helplessness, and guilt look very different to the eyes of God from what they do to man, that God should come down to the very place which men usually abhor, that Christ was born in a stable because there was no room for him in the inn—these are things which a prisoner can understand better than anyone else.—Dietrich Bonhoeffer.

GOD WONDERS ME.   At the close of our church kindergarten year, some of the children were in the city park. One little boy, keenly aware of the vast sky above him and the tall trees about him, exclaimed, "God wonders me!" The exclamation of this child may not be perfect English, but it is an almost perfect expression of the wonder and mystery that surround Christmas.—Chevis F. Horne.

SECTION VII. Evangelism and World Missions

SERMON SUGGESTIONS

Topic: What Is Evangelism?
TEXT: I Cor. 15:1.

I. Evangelism is sharing the good news with people as the apostles did in Jerusalem or as Paul did at Ephesus, Philippi, and other places where Christ was unknown. This work of evangelism has in it a hereditary genius. We inherit the gospel; we do not create it.

II. Evangelism is telling the world and individuals of redemption through Jesus Christ. It is a divine message. It is a supernatural message. It is a Christ-centered message. It is the hope of our survival here and hereafter.

III. Evangelism is beseeching people to turn their lives over to Christ. (See II Cor. 5:20.) It is extending individually and in masses the invitation to a new life. We must urge people to give their lives to Jesus. We must be careful. There is a danger that people will be hypnotized to follow us and not really be converted to Christ. They will become people of Christian suggestion and not people who are genuinely converted. They will be people moved by man's will and not God's will. This means there will be no changed lives and no lasting results.

IV. Evangelism is urgently living the truth. People will be captured for Christ only when they see in our lives his life. Nietzsche said, "If I am to believe in your redeemer, you will have to look more redeemed." He was turned off by Christians whose lifestyle was "Don't do as I do, but do as I say." No person is going to buy a product which doesn't demonstrate its sufficiency and effectiveness.

V. The church is vital to evangelism. (a) When the church exalts Christ by wholesome worship, unreserved dedication to truth, fearless proclamation of the facts, and unselfish love for each person, the world cannot fail to note the challenge. Evangelism is telling, inviting acceptance of, and urgently living the good news. By every possible method we are to tell, beseech, and live our message.

(b) The church must be the living example of what God can do. Without the fact of changed living the people we confront will never *buy* the gospel. They have a right to ask: "Where is the change? Does the product work?"—Jerry B. Hopkins.

Topic: Fishers of Men
TEXT: Matt. 4:19.

Too many of us are hour-a-week Christians, but suppose that we were to become serious about our discipleship. What is required of us if we wish to accept our Lord's offer to make us fishers of men?

I. We must be willing to give people our time. Fishing takes time and patience.

II. We must respect their backgrounds, beliefs, and the degree of their spiritual development. Big fish are more wary than little ones.

III. We must discover what they think is the purpose of life.

IV. We must convince them that some gods are inadequate to the quality of life human beings have a right to expect.

V. We must convince them of the fact

57

that we have a relationship with God and not just an opinion about him.—Gilbert Runkel.

Topic: Why We Don't Witness
Text: Acts 18:9.

I. The first reason for failing to witness is reticence. Most have difficulty unveiling the inner spiritual life. But suppose a reticent person had been healed of a deadly disease and knows how to heal others. And he knew a friend who had it. Would he not share in some way his experience? Would he not lend a book, seek to speak, or in some way share? Would he not at least pray for the person and search for a right moment to share the secret of healing?

II. A second reason we do not share is we have a fear of being thought a hypocrite. We do not live up to all we know. So we profess nothing and need to live up to nothing. Basically it is the result of spiritual pride which is unwilling to admit we are sinners in need of God's continual forgiveness and help.

III. A third reason we shy from sharing Christ is the glib way many approach others, asking, "Are you saved?" They intrude into personality and do not love enough to build a loving relationship. But we do not avoid business contacts because of crude and corrupt businessmen. Neither do the actions of some excuse us for our failure.

IV. For a good many of us the real reason is we have nothing worth passing on. No man is fully won to Christ unless his personality is reaching out to bring others into the experience. It is incredible that we can possess the real thing and keep it as dark as some of us keep our religion. A chill falls upon the Spirit if one contemplates what would have happened if the earliest Christians had done no more to spread this experience than we have done.—Adapted from Leslie D. Weatherhead.

Topic: The Gospel Is for Everyone
Text: Acts 26:18.

I. *Proclaiming the gospel to the Samaritans* (Acts 8:4–8). Conspicuous among those faithful Christians who were scattered from Jerusalem by bitter persecution was Philip, the deacon who fled and found refuge in the city of Samaria, which was a mission field ripe unto harvest. He was the first foreign missionary. Samaria was the first foreign mission field.

II. *Proclaiming the gospel to an Ethiopian* (Acts 8:26–31). Just when Philip's soul-winning efforts were most successful and the prospects for the future looked most promising, the Lord unexpectedly commanded him to abandon his work and go south to a desert where there did not appear to be any prospect of success. Without complaint, Philip obeyed the Lord. He saw a chariot approaching, and the Holy Spirit said, "Go near, and join thyself to this chariot." In that chariot was an Ethiopian eunuch, a man of prominence and distinction who was reading Isa. 53. With eagerness and enthusiasm Philip ran to his chariot and asked him if he understood what he was reading, whereupon the Ethiopian invited him to enter the chariot. Beginning with the passage the man was reading, Philip preached Christ to him, and the man received Christ as his savior the first time he heard the gospel message.

III. *Proclaiming the gospel in Antioch* (Acts 11:19–21). Driven from Jerusalem following the martyrdom of Stephen, certain disciples went to Antioch, the capital of Syria. As those pioneer missionaries preached the gospel of Christ, the Lord placed his stamp of approval upon their witnessing, many were saved, and the first gentile church was established. The church became one of the leading ones in the Roman Empire. There Barnabas and Paul labored faithfully, and through them the Lord wrought great things.—H. C. Chiles.

Topic: Why Is the Great Commission Great?
Text: Matt. 28:18–20.

I. It is great because of the one who gave it—Jesus, the Son of God, the savior of sinners. He gives the commission to save sinners. He makes it great.

II. It is great because of the task assigned—go, disciple, baptize, and teach. What a great task!

III. It is great because of those to whom

it is given—his people through his church. His church has many and varied ministries, but every one of them must have as its ultimate goal the discipling of all men. This is the responsibility of God's people through his church.

IV. It is great because of the power by which it will be accomplished. This is not just a nice thought but a reality. God's commission to disciple the nations must be done by God's power through his people.—T. Hicks Shelton.

ILLUSTRATIONS

DERIVATION.   The priority of evangelism in the preaching ministry of the church is seen in the fact that the great word for the church's message—the word "gospel"—is the very term from which evangelism comes. Evangelism is not just part of the church's task in the world. It comes very close to being the whole of it. It was to one who filled what we could call a pastoral office that Paul wrote the injunction, "Do the work of an evangelist" (II Tim. 4:5).—W. T. Purkiser.

WORLD HUNGER.   The highest aspirations of the human heart in every field of human endeavor find their satisfaction in the gospel we serve. No matter that the night is dark. No matter that the road is long. The world in its secret heart hungers for the message we bear. We proclaim it because it is true. And we are heartened to know that humanity is deeply built to welcome the truth we speak. To dare the Christian mission is to contend with evil, but we wield the weapon of God's love, and all whom he conquers yield joyfully.—The Episcopal Church.

SPREADING THE GOSPEL.   When we turn from the restless entreaties and exhortations which fill the pages of our modern missionary magazines to the pages of the New Testament, we are astonished at the change in the atmosphere. St. Paul does not repeatedly exhort his churches to subscribe money for the propagation of the faith. He is far more concerned to explain to them what the faith is and how they

ought to practice it and to keep it. The same is true of St. Peter and St. John and of all the apostolic writers. They do not seem to feel any necessity to repeat the great commission and to urge that it is the duty of their converts to make disciples of all the nations. What we read in the New Testament is no anxious appeal to Christians to spread the gospel but a note here and there which suggests how the gospel was being spread abroad: "The churches were established in the faith, and increased in number daily" and "In every place your faith to God-ward is spread abroad; so that we need not to speak any thing" or as a result of a persecution: "They that were scattered abroad went every where preaching the word."

EQUIPPED.   The message of the reconciling Christ event must be remembered, rehearsed, and relived until we know it. No persons are sent forth to represent a country into a strange, new land until they are familiar with the meaning and policies of that country. They must be equipped as well as they can if they are to effectively represent that country in a new land. In like manner, we have need to be adequately equipped and prepared to properly represent the King of kings as God's appealers in today's world. A plentiful harvest, some 100,000,000 undiscipled Americans, await God's appealers, equipped with meaning, method, and masterlike winsomeness. God making his appeal to others through us effectively is evangelism in any century.—Hoyt D. Purcell.

RELUCTANT WITNESS.   Samuel M. Shoemaker served as a young preacher and teacher in China. He was attracted to a brilliant young Chinese scholar who was a colleague. He knew he should speak to him about Christ but felt he could not. So he went to an evangelist he knew and asked him to do the task. "Why don't you speak to him?" the evangelist asked. "Episcopalians just don't do that," protested Shoemaker. "I don't believe you," said the evangelist. "I believe the problem is with you and your secret sin."

It was like a knife piercing his heart. "Go

home," said the evangelist, "and examine yourself by the standards of purity, honesty, truth, and faithfulness."

For Shoemaker it was a burning bush experience. He gave himself to Christ in a new way. The next day he went to speak to his Chinese friend. He prayed the whole way that the friend would not be home. But he was home. Shoemaker spoke to him about the savior, and to his great surprise the man became a Christian. This experience was the beginning of a powerful ministry.—Paul M. Werger.

A NEW HEART.   An old Indian chief, who had been taught by a missionary, still had some intellectual problems that kept him from accepting Christianity. "This God you talk about does not seem quite fair to me. Each year he gives the birds a new coat of bright feathers. Even the snakes shed their skins for new ones when the old skins get worn. But we get no new skin. Ours just becomes uglier and more wrinkled every year. Your God is cheating us." "True," responded the missionary, "we do not get a new skin every year, but we can get something far better. God can give us a new heart through his word."

CHRISTIANITY INTERPRETED.   A missionary in Africa once had to make a long trip by automobile. To keep him company he invited his neighbor, a Muslim, to go along with him. The missionary used the trip to explain to his neighbor what Christianity was all about, but his words seemed to be falling on deaf ears. After they had traveled far away from any settlements, the car developed engine trouble and chugged to a stop beside the road. Soon a truck approached and the missionary waved for help, but the driver sped by without even slowing down.

There was nothing to do but to try to repair the car himself. Fortunately for the missionary and his passenger, the problem was not serious, and they soon had it running again.

After several miles, they rounded a bend, and to their surprise they saw the truck that had passed them by the side of the road with its hood up, obviously in trouble. "Honk your horn and wave as you pass him!" shouted the Muslim. "This is indeed sweet revenge!" But the missionary stopped his car and proceeded to lend assistance to the man.

When they had finally gotten the truck running again and were headed back to the car, the Muslim said quietly, "I think I'm beginning to understand what you were talking about when you were trying to explain Christianity to me."—John Wade.

EXTRACTION.   Among the missionaries sent to India by William Booth of the Salvation Army was a beautiful young lady, Elizabeth Geikie. She lived among the natives in a mud hut. One day the villagers took to her a man crazed with pain. She found a huge thorn driven deep into his foot, and only a pinpoint was visible. She had no knife nor surgical instrument, but she had strong teeth. She knelt down, clamped her teeth around the thorn in the man's filthy foot, and pulled it out. The next day that man and his wife accepted Christ as savior.—John R. Brokhoff.

QUESTION.   One evening a dinner was given in honor of Sir Wilfred Grenfell at a church in New York City. Sitting next to him was a woman who had never met him. Trying to make conversation, she said, "Is it true that you are a missionary?" Thoughtfully he replied with a question, "Isn't it true that you are a missionary?"— John Thompson.

SHARING THE GOOD.   A missionary to Africa sat at a table on the patio of an African village home and watched a black ant crawl up the table leg and onto the table to some sugar that had been spilled there. It ate its desire, crawled back down the table leg, and went out of sight. Soon there were two black ants that crawled up the table leg, onto the table, and into the sugar. They ate and left. Moments later there was a steady stream of black ants crawling up the table leg, onto the table, and into the sugar. What could you surmise other than through their communication system, one had communicated to others, "I have found something good, and I want to share it"? Can you say that about the Christian religion?—Jerry Hayner.

ON DAVID LIVINGSTONE.   Here is a man who is manifestly sustained as well as guided by influences from heaven. The Holy Spirit dwells in him; God speaks through him. The heroism, nobility, the pure and stainless enthusiasm at the root of his life came beyond question from Christ. There must be a Christ, and it is worthwhile to have such a helper and a redeemer as this Christ undoubtedly is, as he reveals himself in this wonderful disciple.—Henry M. Stanley.

GUIDANCE.   A native skipper on the African shores could not understand the pilots of great ships who guided themselves by the stars. "This foreign-going ship," he said, "is a star gazer. I go from headland to headland; I steer by what I know; I keep to terrestrial ground. But he, why he fancies that out of sight of land people can find out what spot they are on by looking at another world through a glass. We are not simple enough to believe that it is from another world that we are going to learn whether it is here we are or there."—Vere V. Loper.

DELAYED RESPONSE.   Tom Dooley, heir to a St. Louis fortune, was a talented musician, a skilled horseman, a lover of sports cars, a brilliant but undisciplined student. The faculty at St. Louis University Medical School asked that, in spite of his excellent academic average, he be disciplined for failure to show the qualities of dependability needed in the medical profession. At this crucial juncture in his life, Dean Melvin Casberg, a son of missionary parents from India, intervened. He personally assumed responsibility for continuing Tom Dooley as a student. Graduation, internship, and military service followed.

There was not much change in Tom Dooley.

Then it happened on July 14, 1954. Dr. Dooley received his temporary additional duty orders to Vietnam to assist in the evacuation of the French and Vietnamese from Haiphong. Through the suffering and the human need, God spoke, and Tom Dooley's temporary orders to Vietnam led to his becoming the outstanding Roman Catholic medical missionary of this century. He was the founder of Medico and, until his death at the age of 34, a twentieth-century example of the fact that a life must be measured by accomplishments rather than in years.—George T. Tade.

MATHEMATICAL POSSIBILITIES.   If a pastor, operating on the principle of addition, should win 120 people to Christ each year through his own preaching and personal evangelism, the church would have made 1,200 converts in ten years, 2,400 in twenty years. But suppose that same pastor should also train just one man in personal discipleship and witnessing and suppose that one should win only one more to Christ the first year and help that new man to grow until he too became a reproducing witness. Then suppose these two each won one more the second year. And suppose the four won four more the third year. In ten years over a thousand people would have been won to Christ, and in twenty years the total would be an incredible 1,032,576.—Leighton Ford.

SPEAKING BOOK.   A missionary was translating the Bible into an African tongue and employed a local man to help him. This man had never seen the book until he began his work. After a while he said to the missionary: "This book is not like other books. When a man reads this book, he hears someone speaking to him in his heart."

SECTION VIII. Children's Stories and Sermons

January 3. Day and Night

A rabbi asked his pupils how they could tell when the night had ended and the day was dawning. "Could it be," asked one student, "when you see an animal at a distance and can tell whether it is a sheep or a dog?" "No," answered the rabbi. "Could it be," asked another, "when you can look at a tree in the distance and tell whether it is a fig tree or a peach tree?" "No," said the rabbi. "Well, then, when is it?" his students demanded. "It is when you look on the face of any woman or man and see that she or he is your sister or brother because, if you cannot do this, then no matter what time it is it still is night."

January 10. A Pinch of Salt

A king asked his three daughters how much they loved him. Two of them replied that they loved him more than all the gold and silver in the world. The third and youngest said, "I love you better than salt." The king was not especially elated with her remark and dismissed it lightly as an indication of her immaturity. But the cook, overhearing the conversation, left salt out of the king's breakfast the next morning. He was thus confronted with the deep meaning of his daughter's remark, "I love you so much that nothing is good without you."

It is amazing what a pinch of salt will do to bring out the flavor of a food. How unpalatable a bowl of oatmeal is when one forgets to put in the salt. We especially come to appreciate this quality in salt when the doctor orders us on a salt-free diet. Foods we have loved before, when properly seasoned, become most uninteresting, if not unpalatable.

Christianity is to life what salt is to food. Christianity gives flavor and seasoning to life.—John Thompson.

January 17. Parable of the Builders

Edwin Markham wrote what he called the "Parable of the Builders." A certain rich man had it in his heart to do good. One day, as he was walking out over his broad estate, he came to a little house down in the hollow where lived a carpenter with a very large family. The rich man sent for the carpenter and put before him the plans for a beautiful house and said: "I want you to build a house just like this over on that sunny hill. Build it good and strong. Employ only the best workmen, and use only the best materials, for I want it to be a good house." Then he went on a long journey and left it all to the builder. After the rich man had gone, the carpenter said to himself, "This is my chance." So he used poor materials and gave poor workmanship that he might make more money for himself. At length the rich man returned, and the carpenter brought him the keys, saying, "That is a fine house I have built for you over on the sunny hill." "Good," said the rich man, man, "I am glad that it is a good house. The house is yours, for you and your children." The builder was brokenhearted. How industriously he had cheated himself. He took the keys and walked away, muttering to himself, "Oh, if I had only known that I was building it for myself."—Homer J. R. Elford.

January 24. What's in a Name?

Names are important. Your name is important to you. However, Americans do not seek to express personality and character in the naming of children as did the people of Bible times.

Some meaningful biblical names include Joshua, Samuel, Ichabod, Emmanuel, and Barnabas. God named some people before their birth—such as Jesus and John the Baptist. He changed the names of others. Abram became Abraham, Sarai became Sarah, Jacob became Israel, and Simon became Peter.

Names are important to God. All of the names accorded to Jesus are of special interest, for "God highly exalted him, and bestowed on him the name which is above every name, that at the name of Jesus every knee should bow" (Phil. 2:9–10, NASB).

The believer too has a glorious name. It is a great privilege to be called by the name of Christ.—Dewey F. Squyres.

January 31. Heartbeat

God has given us many wonderful gifts, but there's one gift that may be more important than any other. I wonder if you would think of it. Perhaps not. You can't see it, and maybe you just take it for granted. I'm thinking of your heart.

While the average human heart weighs just a bit more than one-half pound, it beats 70 times a minute, 4,200 times an hour, 100,800 times a day, 36,792,000 times a year, and about 2,575,000,000 times in a seventy-year lifetime. It's the most efficient pump ever created.

God has given you a heart, but there are strings attached to the gift. You've got to take care of your heart by exercise, eating the right foods, and getting plenty of rest. Then you'll be able to thank God for your heart for 70, 80, or perhaps 90 years.

February 7. Birthday Wish

William Willimon tells about a boy's fourth birthday. His name is Clayton. Clayton's mother told him he could have any kind of birthday party he wanted, so Clayton said he wanted a party where everybody was a king or a queen. His wish was granted, and his mother set to work making all the costumes for the party. She made golden crowns from cardboard, robes out of crepe paper, and sceptors for the kings and queens out of hangers.

The day of the party arrived, and as each guest arrived he or she was given a costume. Everyone at that party was either a king or a queen, and everyone had a great time. After cake and ice cream, they went outside and made a royal procession all the way to the end of the block and back again. All looked like kings and queens, and all believed they were kings and queens. And most importantly, all behaved like kings and queens, that is, with dignity and a sense of importance.

That night when the guests had all gone home and Clayton's mother was tucking him in bed, he said, "I wish everyone in the whole world could be a king or a queen not just on my birthday but everyday."—Mark Trotter.

February 14. Community Builder (Brotherhood Week)

Michael Lewis King, Jr., was born January 15, 1929, in Atlanta, Georgia. He came from a family of Georgia preachers who distinguished themselves as crusaders for justice. Michael's father told him about the great Protestant Reformation leader, Martin Luther. Michael's admiration of the courageous Luther caused him to have his name changed to Martin Luther King, Jr.

Through the influence of the president of Morehouse College, Dr. Benjamin E. Mays, and family models of preachers who were trumpeters of love and justice, Martin Luther King, Jr., was ordained in 1947. King's message of love, justice, and peace has plucked up and broken down many walls that separate persons, churches, and communities from each other. King's message has encouraged the building of community in which the love of God, neighbor, and oneself would be planted, cultivated, and shared by all persons.—Milton E. Owens in *The Secret Place.*

February 21. His Face Said Yes

Karl Menninger told about a time when Thomas Jefferson and some companions were riding horseback across the countryside when they came to a swollen stream. A traveler waited until several had crossed and then asked Jefferson to carry him across on his horse. The President did. When they reached the other side, some of the men asked him why he had gotten a ride with the President. The man responded: "I didn't know he was the President. All I know is that on some faces is written the answer no and on some of them the answer is yes. His was a yes face."

God has a yes face. Yes, I love you. It's my nature. Yes, I'll show you that love. It's my nature. Yes, I'll forgive you. It's my nature. His grace gives me mercy, and his mercy grants me peace.—Jerry Hayner.

February 28. A Little Christ (Lent)

An executive ran to catch a train in New York's Grand Central Station. As he came to the train, the conductor called, "All aboard!" As he dashed for a car, he bumped into a little boy who was holding a jig-saw puzzle. The pieces of the puzzle flew in all directions. The businessman let the train go and helped the boy pick up the pieces. When the job was done, the little fellow looked into the man's face and asked, "Mister, are you Jesus?" Of course he wasn't Jesus, but he was what Martin Luther called a little Christ because he did as Jesus would have done.—John R. Brokhoff.

March 7. Rescuing a Dog (Lent)

Several years ago the king of Greece paid a visit to the United States. Accompanying him during the ocean voyage were his family and several servants and his favorite pet, a small dog.

One morning a servant was out on the deck exercising the dog. In a playful mood the dog raced around the deck and, leaping on the rail, lost his balance and plunged into the ocean.

The servant, horrified by what had happened, rushed to the bridge and asked that the captain turn the ship around and go back and pick up the dog. The captain refused. "After all," he said, "it's only a dog."

"Would you turn the ship around to save a man?" the servant asked.

"Of course we would," replied the captain, "but that's different."

Without a further word the servant hurried to a lower deck, removed his shoes and coat, and leaped into the sea. Seeing what had happened, the captain ordered the ship turned around and recovered both the man and the dog.

In a way, this illustrates how Christ, who knew no sin, became sin for us in order to save us and reconcile us to God.—John Wade.

March 14. Beautiful Hands (Lent)

Are your hands beautiful? Do they remind someone of Jesus?

God's word has much to say about hands—especially the hands of Jesus. Jesus used his hands to serve the multitudes. And while we wait for him to return, we can be busy using our hands to serve others.

What can we do? We can reach out and touch someone with love and encouragement. We can serve the sick, write letters to the lonely, and entertain strangers in our home. We can give a portion of our worldly possessions to those in need. We can help friends and neighbors in their time of crisis.

The Bible says, "Whatsoever thy hand findeth to do, do it with thy might" (Eccl. 9:10). We can have beautiful hands that remind someone of Jesus.—Ruth McKinney.

March 21. Her Question (Lent)

Robert Young was putting one of his daughters to bed, and they were saying the evening prayers. She was listing a lot of people for God to bless—mother, daddy, grandparents, friends, everyone she knew. Finally she got to her want list. She talked about many things that she would like to have or that she would like to have happen. After what seemed much longer than it really was, she abruptly ended her prayer with the question, "Now, Jesus, is there anything I can do for you?"—*Guideposts.*

March 28. Leaving the Nest (Lent)

As Margaret stood at her kitchen window, she heard a commotion in an oak tree. A small bird was chirping loudly. All day Margaret heard the continuous chirping. It awakened her the next morning. When she went outside to investigate, it didn't take long to discover the problem. A bird had built her nest in a small birdhouse. Margaret watched as she fed her babies and was surprised to discover they were nearly as large as the mother. When the mother fed them, she held the food away from the hole, forcing the young birds to reach a great distance for the food. Often she hopped to a limb and chirped to them. She seemed to be saying: "Come on out. It's time to come out." They still refused to answer her call. Suddenly Margaret realized why the mother bird was so upset. If they didn't come out soon they would be too large and would be trapped inside the birdhouse.

For several days the mother called frantically to them, but the fat, stubborn babies remained in the nest, content to be fed. Finally one fat baby bird squeezed through the hole. The others soon followed and began fluttering from limb to limb.

Before the end of the day all of them were perched on the birdbath. The small, dark nest they had almost refused to leave was forgotten.

Like these baby birds, we are sometimes more interested in security than we are in following God.—*Home Life.*

April 4. The Empty Egg (Palm Sunday)

Preparing their minds for a proper celebration of Easter, the Sunday school teacher gave each class member a large plastic egg—the kind stockings sometimes come in—and they were to put into each egg something that was symbolic of the season. On the following Sunday the eggs were opened. What do you think the eggs contained? Things like flowers and butterflies. But one egg was empty. Nothing there at all. The children laughed and said how stupid. "It's my egg, and it's not stupid," one of the boys protested. "The egg is empty, but wasn't the tomb empty?"—Adapted from Craig Biddle III.

April 11. The Story of the Butterfly (Easter)

Have you ever seen a caterpillar? They are little green worms. Fuzzy crawlers that wiggle and crawl on trees.

Last October I was mowing my lawn, when right in the middle of my driveway, I saw a big, fat, wiggly caterpillar. He was green and yellow. He had fuzzy little hairs all over his body and a big horn on the front of his head.

I called my children to see this large caterpillar. He must have been eating for days to be so fat.

We put him in a large jar with some fresh leaves to eat.

Do you know what happened? One morning when we went out to look at the caterpillar, he wasn't there—at least we thought he was gone. But in his place we found something new—a cocoon.

This cocoon is a house that the caterpillar lives in during the winter. It protects him from the rain and the cold.

Any day now the cocoon is going to open. And do you know what will come out of the cocoon? No, not a caterpillar—a butterfly!

Every butterfly that you see fluttering from flower to flower—the yellow ones, the black ones, and the orange ones—all of them used to be caterpillars in a cocoon.

Jesus was like the caterpillar wrapped in a cocoon. After he died on the cross, men put his body in a cave and rolled a stone in front of it. But the cave could not hold him, just like the cocoon cannot hold the caterpillar. On the first Easter Jesus came alive out of the cave—just like the caterpillar had a new body. Easter tells us that Jesus came alive, and we too will be made alive if we believe in him.—Joe E. Trull.

April 18. Our Friend, the Spider

Over 50,000 different kinds of spiders live on this earth. Each of the 50,000 has millions of its own kind. Out of this 50,000 less than a dozen kinds can do any harm to man. The human race certainly has a far poorer batting average than this!

The combined weight of all these spiders is greater than the combined weight of all human beings alive. There are so many of them. An acre of rough grassland in the summertime swarms with one to two million spiders. For the most part they are very tiny ones.

Spiders live practically everywhere—on a newborn volcanic isle of the sea, high on Mt. Everest and higher than people can live, and in mines thousands of feet underground. Many live in water, even in the ocean.

Some spiders travel high above the earth using their silken lines as parachutes. They even cross oceans this way, sailing along above the clouds. The original home of the spider, 300,000,000 years ago, was the ocean.

We will stop our description here, although there are many other interesting facts about our friend, the spider.

Why call him our friend? Because he makes life possible for us. If there were no spiders, insects would eat all our food crops within weeks. Spiders live on insects, catching them in many kinds of traps. Were it not for spiders, our insect enemies would starve us to death within a few months.

Many of God's creatures are like the spider. Because we don't know them, we fear them.

So it goes with people we don't know too. We fear foreigners because we're not closely acquainted with them, and they fear us for the same reason.—Graham R. Hodges.

April 25. Human Beans

I was amused by my son's reference to humans as human beans. This is a common mispronounciation by children of the term human beings. After I had chuckled a bit, I began to think about what he really had said without even realizing it. When you think for a minute about a bean, it gets pretty profound. Take any old bean, leave it alone, and it soon will dry and wither away to dust. It will be totally non-produc-

tive. Take that same bean, place it in the right environment—the warm earth—and give it the right nurture—food and water —and a miracle happens. Within that small, simple looking piece of creation, there is contained a fantastic amount of energy. Able to push up the weight of dirt under which it has been buried, it sends forth a small tender shoot which with proper care and nurture becomes a strong stalk, bush, or vine that produces a bountiful harvest. The same bean planted off by itself will not be nearly as productive as when planted in community. Leave that bean out of the ground and out of the environment for which it was made, and it simply dies.

There is an obvious parallel to us as humans. Left alone or isolated, we wither and die. Planted and not nurtured, we simply become another struggling shoot in the row—far from achieving the potential of the miracle God packed inside us at creation. Given the right environment, nurture, and care, we human beans can get in touch with the source of power that enables us to grow.—William E. Amos.

May 2. The Turnstile

Thomas A. Edison used to take special pleasure in showing his guests around the grounds of his New Jersey home. On the way back to the house there was a fence with a narrow opening and a turnstile that his visitors had to pass through one at a time.

"Why the turnstile?" people often asked. It seemed so unnecessary.

"Each time you pass through," Edison would explain, "you pump eight gallons of water into a tank. We use that water for bathing and drinking."

I like to think that there was always a knowing smile on Edison's face as he told his friends about the work they'd just done unwittingly. Edison was a towering genius. How like him not to overlook the natural energy that God has stored up in every human being, energy too often untapped.

Whenever I think of Edison I am reminded of the divine potential within myself. The strength of a muscle I have yet to flex. The ideas in a corner of my mind I have yet to explore. The unlimited power of love that lies unused within my heart.— Manuel Almada in *Guideposts.*

May 9. St. Francis and the Mason

St. Francis of Assisi met a hard-working mason. "What are you doing, my friend?" the saint asked. He got a rather blunt, what's-it-look-like reply: "I'm working from morning till night." Rather than taking the hint, St. Francis posed another question: "Why are you working?" By now the mason was really beginning to show his annoyance at still another inquiry and snapped: "Such a question! To earn some money." "What do you want the money for?" the saint persisted. The mason, really annoyed by this time, replied, "To buy bread to live." "All right," said the holy man of Assisi, "and what are you living for?" The mason was at a loss for words, but St. Francis supplied the answer, reminding him of our purpose in this world. The gist of the story is that there is an eternal purpose to everything we think and say and do. In his revelation to us in his beautiful and holy words Jesus Christ teaches again and again about the eternal significance of man's life on earth. And he told us quite frankly: "I am the way, and the truth, and the life. No one comes to the Father, but through me" (John 14:6). Christ reveals the supernatural truth about God and man's real reason for living. He is our light shining through, penetrating the ignorance and darkness of this world.—William E. Shuman in *Pastoral Life.*

May 16. The Message of the Flowers (Rural Life Sunday)

When I walked outdoors to my garden, the flowers seemed to be in an attitude of prayer. The blossoms were lifted toward the sunlit rays as if in search of even more light. Their green stems supported them with sturdy strength, firmly planted in God's good earth.

Dew sparkled from the pink, blue, yellow, and white petals, like the innocent tears of little children. Each flower seemed to be listening for some message.

Serenely they seemed to we waiting for instructions. What could be the heavenly message intended for them? Quietly I waited for the answer to my heart's query about the flowers. Suddenly I knew that the flowers understood well their God-appointed mission, and that is just that they be themselves. Wherever they are planted, their responsibility and opportunity is to bloom in radiance at the appointed time and season.

The flowers were telling me that by fulfilling their own pattern of growth they were adding to the beauty of the world and enriching my life. Could I do less for my family and friends than the flowers did for me?—Ruth C. Ikerman in *Sunshine Magazine.*

May 23. Have You Seen Jesus? (Ascension Sunday)

What would you say if I told you that I had seen Jesus?

The truth is that I have seen Jesus. Not through any special vision or dream, but I have seen him. In the smiles of little children and the tear-filled eyes of mothers. Through strong and calloused hands or a tender understanding touch. Moments of joy, pain, inspiration, and relief—he's been in them all.

I've seen Jesus, but not nearly enough. When he returned to heaven, Jesus left us as his substitutes. We are to do what he would be doing if he were still here.

Have you seen Jesus? Maybe, maybe not. But the real question is, have others seen Jesus in you?—C. R. Dick Gibson in *The Lookout.*

May 30. Eyes That Smile

Some years ago the sales manager of an American store engaged Jay B. Idden, a New York stage director, to teach his salesmen how to smile. He had come to the conclusion that a smiling assistant sold more goods. Idden took the men one by one, rehearsed their smiles, criticized them, pointed out their errors, embarrassed them, and finally gave up. The experiment failed. The difference between the manufactured article and the real thing, he discovered, was in the eyes. When the smile is manufactured, it is only the mouth that smiles, and it is really a smirk. The eyes don't light up. They remain hard and unfriendly. It is only real joy that can smile in the eyes.—John Bishop.

June 6. Knowing God

Because I persisted in asking all kinds of questions about God and Jesus, my teacher took me to Boston to see Phillips Brooks, the famous preacher. She felt that if anyone could answer my questions he could. Her intuition did not fail her. The great man understood the heart of a child. He took me on his knee and told me in the simplest language how God loved me and every one of his children. He made God seem so real that I said: "Oh yes, I know him. I had just forgotten his name." After that visit my knowledge of the character and words of Christ grew day by day. I felt more and more of his life deepening down into mine, and I found more and more to be glad of in the world.—Helen Keller.

June 13. The Largest Schoolroom

Sometimes on the last day of school you can hear the girls and boys whooping and hollering all the way home, for vacation has come again. But wait a moment. School isn't really out, for all outdoors is a schoolroom. In it are all boys and girls, all those who have a few more years behind them and think they are grown-ups, and all the older people in the world. Mother Nature teaches in her huge school every day.

Some of the things we learn in the school which is as big as all outdoors are easy lessons and pleasant to remember. From falling snow we find out what it means to be gentle. The birds show us how to make merry music. The stars tell us that we live in such a big place that it cannot be measured. Mountains never use angry words. The grass and trees which seem to die in the winter come to life again in the spring.

We learn hard lessons from Mother Nature too. Bees make sweet honey, but they also sometimes sting unless we are careful. Roses are beautiful, though on their stems we run into sharp thorns. Rains water the fields and make wheat and corn—and, yes, spinach—grow, but once in a while they cause great floods and make people homeless. Soft breezes cool us on hot summer days, but sometimes they become big tornadoes. So from our teacher we learn that things have their good sides and their bad. —Philip Cowell Jones.

June 20. Mr. Fix-It (Father's Day)

Many an American dad is Mr. Fix-It. When the children come running with a broken toy, many a lucky wife can console: "Don't cry. Wait till Daddy gets home. Your father can fix it."

"Daddy can fix it"—anything, everything! A bike, a pair of roller skates, broken toys, and even those antiques his wife drags home from auction sales. Patiently, cleverly, with glue and tape and nails and paint—and love and imagination and patience. Whatever it is, if it's dear to its owner, somehow, someway, he'll devise the means of its salvation.

Mr. Fix-It, Mr. Handyman, Father, Daddy, Pop, or Dad—whatever his title— he'll analyze the whole thing wisely and come up with the proper solution. Report cards, budding romances, times of illness, worry, family strains, problems at school or church—don't worry, talk it over with Dad.—Jewel Hill.

June 27. The Flower God Needed

One day God decided to sow some violet seeds along the roadside to beautify his earth. As he scattered them, one little seed rolled over the curb into the paved gutter. "O God, don't leave me here," begged the little seed.

"Don't fret, little seed. You are just where I want you to be. That is the spot I want you to beautify," explained God.

"But I can't grow here. There's no soil. What will I eat?" questioned the little seed.

"I'll nourish you," continued God. "I have a special assignment for you. I have some folks who will be needing encouragement, and I have planned for you."

The little seed interrupted, "But it would take a miracle for me to do any good here."

"I know it. I've got a miracle just your size. I have it all arranged with an ample supply for your every need," explained God.

"But I've got some problems about miracles," said the seed.

"I know. I do too," God confided.

"You do too?" asked the surprised little seed.

"Yes," said God. "I draw up these miracle contracts and everything is fine until I get to the bottom line. That line usually causes me trouble."

"Why is that?" asked the seed.

"That is the line where I need your OK and signature before I can put the miracle into operation. You always have your own plans, and I must find someone who is willing to OK my contract," said God almost wearily.

"But what would my part of the contract be if I signed?" asked the seed.

"Just be willing to stand, to grow, and to bloom," answered God.

"Then I am willing, Lord. I will sign," the seed said.—Arlene Anderson in *Church of God Evangel.*

July 4. Our National Anthem (Independence Day)

In 1931 Congress officially recognized "The Star-Spangled Banner" as the national anthem. It came about in a dramatic way. During the War of 1812 the British took William Beanes, a Baltimore lawyer, as a prisoner and placed him on a British warship anchored in Chesapeake Bay. In an attempt to secure Beanes' release, President Madison sent two envoys, John K. Skinner and Francis Scott Key, to the warship to plead for Beanes' release. Soon after Key and Skinner arrived on board the warship, the British opened fire on Fort McHenry, which protected the city of Baltimore.

The battle started on Tuesday, September 13, and continued all day and almost all night. Key and his friends realized that the fort had little defense and were certain that it would fall to the British. The men paced the ship's deck all night waiting for the dawn and the clearing of the gun smoke. Early in the morning the mist broke, and the men could see the American flag still flying over the fort. Reaching into his coat pocket, Key pulled out an unfinished letter and wrote these immortal words: "Oh! say, does the Star-Spangled Banner yet wave o'er the land of the free and the home of the brave?"—Thomas J. Fleming.

June 11. Backyard Views

A high school teacher in New York City asked her pupils to write on the subject "The Backyard Side of Life." Two lads from the same slum district turned in two opposite views. One wrote of the backyard sordidness, the litter-strewn lots, the piles of refuse and half-open garbage cans, and the vulgar people in various stages of nudity. The other wrote of the urge of all human hearts to bring a bit of beauty to life even in the slums. He described the plants he saw which lined the porch rails and fire escapes, the geraniums in tin cans placed on windowsills, and no backyard so poor it was not brightened by a bit of color. Which of those two lads do you think will rise above the slum he lived in? —Joan Bradshaw.

July 18. Drops of Water

The rainbow is one of nature's most beautiful wonders. Millions of tiny drops of water act together to reveal the rich colors of light which are otherwise invisible to the naked eye. Each drop of water reflects and refracts a sunbeam until it reveals one of the seven shades of light to any person standing with his back to the sun. God expects each of his children to function as those drops of water. Our daily lives are to reflect the magnificent glory and character of Jesus until the unbeliever standing with his back to the Son sees and understands the richness of his love.— Chuck Kelley in *Proclaim.*

July 25. The Emperor's Mirror

An ancient Chinese parable tells of an emperor who was so insecure, so lacking in confidence, and so tension-torn that he kept himself sheltered in his palace. In an attempt to bolster his self-confidence he would gaze at his reflection in a large mirror. In this way he would assure himself that he was a great ruler. His sole goal in life seemed to be to impress himself with his own importance.

While he remained interested only in himself, his people were being hoodwinked by officials who confiscated their lands. Reduced to a state of extreme poverty, they were hungry and worn. Misery abounded in the streets.

A member of the palace staff, realizing the need for the emperor to take action, devised a plan. One night he removed the mirror. In its place he cut a window in the wall, the same size and shape as the mirror.

When the emperor arose he proceeded, as was his custom, to stand before the mirror. This time, instead of his own reflection, he saw his subjects in the street below, huddled together in their misery. He saw weary women carrying burdens on their backs. He saw hungry children looking for scraps of food. He saw tired old men and young men in rags. The emperor cried out, "What happened to my people?" The loyal friend who had engineered the plan told him what had happened. Losing all care for himself, the emperor went out among his people. He took personal interest in his subjects. Prosperity returned to the land, and the people were content and hungry no more.

Christ does this to you and to me. He transforms the mirror in our lives to a window. He causes us to forget about ourselves and become interested in people and their needs. He gives us the self-confidence we need to respond to those who are hurting. He gives us a purpose in living.—Donald L. Germain.

August 1. Where Jesus Lives

A pastor was trying to explain to a group of nursery school children how Jesus still stays with us to help us. He told them how we are Jesus' hands and feet, eyes and voices in this world today, and then he asked, "Where do you suppose that Jesus lives today?" Almost all the children immediately responded, "Jesus lives inside of us!" All the children said that except for one child. He kept looking at his hands and his feet. Then he looked at the huge picture of Jesus that hung in the classroom. Evidently he was thinking: "I'm so little and Jesus is so big. How can that big guy fit inside of little me?" And finally he asked the minister, "If Jesus lives inside of me, it seems to me that he ought to be sticking out some place!"—David G. Maze in *The Clergy Journal.*

August 8. The White Stone

"I will give to him a white stone, and in the stone a new name written" (Rev. 2:17).

In the first century when two friends were separating, it was not unusual for them to break in half a white stone with each friend taking a half. Although years might pass and circumstances alter their appearance and station in life, if when they met and proffered to each their half of the white stone, upon matching, their friendship was completely renewed and restored.

When we accept Christ as savior, he also becomes our friend and thereafter constantly holds out to us the white stone of friendship, waiting for us to match his.—Tom J. Madden.

August 15. The Little Bird That Tried

A man saw a sparrow lying on its back looking intently at the sky. "What on earth are you doing?" asked the man. "Well, I heard the sky was going to fall," replied the tiny bird. The traveler laughed and said, "And you think with those spindly legs of yours, that you can hold it up?" The brave little creature remained in position and declared, "One does what one can."—Bevel Jones.

August 22. Reverence for Life

A bumper sticker, "OUR WORLD: LOVE IT OR LOSE IT," caused me to recall Albert Schweitzer's "Reverence for Life." Not just reverence for the gifts of life but for life itself, which God gave to the world as his crowning gift. The greatest thing a man can do is to reverence life and the God who gives it. The worst thing a man can do is to abuse it by word or deed. Dr. Schweitzer would never burn a field. He said, "Think of all the insects I would burn in a fire like that!" When he ate grapefruit, he always spilled a spoonful of the juice on the floor for the ants. To those who tried to drive the ants away, he would say: "Leave them alone. They are my ants." In reverencing life he reverenced God.—John Thompson.

August 29. The Frog That Became a Prince

A squat, ugly frog sat disconsolately on a drifting lily pad. He didn't know where he was going. His life lacked purpose, reason, and meaning. He was sick of being ugly and a nobody. Eventually he drifted toward shore where a beautiful princess asked, "Are you one of those frogs that used to be a prince until a spell was cast upon you?" "I haven't the froggiest notion," he replied. Thereupon she kissed him, and a handsome prince stood before her. They were married and lived happily ever after. The duty of the church is to kiss frogs.—Myron J. Taylor.

September 5. How Well Do You Do Your Work? (Labor Sunday)

Tomorrow is Labor Day when we honor all workers, not only members of great trade unions, but also all people who do their work faithfully, conscientiously, and dependably. If you do the little chores that are given to you in that manner, then it's a day when you too should be honored. How well do you do your work? With as little effort as possible and lots of complaining or the best you can?

More than 200 years ago, Antonio Stradivarius made a vow. "Other men will make violins," he said, "but no man shall make a better one." So far, experts say, no one has. Stradivarius violins today are worth as much as $300,000. A Stradivarius violin, with the maker's label dated 1733 on the back, was sold for $297,250, equaling the world auction price record for any musical instrument.

We can't all make violins, but we can so do our work that we can be called workers together with God.

September 12. Scattered Feathers

A woman came to St. Francis of Assisi, admitting that she had been guilty of malicious gossip. She wanted to know how she might find forgiveness. He told her to pluck a goose, lay one feather on the doorstep of each person she had wronged, and then collect the feathers again. Of course, by this time they had been scattered over the village by the wind, and she came back empty-handed. He gave her this counsel: "You can never recall those words you have spoken. They have been carried on their way, doing harm, and no reparation is possible. Ask God to forgive you."—Greer S. Imbrie in A.D.

September 19. What the Mirror Tells Us

Are we pleased when we look in the mirror? What is our life reflecting? The place of mirrors in our lives is mentioned by the apostle Paul in a most telling way in I Cor. 13:12: "For now we see through a glass, darkly; but then face to face." He speaks of the mirrored reflection that reveals to us in part the way we are.

There is a funny thing about mirrors, one that we often forget. They show things in reverse. The part on the right side of your hair shows up on the left in the mirror. After awhile we come to think of ourselves in an opposite way to the way others see us. What we see in a glass does not provide the dimension of what others see in real life.—Evaline Echols in *Church of God Evangel.*

September 26. Beside Still Waters

A curious thing happens when you approach still waters. At first you see distant trees and hills outlined perfectly in the water—all upside down. You see a topsy-turvy world. Everything is inverted. But as you draw nearer the inverted world diminishes and the heavens begin to fill the scene. Bill Popejoy in *Goodness, You're Following Me* observes: "When you stand beside still waters you see yourself in heaven's backdrop. And that's the way a man needs to see himself. Otherwise, we will be continually comparing ourselves with others, and will 'fall short of the glory' (Rom. 3:23)."

At times it is necessary for the Shepherd to lead us "beside the still waters" to remind us who we are, where we came from, and where we are going. We must be willing to be led by these mirrored waters in order to see ourselves as God sees us.

Otherwise, our lives will be totally out of perspective. In the *Living Bible* translation, II Cor. 3:18 says: "But we Christians have no veil over our faces; we can be mirrors that brightly reflect the glory of the Lord. And as the Spirit of the Lord works within us, we become more and more like him."

The good Shepherd is aware of our human fears and frustrations. He goes to great lengths to lead us beside the still waters in order for us to see ourselves as he sees us.—Evaline Echols in *Church of God Evangel.*

October 3. The Chair of Honor

In the massive castle of Kentworth lived the mighty Reginald and his courageous Hundred Knights. In this castle, among many ancient relics, was a chair called "Perilous Seat." It was reputed to be the seat on which Christ sat at the Last Supper. The privilege of sitting on this chair was one of the greatest privileges that came to any individual in a lifetime. To be deserving of such an honor was no easy task. Such a knight must be pure of heart and strong of arm. He must be absolutely trustworthy and honest, a friend of the friendless and a helper of all those in need.

Young Gerhard was disappointed when his fellow knights went off to battle and he was left to guard the castle and its occupants, who were mostly women and children. But he performed each duty with care, saying to himself: "If I would neglect a smaller task, I might neglect a more important one. I will be trustworthy."

A half year passed and the warriors returned, their grim faces showing signs of hardships and their armor the signs of many rugged battles. They found everything ready for their unexpected return—their ladies and children happy and well cared for. At the welcoming banquet the moment finally came for the aged leader to select that person who had lived as the most pure and trustworthy knight. Each was hopeful that the lot might fall on him to sit on the seat where Christ once sat.

Slowly the leader moved along the table until he came to young Gerhard, the knight who had been required to stay at the castle while the others went to battle.

Grasping Gerhard by the arm, the leader led him gently toward the seat of honor, saying: "Here is one who has done his humble duties with all diligence. No word of complaint has passed his lips. His shall be the coveted reward."—Homer J. R. Elford.

October 10. The Door That Wouldn't Open

Houdini, the famous magician and escape artist, could get out of any jail, handcuffs, or strait-jacket that he ever tried. That is, all except one.

That one place was a little jail in the British Isles. Houdini worked at the cell lock for more than two hours. He worked with that terrific speed that usually unlocked doors in thirty seconds. But he couldn't get the lock to spring. Finally, tired by his strenuous efforts, he leaned against the door. It swung open. It had never been locked!

Life is something like that, isn't it? We build up barriers in our minds that do not exist. We lock ourselves up in the jail of failure by doubts and fears that live only in our imagination.

Some of us have stopped trying because of past failures. We think there is no use. We assume that the door to success has been locked against us. Maybe, if instead of sitting down and giving up, we would just lean against the door, it would swing open.—*Sunshine Magazine.*

October 17. Which Boy Disobeyed His Father?

Once upon a time Jesus went to the temple. People gathered around him to ask questions about God. Instead of answering them, he told them a story about a father and his two sons.

"A certain man had two sons," Jesus said. "One day the father said to the first one, 'Son, I want you to do some work in the vineyard today.' "

It might have been a hot day, or the boy might have planned to do something with his friends. Whatever the reason was, he said, "No, I won't go."

Then later he felt sorry. So he changed his mind and did what his father asked him to do.

In the meantime the father went to his second son and said, "I want you to do some work in the vineyard today."

The second boy was always respectful. He never talked back. So he said, "Yes, sir, I'll go right now."

But as soon as his father's back was turned, he slipped away. He wasn't going to spend a hot day pruning grape vines.

Jesus asked, "Which of the two did what their father wanted?"

Before you answer, you should know something about families in Jesus' day. One of the worst things a person could do was to be disrespectful to his father. It was considered so wrong that it just was never done.

So if someone who heard Jesus tell that story didn't think about it, he would say the second son was the good son. For he was polite to his father, and the first son was disrespectful.

How would you have answered the question?

The people to whom Jesus asked the question said it was the first son who really obeyed his father. And Jesus seemed to agree. For he went on to tell them that some people who used to disobey God but changed their ways would enter God's kingdom before other people who promise to do what God wants but really don't.
—*The United Church Observer.*

October 24. Resisting Temptation

A group of young people were discussing how to resist temptation. One girl offered her answer to the problem. "When I became a Christian," she said, "Christ moved into my heart. When I hear Satan knocking at the door of my heart, I'm afraid to answer the door because he may beguile me into letting him in. And so I send Jesus to answer the door. When the devil sees our Lord, he knows that he has the wrong address and leaves in a hurry."
—John Wade.

October 31. The Book They Found in the Temple

Josiah became king when he was only eight years old. His reign began in a troubled time marked by intrigue, murder, and almost a century of apostasy and idolatry.

Even as a boy he walked in the way of the Lord. When he was twenty-six years old, during repairs on the temple, the book of the law was found. Somehow God's word had been set aside and lost for years in the temple. And it appears from the account given in II Kings that this was the only copy left.

When the king saw the book, he wanted to know the meaning of it. Before long he staged a public reading of the law before all the people, and they all covenanted with him to keep it and obey it. This incited a revolution in righteousness. All the idolatrous priests were deposed, the houses of the cult prostitutes were destroyed, the horses dedicated to the sun god were put away, the high places for foreign idolatry were broken down, and the very stones of the pagan altars were ground into dust.

Then the king commanded the people to keep the passover. "Surely such a passover had not been celebrated from the days of the judges who judged Israel, nor in all the days of the kings of Israel, and of the kings of Judah" (II Kings 23:22, NASB).

The word of God can also be lost when there are hundreds of millions of copies available. Unread and unheeded, the Bible is lost to man just as was that one copy put away in a hiding place in the temple.

When the word is discovered, then we are also discovered. His book speaks to us in our needs, rebukes our idolatries, and calls us to repentance and devotion.—George Alder.

November 7. God's Telephone Number

Have you learned how to use the telephone? How to dial? How to answer? What is a phone for?

Did you know that you and I have a way to talk to God? The number is P-R-A-Y-E-R.

This telephone we have for talking to God is better than the telephone we have in our house. Do you know why?

The telephone of prayer is one that can be used anytime and anywhere. You don't need to search for this phone. You have it with you always.

The line is never busy. When you talk, you never get a buzz-buzz-buzz busy signal. God is always waiting to hear you talk to him.

You never get a wrong number. When you dial and talk with God, you always get him—never someone else.

If you listen, you will always get a personal message from God. He has something he wants to say to you.

So prayer is like talking and listening on a telephone. Prayer is talking to God. It is like picking up the telephone in the morning and saying: "Good morning, God, this is (*name*). I am happy today. Thank you for the beautiful world all around me. I am so glad I can talk to you. Do you have something you want to say to me? I'm listening."—Joe E. Trull.

November 14. Adding to the Light

Back in the early days of America there was a certain church building built without any central lighting. There were no large chandeliers hanging from the ceiling, but just individual candle brackets along the walls. Each worshiper was to bring his own candle. We can be sure that when all were there the room was filled with light. And in whatever number the members of the congregation were not present, there was darkness to that degree. That is certainly true for us too.—*The Clergy Journal.*

November 21. Gratitude in Action (Thanksgiving Sunday)

Appreciation is gratitude converted into action. It is being so thankful for the good that has come our way that we want to pass it on to others. It is thanking God by helping our fellowmen. If we have strength, appreciation means helping the weak. If we have faith in God, it means encouraging the discouraged and cheering the hopeless. If we have enough food and clothing to keep us alive, it means giving to those on the thin edge of starvation and nakedness.—Harold E. Kohn.

November 28. A Fable (Advent)

A certain nobleman wore a splendid ring. The ring had mystic power to make its owner a person of fine character. The power had worked on this man, as it had on his father and on his father's father before him, for all were known for their nobility of soul.

But the present owner had three sons. He could not choose among them when it came time to bequeath the ring. So he took it to a goldsmith and ordered two copies. The goldsmith crafted well. So exact were the copies that not even the nobleman could be certain of the original.

The sons were delighted for a while. Then delight gave way to strife as arguments rose over which son had the real ring.

The case was taken to a wise judge. He asked the sons to tell him the meaning and purpose of the original. When he understood, he said: "You must be the judges of this, for only you can offer proof. If each of you believes the real ring is the one you wear, go out and demonstrate it by the character it is supposed to fashion." And each son by his believing became as the father.—Bennett J. Sims.

December 5. The Darkness Doesn't Last (Advent)

December brings the shortest days of the year. More darkness. Little light from a sun that seems lost in the southern sky. But then things turn around. Before December has gone the days are just a tiny bit longer. All over the northern parts of the earth, through ages and ages, peoples have held celebrations when the sun was reborn and when there was even a little more light. For even that much is all the promise that is needed.

That is really why we have Christmas on December 25. The people who became Christians in the first generations were used to a celebration at this time of year—a birthday party for the sun, earth's best friend. But Jesus was like that too, a sun, the light of the world. And so this solstice time has become his birthday anniversary.

Advent is the way we keep these darkest days of the year as a preparation. Advent happens in the dark, and it is filled with our fears. Few of us ever really get over being scared of the dark, so this season lets us be the frightened folks that we are.

Only frightened people can really keep Advent. "Be comforted!" "Don't be afraid!" Prophets and angels shout and sing through the Advent nights with that message. It is the hint of a promise. To keep Advent is to live by God's promises that are stronger than our fears.—Gabe Huck adapted from *A Book of Family Prayers* (Seabury Press).

December 12. The Manger Scene (Advent)

For many Christians the nativity is kept fresh in their minds by the displaying of the crèche or manger scene during the Christmas season.

This custom began in the church during the Middle Ages. Simple guild folk and village priests began to enact scenes from the life of Christ. Usually the babe in the manger with Mary and Joseph was the chief scene. Other figures, such as the wise men, shepherds, and angels, were often included.

A popular legend gives the honor to the gentle priest, St. Francis of Assisi, for assembling the first enactment of the birth of the Christ child. His heart was filled with tender compassion for the simple peasants who could not read. He wished to teach them the Christmas story and its true meaning. So in a cave on an Italian hillside above Greccio, St. Francis assembled a manger scene, using real people as Mary and Joseph. In the manger he placed a waxed figure of the baby Jesus. In the quiet of the night a simple mass was read to the country folk who had gathered. With tears flowing down his face, he urged the people to accept the love that God had extended to them through the birth of the savior and to depart from their hatred and sin.—Rose Kyllo.

December 19. The Story of "Silent Night" (Advent)

A tragedy occurred in the Church of St. Nicola in Oberndorf, Austria, on December 24, 1818. The organist had come prepared to rehearse for the annual Christmas program. Imagine his alarm when he discovered that he could not get a sound from the organ. Investigation revealed that mice had industriously knawed holes in the leather bellows which supplied the wind for the organ pipes. It was impossible to repair the organ before the Christmas program. What could be done?

Father Mohr, the parish priest, had just returned from a night call made at a home where a new baby had arrived. The sight of the child in the arms of its mother inspired him. On the return home he walked through deep snow. Overhead the stars twinkled, while on the white landscape there was silence. He hurried into his study to give his inspiration free rein. So it was that "Silent Night! Holy Night!" was written.

On learning of the difficulty with the organ, Father Mohr hastened to his friend, the village schoolmaster, Franz Gruber. Could he write the music for his poem?

It is said that Gruber composed the tune in less than an hour. Hastily gathering together a quartet composed of himself, Franz Gruber, and two women, Father Mohr presented the new carol at the Christmas service. It was sung a cappella. The reception of this new carol was most enthusiastic. No one missed the organ! And so it was that our beautiful "Silent Night! Holy Night!" came to be.

December 26. A Legend

A liberated slave went to see President Lincoln and assured him that he would not accept his freedom as a gift and that he proposed to pay for it. He threw a silver dollar on the President's desk. The kindly Mr. Lincoln tried to show the man that he could not pay for his liberty and that the very fact he thought he could indicated that he did not fully appreciate the priceless gift. When the freed man insisted, the President took him to the window and showed him the row on row of soldiers' graves across the river in Arlington. He asked him how his money could pay back the lives that had been given that he might live in freedom. When the poor man asked what he might do, he was assured that he must walk the world with gratitude and live like a free man.—Orva Lee Ice.

SECTION IX. Sermon Outlines and Homiletic and Worship Aids for Fifty-Two Weeks

SUNDAY: JANUARY THIRD

MORNING SERVICE

Topic: A Constant Call to Renewal

TEXT: Phil. 3:14–15.

I. Pressing on, one must be receptive to new inspirations. (a) Everything worthwhile in life comes as someone feels deeply, is sensitive to, or emotionally enters into some new experience of discovery or understanding. There are those who miss the whole meaning of life because they never lose themselves in some new inspiration of truth, beauty, or meaning and enter into the joy of it.

(b) This is the secret of all of life's gifts, from a Watts studying the way steam was able to lift the lid off a teakettle to the power of a steam engine; from a Handel, in the depths of despair over debt and hardship, rising to the heights of a Hallelujah Chorus; or a Browning, lifted through love to dimensions he never thought he could feel and then giving the world the wisdom of his thought through the music of his poetry. The same has been true for countless others—world famous or unknown.

II. The constant call to renewal reminds us that we can have a new year through the creation of new attitudes.

(a) For most of us a new year does not mean any appreciable change in outer circumstances or conditions. It will be the same job, the same problems, and the same self to live with. If anything is going to be new, it will have to come through a new attitude. Part of the blessed hope of our faith is the knowledge that, although we cannot change outer circumstances, we can be masters of our reaction to them. We do not need to live at the mercy of events.

(b) This is what Paul meant when he wrote: "I have learned in whatsoever state I am therewith to be content . . . I know how to live when things are bad and when things are good." It is far from saying that Paul was satisfied with all outer circumstances. He too had the brooding heart that yearned and hoped for a better day with finer circumstances and conditions. To that end he set about to change some things that bothered him but which he would not let overwhelm him.

(c) Inwardly he found an attitude of heart, mind, and soul that would let nothing crush his spirit. He was saying, "I can take anything the world can throw at me and more, because I am armed with a strength that nothing can break." With his acceptance of things as they were, he also held an attitude which said, "In all these things we are more than conquerors through him that loved us."

III. The constant call to renewal reminds us that we can have a new year as we join our lives to some cause greater than ourselves.

(a) Something bigger than ourselves helps us push back the horizon, starts us

76

growing in new endeavor, thought, and action, and life's limited vista begins to offer breath-taking possibilities.

(b) This was the method of our Lord. In a defeated day he linked the lives of his followers to the kingdom of God. Immediately their little worlds gave way to the infinite possibilities of God's vastness and man's potential in the image of God. So people who were quite ordinary in their little lives became great individuals through a new love and cause and left their mark on all humanity.

IV. The constant call to renewal involves a renewed program of personal prayer.

(a) Prayer holds the greatest resources for maximum experience in the Christian life. Here is where our enthusiasm is rekindled, our perspective enlarged, and our sense of the presence of the Almighty reinforced.

(b) In I Thess. 5:17 Paul writes: "Pray without ceasing," or in another translation, "Pray constantly, give thanks in all circumstances; for this is the will of God in Christ Jesus for you." Life for him was filled with prayer, and it can be the same for us.

(c) Prayer is a gift of God, a great source of spiritual power, and the channel of God's Holy Spirit as we open ourselves to him. The constant call to renewal means using this great spiritual tool, developing our ability, and enlarging our capacity until consciously and unconsciously our lives become a total prayer experience, not necessarily in the formal words we say or the particular posture we may assume but in a sense of communion with God constantly. So his peace, presence, power, patience, and perceptivity will give us the grace to be and to become sons of God in Christ.—Allan J. Weenink.

Illustration

STRIKING IMPRESSION. A man who had not read the Bible for a long time was persuaded by a friend to read carefully the first three gospels. When he had finished, the friend asked him if he had had any strong impressions from his reading. The man thought a moment and then said: "I was deeply impressed by Jesus' use of time. He seemed to use time in a different way than many people do. In many ways he seemed to use time for things that would have seemed unimportant to many people."—Halford E. Luccock.

Sermon Suggestions

WHAT IS THE PURPOSE OF LIFE? Text: John 18:37. (1) The purpose of life is to live. (2) The purpose of life is to love. (3) The purpose of life is to reach, to give, to spend, and to sacrifice for others. (4) The purpose of life is to bear witness to Christ not only in a proclamation of words but also in what we think and do, trying in some small degree to release in the world his spirit of reconciliation and redemption. —Theodore P. Ferris.

HOW LONG IS LIFE? Text: Luke 10:25. (1) As long as you laugh. (2) As long as its loyalties. (3) As long as it loves. (4) As long as it lifts.—Wesley P. Ford.

Worship Aids

CALL TO WORSHIP. "He that dwelleth in the secret place of the most High shall abide under the shadow of the Almighty. I will say of the Lord, He is my refuge and my fortress: my God; in him will I trust." Ps. 91:1–2.

INVOCATION. Our Father, we thank thee for thy word and for the eternal truths which guide us day by day. We thank thee most of all for the living word, Jesus Christ, and the sureness of his presence. Teach us how to turn unto thee so that thy thoughts may be our thoughts and thy ways our ways.

OFFERTORY SENTENCE. "Every man according as he purposeth in his heart, so let him give; not grudgingly, or of necessity: for God loveth a cheerful giver." II Cor. 9:7.

OFFERTORY PRAYER. We give thee thanks, O Father, that through our tithes and offerings thou dost give us an opportunity to illuminate the dimness of the future and to glorify our present life with the word of him who is the light of the world.

EPIPHANY PRAYER.   Father, we come to worship with the songs of Christmas still in our hearts. We celebrate this day the joy which the wise men found when they came to celebrate the birth of Christ. They also came to worship and give praise to the Savior as we do this day. There was anxiety and anticipation as they traveled the miles, just as we find anxiety in our own hearts as we search for truth of life only found in Christ. Yes, Father, there is much anxiety as we face the possibility of life. As we face these anxieties we sometimes falter and sin. Forgive us our sins and free us from the bondage which sin may create in our lives. Help us to seek the Christ event in our lives as we worship. Challenge us to give of ourselves the way the wise men gave of themselves. The wise men were given a star to follow, a light to lead the way. So we also have been given a light in the life of your Son to lead us through the difficult and joyous times of life. Help us this day, as we worship, to see clearly the light which shines in the darkness to lead us. May we see that light even through our hurt, our hunger, our loneliness, our despair, and our grief. Father, not only would we ask to be helped to see the light but also for the light to shine through our lives. Brighten our faces for the new year. Brighten them with the peace and joy which only may be found through you. Help us to light the path that others may see the faith we have in your will and your way. As in the epiphany of old, it is in the revealing and appearing that we joyously say, "Go, tell it on the mountain, that Jesus Christ is born."—James R. Rosenburg.

EVENING SERVICE

Topic: Follow That Star (Epiphany)
SCRIPTURE: Matt. 2:1–12.
Follow that star! How do you do that? How's a person led into a greater realization of the person of Christ? How do you

appropriate more of his life into yours? How do you come to a closer walk with God? What is most effective in leading you on like that? There are four points to that life-determining, guiding star.

I. The first is to take some time every day to reflect on the person of Jesus. What were his priorities? What motivated him? How did he relate to those about him? How did he face the problems and possibilities which confronted him? Weatherhead spoke of "mental anchorage." There is no better place to anchor our thoughts as we face each day than the character of the Lord of life. After we get a good mental picture of him—his goodness, his faith, his courage, his love for God and others, and his resourcefulness—we can more successfully translate his life and way of doing things into our contemporary scene.

II. A second point in the star which leads us to him who is the source of life is the regular use of the scriptures and other Christian literature.

(a) Luther wrote of the Bible as the cradle of our Lord. Christ comes alive for us when we go to that place where he is revealed. If we go there often, he will grow on us and we will grow more into his likeness. Although the story is the same each time, we are not the same. It has something new to say to us at every stage of our growth. Other sound and sensible Christian literature may well point us in the direction of life that shall richer, fuller be.

(b) T. S. Eliot spoke of our age as one of moderate virtue. Maybe we are too easily satisfied with where we are on the road to a closer walk with God. To be moderately Christian may seem to be enough, but it's like being moderately well.

III. A third point on that guiding star toward an immoderate, warm, and wonderful Christian life is that of being alert to recognizing Christ in the lives of other people and in the world around. Our Lord is not entombed anywhere—not even in a holy book. He is alive and well out in the contemporary world—in people and places and things. I have seen him in the attentive, efficient, and tender care of a nurse in a hospital, in the forceful but compassionate confrontation of a drug counselor, in the firm but caring discipline of a father or mother, in the caustic criticism of hypocrisy in modern life, in a contemporary drama, and in the radiant rays of a winter sunset. "The heavens declare the glory of God and the earth shows forth his handiwork." He who has eyes to see let him see and be led into the presence of God.

IV. A fourth point toward an in-depth experience of the life that is in Christ is to make that goal the number one priority of our lives. The wise men left everything and pursued the star until "it came to rest over the place where the child was." They would not give up. God assures us in the scriptures, "If you truly seek me you shall surely find me" and "Ask and you will receive, knock and the door shall be opened to you." Everyone of us can be brought to a new understanding of our Lord's grace and goodness, to a deeper relationship in his love, and to a closer walk with God. We can come to Bethlehem again and see. But to do so we must ask and seek and work. We must follow the star that leads to life. —R. E. Lofgren.

SUNDAY: JANUARY TENTH

MORNING SERVICE

Topic: Hope in the Lord
SCRIPTURE: Ps. 42; Rom. 8:18–25.

Our problem when adversity strikes is not so much to find some kind of hope as it is to find a hope we can trust. There are false hopes. Even when our hope is sure, there is still the need for nourishing it and utilizing it creatively.

I. The first thing we need to do in dealing with our adversity is to recognize that some things are truly hopeless in our lives. William F. Lynch remarks that we need to recognize "that there are situations we cannot handle, things we cannot do, tasks which for us would be hopeless."

(a) Not everything can be hoped for. We are limited human beings and cannot accomplish all we would wish. There are ideals that shall remain hopeless to fulfill. There are paths to accomplishment which dead-end for us for lack of abilities and skills. There are physical accomplishments that may be hopeless for us because of the limitations of our bodies. We are subject to diseases that can cripple us, to accidents that can permanently put out our eyes, and to death that gets us all.

(b) Our lives are always a mixture of hopelessness and hopefulness. The critical need is to separate them out and keep them apart. Too often we tend to recognize something that is truly hopeless in our lives and then let it color all our living. If that is hopeless, we say, then everything is hopeless. This is just not the case. Life shall always have its hopeless aspects. Keep separate that which is hopeless and that which is still possible.

II. Having identified what is not hopeless in our adversity, we need to work actively to overcome it with a kind of relaxed attitude. We do not know what the answer may be, but we believe earnestly that change is possible. We believe that there is a new and healing power that breaks into life.

(a) There are powers of creativity within ourselves that can be tapped. Circumstances change to give a new perspective on our problems. Ours is a God who is always in the process of creating us and giving us all kinds of new possibilities in the midst of trials and tribulation. Hope counts on the creative power of God who out of death can bring resurrection—newness of life. He is at work to set us free from those captivities that bind us tightly.

(b) We need a patience that will give us a certain relaxed attitude toward our problem. Gabriel Marcel spoke of "the secret affinity between hope and relaxation." He observed that when adversity strikes we tighten up to resist it and in the process become so tense we cannot respond creatively.

(c) If hope is to serve us creatively, we must take our time. We need to let our hope take hold so that in due time new possibilities will open to us. This is why our being able to talk over our problem with a pastor or counselor or close friend can help. In sharing our concerns we unstop our bottled emotions, let someone else share the burden a bit, and lay out our problem before another for more objectivity and in the process relax. New possibilities begin to open up as you let go some of your fighting tensions.

(d) Hope is patient, recognizing that life requires us to stand up under difficult circumstances and to await confidently the good that shall in God's own time emerge. Instant victory is not required. We can trust the future because the future belongs to God. The apostle Paul wrote, "But if we hope for something we cannot see, then we must settle down to wait for it in patience" (Rom. 8:25, PHILLIPS).

III. As difficult as it is for us to hope patiently, it is even harder for us to be clear about the object of our hope. What can we properly hope for in the face of our adversity? Our natural tendency is to be quite specific in our hoping. I hope I shall soon recover from my illness. I hope that somehow my marriage partner will see the light and end our destructive relationship. I hope my impossible boss will be promoted and get off my back. I hope the judge will be lenient with my wayward son or daughter. We turn our hopes into prayers, asking God to do this thing or that.

(a) As Christians we need to see that our hope ultimately is not for anything; it is not a hope that something will happen. We hope in God. The psalmist puts the matter simply and to the point: "And now, Lord, for what do I wait? My hope is in thee" (Ps. 39:7, RSV).

(b) To hope in specifics—counting on a good grade, getting the job, or finding the cure—is to end up at some point disappointed, bitter, angry, and unbelieving. When our specific hopes do not materialize, we either conclude God is powerless and evil or that we have no faith. It probably takes a stronger faith to trust God for an answer than to be specific in our requests to God.

(c) Our hope in adversity springs from that kind of a trust in a loving God. We

hope in God. God in his love never leaves us without creative possibilities. Sometimes we do not discover them till we recognize that our specific hopes shall never be realized. There is no guarantee from God that we shall never suffer, that we shall not lose our faculties, or that frightfully evil things shall not happen to us or to our loved ones. In the mystery of God they do happen, and yet he is good and he helps us face them creatively and with integrity. Our hope is in the Lord from whom neither life nor death can ultimately separate us.

IV. Hope founded in God is more a process for living than an answer to a problem.

(a) When we hope in God we are opening ourselves to a future which transcends the solution to any specific problems we have. We may be hoping for an answer to our difficulty, whereas God is in the process of creating us to be whole persons. For those who hope in God he opens up a future full of possibilities, regardless of circumstances.

(b) What searing difficulties are you now facing? Do not despair. Take hope. Hope in God. Trusting in him, look honestly at your life and separate out its hopeless elements from those with possibilities. Don't let your despair over specifics contaminate what is sound and good and fruitful in your life.

(c) Hoping in God, you trust his future for you. Hoping in God, you find the strength to be patient. Hoping in God, you see him not so much a solver of problems as the maker of your life. He is one who is creatively present to make of you the vitally alive person he has in mind. That takes a lifetime. Hoping like that takes us down paths we did not choose and calls for endurance of painful trials we seek to avoid but leads us ever closer to him.—Colbert S. Cartwright.

Illustrations

VISION OF CHRIST. In one of the art galleries of Europe there is an old Greek statue of Apollo, a beautiful figure of physical perfection. A man stood to one side and watched the crowd as they looked. Invariably, he said, a change came over those who stood before it. The people straightened up, put their shoulders back, and stood a bit taller. They were influenced by beauty and perfection, the lifting power of loftiness. The habitual vision of Christ does that to the human spirit, adds courage to life and points the soul upward to the face of God where there is beauty and perfection.—Joan Bradshaw.

ONE THING LACKING.   Leo Tolstoy declared that Jesus came and lived and died and lives again and that in his blessed appearance he taught his followers how they were to live. In the centuries that have passed since that appearance of Christ, his followers have built a great church in his name. They have established impressive religious services often marked by ritual and dignity and order. They have set aside thousands of men to minister to this church and trained them in schools of theology devoted to expounding Christian truth. They have written whole libraries about this truth. All these things, Tolstoy pointed out, they have done with great zeal. But there was one thing which they have left undone. And that was to live as he had taught them to live—to conform their lives to his.—William Barclay.

Sermon Suggestions

LIVING ALL ONE'S LIFE.   Scripture: Rom. 12:9–21. (1) Develop a sincere interest in other people. (2) Don't worry about whether you are given credit for the good you do. (3) Express genuine love and concern toward others. (4) Keep the fires of the spirit burning brightly by planned and persistent effort. (5) Become acquainted with that great body of spiritual literature we call the Bible. (6) Steadfastly maintain the habit of prayer.—Nenien C. McPherson, Jr.

WHAT IS GOD LIKE?   Scripture: Acts 17:16–34. (1) An existing God. (See v. 23.) (2) An eminent God. (See vv. 24–26.) (3) An embracing God. (See v. 27.) (4) An

exacting God. (See v. 30.)—Brian L. Harbour.

Worship Aids

CALL TO WORSHIP.   "Oh that men would praise the Lord for his goodness, and for his wonderful works to the children of men! For he satisfieth the longing soul, and filleth the hungry soul with goodness." Ps. 107:8–9.

INVOCATION.   Almighty God, fountain of all good, kindle in us insight and aspiration, that this hour of prayer may be a moment of time lived in eternity. Open our ears that we may hear. Soften our hearts that we may receive thy truth. Reveal thyself to us that we may learn to find thee everywhere.

OFFERTORY SENTENCE.   "If there be first a willing mind, it is accepted according to that which a man hath, and not according to that which he hath not." II Cor. 8:12.

OFFERTORY PRAYER.   Dear God, help us to become unobstructed channels that thy love may flow through us to others and our gifts may be used for the proclamation to all men of thy saving goodness.

PRAYER.   We gather together from our small worlds, O God, to worship in this church. Your grace binds us in fellowship. Your spirit makes here a communion of faith.

We would not profane your sanctuary with casual, thoughtless prayer, listless singing, or dull minds. To do so is to miss the glory of a gladdened hour. Turn us now, by ways of your own, to some vantage point of spiritual insight from which we may gather new knowledge of love sufficient.

Accept humble thanks for men who founded this church in their faith, for those yesterday and today who entered it devoutly, for all laborers who have cherished it against time's slow ruin, and for those who want, above all else, this sanctuary to be a light in which all men shall see their best and glorify your name. Accept our gratitude for the treasures found here in worship.

Let all the beauty we have known, all the truth our minds have found, and all the goodness our souls have met rise in praise.—Kenneth Watson.

EVENING SERVICE

Topic: Does God Care?

SCRIPTURE: Luke 5:6–11.

Does God care? This is a universal question. The apostle Peter's answer came when times and circumstances were far more difficult than now. Peter gave three specific directives and three definite assurances about how to deal with the question.

I. *Three directives.* (a) "Humble yourselves therefore under the mighty hand of God."

(1) Most of us do not find this natural. We fight God with our feelings and bitter words. We fight him by backsliding.

(2) Our duty is to surrender, not to fight. Initial resentment is almost inevitable. Surrender liberates us.

(b) "Cast all your anxieties on him" (RSV). (1) Instead of worrying about conditions we cannot change or change fast enough, trust God to work out everything for the best. This applies to our health, after we have taken every reasonable medical measure; our job, assuming we are doing our job well or preparing well for another one; and the security of our home, provided that we are working at making the marriage a success.

(2) It does not mean using God for an escape from the results of laziness or general orneriness or an absolute guarantee against sickness, unemployment, or divorce.

(c) "Be sober, be watchful" (RSV). We cannot afford to be off our guard for one moment. (1) Evil continually threatens.

(2) Faith is not a narcotic to put us to sleep while the devil does his dirty work with us.

(3) If we really believe in God, we can dare to look the worst in the face. God is greater and stronger than anything.

II. *Three assurances.* (a) "He cares about you" (RSV). (1) We know this by revelation. The testimony of the Israelites was "Hitherto hath the Lord helped us" (I Sam. 7:12). The same could be said about the entire history of the Israelites. The coming of Jesus Christ—the fact of his coming, the style of his life, and the meaning of his death.

(2) We know this by experience through daily mercies, through special providences, and through answered prayer.

(b) The words of Peter—"After that ye have suffered a while"—indicate:

(1) A passage of time brings one phase of our existence to an end as another better phase begins.

(2) God does not put on us more than we can bear.

(c) Suffering produces some wonderful fruits: personal spiritual progress (Rom. 5:3–5) and an awareness of the troubles of others, sensitivity to their needs, and generosity and charity toward them. "The God of all grace . . . will himself restore, establish, and strengthen you" (RSV).—James W. Cox.

SUNDAY: JANUARY SEVENTEENTH

MORNING SERVICE

Topic: Ambassadors of Christ (Missionary Day)

TEXTS: John 20:21; II Cor. 5:20.

What does it mean to be an ambassador, to be one sent by God, as Jesus Christ was himself sent by the Father?

I. An ambassador before acting receives a commission from the power for whom he or she acts. This commissioning is a mark of trust in the ambassador's ability and training, in his or her integrity, and in the ambassador's loyalty.

(a) In this church there are two manifestations of this commissioning, baptism and confirmation.

(1) In baptism we are commissioned by God as bearers of the ministry of reconciliation in the new nation of the called

people of God, the one, holy, catholic, and apostolic church. Baptism is one of two sacraments ordained by Jesus Christ as necessary to our salvation. For through faith it confers an estate, a permanent and responsible relationship with the God who made us and who through the Holy Spirit empowers us to be new persons in Christ Jesus.

(2) In confirmation we are also commissioned in this church in the doctrine and discipline of Christ as this church has received the same. So we are under orders within something.

(b) Any ambassador before acting receives a commission from the power for whom he or she acts. This gives the ambassador standing, for these are the ambassador's reliable credentials.

II. An ambassador acts not only as an agent but as a representative of his sovereign. We are representatives of Jesus Christ, the reconciler, and behind Jesus stands God. We do not hold this office of ambassador or representative from any human being, however important a personage he or she may appear to be to us. We hold this office from God, and this involves both a mighty burden and a high responsibility.

(a) How should such a representative act? He or she must act responsibly, intelligently, loyally, and without consideration for his or her own feelings or for his or her own person. Any other interpretation of this ambassadorship is a disservice to our sovereign Lord and a disservice to the healing ministry of reconciliation on which you and I are now sent.

(b) The ambassador's duty and high privilege is not merely to deliver a message but precisely to be a diplomat, to deliver that message with grace and with authority and with tact and with a maximum amount of effectiveness, and to watch for opportunities so that the ambassador may place that message before his or her sharers in the best possible light. This is at least a part of what St. Paul meant when he says of his own commissioning that he becomes all things to all men that he may by all means save some. That requires sensitivity, mature

judgment, and unswerving dedication.

III. As ambassadors of Christ Jesus, sent by him, commissioned by him, each of us is committed to the ambassadorial office in international affairs. A Christian speaks at all times in the name of his Lord, not in his own name. A Christian is not responsible for the message he or she is called upon to deliver. He is only responsible for transmitting that message acceptably, accurately, and winsomely so there may be no misunderstanding and as little hypocrisy as possible.

(a) The message is God's message, and as God's message to every man, woman, and child in this world, it is the most important message that people ever receive upon this earth as long as they live here.

(1) It's the offer of forgiveness and renewal, of reconciliation with the most high God who made us and with the men and women with whom we live, and it's the promise of restoration to the father who sent us.

(2) It's a plea, on the part of a loving, hurting, caring Father—a plea to broken, rebellious, lost sons and daughters to come home even if they do not know that they are lost.

(3) It's the offer of power to become something that we are not now but can be if in faith and hope we are willing to surrender ourselves into that audacious servanthood, costly servanthood to be sure, which is the gateway to freedom and to life.

(b) The spirit in which the ambassador of Christ Jesus transmits this message of forgiveness and restoration is very important, for he or she is one who pleads and yearns just as his sovereign Lord pleads and yearns. His tone must echo the compassion of a God who loves even unto a very cruel bloody cross, and when he must warn and rebuke, as on occasion Christ's ambassador must indeed do, he or she does so as one who sorrows over sins, the guilt for which he or she must share. He does not merely lift up the cross. He carries it. His sovereign's burdens are his burdens. His sovereign's grief is his grief. His sovereign's joy is his joy.

IV. When we say yes to Christ Jesus, we

are totally involved with him in his cross-centered ministry to a lost world. We must be prepared to write. We must be prepared to speak. We must be prepared to act with our bodies as well as with our minds and hearts for there is simply no gallery for spectators at Calvary's cosmic drama in which a God-man is dying for the sins of the whole world.

(a) There is only the role for participants, for penitents, volunteering out of gratitude, for people with a sense of unlimited liability. We are not privileged to revise our Lord's prayer, as one Frenchman suggested saying, "Our Father, who art in heaven, stay where you are." We have to act in accordance with that plea and to say, "Thy kingdom come on earth," and then to face and accept the risk implicit in that awesome expectation.

(b) John Oman says that all of us are God's instruments. By no setting of our hearts on wickedness or by doing evil with both of our hands can we prevent God from using us in this world. Our folly will serve him when our wisdom fails. But to be God's agent is quite another matter. This we are only when we respond to his call, only when we work faithfully together with him, and only when we find our highest goals in fulfilling his. For Christians there is no greater source of power than this, and there is no deeper joy.—John E. Hines.

Illustration

CONTAGION. Phillips Brooks was a man of such magnetism and strength that young and old sought his counsel and guidance. One young man had a problem that had perplexed him for a long time. So he secured an appointment with Brooks. The student tells how, with careful thought, he phrased his question in advance so he would ask it in the best possible way. When the day came for his appointment, he spent an engrossing hour with Brooks. But as the young man walked up Boston's Beach Street on his way home, he suddenly realized he had failed to ask his question. He recorded later: "I did not care. I had found out that what I needed was not the solution of a special problem but the contagion of a triumphant life."—Donald L. Germain.

Sermon Suggestions

A FAITH FOR ALL NATIONS. Text: Eph. 3:4–6. The international character of the Christian faith has been established. (1) The promises of God which came to Abraham already indicated that God had the nations in view. (2) The nation of Israel from earliest years included people of other races. (3) The prophecies of the Old Testament told of the salvation that would come to the gentiles. (4) Ancient rulers always brought their praises to God. (5) The finished work of the Lord Jesus Christ brought about a salvation in which the gospel message moved away from the Jewish nation as a nation and was shared with all the peoples of the world.—Joel Nederhood.

THE ARMOR OF LIGHT. Text: Rom. 13:12. (1) Putting on the armor of light means accepting Christ's objectives. (2) Putting on the armor of light means accepting Christ's fitness. (3) Putting on the armor of light means accepting Christ's weapons. (4) Putting on the armor of light means fighting in the line with Christ's fellow fighters. (5) Putting on the armor of light means that we begin to participate in Christ's victory. (7) Putting on the armor of light means putting on the character of Christ.—Samuel M. Shoemaker.

Worship Aids

CALL TO WORSHIP. "O send out thy light and thy truth: let them lead me; let them bring me unto thy holy hill, and to the tabernacles." Ps. 43:3.

INVOCATION. O God, in glory exalted and in mercy ever blessed, we magnify thee, we praise thee, we give thanks unto thee for thy bountiful providence, for all the blessings of this present life, and all the hopes of a better life to come. Let the memory of thy goodness, we beseech thee, fill our hearts with joy and thankfulness.

OFFERTORY SENTENCE.   "Give unto the Lord the glory due unto his name: bring an offering, and come before him: worship the Lord in the beauty of holiness." I Chron. 16:29.

OFFERTORY PRAYER.   Awaken us to the claims of thy holy will, O God, and stir us with a passion for thy kingdom, that we may respond at this time with our gifts and also with our lives.

PRAYER.   We thank thee for the church, the beloved community of memory and hope, forever reminding us of our help in ages past, our hope for years to come, the perpetual witness to thy presence in the world claiming men's lives as thine own.

We thank thee for the privilege of bearing witness in this generation in which our lives are set to the truth to which the church has borne unbroken witness through nearly two thousand years that thou art in Christ, reconciling the world to thyself.

We thank thee for the faith of our fathers living still, the most precious thing we have received from the past and the most precious thing we have to pass on to those who come after us. Help us to transmit it unsullied and undimmed that those who come after us may fortify themselves with our example even as we draw inspiration and incentive from those who once worshiped here and now have joined the choir invisible whose music is the gladness of the world.

We thank thee for this church which thou hast entrusted to this people's care and for the great-hearted men and women who have built their lives into it and through it wrought for thee. By what a cloud of witness are we compassed about as we gather here today!

May it go from strength to strength. May it be an ever more potent influence in this community it has served so long. Sunday by Sunday may it lead its people in the true and living way and win to the covenant of promise those who are out of the way. May every Sunday be a little Easter, filled with the joy and the elation of the resurrection morn.—Frank Halliday Ferris.

EVENING SERVICE

Topic: Christ Needs You!
TEXT: Matt. 4:23.

I. To proclaim the gospel—"preaching the gospel of the kingdom." (a) V. 17 gives us the content of Jesus' preaching: "Repent, for the kingdom of heaven is at hand." Does the world need to be called to repentance?

(b) Repentance involves turning from wickedness to Christ. Is Christ the solution to our personal and social wickedness? We have the good news that Christ is the answer to our moral decay. He goes to the heart, the seat of our behavior. He creates a new heart which results in a good life. He is the answer to our social problems because at the base of each problem there is a moral or spiritual problem. Does the world need the church to call it to repentance? Christ needs you as a part of the church to cry out to the world, "O earth, earth, earth, hear the word of the Lord."

II. To teach the truth of God—"teaching in their synagogues." (a) Jesus was often called rabbi or teacher. He came to reveal the truth about God, life, and man. In our day there is a famine of knowing God's truth. Biblical illiteracy exists both in and out of the church. This results in people flocking to far-out religions which are anti-Christian and in moral delinquency because they do not know the will and laws of God. The world desperately needs to be taught the truth of God in the scriptures.

(b) Who shall do this teaching? The state school is not allowed to teach the Bible. The home should teach it but, on the whole, does not. This leaves the church to teach through the church school.

III. To heal people—"healing every disease and every infirmity among the people."

(a) Jesus healed the bodies, minds, and spirits of people in his day. Is there a need for his healing today? The amount of illness in our world is overwhelming. As the body of Christ, the church heals today through faith, medical science, and love.

(b) While physical and mental illness are

real problems today, the greatest illness is in the heart expressed in the cry for love, companionship, and acceptance. People are dying of broken hearts because of loneliness and isolation. Does the world need the church to bring healing? To answer this need Christ needs you in the church to carry out this healing ministry of love.

IV. Though Jesus had all power, wisdom, and grace to carry out his mission of preaching, teaching, and healing, he sought helpers. He called disciples saying, "I need you to help me do the work of God." In the average congregation forty percent of the members are not helping him. In the nation almost forty percent are not connected with a church. This worldwide work of Jesus' ministry is too much for those now active in the church. Through us Christ sends more disciples and directs us to say, "Christ needs you!" —John R. Brokhoff.

SUNDAY: JANUARY TWENTY-FOURTH

MORNING SERVICE

Topic: One in Baptism (Week of Prayer for Christian Unity)

TEXT: Eph. 4:5.

"I am baptized!" Martin Luther often reminded the devil of this during times of temptation and doubt. To the reformer, baptism was that singular spiritual experience reminding him of his union with Christ. This testimony is eminently appropriate to all the members of Christ's body, for the apostle Paul has affirmed our commonality: "One Lord, one faith, one baptism." Water baptism means, essentially, identification with Christ. This is the truly ecumenical dimension of the ordinance. There are at least five points wherein the believer is identified with his Lord.

I. *Identification with his person.* (a) Water baptism is the external sign that an internal work of grace has been effected—regeneration by the Holy Spirit. The ordinance is visual proclamation that the candidate has renounced his former priorities, values, and lifestyle, choosing now a new and living way. It attests that sin has been forgiven and that a higher allegiance has been pledged.

(b) To publicly commit one's self to Christ was in the early church to associate with one deemed an imposter, a blasphemer, one motivated by Beelzebub, whose ignominious death somehow vindicated God's revulsion at him. To publicly identify with Christ today entails no less an embracing of him who is despised and rejected of men, but we have found him to be the Lord of glory.

II. *Identification with his passion.* (a) Paul speaks of our having been "baptized into his death" (v. 3), "buried with him through baptism into death" (v. 4), "united with him in his death" (v. 5), and "crucified with him" (v. 6), and the apostle declares that we have "died with Christ" (v. 8).

(b) Martin Luther contended that the essence of real religion lay in the personal pronouns. This same apostle exulted: "*I* have been crucified with Christ and *I* no longer live, but Christ lives in *me*. The life *I* live in the body, *I* live by faith in the Son of God, who loved *me* and gave himself for *me*" (Gal. 2:20, NIV).

III. *Identification with his power.* Our text speaks of our being "united with him in his resurrection" (v. 5) and "alive to God in Christ Jesus" (v. 11). According to Paul's later commitments, the Holy Spirit has regenerated believers in Christ, infusing them with resurrection power. Here we encounter one of the most marvelous concepts in the word of God—that the same Holy Spirit who raised the dead body of our Lord on that first Easter morning has also effected within us by coincident power a resurrection from deadness in sin to newness of life. (See Rom. 8:11; Col. 2:12.)

IV. *Identification with his people.* (a) Common experiences forge common bonds. Members of Christ's body are bound inextricably together by his blood that has redeemed us and his Holy Spirit who indwells us. Far more positive and substantive are our affinities in grace than the differences that divide. By one Spirit we are all baptized into the one body of Christ (I Cor. 12:13), and varying persuasions on peripheral concerns in no way fracture the unity of the essential relationship.

(b) This basic Christian camaraderie needs urgently to be recognized, cultivated, and demonstrated to the world. Every Christian needs every other Christian for the support and for the gifts which he has to offer. Let us pray for a baptism of love and grace whereby this relationship may be enhanced to his glory.

V. *Identification with his purpose.* (a) The church of Jesus Christ in the world is a caring community. The most pressing need which it is charged to address is the salvation of the lost. Christianity's primary task is, in its irreducible minimum, simply sharing Jesus with those who do not know him as savior and lord. And here is the irony of it all. Jesus increases in one's own life in direct proportion as he is given away to others.

(b) One Lord, one faith, one baptism. God grant that we who belong to him may sense anew that we also belong to each other. By his grace he has made us one; by his grace let us be one.—Donald N. Bowdle.

Illustrations

ACCEPTANCE IN CHRIST. Christ is perceived individually and differently. The practice of our theology begins here by seeing the light of Christ in others who see him differently than we see him. We can do this only as we accept them and the Christ in them, even though we don't accept their opinions. Acceptance of persons in Christ invariably leads to modifications of positions, and that is the heart of Christian decision making. Loyalty to Christ permits us so to live with our differences that we are brought by him to a deeper unity within him and to one another.—John Coburn.

THE IMPERSONAL ONE. One must do this. One must do that. One is not to do anything. One cannot help himself. With one there is nothing to being. With one it is all over. He who contents himself with explaining or asking what he is to do talks and lives in a vacuum. But he who poses questions with the earnestness of his soul on his lips and means "What have I to do?" is taken by the hand by comrades he does not know but whom he will soon become familiar with, and they answer, "You shall not withhold yourself."—Craig Biddle III.

Sermon Suggestions

UNITY IN THE BOND OF PEACE. Text: John 17:22. (1) One in purpose. (2) One in love. (3) One in fellowship. (4) One in the Spirit.

THE BAPTISM OF JESUS. Text: Matt. 3:16. (1) Christ's baptism was the inauguration of his messianic task. (2) Christ's baptism set forth symbolically the great truths concerning his death, burial, and resurrection. (3) Christ's baptism was an example for all his followers. (4) Christ's baptism was a recognition of his need to identify with sinners.—Stephen McSwain.

Worship Aids

CALL TO WORSHIP. "If a man love me, saith Jesus, he will keep my words: and my Father will love him, and we will come unto him, and make our abode with him." John 14:23.

INVOCATION. Grant, O Lord our God, we beseech thee, that now and every time we come before thee in worship and in prayer we may be vividly aware of thy presence, become conscious of thy power and a sense of thy protection, and finally know in our hearts and minds and souls the wonder and the grace of thy peace.

OFFERTORY SENTENCE. "I will freely sacrifice unto thee: I will praise thy name, O Lord; for it is good." Ps. 54:6.

OFFERTORY PRAYER. Help us, dear Father, to be cheerful givers of our time, means, talents, and self to the master that he may use us in the upbuilding of his kingdom.

PRAYER. Lord of the church, you call us to be your people. You mold us into a spiritual but visible body. You give varied gifts by which to spread good news and good works. You minister to us and call us to minister to others.

Lord, we wonder what it would be like if the church were not here. What if there were no leaven of righteousness, no gospel sound, no people to militate against sin, and no loving hands to soothe hurts?

Lord, thank you for giving us opportunities to show our love for you. Thank you for presiding over your church through all the terrors of adversity and all the temptations of prosperity.

Lord, bless you for your unconditioned love. You willed a means by which your work would be done. You chose us—brittle, frail, weak, fragile, vacillating—yet you chose us! We stand in awe of such trust and such responsibility.

Lord, who can number your servants who made entrance and exit on life's stage? No time has ever lacked voices to tell your story. As you continue to empower those who serve you today, you already raise others to take their places.

Lord, we petition continued endowment for those about to enter into their ministry. Called, taught, examined, ordained, and launched, they face the unknowns of the Christian adventure. May their trumpets have clear sounds.

Lord, permit no spectators in your church. Move hearers to become doers. May each fulfill the ministry of his talents.

Lord of the church, we are your people. Never could we be ashamed of you. May you never have cause to be ashamed of us. —Harland Steele.

EVENING SERVICE

Topic: Is There Life Before Death?
TEXT: John 13:3–5.
What does the resurrection faith mean to us in terms of a life before death?

I. The resurrection affirms that life is measured by the quality of our existence, not by the quantity of time. Philip asked: "Lord, to whom shall we go? You have the words of eternal life." He was not saying that Jesus had the keys to endless life. The Greek word *aionios*, translated eternal, does not mean unending. It means having a quality that is other than temporal. The words of eternal life which Philip asserted Jesus had were vital and effective ones for the creation and sustenance of a kind of life that has a quality of eternity. Eternal life is a life that can begin here and now.

II. The resurrection frees us from the past to live in the present and to challenge the future. There is no backward look in a man's experience of Jesus Christ.

(a) Jesus did not reproach Peter for his cowardly denial of him in the courtyard. There was no word of blame. Instead, the next time Jesus saw Peter, he said, "Peter, look ahead; my sheep and my lambs, go feed them!" He didn't castigate his disciples for running and hiding at his arrest. No, when he saw them next, he said: "Go into all the world and preach the gospel . . . and lo, I am with you always."

(b) The resurrection means being alive to the possibilities of a life before death. It means awareness of the love of those about us. It means hearing one another right here and now. It means coming awake to the possibilities of doing something good and creative today. It means the availability of faith, courage, and love. It means that I can take from this day all that it has to give me.

III. The resurrection means that human life has a deep purpose and an abiding meaning. It means something to have been born, to live, and eventually to die.

(a) "Jesus, knowing that he was come from God, and went to God" found the key to the beginning and ending of the bridge that is life. Because the bridge has a beginning and an ending, it has a purpose in its maintenance. And that purpose is not self-gain, self-love, or self-glory; it is loving service.

(b) Life has a deep and abiding purpose because it comes from God and returns to God. And so we, with Jesus, take a towel and gird ourselves for service to man.— Gene W. Burris.

SUNDAY: JANUARY THIRTY-FIRST

MORNING SERVICE

Topic: Worthy Worship
SCRIPTURE: Mal. 1:7–2:9.
I. Worthy worship is worship in which God is honored. (a) The implication of the entire passage is that the true purpose of worship is to honor God. (See Mal. 2:2; Ps. 95:6–7; Rev. 4:11.)
(b) The entire Bible concurs in this understanding of worship. (1) The most common Old Testament word for worship is *shachah*. The word means to have a reverential attitude toward God combined with adoration. (See Exod. 4:31.)
(2) The basic New Testament word for worship, *proskuneo*, means to kiss the hand toward one or to prostrate oneself before someone. Again the idea of honor to God is primary. (See Rev. 11:16.)
(c) People come to a worship service for many reasons—to hear a certain preacher, to watch their children perform, to visit with their friends, to fulfill an obligation, to enhance their business opportunities, or to see what everyone else is wearing. But there is only one acceptable reason for coming to worship, and that is to give honor and praise to God.
(d) Worship is an attempt to focus our attention on him. And if you can leave a worship experience saying with the psalmist, "Great is the Lord and greatly to be praised," then you have truly worshiped.
II. Worthy worship is worship in which man is helped. In the question in v. 9, Malachi implies that the purpose of worship is to entreat God's favor that he may be gracious unto us. Worship is not just something we do to help ourselves. It is not only designed to meet the demand of God but also to meet the need of man. Worship is that experience in which we seek God's best for our lives.
III. Worthy worship is worship in which sacrifice is heightened. (a) Every true worship experience demands some such response. Peter said that the congregation of believers is to "offer spiritual sacrifices,

acceptable to God through Jesus Christ" (I Pet. 2:5). Paul said in his letter to the Romans that we are to offer our bodies as living sacrifices unto God which, he says, is "the true worship that you should offer" (TEV).
(b) If you have been in church but have never been compelled to give sacrificially to the work of God, then you have not truly worshiped. If you attend a service but try to pawn off on God the leftovers and the castoffs of your life, then you have not truly worshiped. If you have been in a service but have never once felt the compelling urge to say with Isaiah, "Here am I, Lord, send me," then you have not truly worshiped.
(c) Real worship is worship in which sacrifice is heightened and in which we are compelled to respond in some tangible way to the grace of God in our lives.—Brian L. Harbour.

Illustrations

DIVINE PRESENCE. How vitalized the church's worship when she knows her Lord is in her midst! Think of the thrill of singing out with all the heart the great songs of the Christian ages when it is Christ himself to whom you are singing and the joy of celebrating the great festivals of the Christian year and the expectant eagerness of coming up to the house of God quite certain that Jesus will be there and Jesus you are going to meet. Who could fail to be moved to the depths by that word of Jesus, "Where two or three are gathered together in my name, there am I in the midst of them"? If our earthbound hearts could be struck vividly awake to the significance of these words, how the lost sense of the wonder of worship would come stealing back upon us.—James S. Stewart.

HOLY HABIT. Some years ago there was a man at the head of Duke University by the name of President Few. One Sunday morning he was seen walking across the campus with his umbrella hoisted to protect his body from the rain. Some friends saw him, stopped their car, and offered him a ride. He got in, and as they drove toward the church, one of the persons in the car said, "Why did you decide to go to church in the rain this morning?" "I didn't decide this morning," he replied. "I decided sixty-five years ago, and I haven't had to ask myself that question since."—Charles E. Ferrell.

Sermon Suggestions

THE COVENANT OF GRACE.   Text: Jer. 31:31–34. (1) Regeneration. (2) Relationship. (3) Revelation. (4) Remission.

SUMMONED BY THE WORD.   Text: Isa. 29:24. (1) The Bible summons us to living principles. (2) The Bible summons us to the spirit of brotherliness and goodwill. (3) The Bible summons us to helpfulness. (4) The Bible summons us to self-respecting independence. (5) The Bible summons us to the giving and serving which the strong owe to the weak and those who have to those who lack.—Robert E. Speer.

Worship Aids

CALL TO WORSHIP.   "Hereby perceive we the love of God, because he laid down his life for us: and we ought to lay down our lives for the brethren. Let us not love in word, neither in tongue; but in deed and in truth." I John 3:16, 18.

INVOCATION.   O God, who makest thyself known both in the stillness and in the flurry of life: come to us as we seek to come to thee in this place of prayer. In music, word, and song lift our hearts to thee, and so purify our thoughts and strengthen our resolves that we shall go forth into the world of tomorrow, confident that thou art with us.

OFFERTORY SENTENCE.   "What shall I render unto the Lord for all his benefits toward me? I will pay my vows unto the Lord now in the presence of all his people." Ps. 116:12–14.

OFFERTORY PRAYER.   Dear Lord and Savior of us all, may we become obedient to thy will both in the dedication of our tithes and of our talents.

PRAYER.   Eternal Father, thou hast been good to us beyond our deserving. Thou hast surrounded us with light and music and beauty and friends. Above all, thou hast placed hope in our hearts. In the face of thy goodness we have been selfish, thoughtless, and rebellious. We who see at once thy goodness and our rebellion present ourselves this day as suppliants for thy forgiveness.

We would be alert to thine every desire for us. If our minds are closed to thy truth, open them. If our hearts are hardened, stir them. If our ears are deaf to the cries of the needy, unstop them. Lay upon us great responsibilities. Revive in us the hardy spirit of our fathers that we may not only complete their work but also in their spirit establish new thresholds of hope for our bewildered world.

Remember in thy mercy the homes where there is sickness and where some of thy children lie on beds of pain. Remember those who are weighted with sorrow through loss of earthly love or who are distressed because of failure to attain. They are thy children and they seek thy light. Let thy benediction rest upon our dear ones and our friends, wherever they may be. Thou didst go with thy Son Jesus Christ when he was surrounded by acclaiming crowds and when he walked alone in the garden of Gethsemane. We pray thee to minister always to those we love whether they be in joy or in sorrow. —Albert Buckner Coe.

EVENING SERVICE

Topic: The Christian's Mental Health
TEXT: Ps. 42:11.

True Christianity does not bring inner confusion but brings peace. True Christianity does not promote a disturbed mind but promotes a sound mind.

I. The Christian has the greatest threat to his mental health—fear—removed. He no longer has to fear death, for through Christ he conquers death. He no longer has to fear the inhumanity of his fellowman, for he can say: "The Lord is my helper. I will not be afraid. What can man do to me?"

II. He does not have to fear tomorrow nor any succession of tomorrows, for he knows that God through Christ has promised to aid him. If he seeks first the kingdom of God and his righteousness, he knows that all the necessities of life shall be added unto him. He knows that he is God's child and that God, being a loving and kind, a tender and compassionate father, is interested and concerned in all his doings.

III. He knows that he has a father that will not give him a serpent when he needs a fish nor a stone when he needs bread. He is certain that his father knows each sparrow in its fall, the very number of hairs upon his head, and his every need, even before he asks.

IV. The true Christian has good mental health because he knows that God is love and that God and love are the greatest forces that exist. God works for him in his own mysterious way, and love works for him in easily demonstrable ways. Love destroys one's enemies in the right way, and these enemies, that have become brothers, now work for the total good of the true Christian.

V. The human being needs to love and be loved more than he needs food and water. And in giving and receiving he is made complete and whole. The Christian does this in God's appointed way. He is serene and happy. God and Christ are on his side, and no real harm can ever touch him.—Max Leach.

SUNDAY: FEBRUARY SEVENTH

MORNING SERVICE

Topic: When Jesus Supplies the Wine
Text: John 2:11 (GNB).

I. The report is as brief and as factual as any story tucked away in the corner of your morning paper. The wine ran out.

(a) That was a social disaster for people accustomed to about seven days of feasting and drinking at a wedding party. We are not told why the wine ran out. Did Jesus and his friends arrive on the last day when supplies were getting low? Or was their addition to the party the last straw for a host who had miscalculated the capacity of his friends? All John says is that Mary whispered to Jesus, "They are out of wine."

(b) This mother had a special kind of confidence in her son. She tells the servants, "Do whatever he tells you." We are told of the Jewish custom of having jars of water at hand for ritual cleansing. Jesus orders the servants to draw off some of the water and take it to the headwaiter. The headwaiter tastes it and finds he is drinking wine. So he calls the bridegroom and says: "Everyone else serves the best wine first, and after the guests have drunk a lot he serves the ordinary wine. But you have kept the best wine until now!"

II. As we look again, the story begins to unfold like a mighty symphony.

(a) Here is a wedding celebration, a banquet, and we are reminded that throughout scripture such a feast is a symbol of the kingdom of God. John deliberately opens his story with a feast, and this is his way of recording what the other gospel writers express with the question posed to Jesus: "Why is it that John's disciples and the disciples of the Pharisees are fasting but yours are not?" John brings us to this party over which might hang the beautiful words from the Song of Songs: "He brought me to the banqueting house, and his banner over me was love."

(b) There is an immediate contrast offered between the rigid religion of the keepers of the Law and the glorious freedom and joy of the sons and daughters of the gospel. Can't you see those six stone water jars standing solemnly there as the symbol of the requirements of the law?

And the presence of Jesus is enough to turn them into the wine of his grace and the sparkling liberty of the new life of faith. The story already glows for us as a commentary on the great word of Jesus later in the gospel, "I am come that they might have life, and that they might have it more abundantly."

(c) Whatever else breaks through to us from inside this story, the new and abundant life that Jesus brings challenges not only the formal religion of the Pharisees but also our own watery, lifeless, and tame interpretation of the gospel.

III. John gives us a feast at the beginning of Jesus' ministry, and he also gives us one at his close. Can you not hear already at Cana an echo of that other banquet where the bread was passed and the wine went round in that upper room from which Jesus went out to meet his death?

(a) What is the meaning of that strange phrase, "My time has not yet come"? In this gospel, Jesus speaks more than once of his time, his hour—and always there is a reference forward to the supreme moment of his crucifixion. So here these mysterious words introduce this quiet miracle, and a sensitive Christian would immediately be reminded of the deeper meanings that attach to the wine. We already hear the whisper of that awe-inspiring sentence, "This is my blood."

(b) In the Bible, blood is life. Here the wine, symbol of new life in Christ, is also the reflection of the life that is being poured out as he goes his healing, loving, and suffering way to the final sacrifice of the cross. The simple story now confronts us with a Christ who loves us unto death, who has transformed the water of a dull and legalistic religion or a shabby secularism into the costly wine of his grace, and a savior whose blood was shed for us. At Cana of Galilee the hour of Jesus was not yet come, but it was coming at Calvary, it was coming at Easter, it was coming at Pentecost, it is coming now as we meet him, and it is coming at the end of time.

(c) It is the Lord of life whom we meet inside the simple story of the wedding, an abundant life that is infinitely more than mere existence, that opens here and now the windows of heaven, and that at the same time inspires us for the sacrificial path of loving our neighbors and supplying their needs. "They are out of wine." Later he was to hear: "They are out of bread." And each time as he supplied their needs his disciples learned how they could draw upon the bread and wine of his grace to go and do the same.—David H. C. Read.

Illustrations

NIGHT OF DECISION. Mahatma Gandhi studied law in London as a very young man but upon his return to India could not find a job. His family sent him to South Africa to handle legal matters for relatives and at the same time to do some growing up.

Gandhi's real introduction to South Africa came a week after his arrival on an overnight train ride from Durban to Pretoria. Four decades later Ghandi would still remember that trip as the most formative experience of his life. Halfway to Pretoria a white man stalked into his first-class compartment and ordered him to the baggage car. Gandhi, who held a first-class ticket, refused. At the next stop the man called a policeman, and Gandhi with his luggage was thrown off the train in the middle of the night.

All alone and shivering in the cold because he was too shy to ask the station master for the overcoat locked in his luggage, Gandhi passed the night huddled in the unlighted railroad station, pondering his first brutal confrontation with racial prejudice. Like a medieval youth during the vigil of knighthood, Gandhi sat in the darkened station, praying to the god of the Gita for courage and guidance. When dawn finally broke on the little station, the timid, withdrawn youth was a changed person. The young lawyer had reached the most important decision in his life. Gandhi was going to say no. Gandhi came out of the long night in Pretoria a new person—stronger, surer, with a clear answer for the world—a no born out of his pain.—William L. Dols, Jr.

A MODERN PARABLE. The kingdom of heaven is as a blind man who arises from sleep. He does not know whether it is day or night, so he opens his door and steps outside. From the morning songs of the birds he hears the day begin. From the warmth of the sun on his face he feels the arrival of light.

The kingdom of heaven is as a blind man standing on the edge of a beautiful garden of flowers. He does not know what lies before him. Yet when a gentle summer breeze moves the flowers softly, he can smell their honey scent and, turning, step into a garden of flowers, even though the gift of sight is not his.

What is the meaning of this parable? The morning songs of the birds are the praises of the redeemed and of the angels. The warmth of the sun is the rise of that great day which lies ahead for all peoples of all nations. The garden of flowers is the kingdom of heaven. The blind man is all on earth who seek that kingdom.—Ronald L. Cobb in *The Disciple*.

Sermon Suggestions

GUIDELINES FOR GIVING. Text: I Cor. 16:1–2. (1) We should give individually. (2) We should give systematically. (3) We should give proportionately. (See Luke 12:48.) (4) We should give liberally. (See Rom. 12:8.) (5) We should give cheerfully. (See II Cor. 9:7.)

GOLDEN THREADS IN LIFE'S FABRIC. Text: Gal. 5:22–23. (1) Prayer. (2) Faith. (3) Love. (4) Self-fulfillment.

Worship Aids

CALL TO WORSHIP. "Lord, who shall abide in thy tabernacle? Who shall dwell in thy holy hill? He that walketh uprightly, and worketh righteousness, and speaketh the truth in his heart." Ps. 15:1–2.

INVOCATION. Grant, O God, that because we meet together this day life may grow greater for some who have contempt for it, simpler for some who are confused by it, happier for some who are tasting the bitterness of it, safer for some who are feeling the peril of it, more friendly for some who are feeling the loneliness of it, serener for some who are throbbing with the fire of it, and holier for some to whom life has lost all dignity, beauty, and meaning.

OFFERTORY SENTENCE. "Take heed what ye hear: with what measure ye mete, it shall be measured to you: and unto you that hear shall more be given." Mark 4:24.

OFFERTORY PRAYER. O thou who art the Father of all, may we live as the children and brothers of all whom thou hast made to dwell upon the face of the earth that thy kindness may be born in our hearts.

PRAYER. Almighty God, we pause in this moment to lift to thee the problems of our country, of our cities, and of our communities.

Our sins are multiplying and our unrest is growing. May we ask of thee again, O God, as we have been bold to do so many times before, that some healing balm be applied to our wounds and that some divine touch be placed upon the troubled minds of men and women.

We acknowledge with shame our failure in being brothers to those about us. We have thought ourselves better, when we were only equal. We have taken advantage, when we should have given opportunity. We have avoided, when we should have approached. We have ignored, when we should have helped.

Now we stand at thy door and knock. Open to us the door that leads into a new day.

Now we stand at thy door and ask. We ask for things that we cannot buy and for things that we cannot build.

Now we stand at thy door and seek. We seek a presence that will relieve our fears.

We lift to thee our leaders. Their task is not man-sized; it is beyond their ability. Unless thy voice whispers a word of instruction, they are without knowledge for this time of crisis.

Let us this hour across our country, throughout our cities, and in our communities see again the greatness of our heritage. Help us to see the unfinished mission that is ours to complete. May a surge of understanding purge our hearts and make us again like brothers.—C. Neil Strait.

EVENING SERVICE

Topic: Forgiving and Being Forgiven
TEXT: Matt. 6:12.

Forgiveness is primarily a relationship which grows out of forgiving and being forgiven. The relationship of forgiveness has characteristics that point to a more joyous way of living.

I. Forgiveness is commitment to others. (a) God committed himself to persons, hoping that the commitment will be returned. His forgiving spirit is an expression of God's nature, not an act he arbitrarily decides to do.

(b) The forgiveness is a fact before any alienating incidents occur. Hoping that people will be reconciled to one another and to him, God expressed his commitment through Jesus. Forgiveness is the commitment that we belong together.

II. Forgiveness is an acceptance of others. (a) God's forgiveness is given in the hope that people will cease hurting themselves and others, express love creatively, and establish relationships of forgiveness which includes accepting others. Acceptance does not imply the approval of insensitive behavior toward others. It suggests that people care enough to confront each other when necessary.

(b) To benefit from God's acceptance, one must recognize the need to repent, to be redeemed and renewed, and to accept the acceptance of God. When one responds to God's or to a person's acceptance and returns the commitment, a relationship of mutual forgiveness is created.

III. Forgiveness is believing that people are innately worthful. (a) God's act through Jesus is a statement of belief in the worth of persons. God's forgiving act not only proclaimed his love of persons but also affirmed the created worth of each individual.

(b) Forgiveness is recognizing the imperfections and evil yet believing in the created goodness of people, which may be buried underneath a cruel, calloused personal history.

IV. When people accept and experience God's forgiveness, guilt feelings vanish and they lose the need to nurse the old hurts which sapped so much energy and caused so much destruction. Experiencing forgiveness is a process in which one is liberated from the painful past to live lovingly in the present with a faith and hope in the future.

V. Forgiveness between persons is God working in people to proclaim his loving nature. It is characterized by commitment to, acceptance of, and belief in the worth of persons. Forgiveness is an attitude toward people and God. Because we have been forgiven, we are forgiving people living in the grace of God.—Loren Broadus in *The Disciple.*

SUNDAY: FEBRUARY FOURTEENTH

MORNING SERVICE

Topic: The Priority of Persons (Brotherhood Week)
SCRIPTURE: Mark 7:24–30.

I. After a first reading of this passage, we are left with a disturbing impression. Jesus seems to condone a narrow attitude of superiority. It appears he condones the idea the Jew is the really first-class citizen of the kingdom, and the gentile world ranks with the dogs. His words are altogether startling in their seeming harshness: "Let us feed the children first; it isn't right to take the children's food and throw it to the dogs."

(a) What are we to make of this? Was Jesus harsh? Is God partial? Are some people more important than others? Are some outside the realm of God's love and concern? Could it be the squalor of Calcutta, the deprivation of old age, the terrible burdens with which some are born—even the fact some people feed their dogs better than many children are fed? Could this be God's design? Another explanation must be possible.

(b) Did not Jesus say and does not the whole of the New Testament demonstrate: "He who comes to me I will not cast out"? It is out of character with the rest of Jesus' deeds and words to think of this in terms of a permit for prejudice. How could Jesus cast out a poor mother bent with concern for her child?

II. It is helpful to think of this story as an acted parable. Jesus stood in the tradition of the prophets who at times acted out the truth of God. What is important, as in the study of all parables, is to look for the salient point. You can get so lost in detail that you lose sight of the tremendous truth herein contained—persons are above conventions in God's priorities.

III. Mark places this story immediately after the stories of Jesus' conflict with the narrow legalism of the Jews. It seems clear he understood this story to be a continuation of Jesus' emphasis on the universality of the love of God. It is a protest against the legalism of the Jews. It is a protest against exclusivism. It is a graphic illustration in which the discussion serves to illustrate the truth that God's love spans the narrow confines of man's mind and society's conventions.

(a) Jesus is in gentile country. The Jews had nothing to do with gentiles. Jesus' presence in gentile territory is evidence he is expanding his role in this symbolic act to the world.

(b) Jesus needed rest and quiet. He had been greatly pressured to conform by the discussions in Jerusalem. He was wearied from the Jews' insistence on orthodoxy. No doubt his mind was reflecting on the debate around Jerusalem, and here he answers the question, "Are some people outside the limits of God's love?" And he demonstrates that they are not.

IV. We do not have for our interpretation of this passage the other factors so important for our understanding. If we knew the look in his eyes, the tone of his voice, and the movement of his body and hands, we could tell more of Jesus' meaning. Words alone are insufficient for the total meaning.

(a) When the woman heard Jesus, she heard a different message than only the written words give. The disciples were resentful of her persistence and impertinent interruption into the much needed rest and renewal period of Jesus. They asked Jesus to send her away. Do you really think she would have stayed if Jesus had lowered the wrath of Jewish legalism on her?

(b) She stayed because she sensed in Jesus a responsive compassion. There are times when interruptions can irritate and be disagreeable, unwelcome frustrations. But Jesus stopped. A case of human need was never an interruption to him. She sensed a tenderness and compassion in him that made him approachable. His words were colored by his tender look and welcome hands.

(c) Matthew says Jesus first said not a word to her. Sometimes silence communicates as nothing else. It does not mean he was stubborn and refusing. He stood there with her with such compassion that silence was the only appropriate response. It was a silence you may have experienced with a loved one when words would have been babble. It was the silence of a friend who stands with you when you've just been told a loved one has died. Jesus' silence was an overabundance of compassion, not a lack of it.

V. Jesus was using the device of all helpers. He probes gently until real motivations are uncovered. He knows the answer but knows it must be hers before real help can arrive. How many counselors know ahead what to prescribe for our health, but we do not accept it because they tell us. We must discover it ourselves. So the bantering is to establish the basis for strength in her after stripping away the false and unjustified. Jesus could not aid until she launched out in faith and complete trust. Their encounter illustrates the truth when faith is present no arbitrary boundaries or conventions of men can hinder, but when faith is absent no artificial supports will help.

VI. Jesus served the person rather than

convention. She got what she needed. In the end compassion won. Whenever man-made conventions conflict with human need, Jesus' priority is the person. Unlike the priest and Levite in the story of the good Samaritan, Jesus stopped to help. There can be no doubt about it. God's love is for all. No person is denied help because of the barriers of prejudice or dogma. Compassion knows no limits in Jesus.

VII. Any person who dwells near the heart of God must share his love for the last as well as for the first, for the outsider as well as the insider, for the person who has not as well as the person who has, for the black as well as for the white, for the red as well as for the yellow, and for the sinner in the house of correction as well as for the saint in the pew.

(a) Emil Brunner wrote, "The Christian knows that above the demands of justice are always those of love—that he should not merely treat his neighbor as a member of an order of justice but also and above all as a brother, as a man who, as a person called by God, is more than any order of justice."

(b) Jesus' love spanned the conventions of men. It bridged the prejudice of ages. He followed what Goethe later noted, "If one treats a person as if he were what he ought to be and could be, he will become what he ought to be and could be." Jesus treated us all as beloved sons and daughters of God, and so we are.—Joe D. Sergent.

Illustration

VISION. A wise Indian father wished to give his property and possessions to that one of his three sons who showed the most prowess and promise. As a test, he pointed to a mountain bold against the sky and sent his three sons toward it, asking each of them to bring a token to show how far he had climbed up the mountain. The first one returned with a white wild flower in his hands. The father knew that it grew only above the timberline. The second son brought a red flint stone which revealed to the father that he had made it almost to the top. The third son was gone for a long time and returned empty-handed. "Father, where I went," he explained, "there was nothing to bring back, but I stood at the summit and looked out upon a valley where two great rivers join the ocean." And the proud father said to him: "It has been the ambition of my life that one of my sons should see what you have seen. You have nothing in your hand but you have a greater thing—a vision in your soul. This is the greatest of all."—Robert E. Goodrich, Jr.

Sermon Suggestions

BREAKING DOWN BARRIERS. Scripture: Philem. 1:1–21. (1) Barriers are broken when Christians are friends (vv. 1–3). (2) Barriers are broken when Christians pray for one another (vv. 4–7). (3) Barriers are broken when Christians intercede for friends (vv. 8–14). (4) Barriers are broken when Christians accept others as equals (vv. 15–16). (5) Barriers are broken when Christians become burden bearers.—Wayne North.

AN IMPOSSIBLE IMPERATIVE. Text: Matt. 5:43. (1) We must believe that it is possible to fulfill this command. (2) To love our enemies means that we must allow for differences. (3) We can love our enemies by creating an atmosphere for peace.—C. A. McClain, Jr.

Worship Aids

CALL TO WORSHIP. "Delight thyself also in the Lord; and he shall give thee the desires of thine heart. Commit thy way unto the Lord; trust also in him; and he shall bring it to pass." Ps. 37:4–5.

INVOCATION. Heavenly Father, we come before thee in trembling because we are conscious of our many sins and yet boldly because we know that thou dost love us. Forgive us our sins, and help us to become more worthy of thy goodness and love. May we gain that strength from communion with thee which will enable us to walk humbly and righteously before thee and uprightly before the world, manifesting in life's every experience that faith and courage which befit thy children.

OFFERTORY SENTENCE. "If thou draw out thy soul to the hungry, and satisfy the afflicted soul; then shall thy light rise in obscurity, and thy darkness be as the noonday." Isa. 58:10.

OFFERTORY PRAYER. Our Father, help us to trust thee more fully and to accept our responsibility toward thy work and thy children who are our brethren in Christ.

PRAYER. O God, who has made all people in your likeness and who loves all whom you have made, may we not separate ourselves from you by setting up barriers of race and color among ourselves. As Jesus was born of a Hebrew mother, rejoiced in the faith of a Syrian woman and a Roman soldier, welcomed the Greeks who sought him, extolled the virtue of a hated Samaritan, and suffered his cross to be carried by an African, teach us to regard the members of all races as our brothers and sisters and by our loving service on their behalf to show our love to you.

EVENING SERVICE

Topic: The Lessons of Creation

TEXTS: Gen. 1:1, 31; 2:1.

Wholeness is one of the great themes of the Bible. Division is wrong. Wholeness is a prize to be sought after. Unity is the will of God for humanity.

I. In the beginning God created our world as a complete whole and our universe as a unified working entity.

(a) The more scientists learn about our world, our solar system, our galaxy, and our universe, the more we see that all parts are made to work well together.

(b) Most of us are overawed, if not intimidated, by the facts the astronomers throw at us. We learn of a universe of a size beyond our wildest imaginings, filled with stars and planets and other celestial bodies of such vast numbers that we can't deal with them.

(c) One thing is clear—this system is orderly and unified. Although heavenly bodies may be very different from one another, they all exist harmoniously together.

II. In this orderly universe it was clearly God's intention that those creatures made in the image of God, men and women, should also live and work together harmoniously.

(a) The prophets tried to show their people that God is a God of all the earth who cares for everyone, but they were unable to convince their listeners.

(b) Jesus saw quite clearly the universality of God. He emphasized that God was concerned about everyone—Jew and gentile, young and old, male and female, slave and free. In the gospels Jesus shows us time and again that God cares for everyone—the poor and the rich, the hungry and the filled, the Pharisee, the Samaritan, the prodigal son, the tax collector, everyone.

(c) During his lifetime hardly anyone seemed to understand this message which showed a different kind of God, a more caring, loving God than most people had imagined. Few seemed willing to deal with the idea that each part of God's creation, including us, God's human children, is interrelated and that what happens to one of us affects us all.

(d) Perhaps we are finally beginning to acknowledge this truth with its wonderful and frightening implications.—Margie M. Frank.

SUNDAY: FEBRUARY TWENTY-FIRST

MORNING SERVICE

Topic: The Face of Jesus (The Transfiguration)

TEXT: II Cor. 4:6.

There are several verses in the New Testament that speak of Jesus' face, not about his appearance but his demeanor.

I. The first text deals with the transfiguration. This event took place upon a high mountain, perhaps the lovely snow-topped Mount Hermon. Jesus had with him his friends Peter, James, and John.

(a) What happened on that mountain was greatly memorable to the apostles. While Jesus stood before them "he was transfigured," that is, he was transformed in such a way that "his face shone like the sun, and his garments became white as light" (Matt. 17:2). Then they heard a voice: "This is my beloved Son, with whom I am well pleased; listen to him" (Matt. 17:5). It was a soul-shaking spiritual experience for all of them. They were overcome with awe, so much so that "they fell on their faces" in reverence and respect. Jesus had to tell them to "rise, and have no fear" (Matt. 17:7).

(b) In the shining face of Jesus we see the light of God dwelling among men. In the face of Jesus we see the nature and glory of God bursting forth with truth and purity and love on this earth of ours. Seeing the holy face of Jesus portraying to us the essence of the nature of God, we can only say with St. John, "We have beheld his glory, glory as of the only Son from the Father" (John 1:14). The shining face of Jesus as seen in the transfiguration experience is another proof that God has revealed himself most fully to men in the man from Nazareth.

II. A second text which mentions the face of Jesus is one we nearly always hear during Lent. It is St. Luke telling us that "he set his face to go to Jerusalem" (Luke 9:51).

(a) Jerusalem was the capital city of Judea. The ruler of the Roman Empire had an outpost there. The leaders of the Jews, known collectively as the Sanhedrin, also presided there. Jerusalem was the citadel of great power in Jesus' homeland.

(b) Jesus decided to challenge the power structures of his day. He did so because they were corrupt. Jesus was going to Jerusalem to confront the evil resident there that love and justice might triumph.

(c) Jesus could not stand the cruelty being afflicted upon the common people of his day, especially the helpless and the poor. Jesus was disturbed by the oppression of both the military and religious rulers. He knew that nothing would ever be better unless someone confronted the oppressors head-on.

(d) Evil never goes away by merely wishing it so. Evil gives way only when confronted by goodness. That was what Jesus was demonstrating when he set his face to go to Jerusalem.

III. No one engages in warfare with evil without paying a price. (See Luke 22:64.)

(a) Jesus was beaten and cursed and ridiculed. A crown of thorns was jammed upon his head. He was mockingly hailed as a king while blood streamed down his bruised face. Nails were hammered into his hands and feet, spread-eagling him on a cross. Finally they stuck a sword into his side and he died.

(b) When we resolutely oppose the forces of darkness, we can count on opposition and suffering. The cross reminds us of that. The cross symbolizes Christ's suffering to make this a better world. If we are true to him, we can expect to bear our own crosses as we challenge evil in our time.

IV. A final text dealing with the face of Jesus is found in Rev. 22:3-5 in which we see a glimpse of heaven. That is the joyful promise of scripture. We may not know how our Lord appeared during his journey on earth. We know only that he had the shining face of the unique Son of God who set his face against evil and who died in the process. But we know also that he lives now in eternity and that one day we who love and follow him shall see his face. —Charles E. Ferrell.

Illustrations

HOUR OF PRAYER. Paul Tournier decided to put one hour a day aside for prayer. The first time he did it he thought the hour would never end. Restlessly he looked at his watch again and again, hoping that time would pass quickly. At the end of the hour he felt like a child let out of school. But he resisted the temptation to leave immediately. No longer was the pressure on. Now he could relax. And in those moments after the hour of prayer he was transformed. Tournier is convinced that the first hour was God's test of obedience and the real prayer was the whole day that followed which, he said, seemed to be infused with a sense of God.—Craig Biddle III.

NEGATIVE WITNESS. Sinclair Lewis was a self-proclaimed atheist. All of his novels mounted scathing attacks on Christianity and the church. Why?

Lewis started college at Oberlin at age seventeen. He was tall, ugly, red-haired, and not easy to get along with. In his loneliness he joined the YMCA and immediately became involved in the religious activities it offered. He attended services, taught Sunday school, became a Christian, and even announced that he would someday become a foreign missionary. But no one seemed to notice Lewis at Oberlin. No one reached out to him. No one cared. He was homesick and lonely and missed a girl back home. So he left.

In disappointment and failure, Lewis transferred to Yale, hoping to find companionship and friends. It was a new beginning, but the old story was repeated again. Though he taught Sunday school at the YMCA, in a church, and then in an orphanage, he finally gave it all up. His biographer in *Sinclair Lewis: An American Life* writes: "If his religious enthusiasm was dying, it may have been in part because church activity at Yale offered even less by way of human communion than it had at Oberlin." A company of negative witnesses helped drive Lewis to unbelief.—Roger Lovette.

Sermon Suggestions

AS ST. PAUL SEES CHRIST. Scripture: Col. 1:15–25. (1) Christ is the image of the invisible God. (2) Christ is the creator of the world. (3) Christ is the end of the world. (4) Christ is the preserver of the world. (5) Christ is working in the world for the redemption of the world.—Ernest Trice Thompson.

THE CHURCH'S TEMPTATIONS. Text: Luke 9:33. (1) The church's temptation to imprison God. (2) The church's temptation to be satisfied with its past. (3) The church's temptation to offer a despairing world something less than the real God.— George T. Peters.

Worship Aids

CALL TO WORSHIP. "How beautiful upon the mountains are the feet of him that bringeth good tidings, that publisheth peace; that publisheth salvation; that saith unto Zion, thy God reigneth!" Isa. 52:7.

INVOCATION. Almighty God, regard, we beseech thee, thy church, set amid the perplexities of a changing order and face to face with new tasks. Fill us afresh with thy spirit that we may bear witness boldly to the coming of thy kingdom and hasten the time when the knowledge of thyself shall encircle the earth as the waters cover the sea.

OFFERTORY SENTENCE. "As every man hath received the gift, even so minister the same one to another, as good stewards of the manifold grace of God." I Pet. 4:10.

OFFERTORY PRAYER. Our Father, help us this day to remember that we do not live in our own strength but that thou art our help and that from thee cometh even these gifts which we consecrate in Christ's name.

PRAYER.   Heavenly Father, we thank thee for thy word given by inspiration through holy men of old and preserved for us through the efforts of consecrated men who worked with thy blessing. We are grateful to those who under thee carefully copied the scriptures and to those who translated them into the tongues of all the great nations. Hasten the day when all men may have thy word in their own language. May we zealously guard our Bible and its eternal truths, but may we never become guilty of fanaticism, unkindness, prejudice, or dishonesty. Keep us from putting undue emphasis on the bindings of our Bibles or on the beauty of its style, lest its great message of thy love in Christ and his sacrifice for our sins and its guidance for righteous living be neglected. Direct us that we may read our Bible more fervently, understand it more clearly, believe it more firmly, and seek more ardently to spread its truth to all nations. Help us to proclaim thy truth that it may sound above the harsh noises of our times and above the cry of those who would make war. We ask it in the name of him who is the prince of peace.—Armin C. Oldsen.

EVENING SERVICE

Topic: Here Would I See Thee

SCRIPTURE: John 13:1–15, 34–35.

Jesus said he would meet us here at Holy Communion, not under some wall, not at some island rendezvous, not in some relic of the cross—a splinter of wood housed under glass and protected by lock and key. The disciples did not hang around the tomb. They went to the upper room. When they heard the news that the women had seen him, the disciples dressed for dinner. The proof of the resurrection is to be found in the church, especially the church at Holy Communion. There are two reasons why here at Holy Communion more than at any other place we see him most clearly. The first is because we are all sinners and, secondly, because here at Holy Communion we are all summoned.

I. There are not many things that unite us here. We can't say we are all in agreement in doctrine. We certainly can't say we are of one mind on how to apply the teachings of our Lord to the complex problems of the world. If you want to get into an argument among Christians, just start talking about how to apply the Christian faith to the issues that face us as human beings in this world today. We're not united in anything except this—we're all sinners. That's the only thing that church people can be sure they all hold in common. We're all imperfect. We've all fallen short. We're all in need of grace. When we come to the table of our Lord, we're all alike.

(a) That is the only basis upon which there will be any unity in this world. I'm not talking about the cozy groupings of people who think the same way and play the same way. You can make that kind of thing happen whenever you want to. I mean getting to know those people in this world who are really different from you. I mean overcoming the racial, the social, and the economic barriers that traditionally separate people. I mean getting rid of the insidious arrogance that keeps you from communion with other people and that makes you think you're better than other people. I mean the pride that keeps you from saying, "I'm sorry," or the pride that keeps you from saying, "You're forgiven."

(b) That's what Christianity came to do in this world, not to provide a social club for like-minded people. It came to create a whole new community out of the divisions of this world and to bring you new life by reuniting you with all of life. That's what the church is here for, and we rehearse that mission of the church whenever we gather together at Holy Communion. Holy Communion enables us to see the kind of community that God intends for us to have.

(c) In the church we're all alike. We're all sinners. In that equality we come to him, and in that equality he will come to us. He will be seen here at Holy Communion where that unity exists.

II. We are all summoned. (a) In some churches Holy Communion is just for the members in good standing. In those churches Holy Communion is a private meal reserved for members, for the elite. Excommunication means literally to be cut off from the communion. If you didn't believe or if you didn't behave in the right way, you are excommunicated, cut off from the privilege of receiving the sacrament of our Lord.

(b) The church has argued for 2,000 years about who is eligible to receive the sacrament at the Lord's table. Those who say that only those who are church members in good standing can receive it observe what is called closed communion. Those who believe that all are welcome at the table if they can answer the invitation observe what is called open communion.

(c) Jesus has sent the invitation to you. We simply announce it. The summons comes from Christ to you personally to eat with him as his disciple.—Mark Trotter.

SUNDAY FEBRUARY TWENTY-EIGHTH

MORNING SERVICE

Topic: Deep Within Us (Lent)
SCRIPTURE: Mark 1:9–13.

I. In St. Mark's gospel is a straightforward record of the way the early church viewed pivotal events in the life of Jesus. In the scripture two such events are depicted in their simplest form—the baptism of Jesus by John and the temptation of Jesus in the wilderness.

(a) As narrated here we can see how closely interrelated these two events are for an understanding of Jesus' life and work.

(1) By the time Jesus went to John to be baptized in the River Jordan, he was about thirty years old. This was no precipitated decision. For years he must have been pondering the use of his life. Now in an act of clarification he was to affirm publicly his intention for the ministry he was about to begin. He was submitting himself to be the agent of God's purposes for all humanity. That was going to be his appointed mission.

(2) The same spirit which descends upon him like a dove immediately requires something else of him. We read that the spirit drove him out into the wilderness where he would endure the temptations of Satan. The acceptance of his role as symbolized in baptism was not sufficient. Only by enduring the hardest tests that could possibly be presented would he be capable of manifesting his life as God's agent. Only an intention tried by fire would be able to convey the reconciling love of God to people twisted and torn, ransacked and debilitated, and alienated by sin, circumstance, and the absence of faith.

(b) By his baptism Jesus embraced fully and utterly the two-fold nature of his appointed mission. He would manifest the divine love to such a degree that those following him declared that he was the veritable son of God. Yet he would be so undeniably attuned to his fellow human beings in such manner that they affirmed him as their human savior and lord. The creed put it much later, "One Lord Jesus Christ, the only begotten son of God," yet one "who for us and for our salvation was made man"—made human as the epitome of humanness even to the extent of suffering and death—and one "whose kingdom shall have no end."

(c) The church in its ancient wisdom reminds us through this gospel and in the words of one of the Lenten hymns of "the glory of these forty days" we "celebrate with songs of praise," because "Christ, by whom all things were made, himself has fasted and has prayed."

II. We shall want to meditate much about how his own baptism celebrated the way in which his whole life was identified with God's loving concern for the world. But we shall also want to think about how, if we are indeed baptized with the baptism wherewith he is baptized, we are bound in with Christ's purpose and mission. Not only are we called to be open to the divine dimension, but we are called also to be totally human in our identifications and concerns.

(a) It seems strange that we should need to be reminded to be altogether human. Don't we have to be? What else could we be? But the fact is that processes of dehumanization are constantly at work in the midst of our alleged humanness.

(b) This call of Christ to complete humanness is not easy for people to understand, or maybe they just don't want to understand because of the changes it will require in them. Some persons think they are being utterly human even when they show signs of deteriorating into something less than human.

(c) Life can be just a vast and endless plateau for anybody. If life is dehumanized, depersonalized, then we enter a stage of dry rot. Or we try to escape from our meaninglessness in all kinds of empty-ended choices.

III. Surely there is more to life than that we should burn up our days and end with disillusionment and despair.

(a) That need not happen if we remember into whose baptism we have been baptized. For when Christ entered upon his mission he was committed to the whole range of human existence. He was dedicated to the redemption of our total human life. Nothing henceforth was to be alien to him—no one's emptiness, no one's sin, no one's bitterness, no one's disappointments, no one's boredom, and no one's hopelessness. All these he would take unto himself and bear in sacrifice upon the cross.

(b) Likewise he was to take upon himself every bright and scintillant and glorious aspect of our humanness—every happiness, every positive achievement, every victory over darkness and defeat, every creative impulse, every hope, dream, longing, and love. These too he takes into himself and by his sacrifice on the cross enables us to know also the resurrection unto eternal life.

(c) It was no accident that Ps. 51 is often incorporated into the Ash Wednesday liturgy. We don't read of joy only nor of suffering alone. The psalmist saw the wholeness of our humanity when he cried out: "Make me hear of joy and gladness, that the body you have broken may rejoice. Cast me not away from your presence and take not your holy Spirit from me."

(1) Nurtured as he was in the psalmist's faith, our Lord was from his baptism committed to a faith like that. It was a total commitment to life in God and a confident awareness that the complete human experience is of value and concern to us because it is of value and concern to God.

(2) It was that faith into which he was baptized. It was that faith which he tested during the wilderness sojourn. It is that faith into which we, like him, are baptized. It is that faith which will sustain us even as the angels ministered to our Lord while he was among the wild beasts.—Kendig Brubaker Cully.

Illustrations

RELEVANCE.   A missionary was talking to an African chieftain, telling him about the story of Jesus Christ and the importance of the Christian faith. Then he picked out a portion of the New Testament and began to read in the man's language. After a brief period of time, the African leader cried out: "Stop! Where did you get that story? It reads like the story of my own village."—Wayne C. Reece.

SHUTTING THE DOOR.   A woman was trying to turn on the light in a telephone booth. A passer-by stopped and said, "Lady, if you will shut the door the light will come on." Jesus urges us to shut the door on distractions that we may pray to our heavenly Father in secret. He who sees in secret and knows the secrets of all hearts will "reward us openly" (Matt. 6:4). —David A. MacLennan.

Sermon Suggestions

TREES WITHOUT FRUIT.   Text: Luke 22: 32. There are some things that will not please Christ. (1) Fishing without catching. (See Luke 5:4–11.) (2) An empty banquet table. (See Luke 14:15–23.) (3) Sowing without reaping. (See Matt. 13:6–9.) (4) A fig tree that bears no figs. (See Luke

13:3–9.) (5) Lost sheep that are not brought into the fold. (See Matt. 18:11–14.) (6) A lost coin that is sought but not found. (See Luke 15:8–10.) (7) Harvests that are not reaped. (See Matt. 9:36–38.) (8) Proclamation without response.

PREREQUISITES FOR CHRISTIAN LIVING. Text: II Cor. 5:7. (1) Openness. (2) Reverence. (3) Courage. (4) Love.

Worship Aids

CALL TO WORSHIP. "Whatsoever things are true, whatsoever things are honest, whatsoever things are just, whatsoever things are pure, whatsoever things are lovely, whatsoever things are of good report; if there be any virtue, and if there be any praise, think on these things." Phil. 4:8.

INVOCATION. O Lord of light, in this hour of worship in thy house make pure our hearts, and we shall see thee. Reveal thyself to us, and we shall love thee. Strengthen our wills, and we shall choose the good from the evil and day by day manifest in the world the glory and power of thy blessed gospel, which thou hast made known to us through thy Son Jesus Christ.

OFFERTORY SENTENCE. "Therefore, my beloved brethren, be ye steadfast, unmoveable, always abounding in the work of the Lord, forasmuch as ye know that your labor is not in vain in the Lord." I Cor. 15:58.

OFFERTORY PRAYER. O God, who hast given us thy Son to be an example and a help to our weakness in following the path that leadeth into life, grant us so to be his disciples that we may walk in his footsteps.

PRAYER. Our heavenly Father, we come together in thy sacred name making ready for our Lenten pilgrimage to Easter. In worshipful preparation, open our hands to thee, the guide of our lives. Open our eyes to thee, the light for our paths. Open our ears to thee, the teacher of divine wisdom. Open our hearts to thee, the inhabitant of the temple within us. Open our lives to thee, the object of our mission.

Thus may we walk and not stumble. May we see and not forsake the true way. May we hear and not turn from thy holy word. May we love thee and welcome thy presence throughout our inner being. May we demonstrate to others thy truth and not detain thy kingdom from becoming a reality. Through Jesus the Christ, whose life was a Lenten journey of triumph and victory.—Harold A. Schulz.

EVENING SERVICE

Topic: What Will You Do with Jesus?
TEXT: Matt. 27:22.

You must do something with him. Neutrality is impossible. The possession of the opportunity for doing the right thing imposes the obligation to do it. There is no middle course possible here. You must be either for him or against him. You must either take him to your heart or reject him to your ruin. There are several courses open to you.

I. You can deny his divine mission and say he was an imposter. There were plenty in those days who did this, and there are plenty who do the same thing in our day. Some went so far as to say he had a devil. What do you say to that?

II. You can deny your need of any savior. You can say, "I have no soul, and I shall have no hereafter," or you can pretend that you have never sinned and say, "There'll be no judgment, so I don't need a savior." That is what the Sadducees said, and there are thousands who say the same thing in our day.

III. You can openly reject him. Right or wrong, you can simply say, "I won't have him." There are plenty who took this course when he was on earth. They were there in force that day. Instead of taking him to their hearts, they sent him to the cruel tree.

IV. You can pretend to accept him and call yourself by his name, although your heart is far from him. There were any number who adopted that course while he was on earth. He upbraided them, "Why call ye me Lord, and do not the things which I say?"

V. You can treat the whole matter with indifference. There was a crowd in Jerusalem on that day who took no notice whatever of the affair. The shops were all open. The buyers and sellers were all busy. There were marriages and feasts, parties, and amusements in full swing while the Son of God was hanging on the cross.

These people were indifferent. They did not care.

VI. There is one more course you can take. Accept this blessed Jesus as your savior and submit to his authority. Wash every stain away in his blood, enthrone him in your heart as your king, and fight for him all the rest of your days.—William Booth.

SUNDAY: MARCH SEVENTH

MORNING SERVICE

Topic: Risen with Christ (Lent)

TEXT: Col. 3:1.

Everyone who becomes a Christian does so through an actual experience of crucifixion and resurrection. There are five steps of faith in this experience of dying to sin and rising with Christ.

I. We must hear the good news—the gospel. No one ever becomes a follower of Christ unless he hears the gospel. If you will open your heart and mind and listen to the word, you will take the other four steps which lead to the new life in him.

II. We must believe in Christ in our hearts and believe that God raised him from the dead. (See Rom. 10:9–10.)

III. When we believe in Jesus Christ in our hearts and affirm that God raised him from the dead and that he is the unique Son of God, then as a further act of faith we must repent of our sins. In the first Christian sermon on the day of Pentecost when the multitude cried out, "Men and brethren, what must we do?" Peter replied, "Repent ye, and be baptized everyone of you, in the name of Jesus Christ for the remission of your sins; and ye shall receive the gift of the Holy Spirit" (Acts 2:38). Paul calls repentance "the crucifixion of the body" when he reminds the Romans, "Knowing this, that our old man [self] was crucified with him, that the body of sin might be done away, that so we should no longer be in bondage to sin" (Rom. 6:6–10). When we truly repent, we

crucify the old sinful life as Christ was crucified upon the cross.

IV. We must confess our faith publicly, "before men." Paul tells us that we must confess Jesus as lord and that this confession is "unto salvation." It is one of the steps of faith in the Easter experience. (See Matt. 10:32–33.) He who would become a Christian must have the courage to step out before the whole church and confess Jesus as his lord and redeemer.

V. We must be buried with Christ and raised with him in a public act, which symbolizes Christ's burial and resurrection, and in the words of Dr. Gore, "effects what it symbolizes." And so it does, for Christian baptism is always spoken of in the New Testament as a burial and resurrection and is always connected, said James Denney, "with the death of Christ and the remission of sins." (See Matt. 28:19; Rom. 6:3–5.)—Jesse Randolph Kellems.

Illustrations

MARGINAL NOTE. British journalist Hugh Redwood found himself under severe nervous strain facing certain crucial decisions. He was staying at a friend's house and was sitting before a fire in an easy chair. A Bible was on the table beside the chair. It was open at Ps. 59. Opposite v. 10 someone had written an interpretation which kindled his mind. The verse says, "The God of my mercy shall prevent me." The word "prevent" in the classical English means go before—"The God of mercy shall go before me." In the margin he read, "My God in his lovingkindness shall meet me at every corner," which Redwood interpreted as meaning that God provides for us whatever the experience or occasion of our need. God is there before us to provide his power and love.— Hoover Rupert.

TESTIMONY.   Frank Lloyd Wright was testifying under cross-examination in a Chicago court. The cross-examiner asked, "Give us your name." "Frank Lloyd Wright" was the answer. "Your occupation," requested the lawyer. "The world's greatest architect," he answered. "How can you say that?" demanded the lawyer. "Because I am testifying under oath," replied Wright.

If Jesus were testifying under oath, the dialogue would go something like this: "What is this peace that you talk about?" "It comes because I know I am loved." "How can you say that?" "Because I am testifying under oath."—Craig Biddle III.

Sermon Suggestions

THE PEARL OF PEARLS.   Text: Matt. 13:44–46. The parable teaches that the kingdom of heaven is the loveliest possession of all, but what does it mean to possess or to be in the kingdom of God? It means (1) obedience to God and his will, (2) letting God be God in our lives, (3) accepting God's acceptance of us as we are and striving to become what God desires of us, (4) facing life Godward, (5) letting God rule our lives, (6) living under his mastery, and (7) possessing eternal life.— W. Aubrey Alsobrook.

RESOURCES FOR CHRISTIAN GROWTH. Text: II Tim. 1:12. (1) Feed your mind and spirit habitually with the words, thoughts, and affirmations of the Bible. (2) Through prayer regularly accept the privilege of communing with God. (3) Share with others their experiences and your own growing experiences as you learn to walk by faith one step at a time and one day at a time.—Theodore F. Adams.

Worship Aids

CALL TO WORSHIP.   "Thou wilt keep him in perfect peace, whose mind is stayed on thee: because he trusteth in thee. Trust ye in the Lord for ever: for in the Lord Jehovah is everlasting strength." Isa. 26:3–4.

INVOCATION.   We turn our minds unto thee, O God, that thou wilt give us deeper insight into the meanings of the life of thy Son, our Lord. We turn our hearts unto thee that thy love may flow through them. We turn our wills unto thee that thou may guide us in all that we do and in all that we say.

OFFERTORY SENTENCE.   "The end of the commandment is charity out of a pure heart." I Tim. 1:5.

OFFERTORY PRAYER.   Almighty God, whose loving hand hath given us all that we possess: grant us grace that we may honor thee with our substance, and remembering the account which we must one day give, may be faithful stewards of thy bounty.

PRAYER.   We thank thee, our Father, for Christ who would make us anew and who looks at us and opens up our lives, revealing in what places we err, how we ail, and where we fall short of thy good pleasure. We thank thee for Christ who never leaves us where he finds us but in love and compassion bids us mount the steps to a better way. Grant us, O God, a feeling of response when he walks into our lives. Open up our lives and let us be born anew.

We thank thee, our God, for a teacher who abides with us, who lies not in some tomb across the seas, and who moves among us in our time. For his undying interest in us, for the depth of his understanding and for the magnanimity of his soul, for his unflagging sympathy toward us, for the power of his love and for the vastness of his mercy, we give thee thanks. Open our hearts and humble our pride. Forgive our foolishness when we turn from his way and follow after folly. Restore us to a right mind that we may ever know that only in him is life which is abundant.—Fred E. Luchs.

EVENING SERVICE

Meditation: The Incomparable Christ
TEXT: John 17:5.

It is inspiring to contemplate the uniqueness of Jesus. He towers above other human beings as Mount Everest rises above the foothills. His birthday splits history in two, and even the avowed atheist must reckon his calendar by his coming.

It staggers the mind to try to grasp the greatness of his life and the impact he made upon the world—how one person could so live that two thousand years later countless persons are still being transformed by his spirit.

He spoke as never man spoke before, yet he not only taught the truth but he embodied it. His enemies tried to put him to rout and to disorganize him with their trick questions, but it was always they who were discomfited, for his keen mind was more than a match for them.

When they could not conquer him in debate or dispose of him in any other way, they led him to the cruelest death his generation could devise and nailed him to a cross. Yet they could not quench his spirit, for when he was tortured he forgave, and when they thought they were rid of him forever he rose from the grave and vanquished death. He planted an invincible hope in the hearts of all his disciples by telling them, "Because I live, you shall live also."

He founded his church here on earth. No one can ever do that again or needs to. He showed us God as no one had ever been able to do before. He comes into the lives of his followers as friend, redeemer, savior, and lord. He utterly transforms anyone who will walk in his way.

As we ponder the depths of his life and spirit, we cry out, as the centurion did at the foot of the cross, "Truly this man is the Son of God!"—James R. Webb.

SUNDAY: MARCH FOURTEENTH

MORNING SERVICE

Topic: The Story of Two Josephs (Lent)
TEXTS: Matt. 1:24; John 19:38.

The gospels particularly mention two Josephs. One is the Christmas Joseph, and the other the Good Friday Joseph. They stand one at each end of the life of Jesus—the one at his birth and the other at his death.

I. Joseph of Nazareth saw the beginnings of a life and heard the first cry of the infant Jesus. Joseph of Arimathaea may have heard the cry of a dying man on a cross. The Christmas Joseph, a just man and a carpenter, helped Mary, his betrothed, to lay a healthy babe in a crude manger. The Good Friday Joseph, a distinguished, wealthy legislator, carried a dead body to a new tomb. He owned it, and it was conveniently near. No one had yet been buried there.

(a) Joseph of Nazareth apparently had little influence with a Bethlehem innkeeper. True, the city was overcrowded with taxpayers answering a census call, and not many rooms were available. And Joseph was poor. We gather that his temple offering, made when Jesus was presented to the Lord, was a meager one.

(b) Joseph of Arimathaea must have had considerable influence with the mighty Pilate or else his gold was persuasive. The Jewish prohibition against leaving a body on a cross all night was not binding on the Roman authorities. Their custom was to leave the body to decay. But if some money could be made out of the corpse, all the better. In any circumstance it would have taken much courage to face Pilate. Joseph proved he had courage as well as coin. He "requested Pilate that he might take away Jesus' body, and Pilate gave him permission" (John 19:38, PHILLIPS).

(c) Did the Christmas Joseph assist Mary as she wrapped her first-born in swathing bands? Very probably. For the Good Friday Joseph the task was similar but different—not swaddling clothes but a winding sheet. Helped by Nicodemus who had brought an enormous quantity of spices and perfumes, the body of Jesus was prepared for burial. "Then took they the body of Jesus, and wound it in linen clothes with the spices" (John 19:40).

II. Both Josephs were obedient men. One to an angel—"Then Joseph . . . did as the angel of the Lord had bidden him" (Matt. 1:24)—and the other to his conscience—"being a disciple of Jesus, but secretly" (John 19:38, PHILLIPS).

(a) The first Joseph fades from the record. The time of his death is not stated in the gospels. It is doubtful whether he was alive during the public ministry of Jesus. He was not mentioned directly or indirectly, as were the mother, brothers, and sisters of Jesus. Joseph is last heard of when Jesus at the age of twelve became "a son of the law."

(b) Perhaps Joseph's naming of Jesus, as instructed by the angel, was his life's highest moment: "Thou shalt call his name Jesus: for he shall save his people from their sins" (Matt. 1:21). Nothing could merit more the inscribing of Joseph's name on the wall of history's gratitude.

(c) The Good Friday Joseph, it seems, moved from the cross and the tomb into a new era and experience of discipleship. So do all who see in the Christ of the cross their hope of forgiveness from sin. So do all who, in the power of the resurrected Christ, find the barriers to victorious spiritual life rolled away.

(d) The secret disciple, who prudently absented himself from the council of condemnation, fearlessly confronts the tyrannical procurator, pleading for the body of his Lord and willing to pay for it if need be. His membership in the Sanhedrin is thrown to the winds. He acts openly and with speed. Cowardice vanishes. Courage takes over. Nothing counts now but his declared discipleship. The Good Friday Joseph becomes the Easter Joseph, newly alive in Christ, imbued with the power of his resurrection.—General Arnold Brown, The Salvation Army.

Illustrations

GOD'S GIFT.   Two friends met after a separation of many years. One reported that he had married a woman they had both known in school. The other replied, "Oh, what a beautiful gift God has made you!" That remark changed his whole outlook on life. Before the man had regarded his wife simply as someone he had had the good sense or the good luck to marry. Suddenly he realized that indeed she was God's gift to him. And he discovered too how much else God had given which he customarily had taken for granted.—Paul Tournier.

CHRIST IN DISGUISE.   If sometimes our poor people have had to die of starvation, it is not because God didn't care for them but because you and I didn't give, and were not instruments of love in the hands of God, to give them that bread, to give them that clothing because we did not recognize him when once more Christ came in distressing disguise—in the hungry man, in the lonely man, in the homeless child, and seeking for shelter. God has identified himself with the hungry, the sick, the naked, the homeless; hunger not only for bread but for love, for care, to be somebody to someone; nakedness not of clothing only but nakedness of that compassion that very few people give to the unknown; homelessness not only just for a shelter made of stone but that homelessness that comes from having no one to call your own.—Mother Teresa.

Sermon Suggestions

THE PUBLICAN WHO BECAME A PREACHER. Scripture: Luke 5:27–32. (1) The problems Matthew experienced. (2) The promptness he exercised. (3) The passion he expressed.—Hardy R. Denham, Jr.

ON SAYING YES TO LIFE.   Text: II Tim. 4:7. (1) Paul wrote to young Timothy that he had fought a good fight, and for the apostle life was a continual battle. (2) He wrote that he had kept the faith. (3) Paul finished, insofar as possible, the work and task of life.—Frank A. Court.

Worship Aids

CALL TO WORSHIP.   "Having therefore, brethren, boldness to enter into the holiest by the blood of Jesus, by a new and living way, which he hath consecrated for us, let us draw near with a true heart in full assurance of faith." Heb. 10:19–20, 22.

INVOCATION.   Eternal God our Father, who art from everlasting, thou hast made us and not we ourselves. Thou hast set us never far from thee, that we, thy children, may learn the ways of freedom and choose thee with all our hearts. Grant us now thy Holy Spirit, that confident in prayer, we may worship thee with gladness and become as little children before thee.

OFFERTORY SENTENCE.   "To do good and to communicate forget not: for with such sacrifices God is well pleased." Heb. 13:16.

OFFERTORY PRAYER.   O God, help us so to practice by our gifts and our lives the divine principle of goodwill that in our homes, our communities, and among all the nations of the earth men may enjoy the boon of peace.

CONFESSION.   O Lord God, eternal and almighty father, before thy holy majesty we confess and admit without pretense that we are poor sinners, conceived and born in iniquity, inclined to evil, unprofitable to any good, and that, in our depravity, we have transgressed thy holy commandments without ceasing. In so doing, through thy just judgments we obtain ruin and perdition to ourselves. Nevertheless, O Lord, we are grieved that we have offended thee. We condemn ourselves and our vices with true repentance. We desire that thy grace shall be as great as our calamity.

O God and Father, who art gracious and full of mercy, do thou pity us in the name of thy Son, our Lord Jesus Christ. Blot out our sins and vices. Enlarge and increase in us from day to day the grace of thy Holy Spirit to the end that we, truly acknowledging our sins, will be touched with that sorrow which shall bring forth true repentance in us. Through this repentance, O God, cause us to hate sin. Produce in us the fruits of innocence and justice which will be pleasing to thee through Jesus Christ.—*Monday Morning.*

EVENING SERVICE

Topic: The Friend of Sinners

SCRIPTURE: Mark 2:1–12.

Christ's first tour of Galilee ended with his return to Capernaum, the place he resided after his rejection by the residents of Nazareth. As soon as it was broadcast he was at a certain house, a great crowd assembled to see and hear him, expecting to witness more of his mighty works.

I. *The paralyzed sinner.* One man could not come to the house where Christ was because he was a victim of palsy, that insidious disease which deprives the affected parts of the body of sensation or the power of motion. Powerless to move, the man had to be carried by loved ones and friends wherever he went.

II. *The persistent saints.* Four men decided to take this paralytic to Christ. With confidence in the ability and willingness of Christ to cure their friend, they lovingly carried him on a pallet to the house where Jesus was preaching. Their inventive genius and energetic faith were evidenced by their persistence in overcoming all obstacles, even to opening the roof to let the man down into the presence of Jesus. They manifested their faith by their works.

III. *The powerful savior.* Impressed with the faith of the four and because of the faith of the paralytic, Christ bestowed upon the man a priceless blessing, the forgiveness of his sins. Christ forgave his sins and saved his soul before he healed his body, suggesting the soul is of greater value than the body.

IV. *The protesting scribes.* When the scribes and Pharisees heard Christ's words of forgiveness, they accused him of blasphemy. They were right in their contention that God only could forgive sins, but they were wrong in assuming Christ was not God. To the paralytic Christ said, "Arise, and take up thy bed, and go thy way into thine house." The critics were amazed and resentful when the man obeyed Christ.

V. *The publican selected.* As Christ passed along the seashore, he saw Levi collecting taxes. When he saved and called him, Mat-thew's joy was so real he sought occasion to make Christ known to his friends. He invited his friends to a feast at his house where Christ was the guest of honor. He introduced them to the Savior, hoping they would trust and live for him. At this feast Christ ate with the publicans and sinners not because he approved their manner of living but because he wanted to change it.—H. C. Chiles.

SUNDAY: MARCH TWENTY-FIRST

MORNING SERVICE

Topic: The Man Who Might Have Been (Lent)

SCRIPTURE: John 12:3–6; 13:21–30.

I. Frank S. Meade called Judas the man who might have been. He was a person with infinite possibilities. Yet his potentiality never became actuality. For all of his promise as a human being, he was indeed just a might-have-been.

(a) Judas might have been a model for the rest of us to emulate had he lived up to his name. Judas derives from the same Hebrew root word as Judah and means worthy of praise. The two most popular names in first century Judaism were Judas and Simon. These were the names of two Jewish heroes who lived in the second century B.C. In Jesus' day the name "Judas" was given with a great sense of national pride. Jesus had a brother named Judas (Mark 6:3).

(b) Judas might have been a great disciple had he lived up to his calling. Jesus called Judas to discipleship on the same basis as others of the twelve. Judas had infinite potential for good. He was sensitive to the social and economic problems of the poor. He preached and ministered with the other disciples for almost three years. And he was the only one of the twelve disciples to have an official position. He was treasurer for the group—a responsibility Jesus apparently gave him for his unusual ability.

(c) Judas, like all of us, had limitless capacity for good. He had considerable abilities. He lived under the influence of the greatest teacher who ever lived. He enjoyed an enviable environment with the other disciples. Yet he squandered his opportunities. He was like a seed sown in the early spring which never develops. His potentiality never became actuality. He was just a man who might have been.

II. It is interesting to imagine what kind of person Judas might have been had he remained faithful to Jesus and developed his abilities.

(a) The gospel of John focuses upon the man who was. Judas was a man who abused his authority. He was the official treasurer of the twelve. He had concern for the poor. But he was also a phony. Judas used the power of his office and concern for others to enrich himself. He frequently embezzled the funds entrusted to him for his own use (John 12:6).

(b) The fact that something more than money was involved in Judas' betrayal of Jesus is made clear by the text. Thirty pieces of silver was not that much money. It was less than thirty dollars by today's standards. Furthermore, Judas gave the money back. He was the only disciple who attempted to get Jesus released. When his efforts failed, he threw the reward money at the feet of the authorities. His selfish ambitions had led to Jesus' arrest and certain death. Judas was "crushed with sorrow" (Matt. 27:3). And in this state of depression, he committed suicide. This was a very tragic end for one who had so much promise and ability.

III. Most of us, like Judas, have genuine feelings of love for Jesus. There is something deep inside us that is drawn to God.

We all have an inclination toward that which is holy.

(a) At the same time we all have our own ambitions of who we want to be and what we want to do. And there are times when we feel the tension between those two desires rumbling inside ourselves.

(b) If we are not careful, our ambitions will get the better of us. They can cause us to use Jesus for our own purposes. They can lead us to betray Jesus with the mistaken idea that we are doing what is best for ourselves.

(c) The bottom line is clear. If we are to avoid walking in Judas' footsteps, we must surrender our personal ambitions to Jesus instead of trying to force Jesus to comply with our own desires. Remaining faithful to Jesus is the only way we can become the person God wants us to be. If we follow the Judas inclination, which is in all of us, we will only be a might-have-been person. —William L. Blevins.

Illustrations

PERSONAL EXPERIENCE.   G. K. Chesterton differentiated between three great figures in English literature by saying that Carlyle saw, Arnold knew, and Dickens tasted. Carlyle wrote what he saw, Arnold wrote what he knew, and Dickens described what he experienced. Perhaps the distinction is a fine one, but it is there. The disciples saw Christ and to some extent understood him, but above all they had personal experience of him, and what they knew through experience was the surest possession of all. "One thing I know," the commanding certitude, is the supremely important thing.—Ernest Edward Smith.

CIRCLE OF INFLUENCE.   There was once a man in Galilee who seemed to feel that failures and disgraced people had a special claim on him. His own goodness was such that contact with evil must have made him wince. It made no difference. He became known as the friend of sinners. He let his life be burdened by their burdens, cost what it might. Hopeless people, out of whose faces joy and peace had gone, found that in his company they began to hope again. Weak people who wanted to do right but had not stamina enough in themselves and who had stumbled and fallen so often they had lost self-confidence, found they could walk upright when he walked by their side.

As time went on he was surrounded by a strange company whose lives had been broken but by the magic alchemy of love were healed and restored. Lives that were twisted and soiled became straight and clean. Timid people learned to be brave, sad people to rejoice. So changed were they that they could only describe themselves as born anew.

Centuries later, we have come within the circle of his influence. In greater or lesser degree we feel he has given himself to us and for us. In greater or lesser degree we feel impelled to give ourselves to him.—Frank Halliday Ferris.

Sermon Suggestions

KNOWING CHRIST.   Text: Phil. 3:10. (1) Knowing Christ historically. (2) Knowing Christ pictorially. (3) Knowing Christ by hearsay. (4) Knowing Christ personally. (5) Knowing Christ experientially.

NOTHING BUT THE BEST.   Text: Col. 3:1. (1) We must desire the best. (2) To achieve the best will require work and hard labor. (3) To achieve the best will call for patient persistence today, tomorrow, and perhaps through a lifetime. (4) To reach the best in life we need help from above for we cannot attain it apart from God.—John R. Brokhoff.

Worship Aids

CALL TO WORSHIP.   "Now in Christ Jesus ye who sometimes were far off are made nigh by the blood of Christ. For he is of our peace, who hath made both one, and hath broken down the middle wall of partition between us. Now therefore ye are no more strangers and foreigners, but fellow citizens with the saints and of the household of God." Eph. 2:13–14, 19.

INVOCATION. Our heavenly Father, we thy humble children invoke thy blessing upon us in this hour of worship. We adore thee, whose nature is compassion, whose presence is joy, whose word is truth, whose spirit is goodness, whose holiness is beauty, whose will is peace, whose service is perfect freedom, and in knowledge of whom standeth our eternal life. Unto thee be all honor and all glory.

OFFERTORY SENTENCE. "Bring ye all the tithes into the storehouse, saith the Lord, [and I will] open the windows of heaven, and pour you out a blessing." Mal. 3:10.

OFFERTORY PRAYER. O Father of our Lord Jesus Christ, we dedicate these offerings to the fellowship of him, whom to know aright is life eternal.

PRAYER. O thou giver of every good and perfect gift, driven by great hungers of heart and mind and soul, we search the world's mysteries for that bread by which we may be sustained and discover in the broken body of thy Son the only bread that satisfies. Accept our thanks, O God, for this deep mystery. Through his brokenness, we are made whole.

O thou who desirest truth in the inward parts, may we approach worship with integrity, for we know that only the pure in heart—only those who give themselves wholeheartedly—shall see thee. Grant us the courage to give ourselves to that discipline of introspection that strips the soul to its bare essence. Stripped of our every mask, pretense, make-believe, we are embarrassed by our nakedness and cry out to be clothed with thy righteousness. We pray that this occasion may be the moment of truth for many of us as we are awakened to the fact that truth is not merely academic but commands commitment—doing the truth. May we discipline ourselves to follow truth wherever it leads us—to follow it when it leads us out of our ivory tower to the highways of life and to stand for justice, even though we must stand alone; to champion the right, even though unpopular, and to follow it when it leads us out of the cozy enclave of some easy security to hazard life on the frontiers, when it beckons us to follow it up some new Calvary, and when it leads us out of the sanctuary into the marketplace. —John Thompson.

EVENING SERVICE

Topic: Christ Our Substitute
SCRIPTURE: Mark 15:6-15.
All that happened to him at Calvary was for us as he took our place. Consider his substitution on that day.

I. *The sinner Barabbas.* He was a revolutionary against Rome. He may have been a part of that cloak and dagger operation called the Sicarri who, because of their hatred for the Romans, used their daggers in the crowd. He was on death row.

II. *The sinless substitute Jesus.* Neither Pilate nor Herod Antipas found him guilty. "What shall I do with Jesus?" may have been asked in hope that they would release Jesus because of his popularity with the crowds. This is the inescapable question about the unavoidable Christ. Their response was "Crucify him." What is your response?

III. *A suggested comparison.* Origen tells of a manuscript of Matthew in which Barabbas is called Jesus Barabbas. Barabbas means son of his father. Jesus was son of his Father. One was a spiritual messiah, and one was a political messiah. One offered salvation from sin, and one offered salvation from Roman bondage. One offered to save by shedding his blood, and one offered to save by shedding their blood. Jesus refused to be the kind of messiah the other proposed to be.

IV. *A conscious choice.* The people chose Barabbas on the advice of the priests who were successful rabble rousers. They condemned Jesus for political ambition and recommended Barabbas to the crowd for the same reason. He looked like a better hope than Jesus. So the crowd cried, "Crucify him!" They scourged him and led him out to crucify him. And it was all done because he was a willing substitute not only for Barabbas but for you.—William B. Webb.

SUNDAY: MARCH TWENTY-EIGHTH

MORNING SERVICE

Topic: Drawn by the Cross (Passion Sunday)

TEXT: John 12:32.

I. The cross has become a symbol of Christ. (a) Many people before and after his time were put to death on crosses. It was a common method for putting to death those who were condemned for offenses against the reigning powers of this world. It was not until Jesus of Nazareth was crucified upon one of these crude instruments of torture and execution that crosses came to symbolize self-sacrifice on behalf of others.

(b) Here was the first recorded instance wherein someone had it in his power to avoid a cross. He had not committed a crime which called for capital punishment. He had only held to a course of idealism which he earnestly believed to be the way and will of God. By some slight compromise or some elaboration on his principles which would have cleared the issues in the minds of the Roman authorities, he might well have escaped this experience, but he believed that by voluntarily taking up a cross he would fulfill a divine purpose. He had said, "And I, if I be lifted up, will draw all men unto me."

(c) The fact that today we are drawn toward him as he hangs from his cross proves that he was eternally right. Because the cross of Christ has this power to draw us to the one who transformed it from a thing of shame to a thing of worship, we say we have faith in the cross.

II. The cross has become a symbol of his greatest teachings, and on that account we have faith in it.

(a) He had said that love was the greatest of all virtues. He was not the first or the last to say that, but never before had anyone succeeded in actually living out that principle in such a clear and dramatic way. Others had managed to show great love for those commonly known as friends, but there upon his cross Jesus revealed a quality of love which could embrace both friend and foe alike. He could say, as his enemies were driving nails in his hands, "Father, forgive them, for they know not what they do."

(b) It takes a more-than-ordinary degree of love to even be kind to those who wrong us or say unkind and false things about us, and it is a characteristic of many people like ourselves to consider it quite magnanimous not to retaliate by erasing the names of these folk from our Christmas list or refusing to go to a social gathering where these folk are likely to be present or in some other way breaking off all relationships with them. If anyone should really harm us, we would have the law on them before nightfall.

(c) We say, "Yes, we have faith in the cross because whenever we look at it our own petty grievances seem as nothing." The cross inspires us to love as Jesus loved and to love enough to forgive those who are not really deserving of forgiveness but to whom God expects us to extend this blessing because he is continually forgiving us.

III. The cross wins our faith because it inspires us to do our best to be like Jesus.

(a) It is unlikely that anyone would look forward to experiencing a death like his. We know that he did not relish the idea. In Gethsemane he sought to make sure that this was the only way to fulfill the divine purpose.

(b) There are few really conscientious people who do not wish down deep in their hearts that they could live so completely the quality of life God wants them to live that they could find the inner strength to stand by those ideals no matter what the price.

(c) The cross which we are asked to take up may not require death. (1) It may ask, as his cross asked of him, that we be true to the trust imposed in us and that we speak for God no matter how much it may cost us in terms of friendship or prestige. (2) It may mean that we leave some of our cherished ways and follow the way of self-sacrifice which finds us pioneering on new trails.

(3) It may require that we say in the face of criticism and scorn, "I choose Christ."

(d) Because of the mysterious drawing power of the cross, we find it possible to do these difficult things and live the Christlike life. When a cross can help us at these vital points of human experience, we can say with conviction, "I have faith in the cross."—Homer J. R. Elford.

Illustrations

THE EYES OF CHRIST. I cannot and I dare not picture a great assize nor realize the form it might take, but I have my vision and it has its own fear. It is not the fear of a flaming hell. It is the fear of the eyes of Christ, and by the splendor of those eyes, I plead with myself and with you that we live our lives in the fear and in the love of God, meeting our challenges, small and great, not in our weakness but in his strength, remembering always his last words to us on earth, "Lo, I am with you always."—G. A. Studdert-Kennedy.

MINISTERING WOMEN. 'Twas a woman washed Christ's feet with tears and a woman that anointed his body to the burial. They were women that wept when he was going to the cross and women that followed him from the cross and that stayed by his sepulchre when he was buried. They were women that were first with him at his ressurrection morn and women that brought tidings first to his disciples that he was risen from the dead. Women therefore are highly favored and show by these things that they are sharers with us in the grace of life.—John Bunyan in *Pilgrim's Progress.*

Sermon Suggestions

WHY DID JESUS DIE? Text: II Cor. 5: 14–15. (1) Why did they get him put to death? (2) Why did Jesus himself choose to die? (3) What was the meaning of the death of Jesus in the eternal purpose of God?—Donald M. Baillie.

THE THINGS CHRIST TAKES. Consider the resourcefulness of Jesus and what he does with what he takes. (1) He took the loaves in Luke 9:16. (2) He took a little child in Mark 9:36. (3) He took a towel in John 13:4. (4) He took the cup in Matt. 26:27.—Christine McMillan.

Worship Aids

CALL TO WORSHIP. "Worthy is the Lamb that was slain to receive power, and riches, and wisdom, and strength, and honor, and glory, and blessing." Rev. 5: 12.

INVOCATION. Out of our darkness we are come to thee for light; out of our sorrows we are come to thee for joy; out of our doubts we are come to thee for certainty; out of our anxieties we are come to thee for peace; out of our sinning we are come to thee for thy forgiving love. Open thou thine hand this day and satisfy our every need. This we ask for thy love's sake.

OFFERTORY SENTENCE. "For ye know the grace of our Lord Jesus Christ, that though he was rich, yet for your sakes he became poor, that ye through his poverty might be rich." II Cor. 8:9.

OFFERTORY PRAYER. O God, in whose sight a contrite heart is more than whole burnt offerings: help us with these our gifts to dedicate ourselves, body, soul, and spirit, unto thee, which is our reasonable service.

LITANY OF THE CROSS. O God of grace and glory, we acknowledge before thee our unpayable indebtedness; we are the children of sacrifice; our choicest benedictions have been bought with the price of other blood and tears than our own; thou hast given us the inheritance of them that feared thy name:

O Lord, make us thankful.

For all saints and martyrs, prophets and apostles; for all soldiers of the common good who served thee in scorn of consequence and fell on sleep unashamed, of whom the world was not worthy:

O Lord, make us thankful.

For the cross of Christ and his exceeding bitter sacrifice; for the truths which there were brought to light; the love unbounded which there was freely given, and the costly salvation which there visited thy people:

O Lord, make us thankful.

By his loneliness in the garden; by his betrayal and his trial; by the humiliation of his people's hate, the mockery of his thorny crown, and the bitterness of scourging; by the anguish of his cross; by his unfailing faith in thee and love for man:

O Lord, make us thankful.

Eternal God, may we, who owe our spiritual blessings to so great a cloud of witnesses who have suffered before us and to Christ whose cross is our peace, walk as becomes those who are debtors to thy grace. From ingratitude, pride, hardness of heart, and all manner of evil requiting:

Good Lord, deliver us.

From neglect of blessings dearly purchased; from selfish use of opportunities for which good men died; from growing within our hearts the venomous roots of covetousness; from pampering ourselves with vain superfluities; and from all spendthrift wasting of our costly heritage:

Good Lord, deliver us.

Gird us, we beseech thee, with gratitude and fidelity; devote us to the service of mankind with more courageous zeal; free us from the detaining reluctance of our fear, selfishness, and unbelief; and at this altar of remembrance, may we, O Christ, join afresh the honorable company of thy true servants who in sacrificial living share the fellowship of the cross:

Lord, have mercy upon us and grant us this blessing. —Harry Emerson Fosdick.

EVENING SERVICE

Topic: The Cross and the Crown
SCRIPTURE: I Pet. 5:6–11.

Following Jesus involves taking up our cross and bearing much tribulation. While these are a part of the school of faith, they still mean burdens, grief, and pain in our lives. Crosses often severely shake and test faith. Peter advises us how to bear up under our testing and still confidently look for the crown despite the cross.

I. We must humbly submit to the Lord's powerful, guiding hand (v. 6). (a) This is extremely difficult for us to do.

(1) Our sinful ego resists all submission, especially if it means discomfort and inconvenience.

(2) In our quick-cure society we are taught to seek and expect speedy relief from pain and trouble.

(b) Only God and his word can work surrender in us. (1) He gives us his promise that he only seeks our good. (See Jer. 29:1; Rom. 8:28.)

(2) He reveals his power and faithfulness to us.

(c) Burdens, pain, depression, turmoil, disappointment, and grief are all realities in the lives of Christians. Only under the Holy Spirit can humble submission open the way for God's will to be done in our lives.

II. For strength we must depend on the Father's care and grace (vv. 7, 10).

(a) How tremendous is the fact that he cares about us. (1) His grace to sinners is revealed in all that Christ is and does.

(2) It comes to each of us personally as he calls us to faith and to share in his eternal glory. (See Eph. 1:3–12.)

(b) We can confidently look to God for strength and help. (1) Life is filled enough with pressing, straining anxieties.

(2) He urges us to throw our anxieties onto the broad shoulders of his loving care. (See Ps. 37:5; Heb. 13:5–6.)

(3) He promises to supply what it takes to hold our lives together and keep us on a solid footing as we follow his leading through whatever sufferings come to us.

(c) The ifs of daily life that threaten us with sleepless nights or worse come when we bear our crosses alone. We take heart in his promises and are comforted by his presence now and the certainty of his glory hereafter.

III. We must be on constant guard against the devil (vv. 8–9). (a) Satan's goal is to rob us of the gifts of God's grace.

(1) We must remember that this enemy is very real, contrary to modern thought (cf., cults, etc.).

(2) We are most vulnerable to his soul-blinding lies when our hearts are heavy and our eyes filled with tears.

(b) Peter describes well what our defense must be. (1) We must be on guard so that the devil never gets a toehold in our lives.

(2) Resist the enemy with the weapons of our faith. (See Eph. 6:10, 18.)

(3) Remember the commonality of Christian experience in suffering the burdens and problems of life.

(c) Victory over the crosses that the Lord allows to come to us can be had only in his power and grace. We can never praise him enough in return.—Edwin H. Dubberke.

SUNDAY: APRIL FOURTH

MORNING SERVICE

Topic: **Arms Around the City (Palm Sunday)**

TEXT: Luke 19:41.

Jesus entered Jerusalem knowing the risk and the probability that he would die, but he didn't go into the city to die. He went in a final attempt to save the people, which is what the word "hosanna" really means. He was willing to face immense destructive power because he wanted to save the people and because he wanted to throw his arms around the people of Jerusalem. Given the probability of his death, what was this figurative and literal throwing of arms around the people supposed to accomplish?

I. In the face of the cross, Jesus throws his arms around the people to give them comfort.

(a) Sometimes putting your arms around people is what they need most. In the group that greeted Jesus in Jerusalem that day some needed comfort. A woman with her baby—the two of them alone, a helpless infant, a single parent; another rich young man looking for some fusion of his being and his frantic doing; those beside themselves with worry and grief; young and old not sure of their identities; those wearing masks and afraid of what's behind. Sometimes the most important thing that you can do is to encircle a person with your arms.

(b) Jesus was willing to face the cross so he could gather the people in—all the broken bits and pieces. He threw his arms around them all in an integrating love. So

many forces then and now in the city split the nuclear person in a kind of personal nuclear fission. The overflowing love of Jesus brings wholeness, a unity of body, mind, and spirit.

II. In spite of the cross, Jesus throws his arms around the people to give them courage.

(a) Jesus gives us the courage to stand for something good and true and helpful to people. In the immediate moments after the death of Martin, Coretta King wrote that as she groped for meaning she realized that he had been killed during the week leading up to Passion Week. It was somewhat strange, she wrote, yet reassuring that this death would come so close to that of his Lord and Master. For Martin had felt a mystical identity with the spirit and meaning of Christ's passion. The arms of Jesus around him gave King the courage to pick up his own cross.

(b) Jesus gives us courage to obey, courage to discipline, courage to sacrifice, courage to be unpopular, courage even at times to be called unchristian, courage to be in the minority, courage to buck the system, courage in illness, courage in adversity, courage in prosperity when it's hardest to have courage, courage in the face of overwhelming negative power, and courage in the face of our own deaths. He gives us courage to ride into our own Jerusalems and courage to pick up our own crosses.

III. Jesus in the shadow of the cross throws his arms around the people to give them challenge.

(a) If Jesus encircles those who need

comfort with gentle arms and those who need courage with strong and sustaining arms, for the self-satisfied, the dogmatic, and the secure, his arms become the tough, loving arms of challenging love, propelling them and flinging them back into new ways of seeing, being, and doing.

(b) Join the parade, Jesus says, that makes you fully human. Get out of the middle of the road blocking traffic in the present age of the kingdom. Drop your defensive, secure, dogmatic, and petty postures. Examine your aims, your spirit, your claims, and your names. Get out there in the flow of traffic. Reverse your priorities so that people are more important than machines and so that peace is more important than profit and commitment even to the cross more important than security.—James M. Dodson.

Illustrations

TURNING.   In the early church you were baptized at Easter, just as dawn was breaking or rather, in a sense, as it was beginning to dawn on you. The bishop asked you before you underwent baptism, "Do you turn to Christ?" You answered not in words but by turning round from facing the dusk of the west to facing the light of the sky in the east.—Michael Marshall.

CHURCH IN THE TURMOIL.   Hundreds of years ago, so the story goes, a pope commissioned an artist to do a painting which would show the church living and working in the world. After months of hard work, the artist came before the pope and proudly unveiled his masterpiece. The painting showed a wild sea with ships sinking amid angry waves and scattered people struggling in the stormy waters. In the middle of the painting was a calm and peaceful area where the sun was shining on smooth water. There a ship sat quietly, and sitting in it were the pope and his cardinals. The pope frowned in dismay. "Your artistry is excellent," he told the painter, "but this is not a true picture of the church of Jesus Christ."

The church is not an untroubled island in the middle of a troubled sea. The church is in the middle of the world's turmoil, but the church is always going through ups and downs, as if on waves. The church is forever struggling amid that turmoil as it tries to shape the kingdom of God in the world.—Gordon Dalbey in *A.D.*

Sermon Suggestions

IDENTIFYING WITH THE CROSS.   Text: I Cor. 1:23. If you want to know what the cross means to you, then identify with the personalities of Christ's passion. (1) If you identify with the establishment, you can see how disturbing Jesus is to the status quo. (2) If you identify with the women, you see that following Jesus means that you go with him all the way. (3) If you identify with Peter and the disciples, you see that those who love him dearest may be the first to leave him. (4) If you identify with Barabbas, you see that when he says he dies for you he really means it. (5) If you identify with Simon of Cyrene, you learn that if you get too close to Jesus you may carry his cross.—Mark Trotter.

WHAT HIS CRITICS SAID.   Text: I Cor. 15:25. (1) "Never man spake like this man" (John 7:46). (2) "Behold, the world is gone after him" (John 12:19). (3) "Is not this the carpenter?" (Mark 6:3). (4) "He saved others; himself he cannot save" (Matt. 27:42). (5) "Then said the Jews, Behold how he loved him" (John 11:36). (6) "This is Jesus the king of the Jews" (Matt. 27:37). (7) "He made himself the Son of God" (John 19:7).—Charles L. Allen.

Worship Aids

CALL TO WORSHIP.   "Lift up your heads, O ye gates; even lift them up, ye everlasting doors; and the King of glory shall come in. Who is this King of glory? The Lord of hosts, he is the King of glory." Ps. 24:9–10.

INVOCATION.   Our Father, thou who wast received amid the shouts of an earlier day, open our hearts and journey into our inward parts. Help us to lay aside all prejudices, forsake all sins, and overcome all biddings that might bar thy entrance. Let thy entrance into our hearts be triumphant. Conquer our fears, silence our unbelief, and quicken our faith. Lead us through thy Spirit to spiritual victory and conquest.

OFFERTORY SENTENCE. "And whatsoever ye do in word and deed, do all in the name of the Lord Jesus, giving thanks to God and the Father by him." Col. 3:17.

OFFERTORY PRAYER. As thy faithful disciples blessed thy coming, O Christ, and spread their garments in the way, covering it with palm branches, may we be ready to lay at thy feet all that we have and are, and to bless thee, O thou who comest in the name of the Lord.

MAUNDY THURSDAY PRAYER. Our Lord, our heavenly Father, we thy humble servants desire thy fatherly goodness mercifully to accept this our sacrifice of praise and thanksgiving, most humbly beseeching thee to grant that, by the merits and death of thy Son Jesus Christ and through faith in his blood, we and thy whole church may obtain forgiveness of our sins and all other benefits of his passion.

And here we offer and present unto thee, O Lord, ourselves, our souls and bodies, to be a reasonable, holy, and lively sacrifice unto thee, humbly beseeching thee that all who are partakers of this Holy Communion may be filled with thy grace and heavenly benediction.

And although we be unworthy through our manifold sins to offer unto thee any sacrifice, yet we beseech thee to accept this our bounden duty and service, not weighing our merits but pardoning our offenses.

EVENING SERVICE

Topic: Christ Enters Jerusalem
TEXT: Luke 19:37.

The entry of Jesus into the city of Jerusalem on the first day of the week of his crucifixion—the triumphal entry—is one of seven entries that are recorded in the New Testament.

I. Some time after the child was circumcised and named Jesus, he was taken up to Jerusalem to be presented to the Lord in keeping with the law of Moses. On this occasion the devout Simeon took Jesus into his arms and spoke of his future. The aged prophetess Anna was also present.

II. That same chapter tells of his journey into the city at passover time when he was twelve years of age. During this visit he astonished and disturbed his parents by disappearing from the group and amazed those who heard him during his conversation with the teachers in the temple. Following this experience in the city, he returned to Nazareth, was obedient to his parents, and "increased in wisdom and in stature, and in favor with God and man."

III. The third visit to the holy city is recorded in the gospel of John. This gospel places the cleansing of the temple during this visit. On this occasion, apparently, Jesus was visited by Nicodemus at night. Jesus talks about being born of the Spirit, and here is the familiar verse beginning, "For God so loved the world—"

IV. John 5 tells of the fourth visit to the city. On this occasion Jesus healed the man by the pool of Bethsaida and entered into quite a long discussion with his adversaries.

V. The feast of tabernacles was the occasion of the next entry into the city and is recorded in John 17. At this time Jesus went up privately after indicating to his brothers that he would not go at all. About the middle of the feast he went into the temple and taught. And on the last day of the feast, the great day, he stood up and proclaimed: "If anyone thirst, let him come to me and drink. He who believes on me—out of his heart shall flow rivers of living water." This he said referring to the Spirit, which was not yet given because Jesus was not yet glorified.

VI. The sixth entry occurred at the feast of dedication which was in winter. This is recorded in John 10. As in every other instance, Jesus was in the temple. There were those who took up stones to stone him and later tried to arrest him, but he escaped out of their hands.

VII. The final triumphal entry, recorded

in all four gospels, is the only one mentioned in Matthew and Mark.

(a) Immediately after the narrative of the good confession by Peter, we read, "From that time Jesus began to show his disciples that he must go up to Jerusalem, suffer many things, and be killed." After certain events on the journey, the story of the ride into the city is told in eleven verses in Matthew and in ten verses in Mark.

(b) The case is different in Luke. Here the story of this journey to Jerusalem forms a kind of background for a large part of the account. It begins with Luke 9:51: "When the days drew near for him to be received up, he set his face to go to Jerusalem." The Samaritans, through whose country he was traveling, would not receive him "because his face was set toward Jerusalem."—Alan C. Lynch.

SUNDAY: APRIL ELEVENTH

MORNING SERVICE

Topic: The Grave and the Garden (Easter)

TEXT: John 19:41.

The real question of Easter is to rediscover for ourselves what made the disciples glad. You can put it down they were not glad at first. Most of the disciples through most of that dismal day were the most miserable of men. But little by little through confusing, conflicting rumors the truth broke through. Then were the disciples glad. Years later an old man wrote down something that seemed to catch the whole meaning in a sentence: "The grave was in a garden." It seemed to proclaim the victory of God which is what the whole New Testament is about. The place of death opened into the place of life. As we look back in the retrospect of history, some things that made the disciples glad become amazingly clear.

I. *The victory of truth over treachery.* (a) This was the most powerful effect of the resurrection upon the disciples, the restoration of their confidence in the rationality and moral integrity of life, far more important to them than assurance of immortality. What really shook them in the crucifixion was the terrible fear that nothing in the world made sense. They had followed a delusion. They had guessed wrong. Underlying everything Jesus had taught them was his sureness of God, his unwavering certainty that in God's world truth was invincible.

(b) Then suddenly God had let him down. He had relied on truth, and it had failed him. A life like his snuffed out by lies, a bit of political treachery, and a piece of savage brutality. That's what really floored them. It floors us too. It's the problem that's ever with us, the problem of the world's evil and the goodness of God. How often it seems that the best in life is at the mercy of the worst.

(c) See then how timely and timeless is the Easter message, how much it is woven into the stuff of our minds and bound up with the hopes of all good men in every age across the earth. How much we need always to remember that the grave was in a garden, that the final word is not with dying things but with living things, that truth crushed to earth will rise again, that it's not frail or fragile or helpless but tough, deathless, and utterly indestructible.

II. *The victory of triumph over tragedy.* (a) What an amazing paradox it is that so great a tragedy as the cross should turn out to be a victory, that what seemed to be a denial of God become a revelation of God, and that he could take this terrible thing and make it the very instrument of redemption. Where in all your philosophies can you find anything to match the Christian answer to the tragic element in life?

(b) The world has many philosophies about the meaning of tragedy and sorrow, but no one answered back to the deep need in us as creatively and triumphantly as Christ. What we have in Christianity is not another explanation of suffering but a way of facing it to make it fruitful and turn its tragedy into a ministry.

III. *The victory of life eternal.* The grave was in a garden. Life there was stronger than the force of death.

(a) Most of us don't like to think of death. We shove it out of our minds, keep it at arm's length, and speak of it in muffled tones. But not to think of death is not very smart because we all have a date with it somewhere, sometime, and every day we walk through life one step, one pulse beat away from it.

(b) The fear of death, the dread of extinction which is one of man's oldest and deepest fears, has a certain purposeful quality in it. If we did not fear it and fight it and if we had no dread of it for ourselves, our children, and our loved ones, this planet long ago would have been depopulated. We would take no steps to safeguard life and preserve it. There's something in the universe powerfully concerned about keeping life going, and the fear of death is part of that something.

(c) The grave was in a garden. Life there was stronger than death, and from there on in the New Testament there is no misgiving any more.—J. Wallace Hamilton.

Illustrations

NOT YET A CROWN.   Easter will always be a day of high drama, of rolling anthems, and of mighty throngs gathered to praise his name. And so it ought to be. But we must hold our crowns for a while. The Christ is not where the glad hallelujahs are ringing. He is on the Emmaus Road. He is looking for a Zacchaeus or a Matthew or a Mary Magdalene. He is still gazing upon the multitudes with compassion in his heart. He is by our beds of pain. He is where death has come—busy opening the door to the place prepared for those who love him. He is still walking the Emmaus Road—a road that runs through your heart and mind, a road that does not stop until it reaches the gates of eternity. And then, perhaps, he will pause and let us crown him King of kings and Lord of lords.—Ernest Lee Stoffel.

BOLD CLAIM.   In the year 500, Clovis I, king of the Frankish Empire, was converted to Christianity. The first time he heard the story of the crucifixion of Jesus, he was intensely moved by it. He jumped to his feet, unsheathed his sword, and shouted, "If I and my Franks had been there, they never would have done that to him."

Sermon Suggestion

WHEN DAWN COMES.   Text: Matt. 28:1. What are the qualities of dawn that clarify to us the meaning and mission of Jesus? (1) The dawn marks the beginning of something new. (2) The dawn is the most silent force in nature. (3) The dawn is the most irresistible force in nature.—Joseph R. Sizoo.

Worship Aids

CALL TO WORSHIP.   "God hath exalted him, and given him a name which is above every name: that at the name of Jesus every name should bow, of things in heaven, and things in earth, and things under the earth; and that every tongue should confess that Jesus Christ is Lord, to the glory of God the Father." Phil. 2: 9–11.

INVOCATION.   O God, we thank you this Easter morning for the eternal beauty and everlasting power of the resurrection of Jesus. We pray that these days shall see our Christ emerging from the tomb in which our generation has placed him—a tomb which we have closed with the stone of our selfishness and sealed with our hardness of mind and heart. Fill us this day with the spirit of reverence and humility because we are permitted to sing your praise. Help us to remember that we are your children living in your divine presence in our human lives. Make us faithful to duty and worthy of your love, through Jesus Christ our risen Lord.

OFFERTORY SENTENCE.   "It is good to give thanks to the Lord, to sing praises to thy name, O Most High; to declare thy steadfast love in the morning, and thy faithfulness by night." Ps. 92:1–2.

OFFERTORY PRAYER. Our Father, forgive our indifference and neglect, and help us to hear thy call to partnership with thee in making a new heaven and new earth.

PRAYER. Almighty God, whose Son, our Savior Jesus Christ, broke the seal of the tomb and came forth in glory, we laud and magnify thy holy name. Thou hast through thy Son conquered death. Thou hast given life to the sorrowing, and thou hast covered the despairing with light. All honor and glory to thee who hast shown this dark world that thou art life and light.

We pray that new life may come to our homes. We bemoan their lack of hope. There is no sign of Christ in our hearts. We are blinded by activity, earthly rewards, and temporal aspirations. Come into our homes, we beseech thee. Let us see the cross and then the empty tomb. We cannot stand hopeless before such glory. Let thy life so overpower us that we shall be changed.

We pray that new life may come to our churches. Dead customs prevail. Human reason, rather than thy spirit, sits enthroned. Only a few are brought to a knowledge of Christ. We honor tradition but not thy name. Thou who didst in Christ break forth from the tomb, break forth again. Revive thy church that it may be thy temple and a channel of redeeming love.

We pray that new life may come to our world—wounded, broken, disillusioned, and despairing. Lift up before the hungry peoples of the world the risen Christ on Easter Day. Let the empty tomb move us to pay homage. Enter into the hearts of men and let them see Christ as lord over death. Come, thou great deliverer, to our torn world and revive it by thy mighty power.

Thou who art the Lord, the risen Christ, come to us, show us the way and guide us by thy heavenly light.—Albert Buckner Coe.

EVENING SERVICE

Topic: The Easter Trumpet
TEXT: I Cor. 15:52.
I. The first Easter trumpet note is that of certainty. (See I Cor. 15:3–6.)

(a) There is no uncertain, quivering, wavering note in the apostle's certainty of the risen Lord. Paul's Easter faith is based upon innumerable living witnesses bearing unimpeachable testimony and upon his own spiritual encounter with the living Christ, which is the constant theme in all that he writes and preaches.

(b) It is the apostle's assertion that mankind's immortal hope of resurrection of the dead is bound up with the resurrection of Christ. Since he is the representative man, God's ideal for man, and the spiritual head of humanity, his resurrection does not stand by itself. Rather it is man's resurrection also. "Because I live, you shall live also."

II. The second Easter trumpet note the apostle sounds is cheer. (See I Cor. 15: 25–26, 56–57; John 16:33; Rev. 21:1–4.)

(a) Sin crucified Jesus. Sin is responsible for much of the trouble and tribulation and the sorrow, suffering, and separation in the world. Sin separates us from God and the good life, the eternal life and is the real death—not the separation of the soul from the body but the separation of the soul from God. Christ came to solve the sin problem, to make atonement for sin, to bear our sins in his own body upon the cross that "we might be dead to sin and alive to all that is good."

(b) The cross and the empty tomb symbolize the fact that the living Christ can liberate our lives from the enemies of sin and death. This is the good news of Easter. Set the trumpet to the lips and sound the note of cheer for Christ the conqueror is here.

III. Another Easter trumpet note which Paul sounds in this glorious symphony of the resurrection is comfort. (See I Cor. 15:49, 52–53, 55–56.) Perhaps the world today needs comfort as much as it needs censure. Meeting this very need, Christ says, "I will not leave you comfortless. I will come to you." It is a comfort to know that Christ lives, loves, cares, and comforts, that he is concerned about us as individuals, about you and me in our problems and perplexities, our burdens and our sorrows. "Come unto me" is his gracious invitation to all who are weary and

over-burdened, "and I will give you rest."
IV. Paul sounds the Easter trumpet note of challenge. (See I Cor. 15:58.) It makes a world of difference the way we live here as to whether or not we believe in a hereafter. Only as men have had their eyes on the far distant horizon of eternity have they lived life here at its fullest, noblest, and best, for they realize that life here is also lived with Christ who is the resurrection and the life and is directed toward the making and training of faithful souls, who through death pass into that vaster, ampler, freer, fuller, richer, larger, endless life for which all things here are but the preparation.—George Hunter Hall.

SUNDAY: APRIL EIGHTEENTH

MORNING SERVICE

Topic: Symbols of the Season
TEXT: Gal. 6:14.
I. Symbols are important. Often they say more than our words do about what concerns us most. The cross is such a symbol. So is the Easter bunny.

(a) If an observer from another planet chanced upon earth at Easter time, there is no doubt which of those two symbols he would find up front. The cross has never been very good for sales.

(b) We can't blame the secular world for making its kind of good thing out of Easter. What worries me is that Easter bunnies and daffodils and the like may symbolize more than they should about where it's at in the churches too.

II. Clearly the cross is at the center of our story. Paul says it is the very essence of the gospel.

(a) As the primary symbol of Christian belief it does not fit our actual view of the world. It goes against the grain not only of our liberal bourgeois optimism but also our Calvinist religious positivism.

(1) We can't very well ignore it. So we do something even more effective—we trivialize it. It becomes a sentimental illustration of how much God loves us.

(2) But love, divorced from the judgment, justice, and sense of the tragic which are in the biblical account, leaves our interpretation of the crucified Christ lacking all bite.

(b) The doctrinal device by which we remove the reality from Jesus' cross is our way of handling his resurrection. Unlike the original Christian community, whose experience of the risen Christ was such as to make them pay all the more attention to the cross at the center, our concept of resurrection has the effect of removing the cross from the center. It is replaced by daffodils, bunnies, and other pretty symbols.

III. It is understandable enough that we trivialize the meaning of the cross and displace it with something bright and beautiful. Especially in an age of "uncertainty" (Galbraith) and "diminishing expectations" (Christopher Lasch), people need to have something affirmative and unambiguous to hang on to. Who can afford not to sympathize with that? But it is wrong. For two reasons, basically.

(a) It removes the Christian gospel from the sphere of actual human experience and translates it into the realm of religious ideology and spiritual illusion.

(1) It appeals to the human need to win, but it loses touch with the losers. That means that it loses touch with all of us finally, for in the long run there are no human success stories. There are only varying degrees of failure.

(2) Christ's resurrection is no easy, trumpet-blaring declaration of the immediate triumph of the light. It is not a matter of nature (daffodils). It is a matter of sheer grace, perceived by faith not sight (Heb. 11:1). There is a victory but not the kind that could become an instant model for the Junior Chamber of Commerce.

(b) When we make Jesus' death and resurrection the stuff of a success story, we limit its credibility to those who "succeed."

(1) When a rich church smothers its fashionable chancel cross with daffodils, it is making a religious and socio-economic statement with which few of its own members would have any fundamental quarrel.

Indeed, they expect something like that. But both that message and that church are thereby restricted to those who have "succeeded" or who can at least hide for the moment their deeper sense of failing.

(2) Some Christians today wonder why our churches are so lacking in members from the poorer strata of society. The answer has to be traced finally to the sort of message we have been announcing in word and in deed.

(3) When, in the name of providing tranquility and confidence for the dominant social classes, we permit the gospel of the crucified to become an example of a success story, why should we expect to find in our churches oppressed classes and segments of our society who could hardly relate to such an example?—Douglas John Hall.

Illustrations

FACING TROUBLE.   A naval ship was torpedoed, and there were only a few minutes before the ship would go down. The officer saw a sailor on the deck with a broken leg. He moved over to lift the sailor into a lifeboat, but the sailor said: "Go and help those who are really hurt. I'm O.K. Besides, God is looking after me." The officer reflected that that was kind of funny. He said if God is looking after him, how come he's wounded? Then he said: "But I looked around and saw other Christians on that ship who were also wounded, and I noticed they weren't reacting with panic either. It was as if they knew also they were going to be all right." Then he said: "Over the years I've noticed the same thing. You can't tell if a person is a Christian by whether or not he has trouble. You can tell whether or not they are Christian by how they act when trouble comes."—Donald J. Shelby.

BASIC PRAYER.   When it comes to the end of the day, of course one wants to pray about those things that concern one, but I feel the basic prayer of all prayers is "Thy will be done." If we say that and utterly mean it, we have said really all that we can ask of God—that his will should be done

and that we should be vouchsafed sufficient enlightenment to understand and sufficient faith to fall in with that, however hurtful it might seem to our pride, or to our egotism or whatever. That is to me the basic prayer because it is after all in the prayer that our Lord gave us.—Malcolm Muggeridge in *Christian Herald.*

Sermon Suggestions

ANTICLIMACTIC   EXPERIENCES.   Text: John 21:3. (1) Anticlimactic experiences usually are signs of victory and not defeat. (2) Anticlimactic experiences produce, perhaps as nothing else can, a climate conducive to the strengthening of our lives. (3) Anticlimactic experiences remind us that the joys in life come as we strive to reach our goals.—Bob H. Adams.

THE JOYS OF THE HUMBLE.   Text: Matt. 5:3. (1) The inner joy of being at peace with ourselves. (2) The joy that comes from satisfying human relationships. (3) The joy of fellowship with God.—Edward W. Stimson.

Worship Aids

CALL TO WORSHIP.   "Blessed be the God and Father of our Lord Jesus Christ, which according to his abundant mercy hath begotten us again unto a lively hope by the resurrection of Jesus Christ from the dead, to an inheritance incorruptible, and undefiled, and that fadeth not away, reserved in heaven for you." I Pet. 1:3–4.

INVOCATION.   Father God, we come to this place to ask for a new vision of your presence and a resurrected spirit of life within history and beyond history. We come as humble pilgrims, none of us possessing all faith and knowledge but all of us seeking your truth as it lives in our midst. Be with us now, we pray, that we may be aware of you in a special way and, being thus aware, that as we live in the world we may be aflame with your joy.

OFFERTORY SENTENCE.   "Verily I say unto you, inasmuch as ye have done it unto one of the least of these my brethren, ye have done it unto me." Matt. 25:40.

OFFERTORY PRAYER. We praise thee, O God, for thy countless blessings and pray that thou wilt accept these gifts in gratitude in Jesus' name.

PRAYER. Lord of life, whose glory could not be stifled even by death, live in us this day, we pray, with new power. Live in our personal lives to resurrect us to new devotion and service; live in our family life to bring your joy into our homes; live in our relationships with others to make meaning and love prevail for us and for others; live in our community life that your goodness may inspire us to bring health and bread to all; live in the nations that your peace may reign and war may be no more. Lord of life, we need your resurrecting power in these days when the powers of death still threaten us so terribly. Give us faith that you are alive and present. Keep us in the hope that can free us from death's tyranny in this life and the life to come.—*These Days.*

EVENING SERVICE

Topic: We Love the Church
TEXT: Ps. 92:13.
I. Because we love the church, we give. Often unchurched people comment on the amount of money God's people give to his work. It is hard for them to understand the Christian's generosity. And it is even more difficult for them to understand how much joy the Christian receives in giving. Behind it all is a love for God, his church, and its great ministries.

II. Because we love the church, we faithfully attend services. Churchgoing people are sometimes accused by others of going to church too often. Some people think churchgoing people spend too much time participating in church activities. They seemingly are totally unaware of the great blessing the dedicated Christian receives in worshiping God, in fellowshiping with God's people, and in Christian service.

III. Because we love the church, we want to see it grow and prosper. Many times I have witnessed the joy pastors and church members experience when they note church growth—new converts, increased attendance, greater interest, and increased finances. I have also witnessed the deep concern pastors and church members have when their church is not growing. Because they love their church, they care about its growth.

IV. Because we love the church, we want to keep our church facilities looking as attractive as we can. Very often pastors and members work hard to improve the appearance of their church. Because they love their church, they are willing to take time from obligations in their home to beautify their church building. They rightly feel that their church must make a favorable impression upon the community. They know that few people will come to an uncared-for or poorly-cared-for church.

V. Because we love the church, we want to represent it well. We must be concerned with what our church represents. Because we love the church, we want to represent it well in our home, in our neighborhood, on the job, at school, and wherever else we may be.—O. W. Polen.

SUNDAY: APRIL TWENTY-FIFTH

MORNING SERVICE

Topic: The Christian Hope
TEXT: John 11:25–26.
I. We are sure that there is an eternal life. The confidence of Jesus in life eternal is one great assurance of our faith.

(a) In religious matters the supreme rev-

elation of God is the life and teachings of Jesus. When he said, "I go to prepare a place for you, that where I am there you may be also" (John 14:3), he proclaimed the reality of the eternal. If the God whom Jesus revealed were to desert men in their final extremity, he would be no God at all.

(b) If the teaching of Jesus concerning

the Christian hope had become a series of proverbial sayings or philosophic propositions, we would study his thoughts, but we would not claim it as a foundation for our faith.

(1) The teaching carries conviction because it was incarnate in a life. That life was of such quality and character that it could not and did not end in the rockhewn tomb. Jesus, who lived among men, did not remain in that place of death but rose again.

(2) This we believe because of the Bible record, because of the church built upon this fact, and because we have met the living Christ in personal devotion, noble action, and group worship.

II. We cherish the Christian hope because of the existence and vitality of the church. The resurrection gave meaning and power to the first Christian fellowship and can give it to the churches today.

(a) Central to the thought of the New Testament is the phrase, "That I might know him and the power of his resurrection" (Phil. 3:10). Power? Think of the scene on Friday when from his side the nearest fled and death was close in sight. Almost everyone was filled with disillusionment and despair. Only a weary few were left to pay their last respects to the leader who was gone.

(b) Then something happened. From sorrow came joy. From despair came startling hope. From utter disillusionment came great expectation. From helplessness came heroism. Eleven despondent men became the heralds of a new era in the world's history.

III. The Christian hope is that death and frustration are overcome when we live in Christ. Death is the extinction of the body. Frustration is the defeat of the spirit. Both are surmounted by the victory of Christ.

(a) Death becomes an episode by which we are released from the bondage to the present physical body. To the Christian it is a gateway through which the soul of man passes into a nobler life unfettered by the things of earth.

(b) Frustration is overcome by confidence in God's eternal care. Sin, sorrow, and weakness are finally defeated. We do

not fully believe in that which is good until we believe that right is might and will triumph in the end.

(c) We speak of this existence as heaven. This is a symbolic name for our future life, the nature of which we can only surmise from our experience in this present world. If we follow the teaching of Jesus, heaven is that eternal condition of spiritual life in which sin is finally overcome and in which fellowship with God and others leads us into an ever richer and fuller life.

IV. The Christian hope is a hope of fellowship. The ultimate goal of the Christian faith is a fellowship of living personal spirits in which all the sins of society are overcome. It is the hope of a world made perfect.

(a) The source of this confidence lies in our personal experience of fellowship with God and in our experience of fellowship with other Christians in the church. A perfect church on earth would be a foretaste of the perfect society in heaven.

(b) In view of the present continuing state of human society, our belief in God's ability to reconstruct the society of men is childish without belief in the perfect society of the future.—A. Ray Adams.

Illustration

BREATH OF GOD. A Bedouin guide was leading a traveler over a mountain pass. They had spent the night in an oasis in the valley now far below and behind them. As he stopped his camel, he paused for a long moment and then looked ahead at the seemingly endless miles of sand that awaited them. Inhaling deeply the pure, dry, clean wind of the desert, he said: "Can you still smell the fragrance of the orchards behind us? Its headiness is that of wine and its warmth a woman's. But do you now smell the wind of the wilderness? It is the breath of God."—Jerry Hayner.

Sermon Suggestions

SPEAKING FROM THE HEART. Text: Prov. 4:20–24. (1) Let us learn to speak from our hearts our regrets. (2) Let us learn to speak from our hearts our joys, our praise, and our love. (3) Let us learn to speak from our hearts our faith.—Winfield S. Haycock.

RELEASE FROM ANXIETY. Text: Phil. 4: 6–7 (MOFFATT). (1) Prayer achieves release from anxiety by setting things in true perspective. (2) Prayer achieves release from anxiety by bringing our will into line with God's will. (3) Prayer achieves release from anxiety by liberating within us new resources of power for handling the difficult business of living.—James S. Stewart.

Worship Aids

CALL TO WORSHIP. "Know therefore that the Lord thy God, he is God, the faithful God, which keepeth covenant and mercy with them that love him and keep his commandments to a thousand generations." Deut. 7:9.

INVOCATION. Almighty and everlasting God, who givest to all who desire it the spirit of grace and supplication, deliver us, O Lord, from all coldness of heart, from all indifferent wandering of the mind, that we may fix our affection upon thee and upon thy service. Fill us with holy, peaceful, and beautiful thoughts, that with steadfast minds and kindled affection we may worship thee in spirit and in truth.

OFFERTORY SENTENCE. "Every man shall give as he is able, according to the blessing of the Lord thy God which he hath given thee." Deut. 16:17.

OFFERTORY PRAYER. Dear God, help us to become unobstructed channels that thy love may flow through us to others and our gifts may be used for the proclamation to all men of thy saving goodness.

PRAYER. Our Father, we know heaven and earth cannot contain you, much less this house which we have built. Nevertheless, what neither contains nor restrains you helps us to collect and direct us. And we are thankful for this inspiration of your church and for this tangible emblem of your everyday presence in our lives.

We respond to the invitation of rest extended here to our human weariness and to the songs of joy we sing that always enliven and enrich our own celebrations. We are grateful for the assurance of strength you give to match our many burdens and for the promise of peace to meet us, even in the midst of our need of hurt, because you care.

These moments shared together truly represent more, our Father, than we can express or comprehend. You enrich our living and restore our souls. Yet we are ever humbled here by the inescapable images of the cross in word and pew and altar, which remind us life is not lived finally in sanctuary but in service. So now, even as we have come to find rest for our burdens, ease of our hurt, and your touch upon every expression of our own needs, help us most of all to become responsive to the truth of him who said to us, "Life is more than meat, the body more than raiment." Where we have heard too well the stirrings of our own discontent, help us attune our thoughts to the unrest and illease around us. Where we have learned too well the lesson of asking out of our own desires, grant that we may learn more fully both the joy and the responsibility of answering one another's needs. For we pray in the name and power of him whose most earnest requests brought more blessings of comfort and relief to others than to himself.—Paul E. VanDine.

EVENING SERVICE

Topic: Witnessing Without Words
SCRIPTURE: Matt. 11:2–5.
I. By our conversation: "What you hear" (vv. 4–5). (a) Jesus directs John's followers to report to him what they hear. They are to listen to his words, his teaching, and his preaching. They are to listen as he preaches the gospel to the poor.
(b) The unchurched today are not hearing what we say to them about Jesus. They are eavesdropping as we talk to each other in our daily conversations. What we say and how we say it to others reveals the quality of our characters. Jesus taught, "Out of the heart the mouth speaks." Our

speech betrays the kind of persons we are.

(c) Consider some of the qualities of our daily talking that would win the non-Christian.

(1) Trustworthy speech. "My word is my bond." Promises are kept. "A man is as good as his word."

(2) True speech. A Christian speaks the truth at all times. He is honest and factual. You will hear him speak no lies, rumors, or gossip.

(3) Pure speech. The Christian will allow only clean words and stories to come from his mouth. There will be no dirty jokes nor expletives.

(4) Kind speech. The Christian will be heard speaking only good about people, not harsh criticism or judgment. He will put the most charitable construction on his neighbor's actions.

(d) In describing the life of early Christians, Adolph von Harnach wrote, "The new language of the Christians was the language of love in power and act."

II. By our conduct: "What you see" (vv. 4–5). (a) Here is the true test of a Christian and the most effective witness of a Christian. The world may not listen to our talk about Jesus, but they look at our lives. The style of life, the manner of daily living, is what ultimately wins people. Jesus used this method with John the Baptist— "Go and tell him what you see." We need to ask ourselves: "Does the world see Jesus in us? Are we living as Jesus lived?"

(b) Look at the works of mercy and service of Jesus in our text. The blind receive sight, the lame walk, lepers are cleansed, the deaf hear, and the dead come alive. Who could do things like these except the messiah? This work of service reveals Jesus' divine power to heal and Jesus' love that motivated him to help.

(c) Look at the works of Christians today —deeds of service to the poor, handicapped, and oppressed and deeds of love by a people who care and are friendly to strangers.

III. There are times when you can't say a word about Jesus, but you can always witness with your life. Eventually this will create a desire on the part of the non-Christian to find the secret of your beautiful life. Then he will listen to you as you tell him that Jesus is the Christ.—John R. Brokhoff.

SUNDAY: MAY SECOND

MORNING SERVICE

Topic: A Caring Christian Community
Scripture: I Pet. 4:7–11.

We who know God's forgiving and powerful love in Christ are called the church. As we worship and work together, we constitute a Christian community. Our text shows us how we can be a caring Christian community.

I. A caring Christian community is strengthened by its Lord. (a) He leads us to anticipate our final salvation with him in heaven (v. 7).

(b) He strengthens us through our worship. (1) In worship we meet our Lord. We bring to him our sins, doubts, and anxieties. We receive from him his love, pardon, presence, and power.

(2) Our Christian community, the church, rightly emphasizes a word-and-sacrament ministry so that we can glorify God (v. 11) by caring about one another.

II. A caring Christian community is dominated by love. (a) Love shows itself in unselfish concern for the needs of others, perhaps at great cost to us.

(1) Loving those closest to us, other members of the Christian community (I Cor. 12:12).

(2) Loving continuously, even though this goes against the world's way (John 13:35; I Thess. 3:12).

(b) Love covers sin. (1) By refusing to major in the minor faults of others.

(2) By forgiving as we have been forgiven (Matt. 18:22).

III. A caring Christian community is earmarked by service. (a) The ability to serve is God-given.

(1) He gives that ability to every Christian.

(2) Christian service is directed to others, especially other Christians (v. 10).

(b) There are many kinds and opportunities for service. (1) In our daily speech we can share his love with others.

(2) In our daily activities we can reach out as caring Christians by showing Christian hospitality, helping to integrate new members into the congregation, and listening to someone else's problems and joys.

(c) God does not expect us Christians to solve magically the world's problems. Yet he will help us to make life more pleasant for others and for ourselves through our service in a caring Christian community.—Lloyd Strelow.

Illustrations

HEAVEN IN THE SOUL.   During World War II a ship was bombed at her dock in Holland. At the time her captain was in New York. His wife and son were in Rotterdam, which was in ruins, and he had received no word from them. One Sunday after attending worship in one of the New York churches, he stopped to talk to the minister and lapsed into a soliloquy and then into prayer. "God help me," he prayed. "Give your guidance to those who rule. Your kingdom come." His words struggled out slowly: "Watch over my wife and boy. Before they were mine they belonged to you. They are in your hands. Your will be done." Then more slowly still, as if each word were being pulled out of his heart by the roots: "I pray for Hitler. He has great power over the lives of men. Guide him. Help me not to hate him. And help me to mean that, O God. Amen." This is something of the grandeur that comes to a life when heaven gets into the soul.—John Thompson.

SPECTATOR.   Elie Wiesel in *The Town Beyond the Wall* tells of a Holocaust survivor who, several years after the war, is obsessed with the need to return to the small village in Hungary where he had grown up and where, at the age of fourteen, he had been herded one morning, along with all the other Jews, into the village square,

then into box cars for the tortuous trip to the concentration camp. He doesn't know why he feels he must return, but he cannot rest until he has done so.

When at last he stands once again in that village square, he suddenly remembers why he had to come back. On that morning, so long ago, he had glanced up and had seen a face in a window. It was an impassive face, devoid of any emotion, of any caring, of any involvement in the tragic events which were taking place just below. It was the face of the Spectator.

Turning now, he looks up again, and the face is still there.

This the author and the character in his book simply cannot comprehend. To stand in the presence of evil and not to care, to have one's eyes fall on cruelty and inhumanity and not to cry out, to see suffering and remain aloof and uninvolved—this Wiesel cannot understand. Here is how he puts it: "How could one remain indifferent? The executioner I understood. The victims I understood, but with more difficulty. But those others, all those others, who were neither for nor against; who sprawled in passive patience; those who said the storm would blow over and all would be normal again; those who thought themselves above the battle; those who were permanently merely spectators. How can one remain a spectator indefinitely?"—Craig Biddle III.

Sermon Suggestions

THE CHURCH RENEWED AND RENEWING. Text: Matt. 16:18. What are the promising signs of renewal in the contemporary church? (1) The ecumenical spirit that has laid hold of the whole church. (2) The American church is beginning to listen to the world. (3) The church is beginning to be the servant of the Lord in the world.—George T. Peters.

ON BEING FULLY COMMITTED.   Text: Acts 20:24. (1) Commitment to Christ as lord. (2) Commitment to Christ's ministry within the church. (3) Commitment to Christ's ministry in our community. (4) Commitment to Christ's ministry throughout the world. (5) Total commitment to the ministry of Christ.—American Baptist Churches.

Worship Aids

CALL TO WORSHIP. "Sing unto the Lord, sing psalms unto him. Glory ye in his holy name; let the heart of them rejoice that seek the Lord." Ps. 105:2–3.

INVOCATION. As we begin another day, most gracious Father, make us to know that we never drift out of thy love and care. Faces may change and conditions may alter, but thou are never so near to us as when we need thee most.

OFFERTORY SENTENCE. "As we have therefore opportunity, let us do good unto all men, especially unto them who are of the household of faith." Gal. 6:10.

OFFERTORY PRAYER. We praise thee, O God, for thy countless blessings and pray that thou wilt accept these gifts in gratitude in Jesus' name.

COMMUNION PRAYER. Our heavenly father, it is with great and glad thanksgiving unto thee that we meet this hour in this holy place. Here spread before us, poor in spirit and weak in good works as we may be, is the table of thy blessed son, Jesus Christ. Its cleanliness reminds us of a purity of living that we wish were ours. Its simplicity makes us wish our lives were as uncluttered and neat. Its sturdiness bespeaks a strength we wish we felt day in and day out.

In spite of our unworthiness, our frailty, and our sin, thy table stands in our midst, ready and waiting. O Lord, break through our dullness, our shame, or our cockiness, and let us realize that thy presence is as real as this table which is spread before us. May thy message make its way into our consciousness by the persistent presence of the communion table throughout this service of worship. May it remind us of Jesus, who met with his friends at table, shared a meal with them, blessed the food and gave it to them—to all of them, even

to Judas who betrayed him, even to Thomas who doubted him, and even to Peter who failed to understand him—and told them to eat and to drink always in remembrance of him.

Take us, our Father, to the table of our Lord. Tenderly feed us, and then turn us to face once again the demands and opportunities of our daily lives with new faith and fervor.—Jeffrey S. Atwater.

EVENING SERVICE

Topic: Lord of the Home (National Family Week)

TEXT: John 10:10.

To be a Christian means to acknowledge Jesus as the lord of your life. How often we hear that general message and allow it to go right over our heads. Let me bring it down to a specific level. Compare your heart to a home. To make him lord is to invite Christ to dwell in your spiritual home.

I. He goes to the study. This is the control room, the brain where the thoughts are stored. If there is trash and evil and untruth, it has to go because he is lord of our thought life.

II. He goes to the dining room, the room of appetites and desires. If there is an inordinate desire for material things or a worship of money or a lust for pleasure, these have to go because he is lord of our appetites.

III. He goes to the family room. This is the area of interpersonal relationships within the home. If there are inadequacies in our relationships with our children and parents or if there is a lack of effort or commitment to our spouses, this has to be dealt with for he is lord of our family life.

IV. Jesus goes to the workshop. This is the area of creativity in our lives. This is where we use our gifts and talents. If he discovers an abuse of our body or misuse of our gifts or if he sees toys that are contrary to his purpose for our life, these have to go because he is the lord of our creativity.

V. He goes to the living room. This is the room of fellowship and leisure. This is the recreational area of our lives, the intimate area of personal development. If he is not included in this area of our life or if our leisure draws us away from God rather than drawing us to him, some changes will have to be made because he is lord of our inner self.

VI. He goes to the storeroom. It is full of secret sins and bad habits and personal prejudices that we have tried to hold on to. But these things have to go because Jesus is the lord of our personal habits.—Brian L. Harbour.

SUNDAY: MAY NINTH

MORNING SERVICE

Topic: He Took a Child (Mother's Day)
TEXT: Mark 9:36.

I. "He took a child." (a) One of my earliest memories is that of a large picture of Jesus blessing the little children. He has one on his lap, and other boys and girls stand around him. Looking at that picture, before we could read or write, we learned that Jesus is a child's friend. We learned the most wonderful lesson of all—God loves us and cares about us and we have worth even as children.

(b) Long before we were old enough to go to school, we learned to sing, "Jesus loves me, this I know; for the Bible tells me so." We learned about God's love for us and God's caring about us.

(c) Not only did Jesus take children in his arms and bless them, but on one occasion he took a little child and, placing it in the midst of the disciples used that youngster to teach a great truth about the nature of the kingdom of God. We must become as little children if we are to enter the kingdom.

II. Every child has a right to be loved and to be cared for. Not every child has that, but every child deserves affection. Every child has a right to nourishment and health care. Every child has a right to education and training which will equip him or her to live as a useful citizen. These are not privileges alone. Society has the responsibility to provide them. They are the rights of children. We need to focus our concerns.

III. To say that we're to communicate love and worth does not mean that we are to be permissive with our children. It doesn't mean that we are to give them a free hand.

(a) We need to let our children know we have expectations of them. Discipline is required because we love them. They need to know where the fences are. They need to know what is permissible and what is not permissible. We discipline our children because we love them dearly and want them to learn and grow.

(b) We need to strike a balance between anger as parents and spoiling children by being overly permissive. Children are not human pin cushions whom we can jab at will because we happen to be their parents. But neither do children need their parents to be their pals. They can have many pals, but they only have two parents. They need for us to be their parents, emphasizing love and worth and caring discipline.

IV. The children know what our priorities are. They know when we are more concerned about golf than God. They know when we are more concerned about sacking in on Sunday than being in worship. If we have our priorities right, then we set the best example for them. Children need the affirmation of our love. They need to know the expectations of our discipline. They need the example of their parents. And they need their parents' time and interest.

(a) Our children need the example of Christian worship. Even though the youngsters may not be old enough to understand all that's said and done, they understand far more than we imagine.

(b) Our greatest dream for our children is that one day we will be instrumental in placing their hands in the hand of God. This is not automatic. This is not something we can force. There's no guarantee that your children will grow up to be Christians. This church is joining you parents in promising to help you place their hands in the hand of God.—Alton H. McEachern.

Illustrations

UP A TREE.   A boy climbed high into a tree and refused to come down. Throughout dinner, which his parents ate with exaggerated relish in the boy's sight, remarking frequently and fatuously upon the particular delights of the meal, the boy clung stubbornly to his limb, far too high for his father to climb after him. They tried everything, the mother whined frantically to the doctor hours later over the telephone. Everything meant threats, bribery, cajolery, lies, warnings, and screams. "We told him he'd fall and hurt himself. We told him we'd call the fire department, and the firemen would say what a baby he was. We told him he'd catch cold and get sick. We told him there were owls in the tree that would peck his eyes out. We told him he'd get thrashed within an inch of his life if he didn't come down. We've tried everything." "Did you tell him simply that you wanted him to come down because you loved him and wanted him to be with you?" the doctor asked. "Well, no," she said. She called back a few minutes later to say that the boy, who had been waiting for five hours to hear just that, had come right down.—Marshall F. Mauney.

EITHER WAY.   A man told his wife that on a particular Friday he was going into the boss' office to request the raise that he believed he more than deserved. He was quite nervous and upset. When he finally got his courage to go into the boss' office toward the end of the day, the boss agreed that he deserved the raise and gave him even a larger increase in salary than he had anticipated. When he arrived home, he noticed the dining room table was set with the best dishes. There were candles burning. His wife was preparing a delicious meal. He thought to himself, "Someone has called her from the office to tell her." He went into the kitchen, told her the good news, they kissed, and then soon sat down at the table for a delicious meal. Beside his plate was a beautifully lettered note which read: "Congratulations, darling! I knew you'd get the raise. These things will tell you how much I love you." They enjoyed the delicious meal together. When she got up to get the dessert, he noticed a second card fell from her pocket. He bent over, picked it up, and read: "Don't worry about not getting the raise. You deserved it anyway. These things will tell you how much I love you."—Joe A. Harding.

Sermon Suggestions

A MOTHER WHO PASSED ON HER FAITH. Text: II Tim. 1:5. (1) She planted it. (2) She taught it. (3) She lived it.

LIVING YOUR OWN DRAMA.   Text: Heb. 12:2. (1) Every person has a role to play. (2) Every person has an audience to play to. (3) Every person has a script to play from.—Clarence J. Forsberg.

Worship Aids

CALL TO WORSHIP.   "Ye shall know the truth, and the truth shall make you free. God is a Spirit: and they that worship him must worship him in spirit and in truth." John 8:32; 4:24.

INVOCATION.   Lord God Almighty, holy and eternal Father, who dwellest in the high and lofty place, with him also that is of a humble and contrite spirit: we come before thee, beseeching thee to cleanse us by the grace of thy Holy Spirit, that we may give praise to thee, now and forever.

OFFERTORY SENTENCE.   "Therefore, as ye abound in every thing, in faith, and utterance, and knowledge, and in all diligence, and in your love to us, see that ye abound in this grace also." II Cor. 8:7.

OFFERTORY PRAYER.   As we bring our offering today we thank thee, O God, for the happiness of our earthly life, for peaceful homes and healthful days, for our powers of mind and body, for faithful friends, and for the joy of loving and being loved. We pray that these blessings may come to abound throughout all the world and to all people.

PRAYER. Our Father, who from the beginning didst cause the human race to live in families of love, we praise thy name as we worship together. On this festival of the home we remember all families in all conditions. May each of us, through thy spirit of love, learn to live and grow like beautiful flower gardens in the spring. May the happiness of all be shared with one another in the seasons of life.

In our family relations as thy children, O God, we thank thee for the hoe of confession which removes the weeds of sin from our lives and clears the way to nobler expressions of duty to thee. We thank thee for the sunshine of thy radiance brightening our inner temples for profound meditation. We give thee our gratitude for the grace coming upon us like showers of thirst-quenching rain that no one can withhold from thy providential and affectionate hand.

Bless, our Father, our church family in these moments of divine fellowship. Restore our souls amid the pools of prayer fashioned after the manner of thy Son. Refresh our hearts with glad songs and anthems of praise. Inspire our minds with the food of everlasting truth. Lead us into the wide fields of discipleship so thy kingdom may prosper and thy will be done.—Harold A. Schulz.

EVENING SERVICE

Topic: Conquering Depression
TEXT: Rom. 8:28.

I. Believe that God is really greater than your circumstances and the problems that have you down.

II. Turn all those problems over to him in prayer. Do not just say words, communicate with God, take 30–60 minutes. Pray specifically, listing each area of concern.

III. Believe that God has a purpose in your difficult circumstances. What is he trying to accomplish in your life through these circumstances? How are you resisting him?

IV. Recognize that depression is self-pity and must be confessed and forsaken as sin. Do not just patch things up on the surface. Deal with your real problem.

V. Realize that you cannot always have your own way. Submission to life's circumstances is really submission to God's will for your life. Frustrations and anxiety never solve anything.

VI. Acknowledge that there is no valid excuse for staying depressed and determine to do everything necessary to conquer it.

VII. Get up and get out. Face reality with the confidence that God is alive and at work in your life. Remember, sinful thinking—God doesn't love me or he can't help me—is just as harmful as sinful behavior. Wrong actions produce wrong feelings, but wrong thinking also produces wrong feelings.

VIII. Confess and forsake sinful actions and sinful thinking. Think scripturally. Think like a real Christian and then act like one.

IX. Get your priorities in proper order. Put God first, not yourself. Stop trying to make everything revolve around you and your problems. In proper Christian thinking you have no real problems, just opportunities to trust your heavenly Father and see him work in your life.

X. Get involved with the needs of somebody else. Get your eyes off yourself and back into the world. You cease being a missionary when you become a mission field. Jesus Christ has already commissioned you to go to others. Christ-centered thinking is not self-centered or problem-centered. It sees the purpose of God in all things.—Ed Hindson in *Faith Aflame.*

SUNDAY: MAY SIXTEENTH

MORNING SERVICE

Topic: Christ's Response to Human Need

SCRIPTURE: John 9:1-11.

I. Long before Jesus' day the people had been taught that everything that happens is a direct act of God. They believed that the storms, earthquakes, defeat in war, and sickness in body come at God's command. To believe that anything could happen which God did not command would be to lessen his power, they felt. On the other hand, if God is good, why would he cause his children to suffer? The only explanation they could make was to place the blame on man. Man sins and that causes his punishment, they reasoned.

(a) If you saw a father punishing his child, you would reason that either the father is mean and delights in seeing his child suffer or that the child has done wrong and that a reasonable punishment is the obligation of the father. So in the presence of the blind man's suffering, the disciples did not doubt that it was God's affliction because of sin. Their only question was in regard to who sinned, the man or his parents.

(b) Jesus did not accept that theory for a moment. Quickly he said, "Neither hath this man sinned, nor his parents." He did not give the reason for the man's suffering, but he does emphatically say it was not caused by sin. We do know that all sin eventually causes suffering, but it does not follow that all suffering is caused by sin. Jesus made that clear.

(c) Jesus might have taken that occasion to give a sermon on the causes and explanations of suffering, but he does not do it. Instead he said, "The works of God should be made manifest in him." Here is a man in need. Let us not argue about the causes. Better to give ourselves to the work of God which is helping those who need help.

II. Instead of talking about why a man was blind, Jesus set about to help him. That was the theme of his life. Mark tells us, "He went about doing good." Some people are so busy explaining things they do not have time to do much. I doubt if Jesus attended many forums or discussion groups. He was so busy changing people and situations that he had little time for idle talk and speculations.

III. To heal the man born blind, Jesus "spat on the ground, and made clay of the spittle, and he anointed the eyes of the blind man with the clay, and said unto him, 'Go, wash in the pool of Siloam'" (John 9:6-7). The putting of the clay on the man's eyes was for a definite purpose. The people in that day believed that the saliva of a good man contained healing power.

(a) When Jesus put his saliva on the man's eyes, it was for the purpose of arousing faith and hope in the man. As you study his miracles, you learn that he required faith. This man had no faith, so Christ had to help him to create it.

(b) He then sent the man to wash in the pool of Siloam. Why did he do that? Because he wanted to teach the man obedience.

(c) Here we see clearly the two steps Christ requires—faith and obedience. Those are the steps to find the solution to any problem. First, we must believe the answer to it can be found. Then an individual faithfully follows the truth as he discovers it.

(d) When we believe there is a solution of any problem and faithfully take each step God reveals to us, eventually we will find the answer. It may not be the answer we thought we should find, but it will be the right answer. If we want the power of Christ, we must trust and obey.

(e) The blind man was healed. It came through the power of Christ and his own faith and obedience. Whatever our need, he stands ready and able whenever we take the two necessary steps.—Charles L. Allen.

Illustrations

OUT OF HARMONY.   One of the words for sin in the Greek language means to be out of harmony. This word is not used in the New Testament, but it is a descriptive term fitting in very well with the three other words for sin that are used—missing the mark, walking in forbidden territory, and falling flat on one's face. This fourth word means to sing off key, to be out of harmony, to err. In a special way this word fits modern man in his contrived, contemporary world. For from the beginning of what we call civilization, true harmony with the whole world of nature has been almost disregarded. Some great minds, such as that of Francis of Assisi, have known that such harmony is necessary for real contentment, but such persons have had a very hard time trying to convince others that sacrifices should be made to attain this harmony.—George Alder.

OPENING OUTWARD.   When William James was a child, he wrote to a friend about a summer home in New Hampshire which his family had acquired. He was quite excited about it. He wrote, "It is a wonderful house, with all doors opening outward." This was evidently a thrill which lasted in another form all his life, for in a biography of him, it was written: "His delight in human nature was acute and unending, and all his doors and windows opened outward."—Halford E. Luccock.

Sermon Suggestions

TREASURES OF THE FAITHFUL.   Text: Jer. 9:23–24. (1) They feel at home in the universe. (2) They feel adequate for life. (3) They have a sure remedy for failure. (4) They have joy.—Everett W. Palmer.

RELATING TO GOD.   Text: Jas. 1:17. (1) God never lets us off. (2) God never lets us down. (3) God never lets us go.

Worship Aids

CALL TO WORSHIP.   "I will praise thee with my whole heart. I will worship toward thy holy temple, and praise thy name for thy lovingkindness." Ps. 138:1–2.

INVOCATION.   O God our father, who dost dwell in the high and holy place, with him also that is of a humble and contrite heart: grant that, through this time of worship in thy presence, we may be made the more sure that our true home is with thee in the realm of spiritual things and that thou art ever with us in the midst of our common walk and daily duties so that the vision of the eternal may ever give meaning and beauty to this earthly and outward life.

OFFERTORY SENTENCE.   "Of every man that giveth willingly with his heart ye shall take my offering [saith the Lord]." Exod. 25:2.

OFFERTORY PRAYER.   Our heavenly Father, may thy kingdom be uppermost in our minds, our hearts, and our lives. Accept our gifts and with them the rededication of all that we are and have to thy greater glory.

PRAYER.   O Lord, our God, who has created us and who knows our every thought and mood, we set aside this quiet time from our busy lives to give thought to our relationship with you and to reflect upon the meaning of our lives.

O God, because we are weak and undisciplined in matters of the spirit, we pray that you would come more forcefully into our lives. Confront us in new and unavoidable ways that we may develop a sensitivity to your presence in the commonplace. In the people that come into our lives in the week before us, help us to see you challenging us to make the loving response.

Our Father, we intercede this day for all those who are dear to us. Because we know that you intend that life should be good and filled with happy moments and joyful relationships, we are pained when we see those we care about sorrowing, ill, troubled, in conflict or misunderstanding. Enable us to be helpful and supportive in their time of need. And enable us in our own relationships to be constructive rather than destructive. We would contribute to an atmosphere of understanding and acceptance rather than of judgment and comdemnation. Help us to see beneath the surface of one another to the intentions of the heart that we may be free from the restrictions of custom to do the loving thing in every situation.

EVENING SERVICE

Topic: A Theology of Nature (Rural Life Sunday)
Scripture: Rom. 8:18–23.

It is a vision of the created world in the light of Christ that Paul presents in Rom 8:18–23. Here he offers us a guide to a Christian perception of nature. There are three main elements in it.

I. The first is sympathy, community with nature in its suffering. Christians will look on the world with sympathy, not as a slave at their disposal, but as a partner with them in the purpose of God which embraces all his creatures, and more particularly as one which is participant with them in the suffering which is the reflex of the cross of Christ.

II. The second element is the perception of nature in the light of the gospel. The groanings of creation, which are joined in by those who have the Spirit, are heard as the travail pangs of the new creation. Christians perceive the world around them under the sign of hope. Christians who believe in the resurrection cannot restrict their hope to a future life for themselves; they extend it to the whole created world, which, as it proceeded from God in its entirety from the beginning, will, through his faith fulness, attested in the resurrection, pro ceed toward him in its entirety at the end.

III. The third element in the Christian perception of nature is the recognition of the responsibility that rests upon us for the fulfillment of God's purpose with nature. Paul concentrates this responsibility in prayer, but I think we may legitimately expand the concept of prayer to embrace the whole of worship. Worship is an activity to which we are moved by the presence of the Spirit, an extravagant activity in which we exceed the bounds of the comprehensible and an activity in which we become engaged in the transcendent purpose of God.—George S. Hendry. Adapted from *Theology of Nature* (Westminster Press).

SUNDAY: MAY TWENTY-THIRD

MORNING SERVICE

Topic: Come, Lord Jesus! (Ascension Sunday)
Text: Rev. 22:20.

Why does he tarry when he has given the promise of his coming. Three times, in the brief compass of this final chapter of Revelation, the promise, "I am coming soon," is given.

I. Christ tarries and delays his coming because he has made other provision for our need.

(a) What is that provision? Listen to these words which he addressed to his disciples: "I will not leave you desolate; I will

come to you. Yet a little while and the world will see me no more, but you will see me; because I live, you will live also" (John 14:18–19). Jesus means that while he will leave them in physical presence he will come to them in the person of his Holy Spirit.

(b) It means that for each of us there is now grace, power, and strength sufficient for every need. (See Deut. 33:25; II Cor. 12:9.) The strength is not given before it is needed, but when the need arises it is provided.

(c) The coming of the Holy Spirit means that when our day of life is done, the living Christ comes to take us home. (See John

14:2-3.) When that happens death is transformed and transfigured. Then it ceases to be darkness and becomes light. Then it is no longer the end but the beginning of life. And then it is changed from a journey into a far country and becomes going home.

II. Jesus delays his coming because we have not finished our ministry.

(a) What is that ministry? Christ called us to be his disciples, and he established his church to the end that the gospel might be proclaimed to the ends of the earth. Thus before he ascended into heaven Jesus Christ left the church her marching orders in Matt. 28:19-20 and Acts 1:8. Our business as the church of Jesus Christ and our task as disciples of our Lord is to tell the old, old story of Jesus and his love to men and women everywhere.

(b) Certainly much has been done since that day when Jesus ascended up into heaven. The Christian church has grown from a grain of mustard seed to become the greatest of all plants. The Christian church has been established in many parts of the earth. But there still remaineth much land to be possessed. Christianity is still a minority religion, and there are still those who have never heard.

(c) Our ministry is still incomplete and, according to the New Testament, until it is complete, Christ will not return. (See Matt. 24:14.) The tardiness of our Lord is proof not of his indifference but of our failure, and in view of that it behooves us to strengthen stakes and lengthen cords.

III. Christ delays his coming because of his love for sinners. (a) His return will be the day of accounting. His coming again will end the day of grace. It will conclude the day of opportunity. Then every man will stand before the judgment seat of Christ and will answer for the things which he hath done in the body, whether they be good or bad. (See II Cor. 5:10.)

(b) When you realize that, you begin to understand what Peter means when he said, "The Lord is not slow about his promise as some count slowness, but is forbearing toward you, not wishing that any should perish but that all should reach repentance" (II Pet. 3:9). Christ's apparent slackness is in reality the expression of his love for sinners. For them he would hold the door ajar a little longer in hope that still another prodigal will come home.

IV. His coming is sure and certain. (See II Pet. 3:10.) In his own time and in the day of his appointing Jesus Christ will come again. In view of that what manner of persons ought we to be? What is required of us? We need to be ready when he comes. We need to have our robes washed in the blood of the Lamb. We need the oil of the Holy Spirit in our lamps. (See Matt. 24:44.) We need to be found doing the Master's business.—S. Robert Weaver.

Illustrations

EXALTATION. Another word used in the New Testament to refer to the ascension of Christ is exaltation. Alan Richardson writes: "The phrase 'at the right hand of God' meant not a place, but a participation in the sovereignty of God over all things. The exalted Jesus had entered a state and an activity which transcended the limitations of place altogether."

WITH HIM EVERYWHERE. In the days of his earthly ministry, only those could speak to him who came where he was. If he was in Galilee, men could not find him in Jerusalem; if he was in Jerusalem, men could not find him in Galilee. But his ascension means that he is perfectly united with God. We are with him wherever we are present to God, and this is everywhere and always.—William Temple.

Sermon Suggestions

THE GOSPEL OF THE ASCENSION. Text: John 16:7. (1) The ascension was expedient for the spiritualizing of religion. (2) The ascension was expedient for the universalizing of the gospel. (3) The ascension was expedient for the energizing of evangelism. (4) The ascension was expedient for the fortifying of faith.—James S. Stewart.

LIFE OF THE SAVED. Text: Titus 2:11–13. (1) Learning from Christ. (2) Living for Christ. (3) Looking for Christ.—H. C. Chiles.

Worship Aids

CALL TO WORSHIP. "The kingdoms of this world are become the kingdom of our Lord, and of his Christ; and he shall reign for ever and ever." Rev. 11:15.

INVOCATION. Grant, O Lord our God, we beseech thee, that now and every time we come before thee in worship and in prayer we may be vividly aware of thy presence, become conscious of thy power and a sense of thy protection, and finally know in our hearts and minds and souls the wonder and the grace of thy peace.

OFFERTORY SENTENCE. "Upon the first day of the week let every one of you lay by him in store, as God hath prospered him." I Cor. 16:2.

OFFERTORY PRAYER. O heavenly Father, we pray that thy blessings, which are as countless as the stars, may be so used as to bring light and love to thy children everywhere.

PRAYER. Blessed Lord Jesus, who didst show thyself to thy disciples in thy resurrection glory for forty days before thy ascension into heaven, directing and comforting them, let the words spoken to them guide and reassure us in these days of confusion. Meet with us as we worship thee in our troubled world. May our consideration of thy ascension into heaven strengthen our faith and brighten our hope in thy eventual return to take us who love thee, believe in thee, and serve thee to our eternal home in heaven. We are not worthy of thy love. It grieves us that we should so often sin against thee. It comforts us to know that thou art ready to forgive us for thy love's sake. May our highest purpose in life be to serve thee and to take the story of thy love and salvation to the uttermost parts of the earth. In all the disappointments and hardships of

life may we always keep our faces heavenward, lest we become discouraged.—Armin C. Oldsen.

EVENING SERVICE

Topic: The Lord's Return
TEXT: I Thess. 4:16.
I. Some of the believing loved ones of the Thessalonians had died since Paul was there. They were troubled lest at the Lord's return they be taken to heaven, leaving their dead loved ones behind. Paul assures them that they should not sorrow without hope as did pagans who had no hope of life after death (v. 13).

(a) He assumes that they believe that Jesus died and rose again. On that basis rests their assurance concerning dead loved ones (v. 14). The word for sleep is the one whence comes cemetery. It does not teach soul sleeping in an unconscious state until the resurrection. It was a term commonly used for death (John 11:13–14). So their bodies lie in the cemetery. When Jesus returns, they "will God bring with him." This means that the real persons they loved are with him now.

(b) On the basis of what Jesus had taught, Paul says that those alive at his return "shall not prevent them which are asleep" or lie in the cemetery (v. 15). Prevent means go before (precede, RSV). They will not go before and leave behind their loved ones in the cemetery.

II. "Will descend from heaven" is climactic, coming at the end of the sentence (v. 16).

(a) Shout means a cry of command, a military word. Moffatt sees this as a command mustering the saints.

(b) "Voice of an archangel" reads literally "an archangel's call" or voice. Michael is the only archangel mentioned by name in the New Testament (Jude 9). On the basis of Jewish belief Moffatt sees this archangel as Michael mustering the saints and sounding God's trumpet to herald God's approaching judgment.

(c) Paul is using eschatological language to show the power and glory of the Lord's return. The fact that shout, voice, and trumpet are each preceded by *en* (in) shows that they will come in sequence.

III. "The dead in Christ shall rise first."

(a) The use of first does not relate to the resurrection of the saved, to be followed later by a resurrection of the unsaved. In John 5:28–29 Jesus mentions the resurrection of both the saved and unsaved as one event. He is thinking of the resurrection of the dead loved ones in Thessalonica being raised before the living Christians are caught up to meet the Lord (v. 17).

(b) After the loved ones who return with the Lord are raised in their resurrection bodies, those who are alive at that time will experience a change from mortal bodies to immortal ones (I Cor. 15:50–57).

(c) Then they "together with them [the raised loved ones]" will be "caught up together with them in the clouds to meet the Lord in the air: and so shall we ever be with the Lord" (v. 17).—Herschel H. Hobbs.

SUNDAY: MAY THIRTIETH

MORNING SERVICE

Topic: Spirit-Filled Living (Pentecost)
Text: Eph. 5:18–21.

The command "be filled with the Spirit" is a present imperative and means "go on being filled." For the fullness of the Spirit is not a once for all experience which we can never lose but to be renewed each day. As the NEB puts it, "Let the Holy Spirit fill you" and keep filling you as well. Paul gives four wholesome results of being filled with the Spirit.

I. Spiritual fellowship: "addressing one another in psalms and hymns and spiritual songs."

(a) This does not mean that Spirit-filled believers stop speaking to each other and start singing to each other instead. The reference to hymns and psalms indicates that the apostle is referring to church services. Spirit-filled believers love to sing when they assemble for worship, and they sing not only to God but to each other, for they sing responsively and antiphonally, as the Jews used to do, and some of their songs are mutual exhortations.

(b) The venite is a good example, for it begins, "O come, let us sing unto the Lord." None of it is worship to God; all of it is mutual exhortation to worship.

II. Joyful worship: "singing and making melody to the Lord with all your heart."

(a) The Greek probably means in your heart. J. B. Phillips may be right to translate "making music in your hearts for the ears of the Lord!"—an instruction from which unmusical people, unable to sing in tune, have always derived much comfort.

(b) In this case it is silent worship, although at the same time inwardly joyful and melodious. A Spirit-filled Christian has a song of joy in his heart to the Lord.

III. Constant thankfulness: "always and for everything giving thanks."

(a) The grumbling spirit is not compatible with the fullness of the Spirit. Grumbling was the besetting sin of Israel, who were always murmuring against Moses and against the Lord.

(b) The Spirit-filled believer is full of thanksgiving. He gives thanks to God the Father for his fatherly goodness, in the name of the Lord Jesus Christ through whom he has been reconciled to the Father and in whom all spiritual blessings are to be found.

IV. Humble submissiveness: "Be subject to one another out of reverence for Christ."

(a) The Christian submits to Christ and so to other people for Christ's sake. This is important, for sometimes a person claiming to be filled with the Holy Spirit is aggressive, awkward, self-assertive, and brash. But those truly filled with the Spirit exhibit rather the meekness and gentleness of Christ.

(b) These four wholesome results of the Spirit's fullness all concern our relationships. If we are filled with the Spirit, we are harmoniously related to God (worshiping him with joy and thanksgiving) and to each other (addressing each other and submitting to each other). We love God and we love each other, which is not surprising since the first fruit of the Spirit is love.—John Stott.

Illustrations

GRASPING AND INSPIRING.   Spirit is not a mysterious substance; it is not part of God. It is God himself, but not God as the creative ground of all things and not God directing history and manifesting himself in its central event but God as present in communities and personalities, grasping them, inspiring them, and transforming them.—Paul Tillich.

THE SPIDER'S WEB.   The spider's web gives us a graphic picture of the human life pattern. The spider spins long, thin strands and attaches them to nearby objects like anchors. Then it lays cross-strands by circling the structure over and over to create a woven pattern.

We may see these anchored strands as significant times and experiences of our lives—birth, graduation, marriage, and others. The circling strands tie these experiences together with the contributions of other persons, places, and things that influence our way of thinking.

When a strand is broken, the spider reinforces the structure. And after a bad experience, we also make adjustments in life. The experience could be a death or a separation or a financial setback. Sometimes we need to change our direction or location, mend a relationship, alter our way of thinking, or seek new goals in order to hold our structure of life together.—Homer M. Cole in *The Disciple*.

Sermon Suggestions

THE HOLY SPIRIT AND BELIEVERS.   Scripture: John 16:7–14. (1) The Holy Spirit establishes our relationship. (See II Cor. 5:19; Tit. 3:5, NASB.) (2) The Holy Spirit enriches our lives. (See I Cor. 12:7; Gal. 5:22–23; Rom. 7.) (3) The Holy Spirit enlightens our minds. (See v. 12.) (4) The Holy Spirit encourages our hearts. (5) The

Holy Spirit empowers our spirit. (See Acts 1:8, NASB.)—Brian L. Harbour.

THE HOLY SPIRIT AND UNBELIEVERS.   Scripture: John 16:7–11. (1) The Holy Spirit convicts and convinces the unbeliever concerning sin. (See v. 9.) (2) The Holy Spirit convicts and convinces the unbeliever concerning righteousness. (See v. 10.) (3) The Holy Spirit convicts and convinces the world concerning judgment.—Brian L. Harbour.

Worship Aids

CALL TO WORSHIP.   "The Lord is great in Zion; and he is high above all the people. Exalt the Lord our God, and worship at his holy hill; for the Lord our God is holy." Ps. 99:2, 9.

INVOCATION.   O Lord Jesus Christ, who art the truth incarnate and the teacher of the faithful: let thy spirit overshadow us as we meditate on thy word and conform our thoughts to thy revelation that, learning of thee with honest hearts, we may be rooted and built up in thee, who livest and reignest with the Father and the Holy Spirit, ever one God, world without end.

OFFERTORY SENTENCE.   "If ye then, being evil, know how to give good gifts unto your children: how much more shall your heavenly Father give the Holy Spirit, to them that ask him?" Luke 11:13.

OFFERTORY PRAYER.   Our Father, open our eyes, we pray, to the glorious opportunities of sharing with others our blessed experiences of fellowship with one another and with thee.

PRAYER.   Great God our Lord, we thank thee today for thy church. It is thy glory and sometimes, we are sure, thy despair. Yet thou hast entrusted to her the nurture of the saints, the training of children, the proclamation of the faith, and the witness to holy living and confident dying. Give her courage to speak judgment upon every unrighteousness of community and nation, as well as winsomeness in telling and living the gospel to the ends of the earth. May she continue to know the joy of binding up the wounds of mankind and pouring in oil and wine.

Keep clear to believers the assurance that all are priests of the most high, mediating to their fellows the benediction of faith that is transforming their own lives. Make her pastors true shepherds, her scholars clear thinkers, her teachers inspiring trainers, and her preachers great prophets. We pray in the name of the one who loved the church and gave himself for it, Christ Jesus our Lord.—Hillyer H. Straton.

EVENING SERVICE

Topic: The Work of the Spirit
TEXT: John 14:16.

I. The work of the Holy Spirit is interrogation. The Holy Spirit first puts questions into the mind of the unbeliever. This is the convicting work of the Holy Spirit that Jesus talked about in John 16:8–11. As the Holy Spirit works on the hearts of the unbelievers, he plants the eternal questions whose answer can only be found in Christ and thus leads the unbeliever to conversion.

II. The work of the Holy Spirit is identification. Paul wrote to the Ephesian Christians that having believed in Jesus they "were sealed in him with the Holy Spirit of promise" (Eph. 1:13). The word "seal" is the Greek word *sphragizo* which meant the mark of ownership. The presence of the Holy Spirit in our lives is the mark which identifies us with Christ.

III. The work of the Holy Spirit is illumination. After the Holy Spirit has identified us with Christ, then the Holy Spirit begins the ministry that Jesus predicted when he said, "But when he, the Spirit of truth, comes, he will guide you into all the truth" (John 16:13). The Holy Spirit is like a light to the believer. He gives light on the scriptures, on the ethical decisions facing us, on how to pray, and on how to relate to each other. The purpose of the Holy Spirit is to illuminate our minds so that we can know the truth.

IV. The work of the Holy Spirit is that of inspiration. The word that Jesus used to refer to the Spirit, *Paraclete,* is from two Greek words *para* and *kaleo* which means one called aside to help. When you feel courage in the midst of a threatening situation, when you feel power in the midst of a challenge, when you feel hope in the midst of a time of despair, and when you face life with all of its difficulties and are inspired to go on, that's the work of the Holy Spirit in your life.

V. The work of the Holy Spirit is implementation. When Jesus departed he left a big assignment to the church. He said, "You are to go into all the world and preach the gospel to every creature." He left us to carry on his work of reconciliation. How can it be done? In what way can it be implemented? That is the work of the Holy Spirit. "Go to Jerusalem," Jesus said, "and wait for the Holy Spirit. When the Holy Spirit comes, you will receive power." As we walk in the Spirit and as we allow the Spirit to control us and fill us and empower us, as we walk in the Spirit, then we will see implemented in this world the great work that God has left for the church to do.—Brian L. Harbour.

SUNDAY: JUNE SIXTH

MORNING SERVICE

Topic: Community Divine and Human (Trinity Sunday)
SCRIPTURE: John 16:12–15.

There is only one God, and to this one God we offer homage and adoration. The resounding refrain of the people of Israel is as true today as it was thousands of years ago: "Hear, O Israel, the Lord your God is one."

I. For Christians this one God has revealed himself to us not only as one but as a God who is community—Father, Son, and Holy Spirit. Such multiplicity in God does not destroy the unity but rather is the manifestation of the unity.

(a) This may sound like so much theology without much relationship to human life and far from the heart of people wherein God resides. But Father, Son, and Spirit is the Christian God, and any effort to understand something of the revelation that has taken place for us is worth the effort, even if we can never completely understand how the one God can be a community.

(b) Christians call God their father, accept Jesus the Son as their brother, and experience the nearness of the Spirit as teacher, defender, and counselor. Father, Son, and Spirit make Christianity a distinctive religion.

(c) Today we celebrate the feast of the Christian God; we celebrate the feast of the blessed Trinity. Such a celebration does not mean that we are not aware of the presence of our God on other Sundays, but this day we are more conscious that our God has revealed himself as a community of persons. This same God expects us to know him and to love him in the precise way in which he has manifested himself.

II. Sometimes it seems that we Christians could do just as well without our trinitarian God. We tend to speak of God and think of God as one and fail to recall that our God is multiple. There is a community that constitutes our God even as our God is one. Our failure to pay attention to this revelation is our impoverishment. If God has chosen to tell us that he is triune, then this should have some effect on our lives.

III. When we pray we should pray first to God who is our loving parent, our Father. This is how Jesus taught us to pray. We can turn to God as father because we share in the Spirit of Jesus who has been given to us as a gift. We can learn from the life of Jesus, the Son, made like us in all things but sin. His life and his death can give us some direction in our personal lives and teach us to die as the faithful children of a loving God so that we can live eternally in the community that is God.

IV. The Father gives, the Son receives, and the Spirit accepts from both and offers to others. If at the very heart of God there

is relationship, then the giving and receiving and offering to many should characterize our relationships as well. Our God who is triune, who is multiple, and who is community can affect our lives as we pray and as we live.

(a) How marvelous to accept Jesus as a brother and to know the power of the Spirit and feel the support of a loving parent who is God. How wonderful to know that we are never isolated but are called to live a life of community with God.

(b) As a Christian community we gather and celebrate the presence of our God in a sacred meal. We are spirit-filled. We offer our sacrifice joined to that of Jesus to the one God and Father of all. This day we should be more conscious of how we begin all things that are important.—John F. O'Grady in *Pastoral Life.*

Illustrations

ABSENCE.   At the Colinton Parish School one teacher had taught a class to repeat the Apostles' Creed clause by clause, each pupil having his own clause. As the recitation began the first boy said, "I believe in God the Father Almighty, maker of heaven and earth." The second boy said, "I believe in Jesus Christ, his only Son our Lord." So the recitation went on to the boy who said, "He ascended into heaven, and sitteth on the right hand of God the Father Almighty; from thence he shall come to judge the quick and the dead," Then there fell a silence, and it was broken by the next boy who said to the examiner, "Please, sir, the boy who believes in the Holy Ghost is absent today." Lots of folks are absent when it comes to that clause.—Norman Maclean.

WHERE HOPE BECOMES FAITH.   The church at times is thought of as a place, an exercise of ritual, a social institution which works for the general good, or just a group of people who call themselves Christians and think better of themselves. But it is more than that. Its congregations may have all the imperfections of human beings who compose them, yet it is this very human element that gives it greatness.

Often when we gather in God's name hope becomes faith. No other grouping or institution can so encourage us to think beyond our own interests. No other association so easily dares us to be generous, to be kind, or to be tolerant of others. Nor is there any other society in which we can so enjoy reverence, so quickly see the beauty of hope, or receive the inspiration of faith.—Mack Lilly in *The Cumberland Presbyterian*.

Sermon Suggestions

FIGHT THE GOOD FIGHT. Text: Phil. 1: 27. (1) Fight for something in human welfare. (2) Fight for somebody else. (3) Fight for the underprivileged. (4) Fight for the downtrodden. (5) Fight for the good.

AT WITS' END. Text: Job 3:23 (MOFFATT). (1) Wits' end is a place to find truth and where we see our real selves. (2) Wits' end is a place to find answers. (3) Wits' end is a place to find God. (See Job 42:5; II Cor. 1:9, PHILLIPS.)—Bramwell Tripp.

Worship Aids

CALL TO WORSHIP. "We are laborers together with God: ye are God's husbandry, ye are God's building. Let every man take heed how he buildeth. For other foundation can no man lay than that is laid, which is Jesus Christ." I Cor. 3:9–11.

INVOCATION. O heavenly Father, who hast given us a true faith and a sure hope: help us to live as those who believe and trust in the communion of saints, the forgiveness of sins, and the resurrection to life everlasting; and strengthen this faith and hope in us all the days of our life.

OFFERTORY SENTENCE. "Let the beauty of the Lord our God be upon us: and establish thou the work of our hands upon us; yea, the work of our hands establish thou it." Ps. 90:17.

OFFERTORY PRAYER. God of our fathers, dearly do we cherish the blessing which thy church brings to us and dearly do we covet the privilege of sharing through these gifts the proclaiming of thy word until all of the earth shall praise thee.

ORDINATION PRAYER. O God, our hearts are moved by the mystery and holiness of this moment. In all ages thou has been invisibly at work in the depths of the human soul, and even before awareness was given thou wast at work in the life of the one who kneels before us now. In ways both common and beyond all understanding thy eternal Spirit has communed with his spirit, and the subtle pressures of thy will have been felt upon his own. Amid the confusion of this world's voices he has heard thy divine call and responded to it. And now we stand in the mystery of thy divine initiative to celebrate it in holy joy.

O Lord, keep him in the days to come. Accompany him through the temptations he will face. Enable him to stand if testing proves more strenuous than expected. Strengthen him to endure in the long pull. Help him to fear sham more than shame, betrayal more than failure, and thy judgment more than the rejection of the world. Deliver him from all mock seriousness and professional pretense, and may he never forget that his needs are as desperate as the next man's. Grant that in his eagerness to save the world he may not neglect his own soul. In time of success make him humble, and when he fails save him from despair. When, as must be, he comes upon the empty day or the tormented night and when his direction is blurred and life becomes a burdensome darkness, reveal to him in fresh and surprising ways that eternal North Star of the spirit who is Christ Jesus our Lord.

Give him the capacity to grow, our Father, in truth that takes root in the mind and, nurtured, sends deep roots into reality. Give him courage to ask the mighty questions and honesty to admit his ignorance. Give him wisdom which transcends an accumulation of facts and infuses them with meaning. Supremely, give him the capacity to grow into the stature and fulness of humanity as he discovers it in our master.—Taylor E. Roth.

EVENING SERVICE

Topic: By Grace Alone
SCRIPTURE: Luke 7:36–50.
I. To answer Simon's unspoken question, Jesus offered a parable. If two were forgiven a debt, one a moderate amount and one ten times more, who would love the creditor more?

(a) Sinner though she was, the woman provided the services of courtesy, respect, and love which Simon as host should have provided, Jesus tells him. "He who is forgiven little loves little." Simon, blind to his own sin, could experience little forgiveness because he found little need for it.

(b) The world takes God's forgiveness lightly because it takes sin lightly. The woman knew her sinful condition, and she was looking to the Lord to wash her sins away just as she was washing the dirt from his feet. She was looking for a gracious God and found him in the person of Christ. Without saying a word she ministered to Christ and with tears of penitence washed his feet, and although she could not be accepted by the church of her day, that was no reason for Christ to reject her. Rather he forgave her.

(c) Most of this world, like Simon, wants to ignore sin and its gruesome reality. We in our worldly way want to deny our need for forgiveness and convince ourselves that what we do isn't that bad. But our sin and the guilt that precipitates from it are intended to drive us back to God as the only source of true forgiveness, a genuinely clear conscience, and a wholeness in our lives unattainable any other way.

II. Sin must not be forgotten because it has a blood price. In the Old Testament we are told a spotless animal was sacrificed for atonement. In the New Testament, Christ became the ultimate sacrifice. His blood was the costly price paid for our sins.

(a) Perhaps this is why Christ kept such sordid company—prostitutes, tax collectors, and sinners. He came to call the sinners of our world to turn from their ways and be forgiven.

(b) What is the price for this forgiveness? Everything in this world has a price; so too must this. But the cost for us and our sins has been paid by someone else. Our bill was paid at Calvary by Christ.

(c) Forgiveness for us is given by grace alone, not by our own doing. Because he offers us this grace, this unmerited love—"While we were yet sinners he died for us"—we too can come to our Lord and seek and find forgiveness. The sins on our slate will be wiped off—by grace alone.—Olin Knudsen in *Clergy Journal.*

SUNDAY: JUNE THIRTEENTH

MORNING SERVICE

Topic: Don't Blame Your Parents (Children's Sunday)
SCRIPTURE: Ezek. 18:1–4, 30–32; Luke 13:22–35.
I. The writer of the book of Deuteronomy said the problems of his generation were the result of the sins of the previous generations.

(a) The author would be very surprised to be called a Freudian, but he was. Or more likely Freud was really a Deuteronomist. He believed that the sins of the parents are paid for in the lives of the children.

(b) It was a popular belief in Old Testament times and was summarized in a proverb: "The fathers have eaten sour grapes, and their children's teeth are set on edge." That means the misery of the present is punishment for the sins of the past. That is the Deuteronomic view of history, and it was also Freud's view of history and personality. It is ours too to the extent that we blame those who have gone before us for the trouble we face in our time and in our personal lives.

II. There's another way. A hundred years after the book of Deuteronomy was written, Ezekiel came along with this liberating news: "The word of the Lord came to me again: What do you mean by repeating this proverb . . . 'The fathers have eaten sour grapes, and the children's teeth are set on edge'? As I live, says the Lord God, this proverb shall no more be used by you in Israel."

(a) Ezekiel is saying to his generation and to ours, the present is your responsibility. He could see that his generation's fixation on the past and its sins drew their attention away from the present and its opportunities. His generation figured they were stuck with the way things were in their lives because it was a punishment for the way their fathers had lived. Because their fathers had eaten sour grapes, their teeth were set on edge. Ezekiel will have none of this.

(b) The past shapes the present, but it does not determine the present. The past presents the agenda for the present, but it doesn't decide what is going to happen to it. You're not responsible for the way things are in this world. You are responsible for what you do with the way things are. If you are not happy, it's not because of the life that has been given to you. It's because of what you've done with the life that has been given to you. That's what Ezekiel is saying.

III. The important question is "What are you going to do now with the present that's given you?"

(a) If a man came to Ezekiel and told him disagreeable things about his life, how he had been raised, how his parents had made so many mistakes with him, how he had been deprived of the benefits that had been a blessing to other people's lives, and how as a result he now lived a pretty mixed-up adult life, Ezekiel would have replied: "So you are a man with lousy parents, a deprived childhood, and a mixed-up adult life. Now, what are you going to do with it? The past may explain you, but it doesn't excuse you."

(b) You are free only when you can accept the past for what it is and only when you can accept your parents for who they were. And let it be. Then take up responsibility for your own present.

IV. In Luke 13 Jesus is on a hill overlooking Jerusalem. He knows what is going to happen to Jerusalem, and he knows it could have been different, so he weeps.

(a) Jerusalem is repeating the sins of its fathers. Not because it was destined to do so. Not because it was living under some sort of curse. But because it chose to do so. He weeps because it could have been different. It can always be different. That's the meaning of saying the future is a gift from God. It doesn't depend on us. All we have to do is choose it when he offers it to us.

(b) Life is not tragic because things are stacked up against us in this life. That's the Deuteronomic view, which says the die is cast in our childhood or by our parents or by our environment or by something outside of us. The prophetic view is exemplified by Ezekiel and by Jesus that the future is always open, and the only tragedy in this life is that we don't choose it.—Mark Trotter.

Illustrations

DIALOGUE. A small boy tried to show his father a scratch on his finger. Finally, after repeated attempts to gain his father's attention, the father stopped reading and said impatiently, "Well, I can't do anything about it, can I?" "Yes, daddy," his small son said, "you could have said, 'Oh.' "—John M. Drescher.

DRAIN. The *New York Times Magazine* told of the young woman with a new baby saying that she and her husband were startled that their new child was unexpectedly a cash drain and a time drain on the family. The editorialist added, "The idea that the arrival of a new person in the world was siphoning off time and money from another, presumably more important, purpose—and what is more important than what you give a child?—summoned up a vision of the world as a smoothly functioning system of jobs and salaries in which the appearance of human beings was to be regarded as a regrettable disruption."—Richard M. Cromie.

Sermon Suggestions

THREE R'S FOR CHRISTIANS. Text: Luke 2:32. (1) Respect. (2) Responsibility. (3) Reverence.

OVERCOMING FAULTFINDING. Text: Matt. 7:5. (1) Let us face the fact of human imperfection. (2) Let us face the fact of our own faults. (3) Let us face the fact that Christian love is the cure for faultfinding.

Worship Aids

CALL TO WORSHIP. "Both young men, and maidens; old men, and children: let them praise the name of the Lord: for his name alone is excellent; his glory is above the earth and heaven." Ps. 148: 12–13.

INVOCATION. Most holy and gracious God, who turnest the shadow of night into morning: satisfy us early with thy mercy that we may rejoice and be glad all the day. Lift the light of thy countenance upon us, calm every troubled thought, and guide our feet into the way of peace. Perfect thy strength in our weakness and help us to worship thee in the spirit of Jesus Christ our Lord.

OFFERTORY SENTENCE. "This is the thing which the Lord commanded, saying, Take ye from among you an offering unto the Lord: whosoever is of a willing heart, let him bring it, an offering of the Lord." Exod. 35:4–5.

OFFERTORY PRAYER. O Christ, may we walk constantly in thy way and work fervently for those causes which are dear to thee.

PRAYER. Dear heavenly Father, in the quiet tranquility of this moment we listen to you in prayer. We listen for the still, small voice speaking from deep within us.

O Father, let peace like a river fill our souls. We thank you, Father, for the peace we experience after we have worked through a crisis, solved a problem, resolved an inner contradiction, or have been reconciled with a friend. This kind of peace feels like the return of sunshine after a thunderstorm.

Dear heavenly Father, we thank you for the peace we feel when we look at a sleeping baby—soft, helpless, vulnerable, and

yet so full of life. The simple trust of the baby renews our confidence that there is hope and that you are working out your goodwill in our history.

Dear heavenly Father, we thank you for great music which stirs our hearts and throbs in our souls. The peace you give us in these moments is inspiring. We take in new breath. We lift up our hearts in new courage for living. As we lift up our hearts in song we feel your peace flowing again from deep within.—Harold Wahking.

EVENING SERVICE

Topic: Stewardship of the Ninety
TEXT: Luke 17:17.

I. Given as a part of Old Testament law, tithing is probably best known because of Mal. 3:10, that great passage about bringing the tithes into the storehouse. Jesus put his approval upon the practice (Matt. 23:23). Tithing is not only an efficient way of giving but a biblical way—ten percent off the top.

II. Many of us think once the ten percent is out of the way, the rest is ours, scot-free, to do with as we please. In our concern to be biblical, we overlook the fact that stewardship has something to say not only about the top ten percent but also about the other ninety. That's where we do a significant part of our living—in the ninety. And it is where we reveal what we think is important. In the ninety, not in the ten, we publicly and conspicuously witness to what we really believe are the priorities and implications of discipleship.

III. Too often stewardship is promoted on the grounds of what it will do for the steward. Of the tithe God indeed says, "Prove me," but far from being a quid pro quo business transaction, is this not a call to those who already claim to be committed? Commitment comes first. As love can never give enough, so commitment can never give enough and never do enough. Total commitment, like true love, keeps no ledger. Requited love is its own reward. When our attention is focused upon what we hope to get, we are in no frame of mind to give what it takes.

IV. The widow's mites were so great because what she had left was so little. I wonder how we would fare under that kind of measurement? In America, Christian giving for the most part is not terribly demanding. "Give until it hurts," the adage goes. But are we really giving at all if it doesn't hurt? On the other hand, what does hurt mean? Is it anything more than a readjustment to a new commitment, the "expulsive power of a new affection"? Do commitments ever really hurt?

V. Perhaps stewardship is not so much giving up something as doing what one thinks is most important.

(a) God is not so much trying to teach us fractions as to get us to understand that it all belongs to him—the nine dollars somewhere as well as the one dollar in the collection plate.

(b) Maybe the question Jesus is asking each of us—and the one we had better be prepared to answer without embarrassment—is "Where are the nine?"—W. Stanley Mooneyham in *World Vision.*

SUNDAY: JUNE TWENTIETH

MORNING SERVICE

Topic: Crisis and Challenge (Baccalaureate)

TEXT: Phil. 1:20–21.

I. That group of people among us whom we call youth are going through at least five crisis experiences.

(a) There is a growth crisis. This is a physical phenomenon which we all must experience as we move from childhood into adulthood. The body has its changes. But so does the emotional aspect of a person's life. It is a period of moods from extreme joy to extreme sadness. Romances are begun and terminated almost weekly, and the participants cannot explain why.

(b) There is a crisis of identity. They are moving from that period of life when the desire to please parents is replaced by the desire to please and identify with peers. What friends think is very heavy because they're around them in meaningful relationships more than they are around their parents. We never get away from peer pressure. Those of us who are adults are still aware of it. We're image conscious too. But maybe not as much so as are the youth.

(c) There is the crisis of romance. This is the time in life when males and females begin to discover each other and romances are formed. It is a time for dating, falling in love, falling out of love, getting hurt, being jealous, and all of the other things that go with romance. This stage of life can be filled with more anxiety than a person can handle.

(d) There is the crisis of vocation. Who am I? What can I do? Where are my gifts? How do I want to spend the rest of my life? We take one test after the other trying to understand our aptitudes. We talk to counselors. We try our hands at a lot of things. What am I going to major in?

(e) There is the crisis of philosophy. How am I to see life? What's it all about? What is important? What about the Bible? What about God? What about the church? What about other religion? Sometimes during youth or young adulthood, these people who have been very dedicated to God and the church will drift away from their moorings. It will seem to their parents and friends as if they have lost their faith.

II. What can adults do for the youth among us? (a) We can give them an example that is worthy of emulation. There are young people who don't want to grow up. They don't like what they see and don't want to be like some of us.

(b) Adults ought to give patience and love to the youth. In the story of the prodigal son the father not only gave his son the right to make his choices but also the feeling that if he fell flat on his face there was a place to which he could return. It was as if he said: "Son, it's tough out there. Maybe you've got to experience it for yourself to believe it. But listen, my boy, you know the way home. All night long there is going to be a lamp burning."

When the boy got out there and got in trouble, he "came to his senses" and headed for home.

III. What are you living for? There are many philosophies of life.

(a) The first is that which comes from the words of a song, "Life is a cabaret, my friend, so come to the cabaret." Another song says, "Life is just a bowl of cherries." It's the attitude that life is made for fun and fun is made for life.

(b) Shakespeare's character said: "Out, out brief candle! Life's but a walking shadow, a poor player that struts and frets his hour upon the stage and then is heard no more; it is a tale told by an idiot, full of sound and fury, signifying nothing." People who believe that don't live; they just exist, marking time. Their lives are characterized by bitterness, cynicism, and aimlessness. They never hitch their wagon to a star. People who believe that become life's drifters, going from place to place, from party to party, from marriage to marriage, from this to that. Nothing ever satisfies them for they don't understand the meaning of life.

(c) Henry Wadsworth Longfellow said: "Life is real, life is earnest and the grave is not its goal." And it isn't. You and I are eternal. We'll outlast the stars. God made us for glory, for grandeur, and for heaven. He put the very best stuff possible in us—himself. We have his image marked on us. The truly wise person will polish God's imprint in him. He will discover who he is and why he is here and will live every day to the fullest of his being.—Jerry Hayner.

Illustration

A BELIEVER. The great impressario was ill with laryngitis, and the crowd that gathered at the great concert hall that night was angry. They would not hear the beautiful voice of their favorite singer. An understudy would be singing the leading role of the opera that night.

As the curtain rose the understudy stepped forward and sang beautifully. He performed flawlessly throughout the whole first act. As the act came to a close, although he had sung and acted the role as well as the impressario, there was no applause. The sullen audience was silent. They wanted their hero.

Finally from one of the small box seats off to the right there came the sound of one small pair of hands applauding. All eyes turned to see the six-year-old son of the understudy standing, applauding vigorously. And then they heard him shout: "Beautiful, daddy! Beautiful! I believe in you!" And the whole audience erupted with applause.—Bob Roberts.

Sermon Suggestions

MEETING LIFE'S DISAPPOINTMENTS. Text: Heb. 11:40 (RSV). (1) Disappointment may result from our search for certainty. (2) Disappointment may result from our search for mastery. (3) Disappointment may result from our search for real personal experience.—Gene E. Bartlett.

THE ADVENTURE OF BEING YOU. Text: Ps. 8. (1) The Bible is the great textbook that helps an individual to know who he is and to discover life's best. (2) There are basic facts that all individuals have in common in regard to life. (3) The way to discover the true you is through study, growth, and living. (4) To fulfill the adventure of being you, you must know who and what you are in the light of life's highest. (5) To experience the adventure of being you, you must find a frame of reference greater than yourself. (6) The psalmist discovered who he was as he took time to know the creator of the heavens and then turned to the true spirit of life within.—Frank A. Court.

Worship Aids

CALL TO WORSHIP. "And we declare unto you glad tidings, how that the promise which was made unto the fathers, God hath fulfilled the same unto us their children." Acts 13:32–33.

INVOCATION. Most gracious Father, who withholdest no good thing from thy children and in thy providence hast brought us to this day of rest and of the renewal of the soul: we give thee humble and hearty thanks for the world which thou hast prepared and furnished for our dwellingplace, for the steadfast righteousness which suffers no evil thing to gain the mastery, for the lives and examples of those who were strangers and pilgrims and found a better inheritance in peace of soul and joy in the Holy Spirit, and above all for the life, teaching, and sacrifice of Jesus Christ.

OFFERTORY SENTENCE. "Give unto the Lord the glory due unto his name: bring an offering, and come before him." I Chron. 16:29.

OFFERTORY PRAYER. Our Father, enable all Christians to know that their lives may be lived with Christ in God and that their gifts are means by which thy love in Christ may reach into the lives of wayward and needy persons everywhere.

PRAYER. O Lord of all being who art throned afar and whose glory flames from sun and star, we pray that thou wilt in these moments be near to each loving heart.

Enter, we pray thee, into our heart of hearts and, there enthroned, cleanse our lives of sin, refashion our motives according to thy will, and help us by thy grace to rededicate our lives to thy holy purposes and to the kingdom of the Lord Jesus.

So may we by thy renewing of our minds go forth from worship singing thy praises and incarnating in our words and activity the fruit of the spirit as evidence that we have communed with Christ and seek to be his true disciples.

EVENING SERVICE

Topic: Living as God's People

SCRIPTURE: I Pet. 2:9-16.

The grand characterization of gospel people is this: "Ye are a chosen generation, a royal priesthood, a holy nation, a peculiar people." When the church was established, Christ became the life-force of those who obeyed him. Christians have been given gifts of several specialties.

I. *Special privileges and honors* (I Pet. 2: 9-10). (a) "Ye are a chosen generation" (an elect race, ASV). How were those Christians elected? Who elected them? For what purpose were they elected? God chooses or elects any person who believes the gospel truth and obeys the gospel commands (II Thess. 2:13-14).

(b) "A royal priesthood." John wrote of Christ who has "made us kings and priests unto God" (Rev. 1:6). This word reminds us of the offices held by Aaron and his sons. When Aaron was consecrated to that priesthood, he was totally committed to sacred service. He would serve faithfully in holy things. Today all Christians are priests before God, serving under their great high priest, Jesus, just as those priests under Aaron were responsible for serving in the place of sacrifice and worship regularly, handling sacred things conscientiously, careful not to bring offense upon their office.

(c) "A holy nation." Speaking of citizenship in this holy nation, Paul declared, "Ye are no more strangers and foreigners, but fellow citizens with the saints, and of the household of God" (Eph. 2:19).

(d) "A peculiar people." Those claimed by Christ as his very own belong to him and to him alone.

II. *Special conduct before the world* (vv. 11-16). Peter enjoined Christians to abstain from fleshly lusts and thus glorify God in the presence of heathen lifestyles. Heathenism is still with us, and Peter's admonition is still valid. Others may be led to worship and obey God because of the example of Christians. (See Matt. 5:16.) For this reason we are exhorted to be subject to every governmental ordinance for the sake of the Lord. As bondservants of God we can never use Christian freedom as an excuse for doing evil.

III. *Special armaments for suffering.* (a) "He that hath suffered in the flesh." Because of his Christian faith, he has taken a different stance before the world. This may mystify his former associates, but they shall be compelled ultimately to give an account of their own actions before the divine judge.

(b) Whatever God said was necessary, Jesus did. Christians today are placed within the same framework. A person who is willing to suffer for his faith has been disciplined to his loyalty to God and refuses to turn traitor to Christ.—Ard Hoven.

SUNDAY: JUNE TWENTY-SEVENTH

MORNING SERVICE

Topic: The Ground of Our Hope
TEXT: Heb. 13:8.
Our hope is in the God who inhabits eternity, the God whom Jesus called Father.

I. *Always creating.* (a) I saw a motto on a person's desk. It was turned so the visitor could read it. "Please be patient. God is not finished with me yet."

(b) Nor is he finished with you or me nor the universe in which we live. A group of scientists suggested that matter is coming into being at the rate of a nonillion tons a second. A nonillion is the figure 1 followed by 30 zeros, and in Great Britain and Germany it is 1 followed by 54 zeros. A nonillion tons of matter is coming into being every second. Perhaps the figure is only an educated guess or pure speculation. The accuracy of the figure doesn't really matter. The point is that creation is a continuing process. We live in an open universe where the new is always possible.

(c) "Behold, I am doing a new thing; now it springs forth, do you not perceive it?" (Isa. 43:19). God is not finished with us yet and "it does not yet appear what we shall be" (I John 3:2). The Spirit which moved over the void and darkness in the beginning is still blowing in the wind, inspiring the not-yet, the dreams and visions which call us. And in an open universe there is always hope.

II. *Always caring.* (a) If Jesus is the disclosure of God, we can be sure that the Father cares about his creation with an unchanging love—the same yesterday, today, and forever. Not a sparrow falls beyond his notice, and "you are worth more than many sparrows." His love is always seeking even the one who is lost, like a good shepherd seeks the one sheep which is not in the fold, like a woman searching for the lost coin, and like the father watching and waiting for the prodigal son to come home. This is the nature of God's love, and this is the love in which we live.

(b) God's care for you and me reaches for all his creation, all those other persons who live in our world—the peoples of the third world, those who live in the dismal ghettos of our cities and our suburbs, and on and on unto the least and last of all. His unchanging and unending love is concerned that justice and mercy shall be theirs and that they shall know what it is to have hope in their hearts. It is the nature of divine love never to give up on his creation, and the ground of our hope is that he is always caring.

III. *Always redeeming.* (a) It is in this that I find the best understanding of the omnipotence of God. We can best understand his omnipotence by the way in which he is always redeeming—turning tragedy into triumph as in the cross, using doubt to deepen faith, or transforming the lost and wasted life into something splendid and useful.

(b) Always redeeming means that he can never be ultimately defeated in his purpose and can never be completely frustrated in his love and that no person and no situation is ever beyond the reach of God's transforming, redeeming power. There is always hope for "in everything God works for good with those who love him" (Rom. 8:28).

(c) To understand this we do not have to depend upon some theological doctrine or definition. We can see it in history, written in flesh and blood. We can see it happening in the lives of persons around us or in our own experience.—Robert E. Goodrich, Jr.

Illustrations

WILL OF GOD.   Can you look up from your knees when you are at your prayers and say: "Lord, ask anything thou choosest, anything at all, and if it is thy will for me, I will accept it. Even if it means some terribly difficult denial of my own plans and dreams, even if it drives me down a lonelier, harder road than I ever thought I should have to travel, if it is thy will, O God, for me, with unwavering heart I will accept it."—James S. Stewart.

THE NATURE OF RELIGION. The vision of something which stands beyond, behind, and within the passing flux of immediate things; something which is real, and yet waiting to be realized; something which is a remote possibility, and yet the greatest of present facts; something which gives meaning to all that passes, and yet eludes apprehension; something whose possession is the final good, and yet is beyond all reach; something which is the ultimate ideal and the hopeless quest.—Alfred North Whitehead.

Sermon Suggestions

HOPE FOR THE SAVED. Text: Eph. 2:5–6. Paul sets forth three things God does when he saves a sinner. (1) "God hath quickened us." (2) "God hath raised us up." (3) "God hath made us sit together in heavenly places."—P. O. Davidson.

STEADFAST LOYALTIES. Text: I Cor. 15:58. (1) Loyal to such moral principles as honesty, truth, purity, and honor. (2) Loyal to such moral principles as brotherhood, justice, and social righteousness. (3) Loyal to the eternal realities for which the church of Jesus Christ stands and to the vision of a kingdom for which we are to labor.—Theodore F. Adams.

Worship Aids

CALL TO WORSHIP. "It is good for me to draw near to God: I have put my trust in the Lord God. God is the strength of my heart, and my portion for ever." Ps. 73:26, 28.

INVOCATION. Our Father, we thank thee for this opportunity to worship thee and to purify our lives and thoughts by holy fellowship with thee. We ask thee for the grace to forget the rankling past and to press on with joy and confidence to the high calling of God through Jesus Christ. As we strive to be good givers of our lives to others and to thee, help us now to be good receivers of thy grace and mercy.

OFFERTORY SENTENCE. "If any man will come after me [saith Jesus], let him deny himself, and take up his cross daily, and follow me." Luke 9:23.

OFFERTORY PRAYER. Our Father, we thank thee that thou art so generous to us. All that we have is a gift from thee. Help us to serve one another so that we may reflect thy spirit and goodness.

PRAYER. God of glory, center of unbroken praise throughout thy church, we thy people humbly bow before thee in prayer. Gathered here, we affirm our oneness with all thy faithful servants down the centuries. We magnify thy name. We give thee thanks for the church triumphant, for the one clear call by which it summons us to thee. Elevate our prayers to the throne of thy grace that they may fly on winged feet to do thy work on earth.

Lord, hear us as we pray for others. We pray for all sorts and conditions of men, both near and far away. We pray for the coming of that day when every knee shall bow at the name of Jesus Christ, for we know that our salvation is bound together with that of all men.

We name those whose lives touch ours every day—our parents, our children, our beloved, our friends, those with whom we work and play. Thou knowest the heart of each one and dost understand the particular need of each. Feed these persons with thy living bread, O heavenly Lord.

Merciful Father, we cannot forget in our prayers the millions of suffering mankind whose faces we do not know, whose lives do not touch ours, but who are equally precious to thee. May thy healing grace and thy mercy be with them. May the promise of thy deliverance give hope to the millions of homeless and hopeless refugees throughout the earth.—David H. McAlpine, Jr.

EVENING SERVICE

Topic: One Day at a Time
TEXT: Matt. 6:34.

Life comes to us one day at a time. We may waste mental energy regretting yesterday or while away time presuming upon tomorrow. Yet life comes to us simply day by day.

I. In the sermon on the mount Jesus cautions us against anxious concern for tomorrow. "Take no thought for the morrow" does not forbid us to make preparation for tomorrow. A wise person prepares to live his life. The words of Jesus mean that we should not let concern for tomorrow overwhelm us today. You could grow so worried about what the future will bring that you cannot face the present. No amount of anxiety will bring tomorrow sooner, and no thought contains the power to change what will occur when it gets here.

II. Jesus reminds us that each day contains sufficient evil for itself. We live in a world full of trouble. Each day's report of the news brings another burden to lay on our hearts. Two of these put together would be more than we could stand. If you and I can handle one day—today—we have enough.

III. The secret for living one day at a time is found in the Lord's Prayer. "Give us this day our daily bread." God grants us our living day by day. Though he has much in store to give to his children and though he intends the best for us, the Father grants our provision daily. We should live in accordance with his plan.

IV. Tomorrow may not come. Yesterday belongs to the history books. Today is mine. Remember the instruction of our Lord. Take life one day at a time. Live each day to the fullest. That will free your mind from excessive care. That will speak of your obedience to the master. When tomorrow gets here, if it does, you will be prepared for it.—James L. Heflin.

SUNDAY: JULY FOURTH

MORNING SERVICE

Topic: Getting in God's Good Graces
TEXT: Eph. 2:8–10.

How can we find God's favor? What must we do? What attitude must we take toward the task?

I. We may try the way of good works. (a) The way of works is a popular way. It appeals to men everywhere. It is particularly attractive to Americans. We are activists and take pride in our busyness and in our achievements. Some of us are like the man who is reported to have said, "I can show God a thing or two."

(b) The way of works is a way of frustration. Those who attempt this way often fall back in discouragement. After a while they see that their best is not good enough. Or they go along despising other people. Their fancied moral superiority robs them of the experience of Christian love and compassion.

(c) The way of works is the wrong way.

Paul wrote to the church in Galatia, "If justification were through the law, then Christ died to no purpose" (Gal. 2:21). (See Matt. 5:20.)

II. We may travel the way of presumption. (a) The way of presumption is marked with three misleading signs.

(1) One sign says, "God expects little." This appeals to those who resent and resist authority and who are tempted to deify desire.

(2) Another sign says: "God is merciful. Forget your sins." Latourette pointed out that sometimes religious mysticism had a dark side and that there were those "who professed to have a union with God which rendered yielding to the impulses of the flesh a matter of moral indifference."

(3) The third sign says, "The rules don't apply to you." The office holder who fattens his pocketbook with graft, the preacher who breaks the speed limit because he is on an errand for God, or the businessman who carries on a clandestine

love affair because he can afford it and his wife doesn't care—all may blithely go their way, assuming that although the Lord may disapprove such behavior in some people, their own case is exceptional.

(b) What is wrong with the things these signs have to say? (1) God expects much, rather than little, of his people. The noble achievements of many men would not have been made if they had not felt the pull of the impossible. Those who presume that God expects little do far less than what is both right and possible.

(2) The inexorable principle of sowing and reaping goes on, regardless of the easygoing attitude one might take toward the mercy of God and the destructiveness of sin. The moral law of God brooks no exceptions; it was made for all people. Violation of the express will of God by king or clergyman, subject or layman brings unhappy consequences. "Be not deceived; God is not mocked: for whatsoever a man soweth, that shall he also reap" (Gal. 6:7).

III. The right way is the way of grace with works. (a) This way takes into account all the facts from human sin to divine grace. When Jesus prayed for his disciples, he implored, "Sanctify them through thy truth: thy word is truth" (John 17:17). The sanctification of the Pharisees lay in error and presumption; they thought they were set apart to God but were not. Jesus wanted to be sure that those who followed him had a religious life grounded in reality, not fantasy.

(b) This way pays God the highest honor. It is no honor to God for a man to present an offering of money or morality and expect God to be bribed into being favorable. The character of God is magnified and praised when he receives a man and forgives him in spite of what the man is and has done. Such is the grace of God. A man who is saved boasts not of himself but of the merciful God who has saved him. For salvation is "not of works, lest any man should boast."

(c) This way has the highest motivation. Pride and fear may drive men to do daring and spectacular feats. But pride will not save a man from the gnawing emptiness of a life selfishly lived. Nor will fear save a man from self-reproach and

the regret that his fear exacted too great a price in the service of others or of God. But love is different. Love is the motive that more than anything else spurs and inspires the person who has seen squarely his duties toward God and man and has seen them as offerings of gratitude for sins already forgiven rather than as bribes or payments for sins one wishes yet to be forgiven of.

(d) The way of grace with works is really the means of our fulfilling the divine purpose. What is God's will for us? It is God's will that we do good works. Let no mistake be made about that. We do not buy our salvation with good works, for our salvation has been bought already with the redeeming blood of Christ. Rather a life of good works is the outgrowth of the saving work of God in the life of a Christian. "For we are his workmanship, created in Christ Jesus for good works, which God prepared beforehand that we should walk in them" (Eph. 2:10).—James W. Cox.

Illustrations

ACCEPTED. You are accepted by that which is greater than you and the name of which you do not know. Simply accept the fact that you are accepted. When that happens to us, we experience grace, and reconciliation bridges the gulf of estrangement. After such an experience, we may not be better than before, and we may not believe more than before. But everything is transformed.—Paul Tillich.

NARROW WAY. In the Garden of the Gods outside of Colorado Springs the road narrows between massive rock cliffs to the place where it would seem difficult to navigate a motorcycle. As the driver begins to look for a place to turn around, he sees a small white sign. It reads: "Narrows! Yes, you can, a million others have." And what do you know, a minute and a half later, a million and one have done it. —Paul H. Barkley.

Sermon Suggestions

CHRISTIAN CITIZENSHIP. Text: Prov. 11:10. (1) The Christian citizen has a faith to live for and a faith to live by. (2) The Christian citizen renders service through love that will strengthen the nation. (3) The Christian dedicates himself totally in the spirit of Christ to the bringing of the kingdom of God among men. (4) The Christian citizen receives through worship the strength and inspiration to serve the present age in the love of Christ.—Frank A. Court.

KEEPING FAITH IN RIGHTEOUSNESS. Text: Matt. 5:6. (1) To keep faith in righteousness we must believe in human nature and its possibilities for good. (2) To keep faith in righteousness we must give unfaltering support of the ideal that right makes might. (3) To keep faith in righteousness we must have faith in a purposive universe.—Charles F. Jacobs.

Worship Aids

CALL TO WORSHIP.   "Blessed is the man that trusteth in the Lord, and whose hope the Lord is." Jer. 17:7.

INVOCATION.   O God of mercy, in this hour in thy house have mercy upon us. O God of light, shine into our hearts. O thou eternal goodness, deliver us from evil. O God of power, be thou our refuge and our strength. O God of love, let love flow through us. O God of life, live within us, now and forevermore.

OFFERTORY SENTENCE.   "Unto whomsoever much is given, of him shall be much required: and to whom men have committed much, of him they will ask the more." Luke 12:48.

OFFERTORY PRAYER.   We thank thee, O God, for another anniversary of our nation's independence and pray that this rich gift may be an opportunity to serve one another in love.

PRAYER.   Almighty and most merciful Father, who art greater than all our thoughts of thee and who art so deep within us that we cannot escape thee, we have gathered together in a spirit of worship to seek thy face and to pray for thy help in living our lives.

We lay before thee our foreboding thoughts about the world. We live our days now with a sense of danger and of approaching crisis. O God, grant us as a nation and grant to our President and his advisers the courage to master fear, the wisdom to find the main decisions which favor truth and freedom, the self-control to act at the right moment, neither too soon or too late. But above all, Father, grant that our hearts may be stayed on thee that we may be humble enough to recognize that thou thyself art the lord of history and that when we have done our human best we must put our trust in thee and wait in quietness and without fear.

We lay before thee our sense of guilt. We know that we are not the men and women we ought to be. Pride has ruled our hearts and self-interest our decisions. In thought, word, and deed we have sinned against thy holy laws, betrayed our own best selves, and estranged the neighbor whom we were supposed to love. O God of mercy, who hast called us to reason together with thee, let thy promise be fulfilled. Though our sins be as scarlet, let them be whiter than snow. Let our hearts rise up and bless thee. Let us live lives inspired by gratitude for thy great mercy, lives of righteousness and peace.

O God of freedom, who hast made men free and who hast sent thy Son to set us free from all man-made slavery, teach us to cherish liberty, to realize that thy laws of right and wrong, of justice and mercy are the bulwark of freedom, and to give ourselves freely to thy service all our days. —Robert J. Arnott.

EVENING SERVICE

Topic: The Pursuit of Happiness
SCRIPTURE: Matt. 5:3–12.

The subject of happiness has been a favorite one of preachers, philosophers, and poets since the dawn of history. Scientists have avoided the subject because it deals with human emotions and sentiments which do not lend themselves to measurement or evaluation.

I. A survey made by a dozen psychiatrists and psychologists involving over a hundred thousand people found that there was no such thing as a formula for happiness and that its pursuit must be constant.

(a) A study by the University of Michigan's Institute of Social Research found no relation between happiness and money or happiness and the educational level. A high school graduate with money to pay his bills is as happy as a college graduate under similar circumstances.

(b) Another factor influencing happiness, the psychologists found, is expectation. Those who get more in life than they expected tend to be happier than those who achieve less than they expected. Those who seem to have everything are not necessarily happier. After a while they get used to abundance and getting more has no substantial effect.

(c) Good health does not guarantee happiness, and poor health does not rule it out.

(d) People with strong religious feelings are no happier than those without such feelings. Among those with religious beliefs, however, the followers of the most liberal traditions are happier than those with stricter faiths. However, it was found that elderly people with deep religious convictions can be happier than the young or those of middle age.

II. Time was when Christianity and joy were incompatible. (a) The Puritans regarded their religion as too serious to include the lighter side of life. Preachers refrained from telling humorous stories in the pulpit as that was considered sacrilegious. Devout church members lived in the shadows of gloom. Like the comic strip character, they carried their own rain clouds around with them. They even felt guilty when they laughed. An elderly gentleman described one of his aged friends as never happier "than he was when he was miserable." The idea prevailed that suffering must come before one deserved happiness.

(b) In generations past when working hours were long and life was hard, millions looked to the afterlife for their joys. Heaven would supply what they were deprived of on earth.

(c) A realistic view of the present day world would lead us to conclude that we demand instant gratification. We don't want to wait for a post-mortem reward. We want satisfaction here and now.

III. The Institute of Social Research found that the quality of life in a community cannot be measured alone by the size of its library, the symphony orchestra, the number of educational institutions, the employment level, the per capita income, and the recreation facilities. It also involves the number of churches and their effectiveness, the spirit of the people as reflected in their willingness to sacrifice for the common good, and prevailing standards of taste.

(a) Happiness is an elusive element in the human mood. Thomas Jefferson said, "God did not intend for us to be happy all the time or even to be satisfied." George Bernard Shaw observed that "as long as you had a want you have a reason for living. Satisfaction is death."

(b) Just as there is no risk-proof society, there is no perfect prescription for human contentment. But the best that has ever been devised is centered in the basic principles contained in Holy Writ—goodness, love, sacrifice, and caring.

(c) No better route has been found in man's ceaseless search for happiness than that outlined in the beatitudes—"the happy ones" proclaimed by Jesus from the top of a mountain.—Houston Cole.

SUNDAY: JULY ELEVENTH

MORNING SERVICE

Topic: The Everlasting Arms
TEXT: Deut. 33:27.

I. What does this life of ours mean? Is there a purpose in history? What can we make of this universe? Are we just drifting along on a tide that breaks on no shore and ends in nothingness or are we moving toward a destination—some far-off divine event? The deepest need of man's nature is to sense some worthwhile meaning to his life, some light that sheds its ray of hope upon his path, some star of guidance above the dark abyss.

II. We believe that God, who is the ruler of nations and the sovereign lord of life and death, has created us for fellowship with himself and to live in harmony with his will. That is our high calling and our true destiny. God's high purpose gives meaning to our lives. We live our lives within the framework of his love and power.

(a) Jesus taught that our lives are under the surveillance of the heavenly Father who is eternally concerned for the welfare of his children, suffering with them in their struggles, sharing their agonies, and rejoicing in their victories. It is such a faith that "sets up a shaft of everlasting light above the howling senses' ebb and flow."

(b) After the deliverance from Egypt and the perils of the wilderness wanderings, the children of Israel stand at last on the borders of the promised land. About to renounce his leadership, Moses gives them his parting message. He concludes: "The eternal God is your dwelling place, and underneath are the everlasting arms." Such words surely point to the heart of our faith, a faith that makes us more than conquerors over our fears and anxieties, linking us to the infinite resources of the living God.

III. When we look at the world about us and think of the horror, the hatred, the selfishness, the suffering, the misery, and man's inhumanity to man, aren't we left to wonder whether the creator of all does really care and is at all interested in our human agony?

(a) It is a choice of faith against despair, of trust against doubt, and of hope against pessimism. Christians believe that love is stronger than hate, that goodness will conquer evil, and that the cross will outlive the sword.

(b) Something happened on the hill called Calvary, where a man died with love in his heart and forgiveness on his lips, that shatters to dust all kingdoms founded on blood and fear and hate. In the face of the darkness and suffering and tragedy of life, Jesus stood and uttered his beatitudes. Such words fling their rainbow colors across earth's darkest cloud, lighten our heaviest load, and take the sting out of our severest pain.

IV. We know that God is love—a love that will not forsake us nor let us go. The universe is friendly to the best in us, friendly to the hero in our souls, and sympathetic with our hopes and agonies.

(a) Our Christian faith declares that we are of infinite worth in the sight of God and that our little lives have a place in the framework of his purpose. This faith gives dignity to our lives and meaning to our days. Such a faith sustained the brave souls who lived as seeing him who is invisible. (See Heb. 11:36–38.)

(b) Many had to bear what De Quincey called the "burden of the incommunicable." What supported them? The belief that beyond our poor human insight and error and our poor human knowledge and frailty stood the one who knew their worth and placed on their devotion the imprimatur of his approval.

V. Sooner or later life goes to pieces without the encouraging embrace of the everlasting arms. To feel that our lives are walled about with God gives meaning and victory to our poor human struggle. When our faith grows thin and our spirits become weary of striving, "God hoists again the flags of dawn, blows his trumpet from the hills, and calls us humbly back again." Faith such as this makes us feel at home in the universe, and we are encouraged to march breast forward.—Richard E. Gosse.

Illustrations

MESSAGES. The daughter of a preacher was very ill and near death's door. Her father talked to her, and she asked, "Have you any message that I can take to those on the other side when I pass over?" "Yes, tell St. Paul how much his wonderful epistles have meant to me, tell St. John how much he has taught me of the love of God, and give greetings my friends who have gone before." "But," said the daughter, "haven't you forgotten someone? Haven't you a message for Jesus himself?" "No," replied the father, "I have just been talking to him in the next room."—Ernest Edward Smith.

WITHOUT WALLS. A man dreamed that he was at home alone, and as the day wore on he began to hear voices in the basement. Eventually he went to investigate and discovered a man working in a basement office. From the equipment in the room and the drawings that were around, it was obvious the man was an architect. As he conversed with him, he revealed that he was the architect of this man's house. The man not only expressed surprise that he was the designer of the home but also that he had been oblivious to the fact that someone had an office in his basement. The architect told him that there was something else which he had not known. There were more rooms in his house than he had explored. The architect gave him a tour. He opened door after door, showing him rooms he had not known were there. The most striking thing remembered about the rooms was that there were no walls, no boundaries, and no limits. Then the dream ended.

This dream is representative of each of us. The house is each of us. The architect, the designer of the space, is God. The message is that God has created many more rooms in the house than we are aware of—rooms without limits.—Donald L. Germain.

Sermon Suggestions

GOD'S CREATIVE POWER. Scripture: Ps. 104:1–9; Prov. 3:19–20. (1) Creation is an expression of divine wisdom. (See Prov. 3:19.) (2) Creation is the work of a majestic God. (See Ps. 104:1–4.) (3) Creation is controlled by divine providence. (See Ps. 104:5–9; Prov. 3:20.)—Ed North.

AT THE END OF YOUR ROPE. Text: II Cor. 1:9 (PHILLIPS). (1) Sometimes the rope turns out to be longer than we thought it was. (2) Sometimes when a man reaches the end of his rope, he may have to tie a knot and hang on. (3) Sometimes when you reach the end of your rope, you may discover that God has hold of the other end.—Clarence J. Forsberg.

Worship Aids

CALL TO WORSHIP. "They that wait upon the Lord shall renew their strength; they shall mount up with wings as eagles; they shall run, and not be weary; and they shall walk, and not faint." Isa. 40:31.

INVOCATION. Lord, lift us out of private-mindedness and give us public souls to work for thy kingdom by daily creating that atmosphere of a happy temper and generous heart which alone can bring the great peace.

OFFERTORY SENTENCE. "Verily, verily, I say unto you, he that believeth on me, the works that I do shall he do also; and greater works than these shall he do. And whatsoever ye shall ask in my name, that will I do, that the Father may be glorified in the Son." John 14:12–13.

OFFERTORY PRAYER. Our Father, take us with all of our failures and develop us after thine own heart. Give us more of the mind of the master, more of his spirit of compassion, and more of his sacrificial and loving heart.

PRAYER. Eternal God, who is over all, make us to know that you and you alone are God. Forgive us for we have again and again put ourselves at the center of our world. Our pride has been our downfall. We have experienced your judgment upon us as we have played the role of prodigal in the far country and have wasted our substance in ways contrary to your will. We have misused the freedom we have received from you and have failed to be your obedient children. Yet we know your love for us never has stopped. Even though we have experienced your love as wrath and have suffered despair and despondence, we know that you are ever with us, the seeking Father, revealed in the seeking Son, present with us at this very moment as the seeking Spirit. We thank you for not forsaking us. In this moment of worship as we come to ourselves we turn to you in repentance, and by your grace we turn homeward to full fellowship. We thank you for bringing us now from death to life.

Our Father, we would open all the closed doors in our lives to you. We would tear down all of the signs that say to you, "Stay out!" It won't be easy to do this for your penetrating presence exposes all within our living that is crude and cruel and out of harmony with your spirit.

Yet we know that in spite of all that is within us that is painful to face, you are with us as one who loves each of us just as we are. We ask you to forgive us, to renew us, and to set us free to become more and more your true people.—Edward W. Norman.

EVENING SERVICE

Topic: Tests of Conversion
TEXT: I Cor. 14:25.
I. Does a person pay his debts? (a) It was

a feature of the D. L. Moody and Billy Sunday campaigns that the first people to reap the practical benefit of the campaigns were the shopkeepers to whom the converts repaid many a long-standing debt.

(b) As in the case of Zacchaeus, restitution and paying of debts is a mark of conversion.

(c) In a more recent revival which swept a part of central and western Canada, one of the most immediate signs of changed lives was that people paid their debts and made restitution for things taken or gained dishonestly.

II. Does a person mend his quarrels? Nothing could be more blunt than "If anyone says 'I love God' and hates his brother, he is a liar" (I John 4:20). No person is converted so long as he has in his life an unhealed quarrel with another person. No one is truly at peace with God until he is at peace with his fellowman.

III. Does it make a person a better workman? (a) Human nature, left to itself, is both lazy and selfish. It tends to do as little as possible and demands as much as possible.

(b) The converted person works in such a way that he could present his work to God, regardless of who the boss is. He is "ever in the Great Taskmaster's eyes." (See II Tim. 2:15.)

IV. Does a person feel pain at the sight of sin and a compassion for the one who sins? The natural person may be repulsed or repelled by sin and critical of the sinner, but the converted person feels a deep compassion and pain when sin is seen and for the one who sins.—Adapted from William Barclay by John M. Drescher.

SUNDAY: JULY EIGHTEENTH

MORNING SERVICE

Topic: Looking Ahead on Tiptoes
SCRIPTURE: Rom. 8:18–23.
I. Our vantage point for looking ahead is a world full of suffering. (a) Paul describes it well by the use of the word "groan." We groan much (vv. 18, 23).

(1) We groan from the troubles we foolishly bring upon ourselves. (See I Pet. 2:20.) By our sins we bring suffering. We make bad decisions and suffer the consequences.

(2) We groan when troubles come because we are believers. (See I Pet. 3:14.) Because of our faith, we have stood for

what was right and spoken out against some things, and so we have lost out financially or lost some friends.

(3) We groan when God chastises us as children to purify our faith. (See I Cor. 4:17.) The burdens of sickness, trials, and tribulation that he lets come our way to try our spiritual muscles cause us to groan. You know what your burdens are.

(b) We do not suffer alone. All of nature is in waiting, suffering also (vv. 20–21).

(1) Nature did not incur the suffering it endures as a result of its own sin.

(2) When man sinned, God subjected nature to ruin. God cursed the ground. Imperfect man would not get to live in a perfect world. It was made subject to vanity, destined to ruin, no matter what. (See Gen. 3:17–19.)

(3) Paul personifies nature and points out that it does not enjoy its ruin. It groans from the pollution, the ravages of beast and bug, waste, erosion, disease, and depletions. It looks ahead, stands on tiptoes, eagerly waiting the day when it will be delivered.

II. We are looking ahead to the glory to be revealed to us. (a) We have had a taste of this glory through the spirit given to us (v. 23).

(1) The Spirit has attached us to Jesus Christ. Christ has come and walked through the valley of the shadow of death for us. (See Ps. 23.) He groaned for us under the burden of the sins of the whole world. He won our glorious future for us. By faith in Jesus Christ we have the forgiveness of our foolish sins. (See Rom. 8: 1–2.)

(2) When we enjoy the forgiveness of our sins and then find peace with God, we have a taste of heaven. We can feel this in our spirits. And it is good.

(3) The Spirit gives us a taste of this through word and sacrament. We have tasted it in baptism and often through Holy Communion and the proclamation of the gospel.

(4) This taste is just a down payment. It is just enough to put us on our toes in eager anticipation of the complete glory yet to come.

(b) Complete glory will be brought by Jesus Christ (v. 23). (1) He will reveal himself again on the last day in all his glory (v. 18).

(2) Complete glory will be ours when we get the gift of his love—heaven. All things will be made new again. Even the created world will have a new start, doing again what it could when God first made it.

(3) We will be set free from all the things that make us groan. In God's word there is a promise to counter every groan-causing trouble. We receive partial deliverance now and full deliverance in heaven.

(c) This glory makes present suffering unimportant (v. 18). (1) We will still suffer in the future.

(2) Our attention will be focused on what is ahead. Have you never had a pain somewhere which you forgot momentarily because your mind was on something else?

(3) When the time to groan comes again, the glorious deliverance is the thing to put your mind on. Pray for complete deliverance to come soon. Stand on your tiptoes by faith in waiting eagerly with all of nature for the glory of the lord to rip away the vale of tears and replace it with the joys of salvation.—Lowell F. Thomas.

Illustrations

SILENT CHRISTIAN. Two men had been partners in business. One man was a regular attender at church. The other professed no religion at all. One Sunday morning they met in the same tram—the one on his way to church and the other to play golf.

As they separated the latter said to his companion, "Look here, when are you going to give up all this hypocrisy about religion and church-going?"

"I don't understand you," said the other.

"I mean just what I say. When are you going to give up this hypocrisy?"

Much offended, his companion answered, "What right have you to call my religion hypocrisy?"

"Well," said the other, "we have been partners for twenty years. We have met and talked together every day. You know quite well that if what you profess to believe is true it is a very hopeless case for me, and yet you have never said one word to help me to be anything different."—Erskine Hill.

CONJUGATING VERBS. We spend most of our lives conjugating three verbs: to want, to have, and to do. Craving, clutching, and fussing on the material, political, social, emotional, intellectual, even on the religious plane, we are kept in perpetual unrest: forgetting that none of these verbs has ultimate significance, except so far as they are transcended by and included in the fundamental verb, TO BE: and that being, not wanting, having, and doing, is the essence of spiritual life.—Evelyn Underhill.

Sermon Suggestion

WHY SOME CHURCHES GROW. Text: John 4:35. (1) Churches grow when they have a vision. (2) Churches grow when they have a burden. (3) Churches grow when they are well organized and adequately staffed. (4) Churches grow when they have outreach ministries. (5) Churches grow through publicity. (6) Churches grow when they exercise faith, prayer, and hard work.—Raymond E. Crowley.

Worship Aids

CALL TO WORSHIP. "Lift up your heads in the sanctuary, and bless the Lord. The Lord that made heaven and earth bless thee out of Zion." Ps. 134:2–3.

INVOCATION. Mysterious God of creation, we are forever awed by the wonder of life here and now, beyond and forever. The more we learn of nature and existence, the more we ponder the puzzle of your conceptions. Through science and technology we have conquered boundaries unimaginable to our father's father. Yet every answer leaves unknown, though sharper in its reality, the inexpressible nature of your word. The more we discover of the discernible, the more we anticipate our need of the eternal.

OFFERTORY SENTENCE. "Give unto the Lord, O ye kindreds of the people, give unto the Lord glory and strength. Give unto the Lord the glory due unto his name: bring an offering, and come into his courts." Ps. 96:7–8.

OFFERTORY PRAYER. Our Father, help us to love thee so well that we shall have all thy kingdom interests and all thy children at heart.

PRAYER. Our Father, amid the panic and peril that swirl about us, plant new thoughts that will inspire and pronounce wisdom that will guide us. Our lives, we know, are vacant without thy presence, and they are void without thy power. Use this hour to speak the words we need so desperately to hear.

While thy words uplift us, let us remember that we are responsible for lifting others. While thy gospel touches our life, let us be reminded that others await the touch of our life. Send us forth with fresh words for stale lives. Commission us to carry words of hope to hopeless hearts. Engage us to speak words of light amid the darkness.

Too soon do we feel our duties ended and our responsibilities fulfilled. Heighten our sensitivities and broaden our concerns until duty becomes a life and not an event.

May these moments with thee, Father, set our hearts upon new paths—paths of service and discipleship. And may we know that no peace is possible outside thy will.—C. Neil Strait.

EVENING SERVICE

Topic: Keeping Your Spirits Up
SCRIPTURE: Ps. 55:1–8, 22.
Moods are unreliable, and they have their way with us and move on. They come and they go. It is wise to say to them, "This too shall pass!" But not all of us have acquired that wisdom.

I. If moods come and moods go, and we

all experience a wide range of moods, one of the best things we can do is simply to "hang in there"! The rhythm of time, the ups and downs, the ins and outs, just hanging on while the very elemental movement of life occurs is frequently the wisest and best thing to do.

II. Closely related to the this-too-shall-pass awareness that there is a cyclic rhythm to the up and down experiences of life is the importance of a time-perspective outlook on life. If you look at any one day or hour with a pinpointed light, you are focusing in and concentrating on just one infinitesimally small episode singled out from the whole of the life-event. The time perspective is all off. Your narrow beam of concentration puts the whole of the horizon in the dark. You are seeking and singling out this moment in time, this particular experience, this certain person. Your perspective is wrong. All of the available light has been concentrated on this unhappiness or that, and you have thrown into the shadows those large areas of happiness which you have known.

III. The next step is to activate yourself. The worst thing a person can do if he wants to keep his spirits up is to go off into a corner by himself and just think and brood. Keep busy. Get yourself off your hands. Get up, especially when you really don't want to get up. Get busy, particularly if there is nothing you'd rather do than just sit quietly by yourself.

IV. When you're up against the psalmist's experience, set about disciplining your thoughts, sorting out the affirmative from the negative, and allowing the affirmative to stand forth. It is possible to control our thoughts by directing and disciplining our minds. If you are in low spirits, pour out your fears and anxieties, your insecurities and apprehensions. And once you do this, you'll be amazed at how much room there is for sturdy clean thoughts, thoughts that are strong and good and positive, thoughts that are not weights but wings, not problems but powers.

V. The psalmist moved from despair to faith and from depression to a right spirit. In almost every psalm there is this eternal cycle. And so it says, "Cast your burden on the Lord, and he will sustain you." That's not just pious prattle. That's the soundest kind of truth there is. It's been tried and tested by countless souls and not found wanting.—Charles L. Copenhaver.

SUNDAY: JULY TWENTY-FIFTH

MORNING SERVICE

Topic: **Handling Stress Without Strain**
SCRIPTURE: John 14:27–29; 15:1–5.

I. Stress is a natural and normal part of life itself. (a) People who try to avoid stress fail to see that the friction caused by the weight of stress is good for us and is a normal part of our life together as men and women in society. That's one of the reasons why a large truck carrying a heavy load will have better traction on a slippery road than a light, unloaded car. Four men carrying a piano will have better footing on glare ice than one man skidding along by himself without the stress of a heavy burden whose weight can provide him a better footing.

(b) To handle stress without strain, we must stop fighting stress as something alien to our human situation and learn to accept stress as a normal part of our lives. Stress is built into our jobs, into our marriages, and into all human relationships. Our burdens and our responsibilities can help to save us and provide us a sure footing. The loads we are asked to carry will not injure us. They may help keep us alive.

II. Ability to handle stress is in proportion to our ability to be flexible.

(a) Flexibility allows us to give back the energy of friction and of stress without experiencing the damage of strain. When a person takes his first airplane flight in a jumbo jet or in a small craft, he may be apprehensive as he sees the wings of the airplane flapping in midair. But this built-in flexibility in the wings keeps the plane aloft and flying. If the plane design made the wing structure too rigid, the energy absorbed from the friction of the on-rushing air would be stored up instead of discharged, leading to metal fatigue and possible disaster from its overload.

(b) Inflexibility leads us to store up all of the friction and stress of living until physical or emotional fatigue and strain cause some kind of personal blow-up. We find ourselves accident prone or in some form of psychosomatic illness in which we manifest physical symptoms of sickness, but no organic causes are found to explain our illness. By our inflexibility we allow the normal and natural elements of stress to cause harmful strain. Then, like a tire on a car, where friction and heat cause the casing of the tire to bulge, we may finally have a blow-out.

III. The load-limits are a part of our own nature. (a) You may recall seeing a sign when you crossed a bridge telling you what the legal load limit is for that bridge. Or upon entering an elevator, you may notice the inspection certificate which defines the load limit for the size of that elevator. These load limits are established in proportion to the elastic, tensile strength which has been built into the working parts of the bridge or the elevator. Distress points are kept within the normal amount of energy or unit pressure forces which the bridge or elevator has been designed to carry. Strain is the damage done by our loading the materials in the bridge beyond their elastic limit. Instead of being able to bounce back, materials in the bridge suffer some dislocation because they are asked to absorb more energy than they are able to store up or to give back.

(b) Each of us must come to terms with own personal load limits. Our character has its own tensile strength. Our emotional durability may have either a boiling or a breaking point. Our disposition and temperament may have a lower or higher pressure point than found in other people. As we come to terms with ourselves, understanding the propensities of our physical nature and our aptitudes and endowments, we can pace ourselves and avoid letting stress become strain from unreasonable or unrealistic expectations imposed on us by others or by ourselves.

IV. The miracle of God's love and strength makes it possible for us in Jesus Christ to go beyond average expectations and to assume the responsibilities which might otherwise do us in.

(a) With a new serenity of spirit and a peace of mind, without anxiety or worry, we are able to face the challenge of change and uncertainty in our daily lives. By using up the energy of stress in the service of God and of others, we prevent strain. The person who allows himself to store up the memory of every injury and resentment and the stress and friction of life's burdens, without ever helping others and discharging his energies in God's service, discovers that stress invariably leads to strain.

(b) Just as the architect can know his design and building best, so God, who has made you for himself and who has redeemed you in Jesus Christ, knows you best. He knows what you can handle. His life plan for you will not allow you you to be burdened beyond what you are able to bear. God enables us to carry more than our normal share of stress in his mission and service, while his peace provides us the inward attitude of mind and heart which keeps the stress of our burden from becoming strain.—William F. Keucher.

Illustrations

WHEN IN NEED.   A wealthy man was moving into a new house, and his neighbor happened to be a Quaker. The Quakers believe in simplicity and plainness of life. The Quaker neighbor watched as the movers carted in numerous pieces of furniture, a great deal of clothing, and many decorative pieces. Then he walked over to his wealthy new neighbor and said in his quaint Quaker way, "Neighbor, if thee hath need of anything, please come to see me and I will tell thee how to get along without it."—Donald O'Quin.

UNDERSTANDING.   When a trout rising to a fly gets hooked on a line and finds himself unable to swim about freely, he begins with a fight which results in struggles and splashes and sometimes an escape. Often the situation is tough for him. In the same way the human being struggles with his environment and with the hooks that catch him. Sometime he masters his difficulties; sometimes they are too much for him. His struggles are all the world sees, and it naturally misunderstands them. It is hard for a free fish to understand what is happening to a hooked one.—Karl Menninger.

Sermon Suggestions

COMING TO TERMS WITH OUR TENSIONS. Text: Luke 10:41. (1) God has prepared us in advance to meet the strains and tensions of life. (2) We don't have to meet all of the tensions of life at the same times and places. (3) We must give God a chance to pour his strength into our lives.—Homer J. R. Elford.

WHEN YOU SUFFER DEPRESSION. Text: Rom. 7:25. How can you manage your moods of depression? (1) You must accept yourself as you are. (2) You must accept your circumstances. (3) You must try to see your life in relation to what you consider ultimate reality. For the Christian this is God who has shown himself to us in a unique and redeeming way in Jesus Christ.—J. A. Davidson.

Worship Aids

CALL TO WORSHIP. "The Lord is exalted; for he dwelleth on high: he hath filled Zion with judgment and righteousness. And wisdom and knowledge shall be the stability of thy times, and strength of salvation: the fear of the Lord is his treasure." Isa. 33:5–6.

INVOCATION. Most holy and gracious God, who turnest the shadow of night into morning: satisfy us early with thy mercy, that we may rejoice and be glad all the day. Lift the light of thy countenance upon us, calm every troubled thought, and guide our feet into the way of peace. Perfect thy strength in our weakness and help us to worship thee in the spirit of Jesus Christ our Lord.

OFFERTORY SENTENCE. "Give unto the Lord the glory due unto his name: bring an offering, and come before him: worship the Lord in the beauty of holiness." I Chron. 16:29.

OFFERTORY PRAYER. O God, thou giver of all good gifts, in gratitude we bring our gifts on this day of joyous worship. Refine them, we pray thee, in the mint of thy divine purpose and use them to the end that thy kingdom may come and thy will be done on earth as it is in heaven.

PRAYER. O God, who amid the vast and swift changes of our times abidest ever the same, we confess our inability without thee to deal with either progress or decay. We pray for the steadying presence of thy Holy Spirit with all who are confused or in any wise afflicted as new powers, new methods, and new needs unfold before us.

We pray for all who fear change, for all who find their secure ways threatened. Give them faith and courage and the spiritual and material resources to find newness of life within in the midst of newness of life without.

We pray for all who in impatience long for change, who seek escape from present boredom or hardships. Give them faith and courage and the discernment not to embrace in their bewilderment a change for the worse.

We pray for all who accept change and who endeavor to make of it progress and growth. Give them faith and courage to meet every temptation with integrity, all hostility with love, each difficulty with a reasoned determination to serve God and man.—E. Paul Conine.

EVENING SERVICE

Topic: What Christ Offers Through Us

SCRIPTURE: John 9:1–41.

I. An awareness of blindness: "Are we also blind?" (v. 40). (a) Physical blindness is possible but not probable. There are fifteen million blind people in the world. One out of every 1000 Americans is legally blind.

(b) Spiritual blindness was the condition

of the Pharisees in the lesson. What is the cause of it? In v. 41 Jesus implies that sin blinds.

(1) David was blind to his sin of murder and adultery until Nathan opened his eyes with a story.

(2) Baalam could not see the angel with a sword because of his defiance of God's directive.

(3) Because of his despair, Elijah was blind to the 7000 faithful.

(4) Ignorance blinded those who put Jesus on the cross—"for they know not what they do."

II. The light to see (v. 5). Though we have perfect eyes, we cannot see anything without light. In this passage Jesus describes himself as the light of the world. In his light we can see truth.

(a) Light to see who you are (v. 2). When confronted by Jesus, Peter cried, "Depart from me, for I am a sinful man."

(b) Light to see the meaning of life (v. 25). The blind man knew what happened to him. He was definite, certain, and confident. He had it all together. The world asks, "What's it all about?" Christ sheds light on modern man's basic questions: Who am I? Why am I here? Where am I going?

(c) Light to see Jesus as savior (vv. 31–38). The blind man came to see Jesus as messiah. At the transfiguration three disciples "saw no man save Jesus only." It takes spiritual insight to see the Christ in the man Jesus. When this vision comes, we say with Thomas, "My Lord and my God!"

III. If you saw a blind person trying to cross a busy street, would you not take him by the arm and lead him to safety? There are millions outside the church who are spiritually blind—floundering and getting hurt in the traffic of life. Should we not be equally as concerned and helpful by offering sight which comes only from Christ? Because of your witness, someone may say, "I was blind but now I see."—John R. Brokhoff.

SUNDAY: AUGUST FIRST

MORNING SERVICE

Topic: Hallmarks of the Christian
Text: Jas. 2:7.

I. On a piece of silver, gold, or pewter tableware or other articles, one will likely find what is known as a hallmark. It has been placed there to show certain facts, such as the amount of pure silver or gold in the article, the mark or initial of the one who made it, and often a particular style of alphabetical letter which indicates the year or at least the period when the article was made and where the article was manufactured. An experienced collector of such articles puts great store in hallmarks as means for true identification.

(a) As certainly as a collector of rare pieces can immediately identify some articles because of basic characteristics, so we may employ some tests in this regard. Good Christians must have some relationship to Jesus Christ, and the more Christ-likeness they possess, the more of his quality of life they will experience, cherish, and manifest to others.

(b) Basic must be a belief in Jesus Christ as savior and lord. Any who are familiar with the history of Christianity know this was the fundamental affirmation of faith which ran as a golden thread through all the creeds which were formulated from the earliest beginnings to the most recent world assemblies of theologians.

II. Of the many efforts which have been made to fashion specific distinguishing hallmarks which identify a Christian, one is found in the oft-repeated phrase, "A Christian is one who loves, who trusts, who obeys, and who follows Jesus Christ."

(a) Love was central in the teachings and total character of Jesus' life and ministry. He said to his disciples, "A new commandment I give unto you, that you love one another as I have loved you." The love Jesus lived and demands of us is never self-seeking but always self-giving. It is outgoing goodwill which never measures the distance it must travel to bring a person into perfect relationships with God and all people. It is a caring, compassionate quality of life which finds its life by losing its life. When such love motivates and empowers a person, he is thereby bearing one of the distinctive hallmarks of a Christian.

(b) Trust was one of the most distinguishing characteristics of Jesus. It was one of the things which people came to admire most about him and which they sought to emulate. Seeing how implicitly Jesus trusted God to provide for his every need and having shared the fruits of such abounding confidence in God's trustworthiness, the disciples and others came to believe everything Jesus told them about God, about human relationships, and even regarding the indestructability of the soul.

(c) A Christian is obedient to Christ. (1) One dares to speculate that much of the trouble which now exists in many relationships, all the way from the home to the highest echelons of government, has roots in the demise of the principle of obedience. Certainly it is reflected in the moral climate of the world as we find disregard for the time-tested commandments which God wants us to obey if we are to enjoy life in his world.

(2) The Christian who bears the hallmark of obedience has found that if he does not obey our Lord's commands in small things he is without resources when he needs when big issues have to be faced. If we wish to serve in the elite guard of Christ the King, we must be willing to to submit to his disciplines and be obedient to his commands.

(d) A Christian follows Christ. (1) Loving, trusting, and obeying Christ is all for a great purpose. It is to enable us to experience his lifestyle and his very spirit in our own lives. It is not an easy way of life by any measurement. Heaven knows we don't like the disciplined life. We join with the Texas cowboys in singing, "Don't fence me in!" But when we break the tether which binds us to his way—the way which calls for obedience to his commandments —invariably we end up in the wilderness of bewilderment or the desert of despair.

(2) It is by following Jesus, doing the best we can to love as he loved, trusting and being trustworthy like him, and obeying the still, small voice of God within us, as did he, that we experience life worthy of living here and eligible to continue throughout eternity. We follow him through the straight gate and the narrow way and, as he promised, we find life.— Homer J. R. Elford.

Illustrations

HOLY LIVING. Lesslie Newbigin went to Russia and met many young Christians. He asked them how they became Christians when the church is forbidden to use any means of winning converts and when parents are not allowed to teach religion to their children. One youth answered, "The attractive power of a holy life."— John R. Brokhoff.

DOWN DEEP. A piano teacher said to a pupil: "You seem to play the piano with a feather duster. You never strike down deep to the music that is in the instrument." We can play our religion with a feather duster and never strike down deep. Here are the words of a man who did strike down deep to great music: "It is no longer I that live, but Christ that liveth in me." Paul did it in the first century. You can do it in the twentieth.—Halford E. Luccock.

Sermon Suggestions

THE CHURCH ON MISSION. Scripture: Eph. 1:1–10. (1) The kind of world in which we live. (See Eph. 2:12.) (2) The kind of God we serve. (See II Pet. 3:9.) (3) The kind of command he gave.—Alton H. McEachern.

THE LAST BEATITUDE. Text: John 20:29. (1) This beatitude speaks to those whose religious experience is incomplete. (2) This beatitude speaks with special meaning to those who are wistful. (3) This beatitude speaks to those who are passing through suffering. (4) This beatitude speaks to those who feel their lives to be without any meaningful purpose.—Gene E. Bartlett.

Worship Aids

CALL TO WORSHIP.   "I will lift up mine eyes unto the hills, from whence cometh my help. My help cometh from the Lord, which made heaven and earth." Ps. 121: 1–2.

INVOCATION.   O God, whose name is great, whose goodness is inexhaustible, who art worshiped and served by all the hosts of heaven: touch our hearts, search out our consciences, and cast out of us every evil thought and base desire; all envy, wrath, and remembrance of injuries; and every motion of flesh and spirit that is contrary to the holy will.

OFFERTORY SENTENCE.   "Greater love hath no man than this, that a man lay down his life for his friends." John 15:13.

OFFERTORY PRAYER.   Our Father, help us to trust thee more fully and to accept our responsibility toward thy work and thy children who are our brethren in Christ.

PRAYER.   Our Father and our God, we come seeking a deeper understanding of thy ways. Life often seems like a difficult puzzle to us—sometimes a many-splendored thing and sometimes a thing of despair. When we lift our hearts unto thee we are overwhelmed by thy majesty and thy indescribable love for us. But we are also overwhelmed by our inadequacies and our failures and our sins.

When we think about thy great love for us and remember that thou didst create us but little lower than thyself, we are filled with gratitude. But when we realize how we have failed thee, how we have misunderstood thy purpose, how we have rebelled against thee, and how we have often acted like spoiled children, we are filled with disappointment and despair, sorrow and shame.

But we have seen thy love in the person of Jesus Christ. We have known thy ministry. And we know that we do need thee, for we cannot be whole persons without a meaningful relationship to thee and to all others of thy creation. Without such a relationship we are lost and life has neither purpose nor meaning.

Help us, then, as prodigals to come to ourselves and arise and return to our true home. Help us to cut through our preoccupation with ourselves. Help us to become more fully involved in the life about us. As we trudge through our daily tasks, give us the insight to recognize thy purpose and thy presence.—Lyle V. Newman.

EVENING SERVICE

Topic: The New Jerusalem
SCRIPTURE: Rev. 21:1–7; 22:1–5.

Because John is describing a vision, we should perhaps regard it as a pictorial representation of the ideal life on earth toward which the kingdom of God points and toward which we should be pressing. What will be its characteristics? It will be a new heaven and a new earth, new in the sense of being transformed and new in its quality. The emphasis on a new Jerusalem indicates that there will be not only transformed individuals but also a transformed society. In this new society there will be:

I. *Fellowship with God.* Not distant or far away as he seems now so often to be but a present God in our midst. This is suggested by the figure of the bride (21:2, 9) and the son (21:7). The idea is developed more fully in 21:3; 22:3–4;

II. *The end of all evil.* There will be no more sea—the figure of the sea for John meant isolation, loneliness, and separation from loved ones—no more sin, (21:8, 27), no more sorrow (21:4), no more curse (22:3), and no more night (20:25; 21:5). The darkness has been termed humans' oldest fear, the darkness which conceals unknown dangers against which we can never fully protect ourselves.

III. *The fulfillment of all good.* It is easier to describe the evils which can be eliminated than to describe the goods which are to be enjoyed. John falls back here on imagery which only the dull and unimaginative would interpret in exact and literal fashion. No one, it is to be hoped, thinks there will be a city which is a perfect cube—1,500 miles in length, breadth, and height. The figure indicates perfection. So with the jasper walls, the pearly gates, and the golden streets. They describe poetically, not photographically, the beauty and splendor of the new heavens and the new earth—all that one's heart could desire.— Ernest Trice Thompson.

SUNDAY: AUGUST EIGHTH

MORNING SERVICE

Topic: The Ways We Praise God
TEXT: Rev. 4:11.

Our services of worship should include various ways for the people of God to express their praise to God.

I. One of these should be found in the hymnody used in our worship of God. Worship services should include a balance of hymns of praise and of gospel songs.

(a) The hymns express man's praise and adoration of God. Such hymns as "Now thank we all our God," "All hail the power of Jesus' name," and "O worship the king" are examples of our praise to God.

(b) Gospel songs speak of that which God has done for man in Jesus Christ. Such gospel songs as "Amazing grace," "When I survey the wondrous cross," and "Beneath the cross of Jesus" declare the mighty acts of God in human history.

II. We can praise God through our offerings. "Ascribe to the Lord the glory due his name; bring an offering and come unto his courts" (Ps. 96:8). Under the law man was required to give the tithe of all his possessions to God.

(a) The psalmist goes beyond this as he saw the grace of God at work in the lives of his people. The offering of which he spoke was that which is brought to God over and above the tithe.

(b) Jesus taught that man was to be a good steward of all that God had entrusted into his care and to return a portion to that which is first entrusted to his care.

(c) When we look at the grace which God gives to us to heal our brokenness and to restore us into healthy relationships with ourselves, with God, and each other, we see it to be a costly grace, for it condemns our sins and restores us in right relationships with God. It is a costly grace because it cost God the life of his own Son. This same costly grace calls us to become instruments of that grace in the world in which we live.

(d) When we see that the grace of God is a costly grace which we receive as a gift we can give joyously and cheerfully, knowing that through our offerings we are participating in the ongoing ministry of the grace of Christ.

III. We show our praise in our relationships to others. (a) The apostle Paul writing to the church at Rome says, "I appeal to you brethren, by the mercies of God to present your bodies as a living sacrifice holy and acceptable to God, which is your spiritual worship." For Paul the living out of one's faith in relationship to others was and is true worship.

(b) The chief aim of the Christian church is to reconcile people to God. This was Christ's mission and is the mission of the church today.

(1) Rather than to be involved in the missionary outreach to people, it is far easier to fall into the trap of being concerned for the success and prestige of the local church. It is easier to feel that the church's primary reason for existence is for the people who are already a part of the congregation and the upkeep on the buildings and grounds rather than to be concerned for those to whom we have been sent—those persons whose lives and spirits are broken.

(2) They could be the family next door, the person next to you in the pew, or the waif or refugee fleeing for his life. They may be in the hospital or a jail or a hospice. They need the grace of God.

(3) Much of the mental and emotional anguish in today's society could be healed and relationships restored through caring congregations who are concerned about people.—Dale M. Wilson.

Illustrations

WHAT THE LORD SEES.   John A. Broadus left his pulpit and walked the aisle with the ushers. He watched every offering placed in the plate. Some were angry. He returned to the pulpit to say, "My dear people, if you take it to heart that I have seen your offerings this day and know just what sacrifices you have made, remember that the Son of God, your Savior, goes up the aisle with every usher and sees with his sleepless eyes every cent put into the collection plate by his people."—William B. Webb.

FINDING GOD.   Carl Jung was counseling a man who had been in therapy for six months and was getting no better. Finally, Jung said: "Friend, I can't do any more for you. What you need is God." "How do I find God, Dr. Jung?" the man asked. "I don't know," said Jung, "but I suspect if you will find a group of people some place that believe in him passionately and just spend time with them, you will find God." The man did, and he was healed.

Sermon Suggestions

TO BE A CHRISTIAN.   Text: Acts 11:26. (1) To be a Christian is to be a part of the most sacred fellowship of life. (2) To be a Christian is to be a follower of Christ as lord and master. (3) To be a Christian is to be a radiantly happy individual in spite of the sin and evil that engulfs the world. (4) To be a Christian is to accept Christ's love-filled life. (5) To be a Christian is to seek to know God's will and to be obedient to it. (6) To be a Christian is to be loyal to the things of Christ. (7) To be a Christian is to share in the love and fellowship of the church.—Frank A. Court.

THE EVANGELISTIC COMMUNITY.   Text: II Tim. 4:5. When the Christian church discovers its identity, message, power, and mission, what does it do? (1) Follows God's prevenient, seeking Spirit. (2) Finds and reaches out to lost and searching people. (3) Communicates the good news. (4) Invites response to Jesus Christ as lord.

(5) Folds responders into Christ's flock. (6) Makes them disciples. (7) Teaches them to obey his kingdom's mandates. (8) Sends them out in justice, love, and witness.—The United Methodist Church.

Worship Aids

CALL TO WORSHIP.   "Be strong and of a good courage, fear not: for the Lord thy God, he it is that doth go with thee; he will not fail thee, nor forsake thee." Deut. 31:6.

INVOCATION.   O spirit of the living God, who dwellest in thy church and who art holiness, wisdom, and might: come thou now in this hour, fill the hearts of thy faithful people, and kindle within them the fire of thy love.

OFFERTORY SENTENCE.   "Every one of us shall give account of himself to God." Rom. 14:12.

OFFERTORY PRAYER.   O living Christ, help us to know the ecstasy of thine everlasting lordship that we may more perfectly become cheerful givers.

PRAYER.   Creator God, who art beyond space, broader than earth's horizons, and deeper than the ocean, we approach thy holy place desiring to comprehend with our little minds the vastness of thy being. We are blessed in the adventure of divine orderliness. Thy laws are visible among the courses of the stars. Day and night, heat and cold, seasons of planting, growing, and reaping speak of the balance of all thy creation. With thee we declare, "It is good!"

Thou architect of the universe, we see thy hand in the majesty of mountains, amid blue lakes and golden fields. We acknowledge thy image in humankind. The work and progress in the expressions of man only constitute his daily assistance to thee in thy unending creativity. Thou art in the man with the hoe and spade, beside those at the wheel, the bench, and the desk. Thou art in souls and minds where brush and pen tell of thy glory. Viewing this artistry, we see it is, indeed, good.

To thee, maker of heaven and earth, we give thanks for spiritual communication through thy Son Jesus Christ. For the instruments of prayer and worship where spirit with spirit meet in holy fellowship, we are grateful. Upon the radar of thy love we are found. Here we receive goodly direction. May all races of humankind experience a spiritual blending, the re-creation of self, and the adornment of the robes of righteousness and peace. We praise thee in all thy works.

EVENING SERVICE

Topic: Living Today and Tomorrow's Judgment

Text: Matt. 25:21.

A minister prayed the following prayer: "Help me, Lord, to do now what I will wish I had done when I come to the end of the way."

I. I will want to feel that I had taken advantage of every opportunity I had to witness to lost souls.

II. I will want to feel that I had given to God all of the time that rightly belonged to him.

III. I will want to feel that I had lived an exemplary Christian life and was a spiritual stumbling block to no one.

IV. I will want to feel that I had daily maintained a right relationship with God through prayer and his word.

V. I will want to feel that I had practiced and had lived what I had preached to others.

VI. I will want to feel that I had done my best each time I ministered the word.

VII. I will want to feel that I had not been delinquent with my financial obligations to God and the church.

VIII. I will want to feel that I had been an inspiration for good to my family and to those with whom I associated daily.

IX. I will want to feel that I had faithfully performed my duties and had fulfilled my obligations in the various ministerial capacities in which I had been honored to serve.

X. I will want to feel that I had been faithful to the church in every possible way and that I had been an exemplary member.

XI. I will want to feel that the one who died for me and who provided daily strength and grace for me to live a Christian life will be pleased with me and will grant to me a glorious entrance into heaven.—O. W. Polen.

SUNDAY: AUGUST FIFTEENTH

MORNING SERVICE

Topic: The Jonah in Us All

Scripture: Jonah 1–4.

Jonah alternately has been labeled rebellious, ambivalent, peevish, or self-centered. Occasionally modest credit is given him for his forthrightness. Jonah at least admitted his errors. He also never hesitated to argue with God. But Jonah, even on these terms, never has fared well as an example of holiness and obedience. Maybe that is why we like him. He is one of us! He is a crazy mixture of goodness and belligerency, of wisdom and foolishness, and of confidence and confusion.

I. We understand this man because in many ways we are like him.

(a) We believe in God. Indeed, if the Gallup Poll is any guide, the majority of all Americans consistently profess belief in God. But it is not necessarily belief that gets us anywhere, least of all to those places God would have us be.

(b) While we want more than anything else the blessings God bestows, we are not always eager to see our neighbors have those blessings too.

(c) Like Jonah, sometimes our own comfort and the things that constitute it assume greater importance than the people around us. We fluctuate in our convictions and our commitment. We both help and hinder the work of God.

(d) We have our share of complaints

about the way the universe is run, just as Jonah did.

II. If we are like Jonah in these less-than-complimentary ways, we also are like him in being the subjects of God's everlasting love and concern.

(a) God did not give up on Jonah, although Jonah in a sense offered him the chance. "Let me die," the prophet moaned. "Let me be written off." God, in response, only said, "What right do you have to be angry?" God continued to deal with Jonah, not making his life easier, but not giving up on him either. God retained the initiative and continued to deal with this man, and I am confident that the outcome was good.

(b) The record indicates only a fraction of that outcome. It tells how a vine grew up to shelter Jonah from the scorching sun, giving him a brief period of comfort and composure. But the plant was short-lived. It withered and died, the daytime heat becoming worse than ever. From the example of this vine God announced his care for all people. Teaching that Jonah should have compassion for humanity comparable to his vital interest in the vine. The story ends there, still dramatizing God's mercy both to the Ninevites and to his reluctant prophet.

III. If only we could get into our heads the meaning of God's mercy!

(a) Reading the book of Jonah, one quickly sees that mercy meant deliverance from disaster for the people of Ninevah. And mercy—the forgiving, reclaiming love of God—always means deliverance from personal disaster.

(b) The mercy of God not only means deliverance from something; it is deliverance to something. It is the way forward, the pathway out. We are not supposed to stay in sackcloth and ashes. It is intended that we rise up as a people redeemed. In that rising up a whole spectrum of service and sacrifice, of being and doing, and of helping and reaching out is disclosed. Faith issues in works, naturally and inevitably. We become a people who make the Christian difference, wherever we are found.

IV. It is not ours to blame Jonah if his insight fell short. But we must understand our own accountability. Where necessary, we must root out the Jonah in us all. Responding to divine mercy and keenly aware that God has not given up on us or our world, you and I have the responsibility and the privilege of reaching out with a message of hope, of great good news, and of love and redemption. Jonah had his job to do. This is ours.—John H. Townsend.

Illustrations

THE JONAH COMPLEX.   Abraham Maslow describes how Jonah ran away from his commission, turning his back on the great challenge God lined up for him. The Jonah complex means evasion of high destiny and running away from our greatest opportunities because we fear the best more than we fear the worst. We are intimidated by our highest potential.

Why would people recoil from life's peak experiences? Simply because they are afraid of the struggle or don't want to risk failure. Lacking confidence that they have stamina and resources for the climb, they fear default, even disaster, someplace along the way.

For everyone afflicted with the Jonah complex, there is this challenge: stop running from the highest and run to the highest and savor mountaintop achievements, self-affirming encounters, and God-glorifying experiences.—G. Othell Hand.

LIKE CHILDREN.   Humility, because of its basic receptivity to the good of others, makes it possible to receive the joys of union with God. That is why our divine Lord suggested that university professors will have to become as children to enter the kingdom of heaven. They must admit, like children, that God knows more than they do.—Fulton J. Sheen.

Sermon Suggestions

TOO PROUD TO RECEIVE.   Text: I Pet. 5:5. (1) Pride shutters the mind. (2) Pride locks the heart. (3) Pride corrupts the conscience.—Ralph W. Sockman.

COMMON GLORIES. Text: II Tim. 4:2–5. (1) Do your duty. (2) Be loyal to the truth. (3) Keep faith with God.—Theodore F. Adams.

Worship Aids

CALL TO WORSHIP. "Wait on the Lord: be of good courage, and he shall strengthen thine heart: wait, I say, on the Lord." Ps. 27:14.

INVOCATION. O God, we thank you for leading us until this hour. Direct us in the days ahead through the difficult places of decision. When the call seems clouded and the road is in poor repair, grant the boldness to face the future in faith and to fortify ourselves in truth. Help us to be ready to recognize our own inadequacy and your sufficiency.

OFFERTORY SENTENCE. "Therefore, as ye abound in every thing, in faith, and utterance, and knowledge, and in all diligence, and in your love to us, see that ye abound in this grace also." II Cor. 8:7.

OFFERTORY PRAYER. Dear Lord, as we travel the highways of life give us a generous and sympathetic spirit for all people in all circumstances of life.

PRAYER. We come into this service today from a world that beckons us to be elsewhere and tries to make us believe that acceptance comes by power and prestige. We see how efficiently the world conducts its business and its research, and the comparison dampens our enthusiasm when we see the manner and the unchanging attitude with which the work of thy church is done. We see the confidence of the world and the apparent weakness of the church, and our spirits cry out because of concern.

But still we come, knowing with a certainty what the world cannot give to us and that our enthusiasm will be renewed and our spirits will be enhanced by the indwelling of thy Spirit.

We bring our lives—polluted by the sins of greed, anger, and mistrust; darkened by fear, anxiety, and indifference; hurt by sickness, disease, and death; and defeated by doubtfulness and misgivings. We bring our lives because we have been promised forgiveness of sins, light in the place of darkness, strength to bear the hurt, and victory over all defeat. And we now ask of thee the fulfillment of these promises.

Submitting our lives to the workings of thy Spirit, we can depart from this service and be fortified daily to live in accordance with thy divine purposes.

Give us at this time the wisdom to submit our lives completely to thee so that we may be known as those who are followers of Jesus Christ.—W. H. Kirby.

EVENING SERVICE

Topic: Handling Mid-Life Crisis
SCRIPTURE: Ps. 102:1–11.
What can you do to manage mid-life transition or help in mid-life crisis?

I. The person facing mid-life needs to recognize the profound reappraisal of life that often comes with middle age is a natural and even necessary part of becoming a mature adult. Questions and doubts come from deep within—from the most healthy part of the self. The real question is how to make use of such questions and doubts.

II. We need to listen to those other voices in other rooms and try to understand what they are saying even when they are unclear. We ought not to try to deny their existence to ourselves, our friends, and loved ones. This only increases the pain and the difficulty. So often men especially deny anything that will seem to point to their own weakness. This is not healthy and not helpful.

III. Any reappraisal of life cannot be just an intellectual process of making new choices. It always means that there will be emotional turmoil and a lot of pain. Such pain is necessary and cannot be avoided even in our pain-avoidance society. If one is to make a constructive transition through mid-life that will be beautiful, one must endure the pain.

IV. Though our inner voices may tell us to flee, to escape, to evade, or to hide in a cave like Elijah, we need to resist these impulses which have creative possibilities but usually are destructive of sound relationships. We need, hard as it is, to resist having a tantrum—to resist regressing into the grasping, me first, indulgent earlier stage of life.

V. We need to listen to the still small voice of God amidst the changes, conflicts, and pains.

(a) It seems no accident that Ps. 103 was placed right behind the mid-life chronicle of crisis in Ps. 102. This psalm provides real and lasting help to those encountering the pain of the psalmist on the preceding page. This is a testimony to the practical, real life-giving action of God. It is this compassionate, accepting, helping, wholly other voice that the person in mid-life crisis needs to hear or hear again.

(b) In mid-life crisis the creative-destructive polarities of biblical truths are intensified. The person in the crisis has a strong desire for new life, new beginnings, and new creative possibilities. The person wants to do something for the self and others, to participate in new enterprises that advance the human condition, and to contribute more fully to coming generations.

(c) In mid-life a person can come to know more than ever before the powerful forces of beautiful creativity and awesome destructiveness that coexist in the human soul—in my soul and in yours—and it can become the time when they are integrated into a great new integrity that is life restoring and life giving through the love of God.—James M. Dodson.

SUNDAY: AUGUST TWENTY-SECOND

MORNING SERVICE

Topic: How to Be a Winner

Texts: I Cor. 9:24; Heb. 12:1–2.

I. To be a winner in God's eyes, we must seek his will. (a) God has a purpose for each one of us. He has some role for each of us to play, no matter what our place or condition in life. Picture the world as a gigantic picture puzzle with many of the pieces lying loose upon the table. Obviously the picture will be complete only when each piece is in its proper place. You and I are those pieces of the puzzle which God wants to put where we belong, the place which will complete his overall plan. When we agree to let God have his way with us, to put us where he wants us, and to use us for his purpose, then we are on the way to fulfillment.

(b) Being a winner in life has nothing to do with becoming wealthy or famous or being given all sorts of honors and awards. Howard Hughes had all of those, but he was a loser in the sum total of his life. Being a winner has to do with fulfilling the destiny God has for each of us, with an inner sense of well-being which comes from knowing that we have made our life count for something, and with the satisfaction which one derives from simply serving God.

II. Winning involves patterning your life after Christ's life. Jesus said to his friends, "I have given you an example, that you also should do as I have done" (John 13:15).

(a) Those words were uttered just after Jesus had washed the disciples' feet. He was showing them—and us—that the way we become winners in God's eyes is through humble Christlike service.

(b) Jesus showed us the characteristics of a real winner as far as God is concerned. We see Jesus taking time to visit the sick, to minister to the blind, the lame, the mentally ill, those with leprosy, and so on. He took time for little children. He accepted the rejected and the hated. He spoke out for fair play and justice. He insisted on the truth, knowing that it would set men free from ignorance and failure and sham. He showed us the importance of using our talents for worthy purposes, using our money for causes that uplift mankind, and using our time in fruitful and positive ways. He taught us how to forgive, how to take suffering and persecution, and how to stay close to God no matter what happens. No one who ever lived was a greater winner than Jesus Christ.

III. We can win only if we follow God's rules. I refer not only to the ten commandments but also to the new commandment Jesus gave us—that we love one another.

(a) God does not intend for us to live just any old way we please. If everyone did just as he wished, following whatever wild impulse he had, the world would be in complete chaos. There can be success in any area of life only when the basic rules are followed.

(b) It is necessary, no matter what we do in life, to follow the rules which are basic to our work. It is also necessary, if we are to live winning lives, to be conscientious about following the rules which God has given to us.—Charles E. Ferrell.

Illustrations

TWO LIVES.   Lord Byron was a cripple from his youth. One of his close friends wrote of him: "He brooded over that blemish as sensitive minds will brood until they magnify a wart into a huge tumor. His lameness made him skeptical, cynical, and savage." Lord Byron took his lameness and let it destroy the finer qualities of life.

When three-year-old Louis Braille was boring holes with an awl in a heavy piece of leather in his father's harness shop in France, back in 1812, an accident caused blindness. Seventeen years later the totally blind youth invented the Braille system, now used all over the world through which the blind can read and write. Not only did the invention bring "sight" to young Braille, but his tragedy was also the means of helping many generations of blind persons.—Ralph W. Odom.

HELPING HAND.   While George Butterick was chaplain at Harvard, the university decided to give the first doctorate ever granted a woman. Everyone wondered who would be honored. Harvard's honorary awards have always been kept top secret. Everyone gathered on that occasion eager to find out who would be the first woman so honored. Finally her name was called—Helen Keller. And the crowd went absolutely wild, except for the woman who

had been named for the award. She sat quietly in her seat until Annie Sullivan, her teacher, drummed out the splendid message into her palm. After it was over Butterick told the president of Harvard: "We made a mistake today. We should have given two degrees. Helen Keller could never have come to this place had it not been for Annie Sullivan who led her by the hand."—Roger Lovette.

Sermon Suggestions

A RELIGION OF CONVENIENCE.   Scripture: I Kings 12:25–33. (1) A religion of convenience seeks an easy way to discharge obligations (v. 18). (2) A religion of convenience seeks it own gods—something less than the Holy One—develops its own ritual, and exercises excessive and foolish affection on certain religious leaders (vv. 28–29, 31). (3) A religion of convenience seeks a morality of its own (v. 30).—Nolan Howington.

WHEN MAN GROWS TIRED OF FREEDOM. Text: Gal. 5:1. (1) To grow tired of freedom because one has given up outward restraint without getting inner resources until it is wearisome to decide. (2) To grow tired of freedom because one has given up old allegiances without finding an inner loyalty that makes life worth living. (3) To grow tired of freedom because it has become egocentric and individualistic without devotion to the common good. —Harry Emerson Fosdick.

Worship Aids

CALL TO WORSHIP.   "Let all those that put their trust in thee rejoice: let them ever shout for joy because thou defendest them: let them also that love thy name be joyful in thee." Ps. 5:11.

INVOCATION.   O thou who art the light of the minds that know thee, the life of the souls that love thee, and the strength of the wills that serve thee, help us so to know thee that we may truly love thee and so to love thee that we may fully serve thee, whom to serve is perfect freedom.

OFFERTORY SENTENCE. "If you have many possessions, make your gift from them in proportion; if few, do not be afraid to give according to the little you have. So you will be laying up a good treasure for yourself." Tobit 4:8–9.

OFFERTORY PRAYER. Dear Father, help us to be ever concerned to find thy way for our lives, and may we never be satisfied to give thee our second best in return for thy great gift of love.

PRAYER. O Lord our God, we confess that often we do not like the bodies we have. Sometimes we have longed for jobs of others. We would like to do away with parts of our history. We are afraid of our moods and feelings. We wish we had more time. We would like to start over again. We lust after the prestige of others. We think more money will solve our problems. We resent the injustices we have suffered and cherish our sorrows. We want to be appreciated for our small graces. We are enchanted by the past and enticed by the future. We have never really been understood. We have refused to live because we have held out for better terms. Heal us, O God, from the distance we have tried to put between ourselves and life. Restore to us the love of thee and all thy creation. Enable us by thy power to be renewed in our whole lives.—Helmut Thielicke.

EVENING SERVICE

Topic: Does the Gospel Really Work?
TEXT: I Cor. 15:1–2.

Christ and his gospel work. They produce what they promise. The essential message of the church is sound. It is vital. It is workable. It is worth investing in. This is our faith and our confidence.

I. The gospel works because it is based on the premise that persons, character, family, and relationships are the most important things in life. People are more valuable than things. Development of the human mind, body, and spirit are of more worth than making money or proving ideas.

(a) Jesus did not die for a principle as did Socrates. He died for individual sinners—people. Principle was involved, but God didn't have to prove a principle to sinful man. Sinful man needed a savior, so Christ died.

(b) One's character is more vital than one's holdings. "What doth it profit a man if he gain the whole world and lose his own soul?" Character counts in the long run. Under stress we all reveal our true selves. The gospel works because Christ's work changes a man's basic nature, transforming sinful rebels to loyal disciples.

II. The gospel of Jesus Christ shows that it is workable because it has stood the test of time.

(a) The centuries have passed and no matter how theological twists have interpreted the gospel, the basic, Bible-oriented message of salvation, victory, and eternal life have come through as man's only hope. Generation after generation has lived the Christian life in every conceivable climate, culture, political structure, and social arrangement. In each the church has survived when the environment has passed.

(b) Eternity is the final test of the Christian faith. Much of the success of personal Christian living in this world is due to the anchor on faith that we have by knowing that we are destined for eternal life.

III. A third reason why the gospel is a plan that works is that each Christian who lives the life is dedicated to a cause that is bigger than he is. This is no new and novel way of life for serious-minded people. Causes and crusades have always captured the imagination and loyalty of dedicated persons. The Christian faith is unique, for its followers are in the process of giving their lives as their savior gave his, completely and for others. "He who loses his life for my sake shall find it" is not a call to martyrdom but a challenge to life-giving service here on earth that others might have eternal life.

IV. The fourth reason why the gospel works is that God is in charge. Each Christian who thinks seriously about his way of life needs to remember time and again that he is not in a pack of hardworking humans who sacrifice themselves to an ideal. He is a part of the body of Christ. He is a member of the church whose leader is God. The dimension of divinity must always be present in the work of the Christian or he is apart from Christ.

V. The gospel works. But it only works for those who become involved in it and give their lives to him who died that we might have it. Knowing that it works is not the same as demonstrating that it works. All the thinking in the world won't show the workability of Christ's message like one living, breathing example.—Dan Harman.

SUNDAY: AUGUST TWENTY-NINTH

MORNING SERVICE

Topic: Rising Above Cynicism

TEXT: John 2:25 (MOFFATT).

When a man knows the human heart with all its capacity for deception, hypocrisy, cruelty, and betrayal, he finds it very difficult not to become a cynic. Yet this didn't happen to Jesus. You can read every one of his sayings, you can study his attitude in relation to all sorts and conditions of men, and not once do you find a trace of bitter disillusionment. Why? We know the answer. Jesus loved people, and cynicism can no more survive in a loving heart than germs can survive in a sterilizer. Jesus loved people not in a vague, emotional way but in a very practical, positive, and active way.

I. Jesus believed that people could change. (a) What turns the realist into a cynic is the stubborn conviction that he has the clearest possible view of human nature. He believes that he really knows the score. He has removed his rose-colored spectacles, and he sees human nature in the raw—basically depraved, immoral, cruel, and incapable of change.

(1) There is much in human nature that turns the best of us into cynics and breeds within us a low view of our fellowmen. "But that's human nature," says the cynic. "That's the way people are, and nothing you can do will possibly change them."

(2) The cynic may be somewhat less of a realist than he fancies himself to be. If human nature is incapable of change, why do we waste time and money on whole branches of medicine and vast systems of education and social service that have as their goal presisely the recreation of man's nature?

(3) Christianity is a story of changed human lives. It caused a metamorphosis so dramatic that, writing about it, Carl Jung declared that Christianity has produced on this earth a new creature who lives in a new way to which the natural man can no more attain than a crawling thing can fly.

(b) Jesus believed that men could be born again. (1) He believed that the weak could become strong, the crooked straight; that publicans and harlots could enter the kingdom of God; that the poor and oppressed, who, being universally despised, had come to despise themselves, possessed undreamed of capacities.

(2) Jesus never judged a man by what he was but by what God had created him and by what in the grace of God he could become.

(c) To love people is to believe that they are capable of being changed. Such love can be a powerful instrument of change.

II. Jesus knew how to forgive. (a) The cynic is usually a man with a king-sized chip on his shoulder. What he calls his realism invariably has its roots in some slight or some injury that he has suffered, perhaps when trying to be of help to people, so he retreats into a shell of cynicism and makes nasty remarks about the low character of the human race.

(b) We know what happened in Gethsemane was a victory of love over cynicism that reached its climax in his prayer from the cross: "Father, forgive them; for they know not what they do."

(1) The world's salvation was accomplished in that prayer of forgiveness be-

cause it articulated not only the pardon of an earthly Jesus extended to those who drove great nails through his quivering flesh but also the pardon of an eternal God extended to the child of his love who had broken his great loving heart.

(2) God was on Golgotha. The cross was God's final answer to our sin—his way of dealing with our pride, our stupidity, and our betrayal.

(c) Forgiving people has power to change you and thereby remove the roots of cynicism.

(1) You can never again take a low view of your fellowman after you have forgiven him for having hurt you.

(2) By your forgiveness you have exorcised from your heart that sensitive egotism which is the breeding ground of a cynical attitude.

III. Jesus so involved himself in other people's lives that he developed an essential understanding and sympathy for their problems.

(a) The cynic lives in an ivory tower. He stands outside the human situation and turns his back on the very misery he deplores.

(1) The writer of Psalm 1 rates cynicism lower than atheism and even wickedness. The ungodly at least walk, the sinful at least stand, but the scornful are invariably sitting down.

(2) How much safer to be disgusted with life than to take hold of it! How much simpler to condemn people than to cooperate with them! How infinitely more comfortable to curse society than to change it!

(b) Jesus never withdrew into an ivory tower and wrote cynical books about the misery, the depravity, and the hypocrisy of the human race. He did not turn his back on people.

(1) He involved himself in their lives and tried to help them with the very problems that made them the sort of people who could so easily have turned him into a cynic.

(2) Jesus gave himself to all sorts and conditions of men. A publican needing to gain his self-respect or a beggar needing to recover his sight, a rich man worried about his soul or a fisherman worried about his luck, a leper crying "Unclean!" or a woman who had sinned—whoever needed him was not denied him.

(3) At times he felt the futility of it all, the awful discouragement of one who spends himself without effect for others, but he went on spending himself until it took him to the place where it takes every man eventually—a lonely cross outside a city wall.

(c) Our attitude toward people changes when we involve ourselves in their lives.

(1) Because we sit where they sit, we begin to see their situation from the inside, and we become more tolerant toward the foibles and failings about them that tend to make us cynical. We begin to look at them through the eyes of understanding and sympathy. That is why none of the great missionaries or social reformers has ever been a cynic.

(2) Cynicism has its roots in self-centeredness. Jesus taught us that the way to save life is to lose it. What he meant was that the full, happy, well-adjusted life is essentially the outgoing, the unselfish, and the giving life.

IV. A spiritual equation expresses the truth: realism minus love equals cynicism.

(a) If we look at our fellowmen realistically and face up frankly to the very worst in human nature, we shall be tempted to become cynics. And it is no use saying, "Don't let's be cynical" or even, "Let's look at Jesus and try to be more like him."

(b) We shall always be cynical about people until we learn to love them, and only Christ can put that kind of love into our hearts because only he has won the victory over cynicism. He won that victory for us. As we believe in Christ and live with him, we shall begin to see people as he sees them.—Leonard Griffith.

Illustrations

WORKING PRINCIPLE.   Faith is the working principle of daily living, manifest in the tiny tot crossing with her hand in her mother's or in a Columbus crossing the Atlantic when his only chart was one "which faith deciphered in the skies." Faith in some degree is the common heritage of the human race and in the highest degree is the peculiar gift of all noble spirits and the source of whatever bears the impress of greatness.—Ralph W. Sockman.

CREDO. I believe in God as I believe in my friends, because I feel the breath of his affection, feel his invisible and intangible hand drawing me, leading, grasping me; because I possess an inner consciousness of a particular providence and of a universal mind that marks out for me the course of my destiny.—Miguel de Unamumo.

Sermon Suggestions

WHO ARE THESE CHRISTIANS? Scripture: Eph. 4:15–16, 25–32; 5:1–2. (1) Christians are an edified people. (See Eph. 4: 15–16.) (2) Christians are a renewed people who are growing in Christ. (See Eph. 4:25–26.) (3) Christians imitate God. (See Eph. 5:1–2.)—Ard Hoven.

FULFILLING OUR PURPOSE IN LIFE. Text: Phil. 2:5. (1) Who are we? (2) Why are we here? (3) Where are we going?—Lowell M. Atkinson.

Worship Aids

CALL TO WORSHIP. "Ho, every one that thirstest, come ye to the waters. Incline your ear, and come unto me: hear, and your soul shall live; and I will make an everlasting covenant with you, even the sure mercies of David." Isa. 55:1, 3.

INVOCATION. Eternal and ever-blessed God, grant this day light to the minds that hunger for the truth and peace to the hearts which yearn for rest. Grant strength to those who have hard tasks to do and power to those who have sore temptations to face. Grant unto us within this place to find the secret of thy presence and to go forth from it in the strength of the Lord.

OFFERTORY SENTENCE. "And they came everyone whose heart stirred him up, and everyone whom his spirit made willing, and they brought the Lord's offering to the work of the tabernacle of the congregation, and for all his service." Exod. 35: 21.

OFFERTORY PRAYER. O Lord, who hast given us the privilege of life, help us to magnify eternal values and to show forth by our lives and our tithes the Christ, whom to know aright is life eternal.

PRAYER. Our God, creator of all life, we bow in worship because you have made your love for us known through the life of Christ. We come in thankfulness because you have loved us through the lives of Christlike people.

We come in quietness and meditation seeking to understand your love for each of us. We feel secure when we sense your knowledge of our lives and our world. Thank you for knowing us and accepting us as we are.

Forgive us when we make mistakes. Give us comfort and direction when we are troubled or downhearted. Help us to include others in our thoughts and action. Keep us from selfishness. Give us the wisdom and courage to live each day as your children and as brothers and sisters to one another.—Gene N. Branson.

EVENING SERVICE

Topic: The Quest for Inner Quiet
TEXT: Mark 6:31.

The quest for inner quiet is called by a variety of names—peace of mind, peace of heart, personal serenity, inner peace, peace with God, and others. A whole literature has developed around the practical, psychological, and religious aspects of inner peace.

I. It is the singular virtue of the Christian gospel that it is able to meet the alternating needs of persons—the need for challenge to active service and to confront trouble, trial, and temptation and the need for comfort in trustful rest and to relax for inner renewal.

II. The quest for inner quiet is a natural and commendable concern. There is a deep and wistful yearning for it everywhere and by nearly everyone. People desire it as a respite and relief in the midst of life's busy and restless routine. While this seems like a peculiarly modern condition, we find reference to it in the Bible.

(a) Jesus and his disciples had come through a busy day. Then the record observes: "There were so many people coming and going that Jesus and his disciples didn't even have time to eat. So he said to them, 'Let us go off by ourselves to some place where we will be alone and you can rest awhile.' "

(b) This inner peace is also needed in life's critical emergencies. An illustration of this is found in the incident when Jesus and his disciples were caught in a terrible storm at sea. Even the seasoned fishermen of the group panicked in fear. But Jesus was curled up in the stern of the ship fast asleep. They awakened him, and he quickly calmed their troubled spirits (Mark 4:35–41).

(c) The inner quiet that Jesus offers is no complacent acceptance of life as if it were inexorable fate. Nor is it a weak and cowardly resignation to the hardships of life. Neither is it an easy escape from the harsh realities of existence. This peace has at its core a realistic faith which enables people to meet and master all circumstances.

III. A firm faith in the love and truth of God is the indispensable basis for lasting inner peace. Such a faith is nurtured by private devotions as well as by corporate worship—two essential means for practicing the presence of God.

(a) Often overlooked or ignored is the moral requirement for inner quiet. Unconfessed and unforgiven sins dull and destroy inner peace. There is nothing so unsettling as a troubled conscience. The only adequate answer to human sin is divine pardon. An honest awareness of our faults and failures must be coupled with a confident faith in divine forgiveness. Like the psalmist, we need to pray: "I recognize my faults, I am always conscious of my sins. . . . Create a pure heart in me, O God; and put a new and loyal spirit in me!" (Ps. 51:3, 10, GNB.)

(b) Power released through vital prayer is essential for inner quiet. In prayer we recognize the inadequacy of our personal resources to cope with life. In prayer we realize the unlimited resources of divine power available to us. Praying is the act of exposing our needs to the action of God's love—to help, to pardon, to heal, to strengthen, and to inspire.—Emil Kontz.

SUNDAY: SEPTEMBER FIFTH

MORNING SERVICE

Topic: The Dignity of Honest Work (Labor Sunday)

SCRIPTURE: II Thess. 3:6–12.

I. Work is commanded by God (Exod. 20:9). (a) The whole week was symbolically compressed into one day, the Sabbath, and dedicated to the Lord. By refraining from his own efforts on that day, man effectually recognized divine ownership. All time belonged to God, as did the whole of creation.

(b) Six days God commanded men to work. Work is an honorable part of life. In these days man is to do all the necessary work. This command to work also implies a prohibition. The seventh day shall be the Sabbath, and this day shall be kept holy. Through this command God gives direction both for work and rest.

II. Work is a divine attribute (John 5: 17). (a) Jesus was not only suggesting that the Father was working with him in all the actions performed during this earthly ministry, but he was also saying that the Father had been working with him and he with the Father in all their actions previously. Jesus was turning the mind of his Jewish listeners back to God's work from the beginning of creation, and he was claiming to have a part of that work also.

(b) Jesus is saying that God still works, and, as God incarnate, he is still working. He works as the Father works. Those two were in on creation and the giving of the law, and both still work. Work is a divine attribute.

III. Work honors God (Eph. 4:28; 6: 5–8). (a) The thief lives by the labor of others, but the Christian is to live by his own labor. Honest labor, an occupation in a worthy calling, is a part of the Christian life. This honors God.

(b) Our labor is not to be regarded for our own good only but that there may be a means for doing good to others. Our labor becomes a part of our Christian ministry.

(c) The Christian's work should be a labor of love. Then one will be able to express integrity of character through his work. The work of the believer should be done "as to the Lord." In so doing one is able to express the values and virtues of Christ in his work, and the result of this will be to honor God.

(d) Scripture teaches that believers should do all for the glory of God. The glory of God has to do with God's reputation. The work of a Christian reflects the reputation of God. The work of Christians should be honest, thorough, and dependable in order that it may truly bring honor to God.

IV. Failure to work brings God's judgment (II Thess. 3:6–12). (a) Some believers in Thessalonica thought Christ would soon return, and they wanted the rich to share their riches so that they would not have to work. This brings swift judgment. The disorderly brother is pictured as a soldier who is out of line, who leaves his proper place in the ranks and is insubordinate. The command is given in v. 6 to correct this action. The purpose of this command from Christ is to make the disorderly brother ashamed so that he will forsake his wrong action. It also instructs the congregation how to separate such a one from the fellowship if needed.

(b) V. 10 states judgment upon the non-worker. If one fails to work, do not let him eat. Surely those who were unable to work were entitled to support; those who refused to work, even if they alleged religious pretexts, should not be maintained by the charity of their brethren. This truth abolishes all false asceticism, all unchristian disinclination to work and fanatic ex-altation above work, and all self-inflicted pauperism.

(c) There is virtue in honest work. Work has its origin in God. God commands that we work. Man is made in God's image and is capable of productive, creative, and useful work. This will enable man to have his needs met and also remove idleness from his life.—Thomas Tutor.

Illustrations

THE PATIENCE OF GOD. William F. McDowell told how he congratulated the director of an elaborate electrical display on his achievement. He went on to say that he never ceased to marvel at the wonders of electricity. "Yes," replied the director, "and I never think of it without marveling at the patience of God." "The patience of God!" said the bishop. "Just what do you mean?" "Just this," said the director. "Has it ever occurred to you how the creator must have waited through the centuries for someone to break through and discover the vast electrical resources of the universe that were there just waiting to be used?"—Wilfred C. Lockhart.

TINY PUSHES. I long to accomplish a great and noble task, but it is my chief duty to accomplish tasks as though they were great and noble. The world is moved along not only by the mighty shoves of its heroes but also by the aggregate of the tiny pushes of each honest worker.—Helen Keller.

Sermon Suggestions

HOW TO HANDLE LIFE AS GOD'S PEOPLE. Text: II Cor. 9:1, 6–7. (1) Christian stewardship is handling who we are. (2) Christian stewardship moves from handling who we are to the things we handle. (3) Christian stewardship moves from handling who we are and the things we handle to what hands can never handle.—James Lollis.

TRUE RICHES. Text: Luke 12:20. (1) Rich in faith. (2) Rich in love. (3) Rich in character and reputation. (4) Rich in God's graces.

Worship Aids

CALL TO WORSHIP.   "Come unto me, all ye that labor and are heavy laden, and I will give you rest. Take my yoke upon you, and learn of me; for I am meek and lowly in heart; and ye shall find rest unto your souls." Matt. 11:28–29.

INVOCATION.   O Lord, who hast taught us that the love of money is the root of all evil, teach us to care for what money cannot buy—not security but opportunity, not withdrawal from the world but a full participation within it, and not prestige but use. Help us to handle all the goods of life in the spirit of thy Son who out of his poverty made many rich.

OFFERTORY SENTENCE.   "I will freely sacrifice unto thee: I will praise thy name, O Lord; for it is good." Ps. 54:6.

OFFERTORY PRAYER.   God of all good, who hath rewarded our labors, we acknowledge thankfully thy favor and do now dedicate a share of our material gains to the even more satisfying ministries of the Spirit.

PRAYER.   O God our Father, bless all those whose task it is to serve the community, the nation, and the world.

Bless those who have in their hearts a passion for social justice; those who cannot be content as long as some have too little and some have too much; those who labor that men and women may receive a just reward for their work and a good home in which to live; those whose care it is that the workless and the destitute, the homeless and the outcast, and the poor and the needy should be remembered. Deliver them from all bitterness of spirit and wildness of speech, and grant them strength of will and charity of heart.

Bless those whose service of the community is unseen and who are taken for granted; those who clean our streets and repair our roads; those whose day and night work gives us water, light, and heat; those who serve the public in shops and in offices and on the roads and the railways and in the air; those who are engaged on all the many tasks without which the community could not go on. Help them to see their own importance in the scheme of things, and help others not to forget the work of those who serve.

O God, who art the master of all good workmen, grant unto all men joy and diligence in their working and the consciousness that in serving their fellowmen they are serving thee.—William Barclay.

EVENING SERVICE

Topic: Where in the World Is God?
TEXT: Ps. 139:7.

Why is it so difficult for people to experience God?

I. Maybe it is because we are looking for him. A person is lost. The rescuers are looking for the lost person. The one who is lost is looking for the rescuers. In their search for each other they miss each other. That's the way it is with being lost. The lost person should wait right where he is until he is found. God is looking for us. "For the Son of man has come to seek and to save that which is lost" (Luke 19:18, NAS). We should wait and let him find us.

II. Another reason why people find it hard to experience God is that they are looking for him in the wrong places. Mary went to anoint the body of Jesus with burial ointments. She thought she knew where he was. He was dead and in the tomb. But he wasn't there. "Why do you seek the living among the dead?" the angel asked. We may be wrong in looking for God, and we may be looking in the wrong places.

III. The Bible affirms that God is present and that we can find out where he is if we look in the right places.

(a) God is in the world in the Holy Spirit. Jesus promised his followers that he would not leave them alone but would send the Holy Spirit.

(b) God is in the world in the church—his body. God is to be found wherever his church is found.

(c) God is in the lives of his children. We were created in his image. We lost that image in the sin of Adam and Eve, but the image is restored through Jesus Christ.

(d) God is in events. Someone has suggested that history is "his-story."

(e) God is with the needy of every generation. It was no accident that God chose Israel, "the fewest of all peoples" (Deut. 7:7). God did not choose the strong.

(f) God is in nature. One is not led to worship God by the beauty of nature. One starts with faith, then one can observe nature as God's creation and handiwork.—Herbert Carlock, Jr.

SUNDAY: SEPTEMBER TWELFTH

MORNING SERVICE

Topic: Simplifying Life
TEXT: II Cor. 11:3.

How do you go about simplifying your life? There are four important keys we we can turn to uncomplicate our lives.

I. The first has to do with our speech. (a) What does our speech have to do with complicating or uncomplicating our lives? Look at the difference between truths and lies. Truth is always straightforward and simple, but lies are roundabout and complex. Jesus said, "Let your yes be yes and your no be no" (Matt. 5:37). In his day most folks did not answer honestly. If you asked them for their word, they would, by swearing by something unimportant like the gold on the temple door, give you an answer tainted with deceit. We do that too. That's why we're always so careful to read the small print on a contract. That's why we have truth in advertising laws. That's why we give evasive answers to questions asked of us—answers that are not really answers at all.

(b) Even our speech complicates our life. Think of the multitude of rules and regulations there are to follow in our twentieth century society. There were many laws in Jesus' day too—books of them. But Jesus reduced them all to two—to love God with all your heart and to love your neighbor as yourself.

II. "You are what you think," the old adage says. That means, for one thing, if we think about life in simple terms our lives are likely to be simple. If we load our minds with all sorts of extraneous things, our lives will be complex.

(a) That has something to say to how much of television's often worthless fare we take in. It has to do with the kind of literature we read and music we listen to. It has to do with every worthless thing we allow to enter our minds. "As a man thinketh in his heart, so is he" (Prov. 23:7). What kind of unnecessary—and undesirable—burdens do you weigh your mind down with?

(b) Perhaps you could rid your life of a lot of its complexity by ridding your mind of a lot of its superfluous and even harmful baggage. If you are what you think, perhaps by focusing on the simply God-given pleasures of life your lifestyle can come to reflect that thinking.

III. No key for simplifying life is more important than our stance toward possessions.

(a) When you look at the life of Jesus, in addition to the purity of his speech and the purity of his thought life, one of the things you're immediately aware of is the purity of his attitude toward material things. Jesus possessed his possessions; his possessions did not possess him.

(b) Someone suggested there are two ways to be rich. One is in the abundance of your possessions. The other is in the fewness of your wants. When we depend upon Christ to supply us with our daily needs, our wants become few indeed. When we surrender not only our physical needs into his hands but also all of the things that make life complex, our daily tasks turn out to be simple, vital ones, not superfluous, needless ones. We become children again—simple, happy, and unafraid.

IV. When we compare our hectic lives with that of Jesus, we discover an unfathomable difference. Jesus led a life that was busier than any of ours and more hectic than ours will ever be. Yet there was a power and poise about his life that amazes us. What made the difference? How was he able to do what we would so like to but never have been able to pull off?

(a) Two things, more than any others, account for it. He had time for God, for his Father in heaven. He had time for others. It had to do with priorities. Relationships were Jesus' priority—not things, not ambition, not prestige, not power, not any of the things we usually chase after.

(b) True riches and prosperity have to do with relationships, not possessions, power, or prestige. If we could learn that key to reducing our life from complexity to simplicity, we would experience a peace and joy we have always dreamed of but scarcely dared to hope for.—Arthur McPhee.

Illustration

WALLET SCIATICA. When a patient complained of left thigh and lower back pain, a physician asked the man to show him his billfold which was packed so full of money the doctor determined that the wallet was putting pressure on the sciatic nerve and causing discomfort. The ailment was diagnosed as "wallet sciatica," but it could just as easily be described as "miser's misery." Many preachers know from personal experience that when they touch on a man's wallet, they have struck a nerve. Congestion of the pocketbook can prove to be a painful malady, causing the same type of discomfort as a tightly closed hand. There is no doubt that many church members need to lose some weight—from their wallets.—Jim N. Griffith.

Sermon Suggestions

THE FULLNESS CHRIST PROVIDES. Text: Col. 2:10 (ASV). (1) He fills our need for love. (2) He fills our need for belonging. (3) He fills our need for purpose.—James D. McLemore.

WHY SUNDAY SCHOOL? (1) It provides systematic Bible study for all age levels.

(2) It provides teaching during the most strategic time of life. (3) It provides for a need not filled by any other institution. (4) It provides a closely knit fellowship. (5) It provides candidates for membership in the church.—Ray H. Hughes.

Worship Aids

CALL TO WORSHIP. "Make a joyful noise unto the Lord, all ye lands. Serve the Lord with gladness: come before his presence with singing. Enter into his gates with thanksgiving, and into his courts with praise: be thankful unto him, and bless his name." Ps. 100:1–2, 4.

INVOCATION. Great is thy name, O Lord, and greatly to be praised and to be had in reverence of all them that call upon thee. For thou only art God; we are the people of thy pasture and the sheep of thy hand. Therefore we worship and adore thee, Father, Son, and Holy Spirit, ever one God, world without end.

OFFERTORY SENTENCE. "Every man hath his proper gift of God, one after this manner, and another after that." I Cor. 7:7.

OFFERTORY PRAYER. Our heavenly Father, help us to remember that, though Christ offer his companionship, to us belongs the decision as to whether or not we will follow him. May we through these gifts and our witness share with all the world the blessedness that comes to us through thy grace.

PRAYER. Father, we come to worship this day with open hearts. We seek to fill our hearts with the understanding and love which may come through you. We also come with sadness and regret for the ways which we have not followed in your will. We seek to learn more of your will and your way so that our lives will shine as your light around us. We ask your forgiveness for our sins, Father. We cannot be thankful enough for the gift of your Son which you have given us and the life he gave that our sins might be forgiven. Father, help us to remember all that he gave to us. He gave us knowledge through his teaching and through his signs of your kingdom. May these teachings of life remind us daily of who we are and who we strive to be.

Through parables and actions we are able to see the meaning and purpose of life. Christ's parables are still alive in our lives. Through our faith and through our commitment to our neighbors in the world, we come to know the meaning of what Christ said to us. Give us your strength daily to answer the call of Christ in the lives of the sick, lonely, and troubled persons around us. As a child grows so quickly in knowledge and strength, may we also grow quickly in understanding and faith that through all things you and your power will always be with us. May we learn the language of your love which may strengthen the weakest heart. As your Son came to live among us, may we learn to live in our world in peace, always turning toward the path which we know through you.—James R. Rosenburg.

EVENING SERVICE

Topic: Finally, Brethren

Paul's priorities are reflected in his letters, especially as he came to the close of them and said, "Finally, brethren." His closing words dealt with themes of supreme importance.

I. "Finally, my brethren, rejoice in the Lord" (Phil. 3:1). To Paul a Christian's life should be characterized by happiness. Christians should radiate optimism in everyday living, not a superficial and unrealistic attitude of naivete but rather a deep, abiding assurance that although problems exist our God is greater than any of them and "in him who pours power into us, we are able for anything" (Phil. 4:13).

II. "Finally, my brethren, be strong in the Lord" (Eph. 6:10). Paul recognized that Christians in Ephesus must face the opposition of the secular world. To be a Christian has never been easy. Paul pictured the resources available to the Chris-

tian by referring to the armor of the Roman soldier. We are to have our loins girt about with truth, wear the breastplate of righteousness, and have our feet shod with the gospel of peace. The shield of faith will enable us to quench the fiery darts of the wicked. The helmet of salvation is a necessity, and the sword of the Spirit is our constant offensive weapon.

III. "Finally, brethren, pray for us" (II Thess. 3:1). Intercession is the highest form of petitionary prayer and one of the noblest acts a Christian can perform. Satan truly "trembles when he sees the weakest saint upon his knees," and he must tremble four-fold when we are on our knees praying for one another. The words that follow indicate that Paul requested the prayers of his friends in order that "the word of the Lord may have free course," which means he wished to be completely unfettered and unhindered by unreasonable and wicked men as he proclaimed the message of Christ.

IV. "Finally, brethren, whatsoever things are true . . . honest . . . just . . . pure . . . lovely . . . of good report . . . think on these things" (Phil 4:8). Singleness of heart is an absolute necessity if a Christian is to live effectively. Included in this are high ideas and deep convictions in our personal lives. We must decide early that our base nature will not rule but rather our speech shall be clean, our motives pure, and our integrity unquestioned.

V. "Finally, brethren, farewell. Be perfect" (II Cor. 13:11). The word *perfect* does not mean sinlessness but rather complete in character. The verb stem includes such ideas as to adjust thoroughly, to knit together, and to unite completely. This is a different word from the one Jesus used in the sermon on the mount when he said, "Be ye therefore perfect, even as your Father which is in heaven is perfect." The word Paul used here is even more comprehensive concerning completeness and well-roundedness, indicating that we are to be the kind of person who finishes any job that we attempt.—Fred M. Wood.

SUNDAY: SEPTEMBER NINETEENTH

MORNING SERVICE

Topic: Mistaken Identity

TEXT: Luke 3:22 (GNB).

In our gospel passage we have an instance of mistaken identity. The people became so impressed with the words and works of John the Baptizer that they questioned in their hearts whether perhaps he were the Christ, the one God would send to save them. So potentially serious was the mistake that the gospel writer takes pains to counteract the error not once but twice. First, John himself points to the real messiah who is coming in the person of Jesus. Then, when Jesus has been baptized, a voice from heaven says to him, so that all may overhear: "You are my own dear Son. I am pleased with you."

I. It is easy to misunderstand the nature and mission of Jesus. (a) We hail the child of Bethlehem as prince of peace, king of angels, and incarnate deity. We recall the visit of the potentates from the East with their splendid gifts of gold, frankincense, and myrrh. And so we easily fall into the habit of identifying Christ with royal privilege and divine power.

(b) We are not entirely wrong in that. For in the book of Acts we hear Peter speak of him as lord of all and as the one whom God has anointed with power. But it is a strange Lord, who is taken prisoner by Pontius Pilate's guard, and a stranger power, which submits to common execution on a cross.

(c) At the heart of the identity of Jesus there is a contradiction. Christ is lord, as Peter calls him. But at the same time he is a servant. The early Christians, who knew Jesus best, could not help but think of him when they read the opening words of Isa. 42: "Behold, my servant, whom I uphold." Christ is the lord who is a servant, the king who is a subject.

(d) Is it any wonder that he is the object of mistaken identity? Christ defies our everyday categories, and we can speak of him only in words which intensify mystery.

II. His mission is bound up with his identity. (a) This servant-lord champions the oppressed and the imprisoned, says the prophet. His concern is justice rather than privilege. He raises up the lowly and makes the cause of the poor his own, that God's kingdom which is meant for all may be fulfilled.

(b) We need not marvel that this Jesus has been misunderstood. Some who have noticed his concern for the oppressed have seen him simply as a visionary Galilean peasant whose followers mistakenly thought him to be divine. Others have taken the claim of divine lordship so seriously as to miss his concern for human justice and freedom.

(c) Christ is God's riddle come among us, and we wrestle to make sense of the divine-and-lowly presence in our midst. We seek to understand and to make known who Jesus Christ really is in all of his fullness and mystery.

III. What about us? Who are we in relation to who he is? How shall we define our own identity?

(a) It is certain that we benefit from Jesus' ministry. The good news which he came to bring and the kingdom of God which he inaugurated are for us. At his baptism Jesus was proclaimed as the dear Son of God, and through our baptism he has declared to us that we are accepted for his sake. We are God's people by grace.

(1) To say nothing more than that is to have a mistaken identity about ourselves. For while we benefit from the ministry of our lord, we also are called to share in his mission. We are now God's people, servants with Jesus Christ, that the world may believe.

(2) We are claimed by God not for privilege but for service. Through baptism we come to share in the priesthood of Christ, and a priest is one who serves, who works on behalf of others, and who holds before God the hurts and hopes of the world.

(b) In our most honest moments we know that we are too weak and too preoccupied with our own problems and perplexities to worry very much about the rest of the world. Perhaps the church is intended to be God's servant, but we seem to lack the motivation and the strength to do the work which God has committed to the church.

(1) If God came to us only with a request that we serve, there would be reason for anxiety and despair. But God also gives us the power, and we know it. Through our baptism, Jesus Christ shares with us the power of the Holy Spirit revealed following his own baptism.

(2) We have the witness of faithful Christians across the ages that in times of challenge God has imparted strength and has given a power they had not known before. They could do things which otherwise seemed to them impossible. They could make sacrifices which at other times would have appeared too immense to contemplate.—Laurence H. Stookey.

Illustrations

FOOTPRINTS. The ancient Greeks held that when the goddess of Thebes came among them she left her track. Her footprints were in the fields and forests. Passing by a tree that had been blackened by a thunderbolt, she paused, and afterward woodbine sprang up to cover the tree's nakedness. She lingered by a stagnant pool, and it became a flowing spring of pure water. She rested upon a fallen log, and from decay and death came moss, the snowdrop, and the anemone. She had cast her shadow, and wherever it fell, some of her character fell with it.—Homer J. R. Elford.

UNFOLDING LIFE. I have come to believe that appreciating individuals is rather rare. I have come to think that one of the most satisfying experiences I know and also one of the most growth-promoting experiences for the other person is just fully to appreciate an individual in the same way that I appreciate a sunset. People are just as wonderful as sunsets, if I can let them be. When I look at a sunset, I don't find myself saying, "Soften the orange a little on the right-hand corner and put a bit more purple along the base and use a little more pink in the cloud color." I don't do that. I watch it with awe as it unfolds. I like myself best when I can experience my staff members, my son, my daughter, my wife, and myself in this way —appreciating the unfolding of a life.— Carl Rogers.

Sermon Suggestions

LIFE'S IMPORTANT CHOICES. Text: Deut. 30:19. (1) The choice to be, meaning at least in part to fulfill the capacity for which one is intended. (2) The choice to do. (3) The choice to do without.—Wesley P. Ford.

THE MEANING OF BAPTISM. Text: Rom. 6:4 (NASV). Baptism symbolizes a cleansing which brings new life. (1) The new life which the new believer must walk is a life controlled by God. (2) The new life under God is a life of holiness. (3) The new life reproduces life by bearing witness to the Christ who brought life out of death.— James D. McLemore.

Worship Aids

CALL TO WORSHIP. "They that wait upon the Lord shall renew their strength; they shall mount up with wings as eagles; they shall run, and not be weary; and they shall walk, and not faint." Isa. 40:31.

INVOCATION. Lord God Almighty, holy and eternal Father, who dwellest in the high and lofty place, with him also that is of a humble and contrite spirit: we come before thee, beseeching thee to cleanse us by the grace of thy Holy Spirit, that we may give praise to thee, now and forever, in the name of our redeemer, Jesus Christ.

OFFERTORY SENTENCE. "Lay up for yourselves treasures in heaven, for where your treasure is, there will your heart be also." Matt. 6:20–21.

OFFERTORY PRAYER. Cleanse and accept these our gifts, O God, and may they be used according to thy will to redeem, restore, and renew the ministries within thy kingdom.

PRAYER. Grant us, O Lord, that the ears which have heard the voice of thy songs may be closed to the voice of clamor and dispute, that the eyes which have seen thy great love may also behold thy blessed hope, that the tongues which have sung thy praise may speak the truth, that the feet which have walked thy courts may walk in the region of light, and that the bodies which have partaken of thy living body may be restored to newness of life.

Thou hast promised to regenerate us by water and the Holy Spirit and hast given us forgiveness of all our sins: strengthen us, we beseech thee, with the Holy Spirit, our comforter, and daily increase in us thy manifold gifts of grace—the spirit of wisdom and understanding, the spirit of counsel and heavenly strength, and the spirit of knowledge and true godliness. Fill us, O Lord, with the spirit of thy holy fear. Glory be to thee for thine unspeakable gifts.—William C. Swygert.

EVENING SERVICE

Topic: Do You Need to Be Born Again?
TEXT: John 3:7.
I. Nicodemus came to Jesus in the night. Was it also a dark night in Nicodemus' soul? Perhaps he had begun to question what he'd been taught from childhood. Maybe his religion wasn't working for him as he wanted. He longed for a deeper and warmer relationship with God. He had heard of Jesus and had respect for him. Upon seeing Jesus in the shadows cast by the oil lamps, he addressed him as rabbi—no mean title for a Jew.

(a) What Jesus told Nicodemus seemed impossible. You must be born again. How is this possible? Can a man return to his mother's womb and be reborn? No, says Jesus, you must be reborn in the spirit.

(b) Nicodemus went away that night. We never hear about him again. And it is easy for people today—even people in our churches—to turn away from these words. I'm a church member; why should I be reborn? I'm already giving my time and my money to the church; why should I give the notion of spiritual rebirth a second thought?

II. Let me suggest what being spiritually reborn can involve. Hopefully when we know the promise and the joy of Jesus' invitation we'll not turn away. We'll gladly sing, "Take my life, and let it be consecrated, Lord, to thee."

(a) The beginning of a new spiritual life is dawning in those moments when you say to yourself: "I give up. I can't fix this relationship on my own. I can't fix my life without help. I need a source of power and strength outside myself." Maybe a sense of guilt is gripping you. Maybe a feeling of failure is beating you down. Maybe you feel that others don't value you, respect you, or love you. Maybe you don't have self-esteem. Maybe you are doubting beliefs that you've held for a lifetime. Wherever your world is caving in is the point to say: "God, I give up. You take charge of my life."

(b) The new birth Jesus promises is not a passing, fleeting moment. Dramatic conversions may happen in the climate of emotion. People say that a burden is lifted from their shoulders. But this is not the end of it. Conversion that goes to the center of our being and makes us do an about face is a matter of commitment, and commitment is a commitment of the will. Emotion may or may not figure in the experience. The important thing is not what you feel but what you commit yourself to.

(c) Do you need to be born again? We all do. The point of conversion comes when you begin to say: "I can't do it alone. I need God's help." And the test of the genuineness of your religious experience is your lasting commitment to him.—R. Ralph Nichols.

SUNDAY: SEPTEMBER TWENTY-SIXTH

MORNING SERVICE

Topic: The Second Chapter
TEXT: I Thess. 4:15–17 (NEB).

I. The complete story of Jesus has two chapters, one not yet written. The first is entitled: "He comes! The king is at hand." The second is entitled: "He comes again! The king returns." The king has not placed it within the purview of mortal men and women to know the exact hour or day of his return. But we are assured of his return. And both his coming and his coming again belong to the identical imperial tradition.

II. The second coming of the king is implicit in the first coming. We really cannot be first adventist in relation to Jesus until—and unless—we are also second adventists. We are not really candidates for belief in Jesus' first coming until we have plumbed the depth and meaning of his second coming.

III. After the ascension the role of Jesus is different for the disciples and for all people. For Jesus is revealed as the lord of all creation, who divested himself of his awesome royalty before which no mortal human being can stand. He humbled himself, taking the burdens and limitations of this flesh.

(a) Meeting the powers of darkness in this world on their own terms and destroying them.

(b) Establishing a kingdom into which all are invited and in which the only law is the rule of love.

(c) Suffering for them not so that men and women of faith will not have to suffer but so that their suffering may be like his —transforming and redemptive.

(d) Then leaving his subjects for a while, allowing them a time to taste freedom and gain maturing responsibility and a time to lay the groundwork for his coming again in final judgment and in glorious triumph.

IV. It is to the first adventists, whose faith falls short of plumbing the dimensions of the second coming, that St. Paul addresses the sobering observation, "If in this life only we have hope in Christ, we are of all men most miserable." The world will defeat the first adventists every time. It is to the second adventists that St. Paul's reassurance speaks in Rom. 8:38–39.

V. St. Paul is correct in saying, "If in this life only we have hope in Christ, we are of all men most miserable."

(a) Christian commitment is effective here, amid the historical realities, only inasmuch as Christians have "tasted the powers of the age to come." No wonder that St. Paul could end his sweeping analysis of the meaning of the last things (eschatology) by saying: "Therefore, my beloved brethren, be steadfast, unmoveable, always abounding in the work of the Lord, knowing that in the Lord your labor is not in vain."

(b) As Lord Wilberforce was carrying on his struggle for the abolition of England's slave trade against terribly unbalanced odds, Thomas Carlyle said to him, "What you are working for is worth waiting for." The promise of the second coming of Christ is just the reverse for Christians: "What we are waiting for is worth working for." It is worth every effort, every last ounce of devotion, to look ahead to that time when, as Thessalonians describes it, "the Lord himself will descend from heaven; first the Christian dead will rise, then we who are left alive shall join them."

(c) We know that Christ has come. He has redeemed us with his own precious blood. He has guaranteed in his life, death, resurrection, and ascension that evil cannot ever finally triumph. So our labor in the Lord can never be in vain. And even where its goals are not fully realizable, it is still the only labor that is of deathless significance.—John E. Hines.

Illustrations

LOST MESSAGE. In 1935 a bottle containing a note was found on a beach in Japan. The note had been placed in the bottle 150 years earlier. It revealed that the sender and his companion had been marooned by shipwreck on a waterless island. The tragedy was that the message was useless after it was delivered because the doomed sailors had long since been dead.—Jonas L. Stewart.

LAST CHANCE. Phillips Brooks became seriously ill. His illness became so severe that even his best friends were not permitted to visit him. When Robert Ingersoll, a famous agnostic, learned of his ill-ness, he went to visit him. To the surprise of everyone, Ingersoll was immediately admitted to the sick room. Once inside the room, Ingersoll asked Brooks, "Why did you agree to speak with me when you wouldn't allow any of your close friends in?" "Oh, that's very simple," replied the bishop. "I have every confidence that I will see my other friends in the next world. But this may be the last chance I have to speak with you."—John Wade.

Sermon Suggestions

HE BRACED ME UP. Text: II Tim. 1:16. (1) Are there some quiet spaces in your soul where a tired heart and a weary mind can rest? (2) Are you a bringer of good news, or like a tabloid sheet, do you recite only bad news? (3) Is there something about you that says to those whom you meet, "I commend to you my savior"? (4) Does your life open up on something greater than yourself?—Aaron N. Meckel.

THE HOLY COMFORTER. Text: John 14: 16–17, 26. (1) The Holy Spirit is the persuasive comforter. (See Rom. 5:5; II Cor. 5:14–15.) (2) The Holy Spirit is the strengthening comforter. (See Rom. 8: 26.) (3) The Holy Spirit is the hope-inspiring comforter. (See Rom. 15:13.)—P. H. McSwain.

Worship Aids

CALL TO WORSHIP. "We have thought of thy lovingkindness, O God, in the midst of thy temple. According to thy name, O God, so is thy praise unto the ends of the earth." Ps. 48:9–10.

INVOCATION. Almighty and everlasting God, whom the heaven of heavens cannot contain, much less the temples which our hands have built, but who art ever nigh unto the humble and the contrite: grant thy Holy Spirit, we beseech thee, to us who are here assembled, that cleansed and illumined by thy grace, we may worthily show forth thy praise, meekly learn the word, render due thanks for thy mercies, and obtain a gracious answer to our prayers.

OFFERTORY SENTENCE. "It is God who is at work within you, giving you the will and the power to achieve his purpose." Phil. 2:13 (PHILLIPS).

OFFERTORY PRAYER. Help us to remember, O Lord, that a life is a more persuasive testimony than words, that deeds are more effective than argument, and that these gifts are only a portion of the loyalty thou dost require of us.

PRAYER. Our heavenly Father, thou whose name is love, in these moments of worship we sense our being drawn to thee by the cords of an eternal love. We only dare to come before thee because thou didst first love us. We praise thee, for thy love found us in that far country of our own pride, selfishness, and prejudice and through thy forgiveness we have been drawn back to thy house where there is bread and enough to spare.

Help us to comprehend for all days the nature of the ministry to which we have been called and are being called and recognizing that the ministry is not given to individuals but to the church, that it is not the prerogative of professionals alone but the privilege and responsibility of all the people of God. May the wholeness of the church be affirmed in the oneness of our mutual ministry.

Upon the many fronts in the world where our daily lives are lived, may we be faithful to our opportunity to serve in Christ's name. Sharpen our vision to perceive what radical things thou art doing in thy church today for the sake of thy world.

For all who share this fellowship, we pray. Where there is anxiety, grant the poise that comes through a confident faith in thee; where there is mistrust, a faith in the other; where there is despair, hopefulness; where there is weakness, thy strength; where there is fear, the love that casts out all fear.—John Thompson.

EVENING SERVICE

Topic: Dealing with Temptation
Scripture: I Cor. 10:6–13.

"We are set before and behind by temptations and cannot throw them off" (Luther). Temptation is not only the urge to tell a lie or to stay in bed on Sunday morning. Anything in our lives—small and great events, desires and ambitions—can become a temptation when it threatens to tear us away from God.

I. Be aware of it. (a) Be aware that things not evil in themselves can become temptations.

(1) Entertainment can so occupy us and work can so burden us that there is no time to think about our relationship to God.

(2) We can be dancing around the golden calf (v. 7) of success with ambition so consuming us that we refuse to consider whether it is good or bad.

(3) A desire even for such good things as food and the preservation of loved ones becomes a craving for evil (v. 6) if it displaces loyalty to God.

(b) Be aware of subtle temptations to immorality (v. 8). (1) In the sexual innuendos of much advertising in television and magazines.

(2) In the attitudes and actions of people who ignore the divineness of human sexuality.

(c) Be aware of the temptation to complain about God (v. 9). (1) We have the right to complain to God and to bring our troubles and resentments before him.

(2) It is something else to judge God's actions by accusing him of manipulating us.

(d) Be aware of the temptation to grumble against other people (v. 10).

(1) Blaming others for not coming up to our standards.

(2) Venting on them our frustrations and bitterness.

II. Look to God to help us escape it. (a) We cannot cope adequately with temptation by ourselves (v. 12).

(1) Our own fighting powers are so undependable that we succumb again and again. The temptation is beyond our strength.

(2) We get too involved with the fight itself which, after all, is not against flesh and blood (Eph. 6:12).

(b) We must stop squabbling with the demonic powers and look at him who is standing for us and beside us.

(1) Christ stood in the wilderness; the tempter had to flee (Matt. 4:11).

(2) Christ stands at God's right hand; the tempter too must serve him.

(c) Look at the faithfulness of God (v. 13). (1) He permits no temptation to come to us that is not common to man.

(2) Through Christ, our supernatural food and drink (I Cor. 10:3–4), he sustains us in the fiercest temptations.

(3) He always provides a way of escape that differs with different temptations.

(d) The way to deal with temptation is to keep our eyes on our faithful God who will not let us down and who through Christ is able to help us.—Gerhard Aho.

SUNDAY: OCTOBER THIRD

MORNING SERVICE

Topic: A Word at the Table (World Communion Sunday)
Text: Luke 22:20.

Luther says in an essay he wrote in 1519 that a last will and testament has four essential ingredients: a testator who makes the testament, the heirs who are named to receive what is given, the testament itself, and the seal or token.

I. A testament has a testator. (a) One of the important things in any will is the freedom of the maker. If it can be shown that the one who made a will was under someone's influence, was misguided, or didn't know what was happening, the will can be thrown out.

(b) In the Lord's Supper Jesus is the testator. On the night before his death he and his disciples ate their last meal together, the passover supper. During the course of the meal Jesus made his testament freely, and of his own loving will he instructed his disciples in what he wanted done with his gifts.

II. A testament has heirs. (a) The heirs don't make the will or decide its benefits. Sometimes people are disappointed or pleasantly surprised. Once they are named by the testator, they simply receive what has been willed to them.

(b) In the Lord's Supper Jesus names his heirs. He does so in a general way. At the same time he is very specific. This is "given for you," he said to his disciples when they were at supper that night. Then he instructed them to continue to "do this"—that is, they should give his gifts and say "for you." So whoever hears and believes these words, "given and shed for you," is named as one of the heirs.

III. There is the testament itself. (a) This is the decisive moment when the word—whether joyous or painful—is spoken. In the testament the one who has made the will names the heirs and makes the divisions of property, announcing who is to receive what.

(b) In the Lord's Supper the testament is in what has been called the words of institution. Beginning with the words, "In the night in which he was betrayed our Lord Jesus took bread," it ends with the repetition of "Do this for the remembrance of me." The declaration of the gifts is central: "Take and eat; this is my body, given for you" and "This cup is the new testament [or covenant] in my blood, shed for you and for all people for the forgiveness of sin."

IV. A last will and testament has some kind of seal or stamp—a witness showing that it is a legally recognized document. Most wills go off without a hitch, but sometimes the will is challenged.

(a) Luther suggests that the seal or token in a will is something like the bread and wine at the Lord's Supper. With these common, everyday elements, Jesus sealed his testament to his heirs.

(b) That's as far as the comparison goes, Luther said. For Jesus' seal is not dead but living. He invests himself in the bread and wine, coming "in, with, and under" them to express himself and his gifts to us.—James A. Nestingen.

Illustrations

THE LONGEST DAY. The books say that there are twenty-four hours in a day, and that is true. New Year's Day has twenty-four hours. So do Labor Day and next Sunday and my birthday. However, World Communion Sunday has more hours than that. By my determination, it has thirty-nine.

At my desk is a world map showing the 180th parallel. Counting 6 A.M. as the sunrise hour in the Pacific Ocean, I moved my pencil across the twenty-four time zones until I came to 6 A.M. in the last one. That made twenty-four hours. That still left meetings at all times of the day in the last zone, the last, according to my experience, beginning at 8 P.M. and lasting at least an hour.

I put the figures together—twenty-four hours from 6 A.M. in zone one to 6 A.M. in zone twenty-four, six more hours to noon, and nine hours from noon until 9 A.M. Twenty-four plus six plus nine. I was startled to find that there are thirty-nine hours in World Communion Sunday, a thirty-nine hour day with Christians thanking God together around the world. Undoubtedly, it is the longest day in the year.—Lora M. Green in *Response.*

INTERACTION. We human beings want to be where the action is. And some would say that the action is not at the Lord's table. Many would come out of a sense of commitment or obligation, with pious feelings, anxious to return to the world to experience real action.

We do not recognize the action in the Lord's Supper. There is interaction, and that makes it all the more meaningful. Through the centuries Christians have met about the table and have been put in touch with one another and with Christ. At the table we are not observers but participants. We are right in the middle of a dynamic activity. Millions of unseen Christians interact with us as we feast together. Together, in the name and spirit of Christ, we distribute, partake, and consume. And through his action, Christ gives himself anew to his people, cleansing, healing, and renewing.—Clinton C. McCoy in *The Disciple.*

Sermon Suggestions

JESUS AND HIS PEOPLE.   Scripture: John 17:3–22. (1) A living people (v. 3). (2) A faithful people (v. 6). (3) A secure people (v. 15). (4) A mature people (v. 19). (5) A united people (v. 22).—Walter L. Dosch.

EMPOWERED FOR MISSION.   Resource: Acts 2. (1) Empowered with new personal strength (vv. 1–6). (2) Empowered to boldly share (vv. 14–17). (3) Empowered to convince the world of its need (vv. 27 –39). (4) Empowered to live in unity (vv. 41–42).—Thomas Tutor.

Worship Aids

CALL TO WORSHIP.   "The cup of blessing which we bless, is it not the communion of the blood of Christ? The bread which we break, is it not the communion of the body of Christ? For we being many are one bread, and one body: for we are all partakers of that one bread." I Cor. 10: 16–17.

INVOCATION.   Almighty God, the giver and lord of life: we bless and praise thee for thy merciful keeping and gracious care, for all the gifts of thy providence and grace, and for all the blessings which manifest thy fatherhood. We thank thee for the faith which sustains us, the hopes which inspire us, and the light by which we daily walk. We thank thee for Jesus Christ, who by the life he lived, the temptations he conquered, the gospel he taught, and the cross he bore has brought us nigh to thee and closer to one another.

OFFERTORY SENTENCE.   "Every good gift and every perfect gift is from above, and cometh down from the Father of lights." Jas. 1:17.

OFFERTORY PRAYER.   Almighty God, may we trust more and more in thy kind providence, and may our submission to thy will be revealed in the deep devotion expressed through these gifts we offer in Christ's name.

PRAYER.   With this bread broken, Lord, we eat an invisible loaf, given each day in pieces no larger than our need; the broken bread of thy glory shining in the common thing; the broken bread of thy truth nurturing the small words of our lips; the broken bread of thy given life sanctifying the deeds and dreams of love and labor; the broken bread of thy joy glimmering in all the beauty and wonder of the broken lights of eternity through days and nights, through flowers and stars, through age and infancy, and through mercy and faith. With such broken bread we come to the table of him whose life was broken that ours might be mended, to shine at last with his spirit in the doing of thy will on earth where all things are incomplete until thy blessing rests upon them and they are as they were in heaven.—Samuel H. Miller.

EVENING SERVICE

Topic: Remembering Jesus

TEXT: I Cor. 11:24.

I. "This do." The communion is an action through which we proclaim our faith.

(a) The word "do" implies action and not verbal repetition. How easy it is for the Protestant service of worship to be just the latter. It is an encouraging sign that so many people today want more. They realize worship is not only speaking and listening but also doing. In worship we are all involved in an active way.

(b) The command of Jesus is demanding that we break bread and bless the cup in the same way as he did. This is something we do. In the act of receiving and sharing there is enacted a spiritual truth seen by everyone present.

(c) Our communion service should be the family meal of the Christian church, expressing our unity and mutual love. The disciples were present at the institution of this meal by Jesus and were the first to share in this fellowship. We too as members of the family of God join in this act. We have become members by our faith in Christ and his sacrificial death. This is the basis of our fellowship.

II. "In remembrance of me." The communion is an action centered upon Jesus Christ. There are two possible approaches to this second phase.

(a) The first is straightforward and well known. Our time of communion is meant to recall to our memory the events of salvation. We are "to do this"—break the bread, bless the cup, and receive the elements—in order to remind ourselves of the way God has delivered us from the bondage of sin through Christ's death and resurrection.

(b) More is involved than this in the understanding of remembrance. It has been suggested by those qualified that this phrase of Jesus could be better translated as "Do this that I be remembered."

(1) If this is so, an ambiguity arises. Who is meant to be doing the remembering? We, on the basis of Exod. 13:9 ("And it shall be to you as a sign and as a memorial"), automatically say, "The disciples and the church yet to be." But from other parallels when this phrase is used it would appear that God is the one who remembers. This has led to the view that Jesus meant, "Do this that God may remember me."

(2) We continue the work, conscious of many disappointments and failures. We are to be encouraged and strengthened as we meet in fellowship around the table. In waiting upon God we are to ask him to remember Jesus the messiah. We are to pray and act as commanded, for by so doing we hasten the time when the kingdom will come "on earth as it is in heaven." (See I Cor. 11:26.)—M. H. Bell.

SUNDAY: OCTOBER TENTH

MORNING SERVICE

Topic: Jesus Calls a Disciple

SCRIPTURE: Luke 5:1–11.

It is hard to miss the contrast between Jesus the popular teacher—so popular that he was being crowded off the shore of the lake—and Simon and his partners, fishermen who had failed. They had toiled all night and had caught nothing. To use modern jargon, they were losers. But instead of the envy that we would expect to find in such a situation we end up with enthusiasm. What did Jesus do that turned these dispirited men into disciples? When Jesus arrived on the scene, they were in a quitting mood. At the end of the story they volunteer. That is the important miracle in this story.

I. How did Jesus bring this about? (a) Jesus asked Simon to help him. He spoke to him directly. He needed Simon's boat in order to speak to the crowd. His request

was neither flattery nor false sentimentality. He wasn't trying to make Simon feel needed. Jesus did not try to flatter Simon by calling him a fisher of men before he became one. As Simon was to learn, it takes time and experience to become a leader. Jesus asked for all that Simon could offer at the time—an empty boat, empty because of failure. It was converted into a useful boat. Simon was converted into becoming a useful disciple.

(b) It is highly unlikely that this was the first time Simon had heard Jesus speak. He must have heard of Jesus before he met him, and although it is possible that what Jesus said in one session could have persuaded Simon and his partners to forsake all and follow him, I don't think we have to believe in that sort of miracle.

(c) Most likely what turned Simon and his friends into disciples was a longer association which came to a climax in the events described in this story. It was an association in which there had been both teaching and befriending.

II. The second thing worth noting about the way in which Jesus approached Simon is how he dealt with Simon's expression of unworthiness: "Depart from me, for I am a sinful man, O Lord."

(a) Jesus did not argue with him, but he would not allow Simon to use his past as an excuse for shirking. Rightly and compassionately, Jesus understood that what was troubling Simon was fear. "Do not be afraid" was his answer. "You will be a fisher of men."

(b) Compare this reassurance with the dismal view of human capabilities which has colored so much ecclesiastical discussion of people's needs and problems. Obviously Christians are concerned with the relief of hardship, but is it true that everyone needs an education leading to material wealth, public recognition, or political power in order to lead a useful life?

(c) Are the normal tragedies of disappointment, sickness, and death always to be looked upon as problems which necessarily incapacitate those affected by them? E. M. Forster used the phrase, "the aristocracy of the plucky." Perhaps the church ought to recall the fact that it once listed fortitude as one of the cardinal virtues.

III. Jesus impressed upon Simon and his friends that if they wished to be his disciples they would have to make sacrifices.

(a) The story ends with the statement that they left everything and followed him. No one in his right mind is going to give up something he values—such as his livelihood—unless he is offered something of greater value for it.

(b) Renunciation for its own sake is not a Christian virtue, despite the writings of many Christians throughout the ages. Jesus does not ask us to retreat from the world. He does ask us to be realistic. We are limited in what we can do. Often we must make a choice.

(c) There was something in what Jesus said and did that caused these men to decide that they would give up anything that would prevent them from following him. They saw the greater value of what Jesus offered them.

(d) Perhaps one of the reasons the modern church fails to draw many people to the cause of Christ is that the challenges and demands of Christian discipleship have not been stressed.

(e) The gospel was preached by Jesus to the fishermen by the lake. In this way it has been presented to the men and women throughout Christian history who have answered the call to missionary work. If the gospel is presented with the directness, the honesty, and the realism characteristic of Jesus in his ministry, it can evoke the same response today.—Edwin S. S. Sunderland.

Illustrations

SUSTAINING FELLOWSHIP. In Melville's *Moby Dick*, Father Mapple's pulpit is in the shape of a ship's prow—a cutting edge in the deepest waters. The preacher climbs into the pulpit by means of a rope ladder, which he pulls up after him, as if to signify that preachers are not puppets to be manipulated by congregational pressures. While accepting that truth, there is another side we need to see. Freedom to prophesy is rooted both in the call of God and in the congregation of his people. It is the sustaining fellowship which nurtures a climate of freedom and keeps people in dialogue as they listen and learn together what the master's voice is saying.—William Keucher in *The American Baptist*.

RECOVERY OF MEANING. There is an urgent need for all church members to recover the true meaning of certain words; to learn that the laity is really the *laos*, that is, the whole people of God in the world, including, of course, those that have been ordained; to learn that ministry means any kind of service by which a Christian, exercising a particular skill and gift, however humble, helps fellow Christians or fellow human beings in the name of God.—World Council of Churches.

Sermon Suggestions

WAYS LAY PEOPLE CAN SUPPORT CHURCH GROWTH. Text: Neh. 4:6. (1) Start where you are. (2) Let God use you the way you are. (3) Discover and use your spiritual gifts. (4) Don't be content with things as they are.—Leonard Albert.

CHARACTERISTICS OF GOD'S APPROVED WORKER. Scripture: II Tim. 2:14-26. (1) Avoids wordy discussions on religion (vv. 14, 16-17, 23). (2) Takes pride in his work (v. 15). (3) Teaches God's truth (v. 15). (4) Trusts God's foundations (v. 19). (5) Wants to serve, not sparkle (v. 21). (6) Shuns immature impulses (v. 22). (7) Operates with a pure heart (v. 23). (8) Acts kindly toward all (v. 24). (9) Is a patient teacher (vv. 24-25). (10) Remains open to divine intervention (vv. 25-26).—W. Lee Prince.

Worship Aids

CALL TO WORSHIP. "Let us search and try our ways, and turn again to the Lord. Let us lift up our heart with our hands unto God in the heavens." Lam. 3:40-41.

INVOCATION. God of all life, we have come here today alone as persons, together in families, all joined in the community of Christian faith. Though we seek your face in the world of life, we ask your blessing in these moments of withdrawal. Take us not from the world, but prepare us for life in the world. Let us not imagine special privilege for ourselves, but let us encourage common opportunity for all. Give us not love for ourselves alone, but make us instruments of your love in the midst of every human place.—Richard D. Bausman.

OFFERTORY SENTENCE. "Thou crownest the year with thy goodness. . . . Samuel took a stone, and set it between Mizpeh and Shen, saying, Hitherto hath the Lord helped us." Ps. 65:11; I Sam. 7:12.

OFFERTORY PRAYER. O Lord, upon whose constant giving we depend every day, teach us how to spend and be spent for others that we may gain the true good things of life by losing every selfish trait.

PRAYER. Father, in the fellowship and challenge of worship, measure our life by the height of our dreams, plans, and purposes as revealed in the dreams of Christ.

Weigh us, O God, by the strength of our thought, the lightness of our heart, the sincerity of our convictions, and the supreme desire of our life as revealed in daily living.

Value us as workmen in thy great vineyard, measured, weighed, valued in the light of thy purpose for our life, making us ashamed of shoddy work, slip-shod thinking, tasks undone, and the frittering away of life on trivialities.

Give us, above all, in and through worship the inspiration to discover new spiritual values, new visions and dreams, and great convictions as we think of life in terms of being co-creators with thee in the art and joy of living.—Frank A. Court.

EVENING SERVICE

Topic: Thinking, Working, and Praying
TEXT: I Cor. 14:15.

The argument that because God is infinitely good and wise prayer is a superfluity rests on two fallacies.

I. The first is the idea that praying is an attempt to secure from God by begging something which God had not at all intended or had intended otherwise.

(a) Christian prayer is giving God an opportunity to do what he wants and what he has been trying in vain, perhaps for years, to do in our lives, hindered by our unreadiness, our lack of receptivity, and our closed hearts and unresponsive minds. God stands over many lives, like the master over Jerusalem, saying, "How oft would I . . . and ye would not" (Matt. 23: 37).

(b) True prayer changes that. It opens the door to the will of God. It does not change God's plan, but it does give God's plan gang-way. It is not begging from God; it is cooperation with God. In the luminous words of Archbishop Trench: "We must not conceive of prayer as an overcoming of God's reluctance but as a laying hold of his highest willingness."

II. The other fallacy underlying the

thought that the wisdom and love of God make prayer superfluous is the idea that God can do all he wills without any help from us. But he cannot.

(a) The experience of the race is clear that some things God never can do until he finds a man who prays. Meister Eckhart put the truth with extreme boldness: "God can as little do without us as we without him."

(b) If at first this seems a wild statement, we may well consider in how many ways God's will depends on man's cooperation.

(1) God himself cannot do some things unless men think. He never blazons his truth on the sky that men may find it without seeking. Only when men undiscourageably give themselves to intellectual toil will God reveal to them the truth, even about the physical world.

(2) God cannot do some things unless men work. Will a man say that when God wants bridges and tunnels, and wants the lightning harnessed and cathedrals built, he will do the work himself? That is an absurd and idle fatalism.

(3) If God has left some things contingent on man's thinking and working, why may he not have left some things contingent on man's praying? Some things never without thinking, some things never without working, and some things never without praying! Prayer is one of the three forms of man's cooperation with God.— Harry Emerson Fosdick.

SUNDAY: OCTOBER SEVENTEENTH

MORNING SERVICE

Topic: Man's Questions and God's Answers

SCRIPTURE: Ps. 73.

I. Real religion offers every sort of encouragement to seek the truth. (a) In all honesty we must admit that some church people regard those with inquiring minds as the enemies of truth.

(1) Some indeed have made a shipwreck of faith because they will never commit themselves.

(2) Such failures cause some to overlook the needs of many others who seek something better than canned answers.

(b) Our Lord was not content with old explanations. (1) He saw that often they did not work.

(2) He saw that sometimes they interfered with the will and work of God.

(3) He had a healthy respect for what had been revealed in the past and judged the misuse that often had been made of it.

(4) He recognized that God is alive and capable of doing something new and surprising. (See Matt. 13:52.)

(c) Jesus taught us to ask, seek, and knock. (1) To refuse anyone the privilege of raising questions is unbiblical. Consider the questions of the prophets.

(2) No one has ever needed to be afraid to cry to heaven for an answer since Jesus cried, "My God, my God, why hast thou forsaken me?"

II. Some times and places are more promising than others for getting the answers we need.

(a) The moment of despair is a promising moment for the discovery of truth.

(1) Martin Luther received liberating insight when he despaired of saving himself.

(2) Many an alcoholic has started on the way to recovery when he acknowledged his utter inability to help himself.

(3) The psalmist knew despair: "But as for me, my feet were almost gone; my steps had well nigh slipped" (vv. 2–3). Man's extremity is God's opportunity.

(b) Religious insight can come in a thousand different places. (1) Consider Abraham, Jacob, Moses, Elijah, Isaiah, Jeremiah.

(2) Think of the varied testimonies of the members of any church congregation.

(3) All in all the most promising place is the sanctuary, the place of worship (v. 17). We find there a sense of history, companionship in suffering and doubt, and a caring community that signifies the presence of God.

III. God's answers come in his own

ways. (a) You are in for terrible disappointments if you expect final answers to your questions. (See Isa. 55:8–9; Rom. 11:33).

(b) Nevertheless, God does speak and act. (1) He makes his presence known. You may feel like running away. (See Isa. 6:5; Mark 5:7; Luke 5:8.) But you also want to stay. God will overcome your ambivalence by his clear purpose to help, not hurt.

(2) He brings repentance. Eventually you have to admit you were wrong (vv. 21–22). Eventually you have to exercise a daring faith (vv. 25–26).

(3) He guides you. He leads you through the thorny, uncertain way. (See Isa. 42:16.) This is a deepening conviction to all whom God leads (vv. 23–24).—James W. Cox.

Illustrations

APPLICATION.   After attending church one Sunday, Longfellow went home and wrote these words in his diary: "John Ware, of Cambridge, preached a good sermon." Underneath he added these unusual words: "I applied it to myself."—Donald E. Collins.

LANGUAGE OF CONFESSION.   If anyone feels that the language which the church asks him to use is exaggerated—"We do earnestly repent and are heartily sorry for our misdoings; the remembrance of them is grievous unto us; the burden of them is intolerable"—then let him think of slums, sweating, prostitution, and war and ask if the remembrance of these is not grievous and if the burden of them ought not to be intolerable. Let him remember that these horrible things are there not because some men are outrageously wicked but because millions of men are as good as we and no better.—William Temple.

Sermon Suggestions

THE BASIC PROBLEM.   Text: Obad. 1:4. (1) Pride is the basic problem because it closes the door to truth. (2) The proud are beyond the reach of God's help. (3) Pride shuts the door to hope and dooms us to stay the way we are.—Robert E. Goodrich, Jr.

NO NEED FOR OUR FEET TO SLIP.   Text: Ps. 18:36. (1) We are able to stand upon the rocks of affliction without slipping. (2) We are able to stand upon the rocks of discouragement without slipping. (3) We are able to stand upon the rocks of temptation without slipping.—O. W. Polen.

Worship Aids

CALL TO WORSHIP.   "We have thought of thy lovingkindness, O God, in the midst of thy temple. According to thy name, O God, so is thy praise unto the ends of the earth." Ps. 48:9–10.

INVOCATION.   Most humbly do we thank thee, O Lord, for thy mercies of every kind and thy loving care over all thy creatures. We bless thee for the gift of life, for thy protection round about us, for thy guiding hand upon us and the many tokens of thy love, especially for the saving knowledge of thy dear Son, for friendship and duty, for good hopes and precious memories, and for the joys that cheer us and the trials that teach us to trust in thee. O heavenly Father, make us wise unto a right use of thy benefits, and so direct us that in word and deed we may show gratitude to thee.

OFFERTORY SENTENCE.   "Seek ye first the kingdom of God, and his righteousness, and all these things shall be added unto you." Matt. 6:33.

OFFERTORY PRAYER.   Dear Father, help us to be ever concerned to find thy way for our lives, and may we never be satisfied to give thee our second best in return for thy great gift of love.

PRAYER.   Our heavenly Father, we gather together to praise thee for the wonder of thy light in our life. We rejoice in the glory that has been revealed to us through Jesus Christ and for the light that shineth in our hearts even in times of darkness and that the darkness can never put out. For the wonder of the illumined life and the glory that shines in our spirit because of thy grace, we praise thy name. Wilt thou unite our spirits in this time of worship in faith and confidence as we come to thee. We come at thine own invitation who art our heavenly Father and art more eager to give us the good things of life and life eternal than we know to ask.

May we be humble under thy hand, eager in thy presence, and receptive to hear what thou hast to say to us. Grant that in our life of prayer we may lay hold upon the great meanings that thou hast for us, that we may heed thy word when we hear it, and that we may live under thy leading and guiding and direction. So wilt thou make thy sufficiency account for our own weakness and wilt thou fill up the measure of our inadequacy with thy strength. May we always be seeking and acting and deciding and purposing, as those who belong to Jesus Christ. Bless this time of worship and grant that our hearts may be warmed, our minds illumined, and our spirits strengthened because we have come together this day.—Lowell M. Atkinson.

EVENING SERVICE

Topic: On Being Absent from Church
Text: Heb. 10:25.

I. Absenteeism does not kill churches. Does that sound strange coming from a preacher? Well, it's true and preachers certainly should tell the truth. Absenteeism is not the disease but a symptom. Symptoms do not kill. A symptom is defined as "any condition accompanying or resulting from a disease and serving as an aid in diagnosis."

II. Our disease may be a lack of love, unbelief, selfishness, worldliness, and lust. These things in turn produce undesirable fruits in our lives.

(a) A man is more concerned with his own pleasure than with the things of the Lord, so he is at the lake rather than in God's house on the Lord's Day. His real trouble is whatever caused him to be absent.

(b) Another man does not give as he has been prospered. His real problem may actually be covetousness. He wishes to keep for himself what rightfully belongs to God.

III. One of the reasons for our slow progress in the Lord's church is our widespread practice of working on the symptoms rather than the disease.

(a) We harp on one's being absent when we would do well to spend the time in cultivation of his love for the Lord, in enlightening him about the values of regularity of worship and the dangers of neglect, and in building his faith and confidence in God. Introduce him to the joy of saving a soul.

(b) Absenteeism does not kill churches, but cold and selfish hearts will. Covetous hearts will. Lust will. In whatever form it comes, sin will. When we put away sin, absenteeism will die.—Lewis Hale.

SUNDAY: OCTOBER TWENTY-FOURTH

MORNING SERVICE

Topic: Christianity and Healing
Text: Mark 1:40.

I. Health is a wonderful gift of God yet one we do not fully appreciate until we have lost it or are in danger of losing it. Without health, food and life become tasteless. To dwell in the shadows of chronic pain and half-health—no matter how brilliant a mind you have nor how large a check you can write—is to be handicapped in practically everything you do.

(a) God never planned that a man should know the sting of suffering and the distress of disease. Christ said of the woman who for eighteen years had been afflicted with physical infirmity, "Satan hath bound her." He regarded suffering of all kinds as evil, and he used his almighty power generously to relieve it.

(b) No sickness or disease is ever the will of God in the sense that he delights in it. The doctor, the nurse, and the psychiatrist have outstanding opportunity to glorify God in alleviating physical and mental disorders for love of Christ.

II. God gives us an amazing body, "fearfully and wonderfully made." (a) In your lifetime, if it is average, your heart will beat two and a half billion times without a shutdown for repairs, and it will expend enough energy in that time to raise almost four million pounds to the height of the Empire State Building. God makes us strong and sturdy because he wants us to glow with health.

(b) God expects us to take care of our bodies. Buoyant health is not a perpetual gift. The Christian way of living is a healthful way of living. The manufacturer of a machine is best qualified to give instructions on the care and use of the machine. God, who in his infinite wisdom and with his unlimited power created the human body, incorporated the instructions for the care and use of that body in his principles of godly living.

(c) What physician or psychiatrist will deny that contentment; a heart free from envy, hatred, anger, fear, and lust; a heart relieved of feelings of guilt; a body respected as a temple of God; and a body not abused by intemperance are all desirable goals of physical and mental hygiene?

III. We know that there is a remarkable relationship between all parts of a human being—body, mind, and soul.

(a) The *British Medical Journal* said, "No tissue of the human body is wholly removed from the influence of the spirit." A healthy soul, a soul at peace with God and man, will have a salutary influence on the body in which it dwells. A harmonious relationship within an individual and between an individual and his God and his fellow men is the relationship that God encourages and is a healthy relationship. God wants man to be well rather than sick.

(b) Everything that is used to maintain and restore man's health—antiseptics and germicides, drugs and medicine, pharmaceutics and the skills and techniques of doctors and psychiatrists—are not a happy accident of nature but a gift of God, because God wants man to be healthy rather than sick.

(c) Anyone who has observed Christ as he dealt with the diseased and the crippled will know that if Christ, the Son of God, was ready to spend himself as he did in relieving suffering, then God finds no delight in seeing bodies weakened, crippled, and destroyed by disease and accident. The stories of more than thirty individuals who felt Christ's healing touch are written in the Bible for our instruction and encouragement.

IV. We Christians believe in a Lord who today has the same power that he showed and used in Palestine so long ago when leprosy, deformity, and insanity fled at his touch. What is more important, we believe in a lord whose love for us and whose sympathy with our suffering is as strong and as sure as it was when he healed the leper.

(a) Those who believe in Christ as their savior share the trust and confidence of the leper, and their prayer is, "Lord, if thou wilt, thou canst make me clean." No matter how critical their illness and no matter how hopeless the outlook of others, they are sure of Christ's love and they do not question his power. Finally all healing depends on God's blessing.

(b) Does Christ today ever perform miraculous cures? When the arts of medicine and surgery and psychotherapy have done everything that they could without results, does God ever take a hand and accomplish what they could not do? There is no question that he can. A tremendous host of grateful Christian people and an increasing number of those who are in the medical profession answer, "Yes, he does."

(c) Not all who have Christian faith are healed of their diseases and infirmities. Even Paul, that man of amazing Christian faith, suffered to his closing days from a physical affliction. It is mockery and cruelty to say to those whose pain and ailment persist in spite of the best that modern science can do for them and in spite of fervent prayers, "If you'd have more faith, you'd have better health."

V. Christianity is not for those who are merely in search of better health. (a) Christianity is for those who recognize their soul's need, who confess that they are sick with the disease of sin and plead for forgiveness for Jesus' sake, who confess that they are weak and request strength from above, and who confess that they are confused and ask for God's guidance.

(b) How much better it is to be sick and have Christ the savior and eternal life than to be well through using God's gifts for maintaining and restoring health but to have lost one's soul.

(c) In sickness let us gratefully use the healing means God has given and let our prayer be, "Lord, if thou wilt, thou canst make me clean," and let our song be, though our body be racked with pain, "Whate'er God ordains is good." In health or illness, let our daily petition be, "Lord, for Jesus' sake cleanse our soul from all sin," and we'll sing praises to God forever in heaven where pain and sorrow shall be no more.—Armin C. Oldsen.

Illustrations

REVEALING MIRROR.   When Queen Elizabeth I grew old and unattractive, an unfortunate master of the mint incurred disgrace by a too faithful likeness of her cast on the shilling. The die was broken, and only one mutilated specimen is now in existence. The queen's maids of honor took the hint and were thenceforth careful that no fragment of a looking glass remained in the palace. *The Quarterly Review* noted that the queen "had not the heart to look herself in the face for the last twenty years of her life."—Donald E. Collins.

IN LOVE'S SERVICE.   Thorton Wilder's play *The Angel That Troubled the Waters* is laid at the pool of Siloam, where, at a certain hour of the day, the gospel story tells us, an angel ruffles the surface of the water, and whoever at that moment is lowered into the pool is healed. In Wilder's play a physician is discovered in the throng of sufferers gathered expectantly around the pool one day. He suffers from an incurable disease and, like the others, he is seeking a miraculous restoration of wholeness and health. But as he pushes forward he hears the angel of healing speak to him: "Draw back, physician . . . healing is not for you . . . without your wound where would your power come? It

is your very remorse that makes your low voice tremble into the hearts of men. The very angels themselves cannot persuade the wretched and blundering children on earth as can one human being broken on the wheels of living. In love's service only the wounded can serve. Draw back."—C. Thomas Hilton.

Sermon Suggestions

TEMPTATIONS WHILE PRAYING.   Text: Luke 22:42. (1) The temptation to give up. (2) The temptation to give in. (3) The temptation to give out.

STANDING UP UNDER STRESS.   Text: Eph. 6:13. (1) Accept your life. (2) Simplify your life. (3) Let go of your life. (4) Enlist your life.

Worship Aids

CALL TO WORSHIP.   "Trust in [God] at all times; ye people, pour out your heart before him: God is a refuge for us." Ps. 62:8.

INVOCATION.   O thou who art the light of the minds that know thee, the life of the souls that love thee, and the strength of the wills that serve thee, help us so to know thee that we may truly love thee and so to love thee that we may fully serve thee, whom to serve is perfect freedom.

OFFERTORY SENTENCE.   "Offer the sacrifices of righteousness, and put your trust in the Lord." Ps. 4:5.

OFFERTORY PRAYER.   O eternal God, may these gifts represent an inner commitment to love thee above all else and to love our brethren in need because they are loved by thee.

PRAYER.   God of the strong and the weak, of beginnings and endings, of the satisfied and the suffering: there is no experience of life from which you are absent. There is no need you have not known before we could express it. There is no joy you have not entered into and celebrated with us. There is no depth of hurt or sorrow you have not visited ahead of us and prepared a refuge for us, even within it, through your own caring and concern. Yet, we confess, we remain a people who are ever quicker to ask again than to give thanks once. Our prayers often are more vocal with complaints than with gratitude. We are more generous with our requests than with our gifts. And we are too typically more responsive to our own whims than to our neighbor's needs. Nevertheless, our Father, you hold our possibilities before us more than our performances. You keep us always aware that life offers dimensions greater than those we have explored. You have let us glimpse life's broader boundaries through one who has lived in its troubles, shouldered its responsibilities, and shared its joys like each of us. And through him we sense within ourselves from time to time those gifts which you have given that we only have begun to use. Empower us through the power made known in him. Minister to us by the renewal of our sense of ministry. Bless us through the multiplication of our willingness to become a blessing. For we pray in the name of him whose authority was in serving and whose giving of life itself became the example and the strength of living.—Paul E. VanDine.

EVENING SERVICE

Topic: Understanding the Bible
TEXT: Luke 11:28 (LB).

I. Do your study consistently. This will continually keep you in touch with God's word. Heb. 4:12 (NIV) says: "The word of God is living and active. Sharper than any double-edged sword, it penetrates even to dividing soul and spirit, joints and marrow; it judges the thoughts and attitudes of the heart." We all need continually to be sensitive to the teaching of God's word.

II. Do your study systematically. This will help you accomplish your objective. Jumping from one form of study to another or from one book to another, without completing any, is a haphazard approach that will fail.

III. Do your study with pencil and paper. Actually study the Bible. You will find that new ideas make a much deeper impression when they are written down. You will also be able to think more clearly by seeing your thoughts on paper. And mark in your Bible. This is not sacrilegious.

(a) Do your study by original investigation. Follow the example of the Bereans in Acts 17:11 (NIV): "Now the Bereans were of more noble character than the Thessalonians, for they received the message with great eagerness and examined the scriptures every day to see if what Paul said was true."

(b) A personal, original investigation may sound difficult. Don't let it scare you. It is one of the most fun and most profitable ways to study the Bible. To help you get started if you have never done an investigative Bible study before, utilize three steps which will make your study relatively easy.

(1) Read the book or chapter in its entirety several times.

(2) Begin a verse-by-verse analysis of the chapter. In this analysis ask yourself the following questions and write down the answers: Is this verse a command I must follow, a promise I can claim, or an instruction that will help me in life? Do I understand the meaning of all the words in the chapter? Where else in the Bible are there similar teachings? Is there anything I do not understand? What is the writer really saying?

(c) Make a personal application. This is the key purpose of Bible study—to study not merely for knowledge but for how you can live. Here is how you can apply scripture to your life.

(1) State the general problem you need help with.

(2) Write a specific example of this problem from your life.

(3) Write down specific steps you will take to begin changing your attitude, using personal pronouns.—Monte Unger in *Christian Herald*.

SUNDAY: OCTOBER THIRTY-FIRST

MORNING SERVICE

Topic: The Reward of Faith

TEXT: Matt. 8:13 (RIEU).

Jesus' healing ministry demands serious attention from modern Christians, but here the actual healing of the centurion's servant is incidental to the central point of the story. That point is in the faith of the centurion that elicited from Jesus this assurance, "Because of your faith, so let it be."

I. "Your reward shall be equal to your faith." (a) What brought forth these astonishing words from Jesus? The centurion had just said to him: "I am myself under orders, with soldiers under me. I say to one, 'Go,' and he goes; to another, 'Come here,' and he comes; and to my servant, 'Do this,' and he does it." The professional soldier saw the power and authority of Jesus in terms of what he knew best from his own experience—the pattern of discipline and command in military life.

(b) There is an element of naiveté in this. The centurion seems almost to have seen Jesus as a sort of heavenly sergeant-major who can give orders to the denizens of the unseen world. But Jesus saw beneath the surface naiveté. He saw the rudimentary but real faith of the centurion which recognized that Jesus had powers that were, so to speak, delegated to him by higher authority—powers given to him by God.

(c) The centurion's simple statement was an expression of trust in Jesus as a special servant of God, and in that trust was his faith. Jesus then exclaimed with ironic exuberance, "I tell you this: nowhere, even in Israel, have I found such faith." Then he says to the centurion, "Your reward shall be equal to your faith."

II. What did Jesus really mean by that assurance? What is the nature of the reward that faith promises to bring?

(a) Despite the distorted views we sometimes have of the rewards of faith, faith does offer authentic rewards. They are not the kind of rewards we yearn for in our more worldly moments. They are not the rewards that can be held up in front of us to spur us on.

(b) In the life of faith you cannot choose in advance your own desired rewards. God will not haggle with you over the rewards of faith. God does not issue trading stamps for your little religious observances and activities and then let you select your rewards out of a glossy catalogue. You cannot say to God, "If you'll give me such-and-such and do so-and-so for me, I'll have a real go at faith." That is not God's way with us, although at times we seem to think that it is.

(c) Jesus assured the centurion of Capernaum, "Your reward shall be equal to your faith." It has been the experience of the faithful down through the years that their reward has indeed been proportional to their trust in God as he has shown his will and love supremely in Jesus Christ.

III. The centurion of Capernaum did not try to bargain with Jesus over faith and its rewards. He recognized the power and the authority of Jesus that come from God. He simply put his trust in Jesus, and in that trust was his faith. And Jesus gave him this great assurance, "Your reward shall be equal to your faith." A paradoxical but realistic summing-up of this principle was given by Rudolf Bultmann: "Jesus offers rewards to those who follow him without hope of reward."—J. A. Davidson.

Illustrations

WORTH TO GOD.   A. J. Cronin knew a nurse who gave unstintingly of her time and talent to serve the people of her district. Cronin, a medical doctor at the time, said of the nurse: "I marveled at her patience, her fortitude, and her cheerfulness. She was never too tired to rise for an urgent call. Her salary was most inadequate, and late one night, after a particularly strenuous day, I ventured to protest to her: 'Nurse, why don't you make them pay you more? God knows you are worth it?' " Her answer was beautiful and memorable. "If God knows I'm worth it, that's all that matters to me."

TO CHERISH AND STRUGGLE. The church is the only thing that is going to make the terrible world we are coming to endurable. The only thing that makes the church endurable is that it is somehow the body of Christ and that on this we are fed. It seems to be a fact that you have to suffer as much from the church as for it, but if you believe in the divinity of Christ, you have to cherish the world at the same time that you struggle to endure it.—Flannery O'Connor.

Sermon Suggestions

A NEW CHURCH FOR A NEW DAY. Text: John 15:16. (1) Honest recognition of man's contemporary existence. (2) Acceptance of the task to be a unifying force which builds community. (3) Proclamation of a basic faith in the God of Jesus. (4) Willingness to act on institutional imperatives.—Hoover Rupert.

WHAT IS THE CHURCH? Source: Acts 2–7. (1) It is people who share. (See Acts 4:32.) (2) It is people who care. (See Acts 3:6.) (3) It is people who dare. (4) It is people who declare. (See Acts 5:42.)—Brian L. Harbour.

Worship Aids

CALL TO WORSHIP. "O love the Lord, all ye his saints: for the Lord preserveth the faithful. Be of good courage, and he shall strengthen your heart, all ye that hope in the Lord." Ps. 31:23–24.

INVOCATION. Almighty God, who of thy great mercy hast gathered us into thy visible church: grant that we may not swerve from the purity of thy worship but may so honor thee both in spirit and in outward form that thy name may be glorified in us and that our fellowship may be with all thy saints in earth and in heaven.

OFFERTORY SENTENCE. "Whatsoever ye would that men should do to you, do ye even so to them: for this is the law and the prophets." Matt. 7:12.

OFFERTORY PRAYER. O Lord Jesus Christ, who hast taught us that to whomsoever much is given, of him shall much be required: grant that we, whose lot is cast in this Christian heritage, may strive more earnestly by our prayers and tithes, by sympathy and study to hasten the coming of thy kingdom among all peoples of the earth, that as we have entered into the labors of others, so others may enter into ours, to thy honor and glory.

PRAYER. Almighty and everlasting God, who through Christ established the church and who through thy Holy Spirit dost judge, prod, and forgive thy church, today we praise thy name for all those who answered thy call to reform and renew the faith. We thank thee for the prophets who sought to rescue the faith from the kind of hypocrisy that confesses thy name from the lips only and not from the heart and who paid the price of isolation, loneliness, and even exile. We lift up our hearts in gratefulness for Jesus, who rescued the faith from hard legalism and empty ritual, who in himself embodied the message he preached, and who paid the price by being sent to the cross. Our hearts are filled with thanks for the work and thought of Martin Luther, John Calvin, John Huss, Huldreich Zwingli, John Wesley, and all others who were reformers of the faith for their day and who each paid the price to a hostile society.

Make us grateful for those of prophetic voice and thought, for those who reformulate the faith for our time. We confess, O Lord, that it is often easier to pay honor to those men who lived on the growing edge of faith in times past than in times present. Forgive us when we resist those in our own time and in our own associations who for our own good and for the good of the church challenge our dearly held ideas of thought and patterns of action. Make us open to a growing faith and a maturing set of convictions.

Make us, if it be thy will, partners in our own time to the reform of the faith for this time and for this community. Make us willing to pay the price.—Ralph W. Mueckenheim.

EVENING SERVICE

Topic: What We Believe About the Church (Reformation Sunday)

TEXT: Eph. 1:22–23.

I. We believe the church is more than a human institution. She is divine. She originates in God, not man. She has been provided for mankind by God through the life, death, resurrection, and continuing presence of Jesus Christ. She exists among mankind as the body of Christ, trusted to be obedient to the mind of Christ, and commissioned to serve the mission of Christ.

II. We believe the church is a fellowship that joins earth to heaven and time to eternity. She rises above all divisions of nation, class, or race, transcending all human boundaries and barriers.

III. We believe the church belongs to no one nation, class, or culture. She belongs by nature of origin and purpose to Jesus Christ and to him alone. She cannot serve two masters. She can obey but one, Jesus Christ.

IV. We believe, insofar as the church obeys Jesus Christ, she is the strongest friend and bravest support of every human value and worthy institution.

V. We believe there is wisdom available beyond the wit of men, and men need to know and obey this wisdom lest they destroy themselves.

VI. We believe life is a unity. All of it—business and pleasure, government and politics, family life and international relations, education and culture—must be obedient to the laws of the creator. Though men have freedom to disobey, such disobedience brings them to ruin.

VII. We believe God in wisdom and love has shown and does now show men his will and way. He has spoken in the scriptures and supremely in Jesus Christ. He speaks still to those humble enough to be teachable, earnest enough to sense his presence, and brave enough to practice obedience. To this end the church was established.

VIII. The church must be the voice of God. Anything less and she is guilty of betrayal like that of Judas.—Everett W. Palmer.

SUNDAY: NOVEMBER SEVENTH

MORNING SERVICE

Topic: The Shepherd Who Leads, Restores, and Comforts

SCRIPTURE: Ps. 23.

I. God restores souls. He has concern for the spiritual and psychological aspect of our existence—our souls. The Hebrew word used here for restore can have two possible meanings.

(a) It can mean that God recalls or reclaims the sheep that are lost. God is concerned for those who wander from the fold.

(b) A second possible meaning is that God strengthens or refreshes our souls. Is the psalmist deliberately ambiguous? Both of these interpretations are true, and perhaps he intends both.

II. The shepherd leads his sheep to serenity and quiet. God can take a life torn with inner conflict and speak a word of peace. The struggle subsides, and the warfare ceases. Jesus said, "Peace I leave with you; my peace I give to you; not as the world gives do I give to you" (John 14:27). The peace that God gives does not desert us even in the most trying circumstances. We can take refuge under the wings of the Almighty. We can find our peace in him.

III. The psalmist adds a thought that is even better. God is our savior and comforter, but he is also our friend. This is the theme of vv. 5–6.

(a) In these verses the psalmist uses the idea of a great banquet, which was in many cases the symbol of a covenant, a bond of friendship and loyalty, between two people. For Christians the ultimate symbol of God's covenant is the Lord's Supper. There, as Jesus held up the cup, he said "This is my blood of the covenant" (Matt. 26:28, RSV).

(b) God treats us as friends and honored guests at a great banquet. He anoints our heads with oil, an ancient custom indicating honor and respect. God welcomes us with the open arms of friendship, and his friendship does not falter in difficult times —"in the presence of my enemies."

IV. V. 2 says that the Lord guides his sheep to still waters. He knows the way ahead, and his sheep trust him. "Trust in the Lord with all your heart and do not rely on your own insight. In all your ways acknowledge him, and he will make straight your paths." (Prov. 3:5–6, RSV.)

V. God's guidance gives us a feeling of assurance even in the darkest of times. Here again we have deliberate ambiguity. The word translated "valley of death" could have two meanings. In most Old Testament passages darkness is the dominant idea; the darkest darkness is used in reference to death in Job 38:17 and Jer. 2:6. We can safely take it in both of these connections. God is with us in the dark and fearful times, even in the face of death.

VI. "Thy rod and thy staff they comfort me." The rod was a weapon used to ward off attack, and the staff was used to keep the flock in line. One is a symbol of security; the other a symbol of guidance.

VII. "My cup overflows." The psalmist tells what his life with God has been like. God gave more than the necessary; his blessings abound.

(a) God's blessings are above and beyond what we need or merit. His blessings come freely; they surround us. The Christian can look back on his life and see that God has been good. Life is not always easy, but a bright thread of blessing runs through it all.

(b) In v. 6 the word translated follow could be translated pursue or chase. An intriguing picture—God's mercy and goodness chasing after us. In the good times and in the bad, God's goodness pursues us.

VIII. We see in the psalm a clearer picture of the God we serve. He is a faithful dedicated shepherd. He is a host who has invited his friend to a banquet in his honor. He restores us, he comforts us, he befriends us, he leads us, he removes all fear, and he gives us more than we need or could ever deserve. We find this beautiful image in the New Testament as well. In John 10:1–18, a passage of similar depth and meaning, Jesus is pictured as the good shepherd who will lay down his very life for his sheep.—Craig L. Adams.

Illustrations

FRIEND OF SINNERS.   Every morning St. Peter found in heaven a horde of undesirable aliens whom he was certain he had never admitted at the regular hours. Some had never been baptized, some were ignorant of the Bible, and many were soiled and damaged souls who clearly had no right in the celestial precincts. He decided to discover just how this leakage occurred and one night prowled about the ramparts of heaven. At last he discovered a dark corner where a few stones had been removed from the wall since his last inspection an hour before, and a crowd was steadily creeping in. He rushed at them with indignation but was amazed to find the Savior there, helping some of the cripples over the wall. "I'm sorry, Peter," the Lord said. "I know it's against the rules. The poor souls aren't all they should be. Some were never baptized, some of them were not quite orthodox in their opinions about me, and all of them were miserable sinners. But they are my special friends, and I want them here."—Frank Harris.

BUNDLES IN HEAVEN.   In heaven there are vast halls full of shelves piled with bundles. A newcomer asked what those bundles were. The reply: "They are answered prayers that never have been called for."

Sermon Suggestions

OPEN YOUR EYES.   Text: II Kings 6:17. (1) We are blind to our blessings. (2) We are blind to the hurt of others and their needs. (3) We are blind to our spiritual resources.—Alton H. McEachern.

CERTAINTY. Text: Rom. 8:38–39. (1) Death cannot separate us from the love of God. (2) Loneliness cannot separate us from the love of God. (3) Guilt cannot separate us from the love of God. (4) The bitterness, the hatred, and the contempt of man cannot separate us from the love of God.—George T. Peters.

Worship Aids

CALL TO WORSHIP. "I will instruct thee and teach thee in the way which thou shalt go [saith the Lord]. I will guide thee with mine eye. Be glad in the Lord, and rejoice, ye righteous: and shout for joy, all ye that are upright in heart." Ps. 32:8, 11.

INVOCATION. Our heavenly Father, who by thy love hast made us, through thy love hast kept us, and in thy love wouldst make us perfect: we humbly confess that we have not loved thee with all our heart and soul and mind and strength and that we have not loved one another as Christ hath loved us. Thy life is within our souls, but our selfishness has hindered thee. We have not lived by faith. We have resisted thy spirit. We have neglected thy inspirations. Forgive what we have been, help us to amend what we are, and in thy spirit direct what we shall be, that thou mayest come into the full glory of thy creation in us and in all men.

OFFERTORY SENTENCE. "We then that are strong ought to bear the infirmities of the weak, and not to please ourselves." Rom. 15:1.

OFFERTORY PRAYER. Dear Father, may we ever give thee a definite, consistent, and heartfelt service.

PRAYER. O God, who didst send thy Son to bring peace on earth, give us the peace that comes from knowing that thou art our loving Father and that Christ is our savior from sin. Help us to strive for peace and not lose heart, even when the world seems determined to destroy itself in war. As we remember those who died for us in battle to preserve our peace and liberty, make us willing unselfishly to sacrifice that we may retain our liberties in righteousness. When evening comes may we be able to say honestly, "We did all we could for the cause of peace this day." Transform the hearts of men everywhere through the gracious working of thy Holy Spirit that they may place peace above selfish interests and work untiringly to solve all conflict. Let thy kingdom grow and prosper that men everywhere may love thee and that the nations of the world may live together like brothers. Be with those who would be at peace. Be with our loved ones wherever they may be. Stay close to them that they may ever be close to thee, and be with each of us always in Jesus Christ.—Armin C. Oldsen.

EVENING SERVICE

Topic: The Church as a Monument or a Ministry

TEXT: Acts 7:48.

The programs of most churches can be divided into two categories.

I. One of those categories is maintaining monuments. The major thrust of those congregations is to erect a building and to maintain it.

(a) Almost every issue of one church newsletter carries one or two articles about a bazaar, rummage sale, or some other kind of money-making project or special appeal in order to get enough money to pay the monthly building note or the utility bill. This congregation obviously is concerned with maintaining their beautiful building. Everything they do is building-oriented.

(b) Are such congregations simply maintaining monuments? In this day and time it is easy for a congregation to get bogged down in the monument trap. It is easy for congregations to think that the most important task they have is to maintain the church building.

(c) One might question if a congregation that is primarily interested in maintaining the church building really understands its mission as the body of Christ in the world today. One might question if these congregations have ever developed a mission statement. Over the years maintaining the monument may have become their purpose, and all of their goals are centered around this purpose.

II. There are some churches that reflect a genuine desire to be an effective, active, positive, ministering-to-others congregation. These churches seldom mention the building, and any money-raising project generally goes for some charitable purpose.

(a) Somehow these congregations have evaluated their particular purpose and de-cided they want to do more than maintain a church building. They have developed a mission statement that includes words like sacrifice, others, service, giving, loving, helping, and caring.

(b) It is doubtful that Jesus ever intended for his followers to become caretakers of monuments. He did intend for his followers to be ministers and servants. May God lead us to struggle through the process of evaluating our task and determining our mission in the community and in the world. May God lead us not into maintaining monuments but into ministry. —Tommy Thompson.

SUNDAY: NOVEMBER FOURTEENTH

MORNING SERVICE

Topic: You Can Take It with You (Stewardship Day)

TEXT: Matt. 6:20.

I. Jesus in the sermon on the mount contrasted two forms of treasure—material and spiritual, earthly and heavenly.

(a) The text is his conclusion as he calls us to lay up for ourselves treasures in heaven. Moth, rust, and thieves cannot take them from us. We have a choice between two masters—Mammon, the god of things whose religious adherents are materialists, and God, who calls us to give our dominant devotion to securing the wealth of spiritual values. We cannot do both. (See Luke 16:13.)

(b) Jesus calls us to base life not on the worldly treasures of money, power, and fame. Rather we are to base life on ultimately heavenly qualities—love, generosity, gratitude, kindness, and trust. This provides fulfillment for life here and in the hereafter as well. These values you can take with you.

II. Money is an integral part of human life. (a) Jesus did not condemn money and material goods as such. He was a carpenter who was in business and received compensation for his products that in turn supported the economic needs of his family. He was friend to rich and poor alike.

What Jesus did condemn was the person for whom money and property were life's ultimate value and their pursuit life's dominant purpose and goal.

(b) In Luke's version of this passage he tells the parable of the rich fool. He had too much grain to get in his barns and too much wealth to use. So he planned bigger barns to store the wealth, only to discover that death was to rob him of the enjoyment of that accumulation. He earned his wealth honestly. He gave a lifetime of effort to that accumulation. But he was self-centered in the effort. He ignored God, he was unconcerned about others, and spiritual values were irrelevant. He died a pauper, having burned himself out, and lost his soul in the process. He found that you can't take it with you.

III. It is easy to lose the things money cannot buy. (a) Jesus was saying that life's greatest treasures lie in the realm of the things money cannot buy. They lie in an unpurchasable realm. Dr. Fosdick said: "You cannot buy in any market a clear conscience or genuine affection or inward spiritual power or deathless hope. They move in the unpurchasable realm." He added that everything that money can buy depends for its ultimate worth, for the purpose it serves, and for its final effect on human life, upon the things that money cannot buy.

(b) If we confine ourselves simply to the search for happiness through money, we will be sorely tempted to forget the things that money cannot buy. We will have means, but will we find meaning? We will have economic forms of security, but will we settle for them alone and try to eke out life without spiritual significance and moral purpose? Happiness consists not in the things that money can buy but in the things that money cannot buy. Jesus said this is the kind of treasure worth saving, for neither moth nor rust nor thieves can take it from us as they can our material things.

IV. Christ calls us to accumulate the wealth of the spirit. (a) The rich fool in Jesus' parable was so busy accumulating grain and building barns in which to store it that he had little time to accumulate the wealth of spiritual things. Is that a picture of your life and mine? We spend a good bit of our time securing the means for livelihood. And Jesus said that is needed in this life. But has it become such an obsession with us that we have little time for anything else?

(b) We are called to store up in our minds and hearts the truth that makes persons free, the faith that gives life meaning, and the hope that gives life a future. These are not tangible things. These are the invisible things that make up the wealth of the spirit. Jesus said you can take with you the wealth of the spirit which comes from your deeds of kindness and the character you are fashioning here.—Hoover Rupert.

Illustrations

THE WIDOW'S MITE.   Gordon Cosby told about his early years of ministry in a small church in a railroad town just outside of Lynchburg, Virginia. One day a church deacon spoke with him, saying: "We have in this congregation a widow with six children. I have looked at the records and discovered that she is putting into the treasury of the church each month $4—a tithe of her income. The deacons want you to let her know that she needs to feel no obligation whatsoever, and free her from the responsibility." Cosby, reflecting upon this incident, explained: "I told her of the concern of the deacons. I told her as graciously and supportively as I knew how that she was relieved of the responsibility of giving. As I talked with her the tears came into her eyes. 'I want to tell you,' she said, 'that you are taking away the last thing that gives my life dignity and meaning.' "—John H. Townsend.

STRANGE CALCULATION.   God's arithmetic is strange. He uses a calculation based not on amounts but on attitudes and not on quantity but on quality. He considers not only the sum that we give but also the share that we give. For him the gift which counts is the gift which costs. True giving has to be measured according to what is left, not only according to what is given. It is not so much the size of the gift but the sacrifice involved in the gift.—Harold Freeman.

Sermon Suggestions

WHY WE TITHE.   Text: Lev. 27:30. (1) Because we love God for who he is. (2) Because of what he has done for us. (3) Because it is God's plan of finance for his kingdom. (4) Because tithing brings us real joy. (5) Because our church needs it. (6) Because missions need it. (7) Because we love to have the blessings of God poured out upon us. (8) Because it is the greatest investment we can make. (9) Because of the safety of our treasure. (10) Because we do not want to be robbers. (See Mal. 3:8–9.)—John E. Barrow.

COMMITMENT.   Text: Matt. 9:29. (1) The content of commitment. (2) The intensity of commitment. (3) The behavior of commitment. (4) The style of commitment.—Ross Nicholson.

Worship Aids

CALL TO WORSHIP.   "Bless the Lord, O my soul: and all that is with me, bless his holy name." Ps. 103:1.

INVOCATION.   Merciful God, forgive the halting nature of our discipleship. We confess that so little of thy love has reached others through us and that we have borne so lightly wrongs and sufferings that were not our own. We confess that we have cherished the things that divide us from others and that we have made it hard for them to live with us. And we confess that we have been thoughtless in our judgments, hasty in condemnation, and grudging in our forgiveness. Forgive us, we beseech thee.

OFFERTORY SENTENCE. "Go, and sell that thou hast, and give to the poor, and thou shalt have treasure in heaven: and come and follow me." Matt. 19:21.

OFFERTORY PRAYER. We pray thee, O God, to give us sight to see the Christ, the insight to chose him, the steadfastness to follow him, and the stewardship of loyalty represented in these gifts offered in his name.

PRAYER. O thou eternal God, creator of men and nations, make us into men and nations that fear, honor, love, and serve thee in all ways. When we consider all the ways in which we have dishonored thee and each other, we wonder at thy patience. We wonder that we have been able to tolerate each other. Yet thou hast given us and all thy children the capacities to grow, to develop, to forgive, and to forget. We have as many positive qualities as negative, but we fail to nourish the positive.

We acknowledge that we run our lives on flimsy excuses, bad religion, poor relationships, and low purposes. We live from game to game, from meal to meal, from love affair to love affair, from one night of television to the next, and the interims are filled with routines from which we do not know how to escape and we are afraid to exercise any imagination. Even our pride is so abused that we belittle thy efforts to lift us up to make us real men, and we refuse to believe that any outside influence is what we need.

Put us in touch with reality. Teach us individuality and responsibility, independence and mutual affection, and when to be aggressive and when patient. Teach us

to man our own vessels and not criticize school or church or government for failing to do what we should have done in the first place. Teach us that no institution, not even a congregation, is larger than the vision of its people but that it can be as large as the love and mercy and providence of the Almighty.—David V. Pettenger.

EVENING SERVICE

Topic: Gratitude and Pride
TEXT: II Thess. 1:3–4.
I. When Paul's first letter to the church in Thessalonica failed to have the desired effect, he wrote Second Thessalonians from Corinth shortly afterward.

(a) He used good psychology by bragging about them before dealing with remaining problems about the second coming of Christ. You can always find something good to point out about people before dealing with their faults. In v. 3 Paul gives thanks for his readers, and in v. 4 he expresses his pride in their Christian fortitude while undergoing difficulties.

(b) "Bound" expresses a sense of obligation "to keep on giving thanks" (present infinitive) to God concerning the Thessalonian Christians. "Meet" renders a word involving scales or balances. A. T. Robertson says that bound points to the divine side and meet points to the human side of the obligation.

(c) He is obligated to God to express this thanks. He is obligated to his readers to do so. Thus the two balance out.

II. Paul's gratitude rests on two bases. (a) Their faith keeps on growing exceedingly. It super-grows or increases in spite of outward trouble. It pictures faith as a tree growing or flourishing beyond measure.

(b) Their love toward each other abounds despite outside enemies. Note "every one of you," literally, "last one"— none is left out. So often trouble from the outside produces friction on the inside. Not so here. This is in response to Paul's words in I Thess. 3:12. The word in v. 4 for persecutions is used only of religious persecution. Tribulations means to be in a tight place with seemingly no way out, like grapes in a winepress.

III. Paul says that he boasts about this church to other churches. He did this to challenge others to do likewise. (See II Cor. 8:1–7.)

(a) Patience means abiding under. It was used of athletes and soldiers who could take all their opponents threw at them yet had reserve strength with which to countercharge to victory.

(b) It is no wonder that Paul was both thankful and proud of this church. It would be true of any similar group today. —Herschel H. Hobbs.

SUNDAY: NOVEMBER TWENTY-FIRST

MORNING SERVICE

Topic: Murmurings (Thanksgiving Sunday)

Text: Matt. 21:31–33.

I. The Pilgrims were devout men and women of God who gave thanks to their loving, caring Father in the midst of all conditions of life.

(a) They arrived at Cape Cod "with no friends to welcome them, nor inns to entertain nor refresh their weather-beaten bodies." In the winter they experienced weather that was so sharp and violent that one-half of their number died. Food was so scarce that they were reduced to living daily on five grains of corn for each person. But spring came. And then summer. And soon the fall harvest appeared—a good harvest. And Governor William Bradford set aside a special day of thanksgiving to God.

(b) The giving of thanks to God was always a natural response on the part of the Pilgrims, and it was never to be associated with the absence of hardship—as so many of us think today. The Pilgrims understood thanksgiving in its fullest biblical sense. The Lord was with them. He did watch over them. He would sustain them. He would give them the courage and strength to persevere. So, instead of complaining, they found cause to be grateful and joyful. "The Lord was with them in all their ways," they wrote, "for which let his holy name have the praise forever, to all posterity."

II. In our time there are danger signals that the concept of gratitude is eroding.

(a) The kjv has a very special word for this condition of life. It is called murmuring. Let us hope we never lose this word from our vocabulary because when you pronounce the word "murmur" or "murmuring" over and over again, you can sense the power and action of what is happening—the half-suppressed grumblings, the contemptuous complaints offered in a corner, and the lecherous side comments. We don't think that we have been heard. We don't think that others are behaving the way that we think they should behave.

(b) The Bible is full of murmurers or, as we call them, complainers. "And they murmured against the good man of the house." Who? Those laborers who received their exact wages for which they contracted. "And the scribes and the Pharisees murmured against the disciples because they dined with publicans and sinners." "And the Jews murmured against Jesus because he said, 'I am the bread of life.' "

III. In today's gospel we are cautioned by our Lord to live each day consciously in God's presence. We should not be anxious or overly concerned about the security of our existence. Seek God's will and his kingdom, and all manner of things will be given to us.

(a) It was not by accident that the church directed this passage to be read on Thanksgiving Day. The joy of giving thanks is directly related to a life that is free from anxiety and frustration. The key is to live each day consciously in the presence of God.

(b) While Jesus is certainly not against planning an honest retirement or saving for our children's education or providing health insurance for the future, what he is discouraging in today's text is taking flight into a world of fantasy and pipe dreams which can only cause frustration and cynicism, those ancient enemies of a thankful heart. What he is discouraging is an hysterical concentration on future events. He is discouraging that false kind of security that comes from closing our eyes and wishing that the present predicaments would go away.

IV. The inescapable fact is that all we have is now. The past belongs to history, and the future belongs to God. If we will rearrange our priorities and if we will seek God's will in all matters, then our Lord assures us that the Father who looks after the birds of the air and feeds and nourishes them will also take care of our needs.

(a) That condition of life demands a faithful response on our part. We must stop being overly obsessed with our needs. We must learn to take our eyes off ourselves and focus on God. It is a matter of discipline. It is a matter of living each day in God's presence and reminding ourselves of the obvious but often forgotten eternal truths: "This is the day the Lord hath made. We will rejoice and be glad in it." "God has given me this breath of life. Thanks be to God." "The earth is the Lord's and all that therein is."

(b) When we pay attention to the present, a peculiar thing happens. Suddenly each moment is no longer sandwiched between the past and the future. Suddenly we can stand still in it. In the light of one eternal moment we can begin to look at ourselves and at life in a joyful, new way. Life no longer is something to be endured but rather to be enjoyed. As we begin to enjoy and reverence each day, a grateful heart begins to find expression.

V. Here we come to the heart of thanksgiving. (a) Thanksgiving begins with the awareness of God. We feel his living presence with us, among us, and in us. He is at the very heart of life. Thanksgiving breaks forth from our lips when we begin to experience an interplay between God and ourselves. Thanksgiving finds expression when we provide those quiet moments for God to act upon us, and instead of rushing through life as directors of our own destiny, we allow God to be God.

(b) Thanksgiving takes form on our lips when we discover that among the tensions and bewilderment of our world and our society, amid the changing nature of Christ's bride, the church, and when our congregations and our homes sink into angry times of stress and strain, there still breaks forth the living loving presence of Emmanuel—God with us. —Frank S. Cerveny.

Illustrations

THANK YOU. A restless child in an airport was given some candy by a waiting passenger. The child's mother tried to get the child to say, "Thank you." The passenger remarked, "He doesn't have to say 'thanks.'" To which the mother replied, "But if he learns to, he will be a better person." One does not have to say thanks. There are no laws which compel us to thus express our gratitude. If we learn to be grateful and practice the expression of that gratitude, then life takes on that extra quality of living which distinguishes between mere existence and the abundant life.—E. Paul Hovey.

THANKSGIVING DAYS. Charles Dickens said that we are somewhat mixed-up here in America. He told an audience that instead of having one Thanksgiving Day each year we should have 364. "Use that one day just for complaining and griping," he said. "Use the other 364 days to thank God each day for the many blessings he has showered upon you."—William Folprecht.

Sermon Suggestions

GRATEFULLY YOURS. Text: Eph. 5:20 (RSV). (1) Gratefully yours, O Lord, because thy love has saved us. (2) Gratefully yours, O Lord, because we cannot drift beyond thy love and care. (3) Gratefully yours, O Lord, for all things, because we cannot imagine anything not from thy mind and heart nor can we believe that anything in life cannot be used by thee for a good purpose.—David A. MacLennan.

JESUS USED SCRIPTURE. Text: II Tim. 3:16. (1) Jesus used scripture to differentiate between doctrinal truth and error.

(See Mark 12:24.) (2) Jesus used scripture to reprove the devil during temptation. (See Matt. 4:1–11.) (3) Jesus used scripture as correction. (See Matt. 21:13; Isa. 56:7.) (4) Jesus used scripture for instruction in righteousness. (See Matt. 5:21, 27.) —George L. McGlothin.

Worship Aids

CALL TO WORSHIP. "O come, let us sing unto the Lord: let us make a joyful noise to the rock of our salvation. Let us come before his presence with thanksgiving, and make a joyful noise unto him with psalms." Ps. 95:1–2.

INVOCATION. O God our Father, giver of all good things, we are grateful for the Thanksgiving season of the year when we come with gratitude for bountiful harvests filling granary and bin. Give us such a spirit of thankfulness that every day and every season and all thy continuing gifts may be occasions for thanksgiving and all the year be blessed with an ever-continuing gratitude. As thy mercies are new every morning, so may our praise rise to thee each day and hour.

OFFERTORY SENTENCE. "Offer unto God thanksgiving; and pay thy vows unto the most High." Ps. 50:14.

OFFERTORY PRAYER. Not by words only, O God, would we offer our thanksgiving for so many loving expressions of thy concern for us but also in Christ's name we dedicate these gifts that through them we may participate in the work of thy ever-widening kingdom.

PRAYER. O God our Father and Creator, we thank thee that we are human beings. We thank thee that long before we came to light upon this planet we were in thy thought and thy intention. We thank thee that we are not mere children of chance, a strange accident in a universe that might have been better without us, and not creatures of a moment only, some trifling experiment or some mistake to be wiped out of this fair universe to restore its balance and its beauty. We are here be-cause thou didst call us from the dust. The manner of our coming we but dimly know, yet that we are here because thou didst summon us into being, we believe, and we thank thee.

For thy mighty power that created us, for thine infinite mind that conceived us, and for thy sovereign will that set us on this earth, we thank thee. That in this vast universe we have any place is wonderful, and that our place is so near to thee is past our comprehension. Yet by the hand and mind and will of the Almighty we are here, created freely by thee, in freedom and for freedom, and we are grateful. We humbly rejoice that thou desirest our hearts in freedom, that thou dost not compel our love, that thou who couldst blast us into nothingness dost continue us in being, and that thou givest us the means of life and dost crown our lives with lovingkindness, and yet for all this wilt not compel our souls but wilt rather take the free service even of a few than to force the obedience of any.

And so we thank thee that thou hast created us for fellowship with thyself. We seek companionship among thy other creatures, and we rejoice in this. Yet amid all the ties that bind us, we are not at peace until we find thee. We thank thee that in thy fellowship we are lifted above ourselves, above the world, and above all that time and change can do against us. We thank thee that thou hast not set eternity in our souls in vain and that we are not doomed to grope within walls that have no door or to sit in darkness with no window to the sky, but that thou hast set us in a mansion also of thy devising and fashioning, wherein we can both serve thee and find thee.—Kenneth J. Foreman.

EVENING SERVICE

Topic: How God Speaks to Us (Bible Sunday)

TEXT: Heb. 1:1–2.

Communication is God's problem too. How does God, who is spirit, communicate himself, his nature, and his will to mortal man? God speaks with many voices, according to the Bible.

I. God speaks through nature for those

who would see him there. "The heavens are telling the glory of God; and the firmament proclaims his handiwork" (Ps. 19:1, RSV).

II. God can speak within the human conscience. (a) His still small voice confronts us there. Moffatt translated Prov. 20:27: "Man's conscience is the lamp of the eternal."

(b) Man has a sense of right and wrong —a sense of ought. Kant said that two things filled him with awe—the starry heavens above and the moral law within.

III. History is an avenue of communication for the Almighty. (a) We can trace his activity there. It is still "his-story." And it has a goal. The divine purpose is being worked out in history with an outcome which is certain.

(b) Think about the ways in which we communicate human love. We write notes or letters. We give extravagant gifts. The ultimate communication of love is the gift of oneself in total commitment.

(c) In much the same way God communicates his love to us. He has given us the scriptures—God's love letters. He has given us his providential care and the gifts of the good earth. God's supreme communication of his love for man is the gift of his Son—the incarnation and the cross.

IV. Focus on the communication of God's nature, purpose, and love in the scriptures.

(a) The Bible is the word of God. It is our primary source of knowledge about our maker. The Bible's message becomes the word of God to us as we receive and appropriate it. The same Holy Spirit who inspired men of old to write the Bible inspires us today as we read it and practice its teachings.

(b) This dynamic truth of inspiration is symbolized in the seal of Southern Baptist Theological Seminary in Louisville. It depicts a descending dove above an open Bible with rays of inspiration surrounding both. The Bible is not simply a book of our finding God. Through its message, energized by the Holy Spirit, God finds us.— Alton H. McEachern.

SUNDAY: NOVEMBER TWENTY-EIGHTH

MORNING SERVICE

Topic: Ready or Not, I Am Coming (Advent)

SCRIPTURE: John 1:1–17.

When you played hide and seek, the cry, "Ready or not, I am coming," was a warning. It did not come as a surprise. You knew the count-down had already begun, and he would be coming.

I. It was the same with the coming of Christ into the world. They should have been ready, for God had been telling them and preparing them for it over a long period of time.

(a) The Jewish law, teaching the righteousness and holiness of God and the duty of man, was a schoolmaster preparing them for Christ's coming. There was a preparation in the Jewish worship and sacrifices. Every altar that smoked with its victim pointed to Calvary and prepared the hearts of men to hear the message of the gospel, "Behold the Lamb of God, which taketh away the sin of the world." Every chant of the Levite choir in the temple was an echo of the everlasting song of the redeemed. Even the persecutions and dispersions of the Jews prepared the way for the preaching of the gospel, for the synagogues which were planted all over the Roman world were the first pulpits for the apostles.

(b) God wanted Israel to be prepared for the coming of the savior. That is why he moved the prophet Isaiah to say to the people 700 years before the actual birth of Christ, "Prepare ye the way of the Lord." That is why he sent John the Baptist into the wilderness of Judea to preach repentance so that the hearts of the people might be ready for Christ's coming. One cannot read the Old Testament without observing numerous intimations that a messiah was coming. Peter said to the Roman centurian, Cornelius, "To him bear all the prophets witness." If the people were not ready, it was not God's fault.

II. "When the fullness of time was come," said St. Paul, "God sent forth his Son, to redeem them that were under the law, that we might receive the adoption of sons." As far as world history was concerned, the fullness of time had come. Materially and culturally, the world was ready.

III. Some were not ready. (a) Herod was a nominal Jew who subscribed to the Jewish faith, but he was not ready for the messiah. He was interested only in himself. How could one who ruled ruthlessly with an exalted opinion of himself have any place for Jesus? A ruler like that could never be ready for a heavenly king, one who might threaten his autonomy, deflate his ego, and challenge his methods.

(b) The innkeeper was not ready. He had made a lot of preparations, but his preparations were all for business. This time of census taking was to be the big business boom of the year, and he had all he could do to take care of that. When Mary and Joseph came rapping at his door, he had no room for them.

(c) "He came unto his own, and his own received him not." Why? For some it was their business, for others it was personal greed and lust for power, and for some it is their sense of sin that keeps them from welcoming him. Many, like Augustine, want to accept Christ and become a Christian—"but not now." And often it is perfectly innocent pursuits that keep us from finding Christ.

IV. There will always be people who miss God's greatest gifts, but there have always been people whose hearts are ready.

(a) Mary and Joseph and Elizabeth were ready. The shepherds and the Persian astrologers were ready. So was the aged Simeon for whom the one prayer was that he might live to see the promised one before he died.

(b) How will it be in your home this Christmas? Will it be a time of bedlam, or will it be a day of joy in observance of the birthday of Christ? Will our hearts and

homes be open to him? Ready or not, he is coming.—Cleo Y. Boyd.

Illustrations

MORE LIGHT.   A few days before Christmas a small girl, shivering on the streets of a large city, slipped inside a church to warm herself. Hearing the minister say, "Jesus is the light of the world," she approached him after the service and asked if what he said was true. "Why, yes," the minister said. "Then," said she, "I wish he would come down to our alley 'cause it's awfully dark down there."—Jim N. Griffith.

FORGOTTEN.   A story in the broadcast news told of a man who notified the police that his car had been stolen from a parking lot. Worse still, he had left his wife sitting in it. After a frantic search the man suddenly and sheepishly remembered that he hadn't parked in that lot after all but in another one down the street. The police graciously declined to scold their client for wasting their time. They figured the wife would take care of all the necessary excoriations.

A lot of people have forgotten where they parked the Christmas spirit and are searching in all the wrong places for it. Some are looking all up and down Nostalgia Lane for it, yearning to be children again so someone can dump all the goodies in their laps. It is more blessed to give than to receive, but let's face it—receiving is much more fun and a lot less work.—Ralph A. Cannon.

Sermon Suggestions

ON COMING IN SECOND.   Text: John 3: 30. (1) There are times when it is more important to lose than to win. (2) We must settle for what life hands us. (3) A race worth winning is a race worth losing.—Clarence J. Forsberg.

RESPONDING TO CHRIST.   Text: Phil. 3: 12–14. (1) A steady purpose: "One thing I do." (2) Forgetting the past: "Forgetting what lies behind." (3) Reaching forward:

"I strain toward what lies ahead." (4) Unceasing effort: "I press on toward the goal."—Ernest Trice Thompson.

Worship Aids

CALL TO WORSHIP. "O Zion, that bringeth good tidings, get thee up into the high mountain; O Jerusalem, that bringeth good tidings, lift up thy voice with strength; lift it up, be not afraid; say unto the cities of Judah, Behold your God!" Isa. 40:9.

INVOCATION. Dear Christ, who art the light of the world, shine, we pray thee, so that all who walk in darkness and dwell in the land of the shadow of death may have the light of life. May thy word at this season be for us a lamp unto our feet and a lamp unto our path.

OFFERTORY SENTENCE. "He that hath a bountiful eye shall be blessed; for he giveth of his bread to the poor." Prov. 22:9.

OFFERTORY PRAYER. Accept, O Lord, these offerings thy people make unto thee and grant that the cause to which they are devoted may prosper under thy guidance, to the glory of thy name.

PRAYER. Almighty God, we give thee thanks for the mighty yearning of the human heart for the coming of a savior and the constant promise of thy word that he was to come. In our own souls we repeat the humble sighs and panting aspirations of ancient men and ages and own that our souls are in darkness and infirmity without faith in him who comes to bring God to man and man to God. We bless thee for the tribute that we can pay to him from our very sense of need and dependence and that our own hearts can so answer, from their wilderness, the cry, "Prepare ye the way of the Lord." In us the rough places are to be made smooth, the crooked straight, the mountains of pride brought low, and the valleys of despondency lifted up. O God, prepare thou the way in us now, and may we welcome anew thy holy child. Hosanna! blessed be he who cometh in the name of the Lord.—Samuel Osgood.

EVENING SERVICE

Topic: John Prepares for Christ's Coming

SCRIPTURE: John 1:6–8, 19–34.

I. The fourth gospel contains limited information about the ministry of John the Baptist. From the other gospels and non-Biblical sources, we know that John the Baptist had a successful ministry near the Jordan. He attracted large crowds who came great distances to hear him proclaim the day of judgment. The Baptist was so successful that news of his ministry reached Jerusalem where the religious status quo became suspicious of this upstart from the desert. The Jerusalem Jews sent a delegation to interrogate the Baptist. The gospel of John records this investigation.

(a) They wanted to know John's identity. Because John was engaged in eschatological preaching and performed baptism, an eschatological action, the delegation asked if he was one of the eschatological figures that the Jews were expecting. The Baptist said he was not the messiah. He said he was not Elijah, who had been taken up into heaven and was thought to be returning. The Baptist was not the prophet who would re-establish the law of God in Israel.

(b) John's negative responses led the committee from Jerusalem to ask, "Well, then who are you?" John answered by quoting a verse from Isaiah. He saw his ministry as preparing the way for God to come to his people. For him it was not a question of who he was but who was coming after him.

(c) When John the Baptist refused to claim the authority of any of the expected messianic figures, the delegation wanted to know by what authority he did baptize. Again John the Baptist shifted the focus of the question from his own person and from his activities to the coming Christ. John explained his baptism in terms of preparation for another.

II. John the Baptist came to bear witness to the true light who came to enlighten every man. As the herald of the word, John attracted a large following. Many became devoted to John, and after his death these devotees formed a sect to venerate John the Baptist. The fourth gospel indicates that John consistently pointed away from himself to the one who was coming after him and yet who was before him.

(a) Often the contemporary church loses its integrity at this point. There are some super preachers who allow themselves to be lifted up by their followers while the preachers are supposed to be lifting up Jesus Christ. Also in subtle ways we allow our churches and their programs to become the focus of our witness, push-ing aside the one who has come and is coming again. Evangelism becomes manipulative, and the work of the church becomes just another activity.

(b) The model that characterized the ministry of John the Baptist is important to faithful evangelism. The Baptist did not ingratiate himself and his ministry but pointed away from himself and always to the coming Christ. The church's task of evangelism is to prepare the way for God's grace to work in the world. As we allow God's love to be present in our lives and through us to touch others, then we are evangelists. As a herald of Christ, John has pointed the way.—David and Nancy Arant.

SUNDAY: DECEMBER FIFTH

MORNING SERVICE

Topic: In the Fullness of Time (Advent)
TEXT: Gal. 4:4.

I. There is in God's coming a sublime mystery. "In the fullness of time God sent forth his Son." The statement generates a mood of awe and wonder; the New Testament lives and moves and has its being in an atmosphere of wonder and mystery.

(a) The revelation of God in Christ is the central mystery of the Christian faith. It is a fresh reminder that mystery and wonder are basic ingredients of life, if we but have the eyes to see it. It is a dimension of life of which we need to be reminded often in this day of sophisticated intellectualism and cold, calculating reason.

(b) We need not make any apology for the mystery surrounding the life born on Christmas night. It is the remarkable blending of the divine and human: "The hopes and fears of all the years" were met at Bethlehem that night. For whenever divine and human forces coalesce, like the stars that blended to form the star of Bethlehem, there is born a brightness and a hope, no matter how dark the night. And this is the essence of mystery.

II. "In the fullness of time, God sent forth his Son." There is a sublime mystery of life communicated in that statement.

(a) It reflects the fact of God's divine action in human history. One of our newer translations says, "When the time was right God entered the world in the person of Jesus." Only a casual study of history will demonstrate that the entire historic setting of the first century seemed to be in unique readiness for what was to transpire. Even such mundane things as the unity of the Roman Empire—the routes of commerce, shipping lanes, Roman highways, and the Greek language commonly spoken in all provinces of the empire—all conspired to make the transmission of the gospel possible.

(b) This is what Paul meant when he spoke of the fullness of time. God is the God of history. He moves and works, and he judges and redeems the affairs of humanity. From Genesis to Revelation the Bible views history as history-under-God.

(c) We speak of humanity's search for God. So does the Bible but only because it first speaks of God's search for mankind. Jesus is what we mean by God, and Jesus is what God means by being human.

(d) The mystery of God is always breaking in on our human pilgrimage. You and I, indeed all life, are gripped in mystery in birth and death and in disaster and sudden tenderness, and we respond to that mystery in worship and in our daily lives. Such is the very nature of faith.

(e) Mankind in the Bible is always on tiptoe, straining his eyes for the first light of dawn. It is that light that dawned at the stable in Bethlehem. We are so accustomed to it that we miss its startling newness. There is movement in the biblical understanding of history, but let us never confuse it with our fuzzy ideas of progress. In the Bible history is life-drama with plot and pilgrimage and denouement. History is the divine encounter, and in Christ mankind has been encountered by his God.

III. "In the fullness of time, God sent forth his Son, born of woman, born under the law." In Christ is sublime mystery; in his coming you see decisively God's action in history. In him you find fulfillment of life.

(a) The advent of Christ is not just a day long ago and far away to be remembered; it is a contemporary experience.

(b) The Christ-event is an on-going process. God has never left humanity without it. Men and women who walk in darkness do so by preference, not because the light is unavailable to them.

(c) The light of God's knowledge and love did not begin with the advent of Christ. The purpose of his coming was to let men and women know what was already available to them. The divine love that forms the warp and woof of the universe found its fulfillment in him. It was God becoming what we are so that we might become what he is, thus fulfilling our divine humanity.—Robert L. S. Brown.

Illustrations

FULLNESS OF TIME. Religiously, it was the fullness of time because Judaism had firmly established the understanding of monotheism. Culturally, Alexander the Great had spread the Greek language over most of the civilized world three centuries earlier. It was then established as the international language by which the gospel could be communicated. Governmentally, the Romans furnished a system of law which made it possible for the gospel to grow in relative stability. Logistically, the system of Roman roads made travel by missionaries very possible. Indeed it was the fullness of time for a savior.—Ernest White.

CHRIST'S COMING. During Advent we think of the coming of Christ both in terms of what began 1982 years ago and of the fullness of his coming still to be experienced. In this combination of backward look and forward look there is a creative tension between what has already been realized and what we anticipate. The tension is illustrated in a striking way whenever we repeat the Lord's Prayer. We say, "Thine is the kingdom," yet we pray, "Thy kingdom come." God's reign is inaugurated, yet the consummation of it still lies beyond our ken. There is no real conflict between those two aspects of reality. Christians believe in the coming victory of Christ just because they have experienced his present power. An early Christian writer resolved the paradox by saying: "We do not yet see everything in subjection to him, but we see Jesus" (Heb. 2:8–9).—Samuel McCrea Cavert.

Sermon Suggestions

JESUS, THE SON OF GOD. Text: John 20: 30–31. How can we know for certain that Jesus is really the Son of God? (1) The testimony of his supernatural conception. (See Matt. 1:24–25.) (2) The testimony of his sinless life. (See II Cor. 5:21; Heb. 4: 15; I Pet. 2:22.) (3) The testimony of his spectacular resurrection. (See I Cor. 15: 14–17.) (4) The testimony of his stupendous impact on history.—Brian L. Harbour.

UNFINISHED BUSINESS. Text: Phil. 3: 13–14. (1) Out of the incompleteness of life come most of life's tensions. (2) Out of the incompleteness of life come most of life's opportunities. (3) Out of the incompleteness of life come most of life's charm, romance, and happiness.—J. Wallace Hamilton.

Worship Aids

CALL TO WORSHIP.   "Arise, shine; for thy light is come, and the glory of the Lord is risen upon thee. Lift up thine eyes round about and see." Isa. 60:1, 4.

INVOCATION.   Our Father, help us during this special season to remember the many ways thou hast pointed out to us the coming of our Lord Jesus Christ. May we be ever mindful that thou wilt not let us sit in darkness, but if we are receptive we will see the light of thy many signs in the prophets, in the lives of our neighbors, and in the eyes of our family.

OFFERTORY SENTENCE.   "Remember the words of the Lord Jesus, how he said, It is more blessed to give than to receive." Acts 20:35.

OFFERTORY PRAYER.   O God, who didst give to us the gift of thy Son, stir us with such love toward thee that we may gladly share whatever thou hast entrusted to us for the relief of the world's sorrow and the coming of thy kingdom.

PRAYER.   Speak to our consciences, we pray thee. May an arresting word from thee stop some soul here who is traveling a wrong road. Show us the falsity of our excuses and evasions, and grant us an hour of honest dealing with ourselves and thee. From our ill tempers, our unkind moods, our hasty words, and our cherished vindictiveness, good Lord, deliver us. In the quiet of this hour may we be born again into a better mind and a more worthy life.

Speak to us in memory, we pray thee. May recollections of the homes from which we have come, of friends whose affection and fidelity have sustained us, and of sacred hours when we have been certain of thy guiding hand, cleanse and reassure our hearts. Above all in this Advent season may the light of the knowledge of thy glory, which we have seen in the face of Jesus Christ our Lord, stir us all to gratitude and devotion. Thanks be to thee for him, for his coming to redeem us, for his life and teaching, and for his trag-edy and his triumph. He is the way and the truth and the life. O God, make that not only our belief but our conviction and our experience.

Speak to us in our hopes and our ideals, we pray thee. Save us from conformity with the low standards of the world. Grant us higher thoughts of Christ's purpose for us, a nobler philosophy of life's meaning, loftier goals for our devotion, and worthier aims for our aspiration. Because we have worshiped thee here, may the character and mission of Jesus, the ends for which he lived and died, grow vivid in our thought. Beget hope in us that by thy grace we may rise above our meaner selves, outgrow our littleness, and render some Christlike service to the world.

Speak to our wills, we pray thee. O God, who hast given us the power of decision whereby we can take either the right way or the wrong, can choose either the blessing or the curse, and may we choose life and not death. To some soul here today, standing at the parting of the ways, may thy guidance come. May some decisions be made here whose fair fruition will make future years useful and joyful.

Speak to us through the need of the world, we pray thee. We believe in thee, but how can we believe in man? The corruption of his life and the viciousness and violence of his deeds tempt us to disgust and cynicism. Create in us fresh faith in mankind. Help us to look on men and women with the merciful eyes of Christ. Thou Son of God, whom men crucified and yet who didst believe in man, in his possibility and destiny, send us out from our worship restored in confidence that justice can conquer greed, that peace can overcome war, that love is stronger than hate, and that life is mightier than death. —Harry Emerson Fosdick.

EVENING SERVICE

Topic: The Christmas Verb

TEXT: John 1:14.

The word "became" is an important word as we consider this verse and the meaning of Christmas.

I. The word was already existing in the beginning. He was with God, and he was

God. He participated in creation. (See Col. 1:16.)

(a) Jesus became flesh, a human being. "He became like man" (Phil. 2:7, TEV). Jesus became that tiny babe who was laid in a manger.

(b) Jesus became a grown man, following the human principle of growth. (See Luke 2:40.)

(c) Although Jesus was sinless, he became a sinner by taking our sins. He chose to be a sinner not because of his sins but because of our sins. (See II Cor. 5:21.)

(d) He became our savior by taking our place of punishment and death. He died on the cross when in reality we should have been nailed to Calvary's tree. (See Phil. 2:8.)

(e) Then came the glorious resurrection. Jesus completed his earthly mission —and the purpose for which he came on that first Christmas—by rising from the grave. (See I Cor. 15:20.) Jesus became the first of many who would overcome death.

(f) Because of what Jesus became, we will become like him.

II. Perhaps the real question of Christmas is "What have you become because of what Jesus became?" Have you become a believer? Have you become a forgiven sinner, grasping the promise of eternal life? Have you become a witness of the message of Christmas?

III. When Jesus chose his first disciples, he said to Peter and Andrew, "Come ye after me, and I will make you to become fishers of men" (Mark 1:17). The power and love that made Jesus become flesh, become a man among men, become sin for us, become obedient to death on the cross, and become the first fruit of the resurrection is now available to us through Jesus Christ who will make us to become fishers of men.—Alvin C. Shackleford in *Baptist and Reflector.*

SUNDAY: DECEMBER TWELFTH

MORNING SERVICE

Topic: Preparing the Way (Advent)
TEXT: Matt. 3:3.

I. In ancient times when a king set out to visit some place in his dominion men went before him to prepare the way. That is to repair the road, get rid of obstacles, and to provide resting places. And so Isaiah assured the exiles of Babylon that God would prepare the way for their deliverance. God would come and lead them across the desert back to their own land.

(a) John the Baptist declared, "Prepare ye the way of the Lord, make his path straight." John knew their Lord was at hand, but they must prepare his way. To make straight in the desert a highway for God was to prepare the way for him.

(b) "Prepare ye the way of the Lord" are words which constitute a call to us as we make ready our hearts to celebrate this Christmas—remembering the coming of Christ. Christmas comes and goes so quickly with its wonderful message of comfort, hope, and cheer. But the bright dawn that rose upon the world with the advent of Christ often seems an illusion.

II. What can we do about it? How can we prepare his way? (a) We can pray. This is a good way to prepare for his coming to us at Christmas time. Jesus with urgency told people to pray and not to faint. Many obstacles in God's way can be removed through prayer. Every revival of religion has been preceded by persistent and undiscouraged prayer. Through prayer let us prepare the way of the Lord.

(b) We can prepare God's way by making room for Christ in our own attitudes and actions so that men can catch some glimpse of his shining face. Our lives can and must reveal the gospel in action. They can illustrate the story of Jesus so that to the many lives our lives touch it can be true.

(c) We can prepare the way by being concerned for the welfare of the multitudes about us.

(1) Poverty and sickness were evil to Jesus and must be got out of God's way. They were obstacles to Christ's kingdom.

Valleys where people were sunk deep in depression had to be leveled up and mountains of human pride or selfishness that stand in God's way had to be brought low. What of the region beyond?

(2) The world mission of the church has always put hospitals and schools among the priorities. To open the mind to knowledge and to get rid of disease are not only a preparation for the gospel, but they can also be and often are the medium of the gospel. They proclaim the truth that people really matter and all individuals are sacred. In the work of the gospel we must use every kind of service which will develop men and women, set the mind free, and give liberty to the human spirit.

III. To prepare God's way we must proclaim the message of his love. The message of God's love in Christ is not a theory. It is a light that breaks into the mind and shines in the heart.

(a) "You shall be my witness," said Christ to his disciples before his ascension. A witness is one who tells what he has seen and relates his own experience. To see Jesus and to show him to others is the business of every Christian.

(b) We can all do something to prepare for the entry of Christ into our community, country, and world. The best way to prepare the way of the Lord is to give him abundant welcome to the heart. "Come into my heart Lord Jesus" is the best way to prepare the way of the Lord. And to prepare the way of the Lord is to have a truly Christian Christmas.—Ernest Edward Smith.

Illustrations

MOTIVATION. Thomas Langford told of a French priest who extended himself to get a sewage system in his village. When asked why he worked so hard at such a task, he replied, "Because I believe in the incarnation." What a contrast! A sewage system and the incarnation! But the reality of the incarnation seen first at Christmas is the source of motivation for all we are and all we do in Christian mission.—Edward L. Tullis.

BY FAITH. *Caspar:* I looked for wisdom —and behold! the wisdom of the innocent.

Melchior: I looked for power—and behold! the power of the helpless.

Balthazar: I looked for manhood in God —and behold! a God made man.

Caspar: Up and to horse! Make haste! for the star has moved on before us, and the east is pale with the dawn. We must ride by faith.

Melchior: Following the light invisible.

Balthazar: Following the star.—Dorothy L. Sayers from *He That Should Come.*

Sermon Suggestions

RESTORING CHRISTMAS. Text: Luke 2: 18. (1) We will restore the wonder of Christ's coming. (2) We will restore the values of life. (3) We will restore the presence of hope. (4) We will restore the spirit of caring.—James E. Carter.

HAVE YOU DISCOVERED CHRISTMAS? Text: Luke 2:10–11. (1) Christmas is an event. (2) Christmas is good news. (3) Christmas is an experience.—Richard Bodey.

Worship Aids

CALL TO WORSHIP. "Lo, the star, which they saw in the east, went before them, till it came and stood over where the young child was. When they saw the star, they rejoiced with exceeding great joy." Matt. 2:9–10.

INVOCATION. Hushed be our hearts, O God, by the mystery and the wonder of the birth of the Christ Child. Make us truly wise with the wisdom of a little child that once again the highest truth may be born afresh in our hearts. Let not our souls be busy inns that have no room for thy Son, but this day throw wide the doors of our lives to welcome our holy guest.

OFFERTORY SENTENCE. "Thy prayers and thine alms are come up for a memorial before God." Acts 10:4.

OFFERTORY PRAYER. May we find it to be a joyful experience, O Lord, to offer these gifts in the name of Jesus. Grant unto us the wisdom of the men of old who found a token in a star, worshiped the child as a newborn king, and made offerings at his feet.

PRAYER. Our heavenly Father, we thank thee for this season of the year when we are more ready to respond to thy love which comes to us with such tenderness and grace. The touch of the Christmas spirit comes upon us and takes us out of ourselves and makes us ready to give and to share and eager to make happy and joyful not ourselves but others. We know it is the spirit of Christ that makes us thus. May it control all our thoughts and wishes, our words and deeds, and pervade all our lives so that we may celebrate Christmas in the deepest and truest sense. We pray also that we may have this spirit of Christ all through the year and that he may be in the center of our lives and not we ourselves. And may thy gracious love so work through us and thy Holy Spirit so use us day by day that we may become coworkers with thee in thy great work of redemption and that we may have our share in making men and institutions more Christlike and more ready for thy rule.—Julius A. Brewer.

EVENING SERVICE

Topic: Isaiah Speaks of the Messiah
TEXT: Isa. 9:6.

In the beautiful hymn we have a description of the messiah. Looking ahead, it offered hope; looking back from today, we see fulfillment. Isaiah's descriptive language helps us to see Jesus and have a broader understanding of the messianic task.

I. "A child . . . a man" helps us understand who he is and what he does. From the humble beginning as a child, he grew to become a man in whom was revealed his nature and work. The government on his shoulders referred to his role as ruler in the total realm of nature as well as in the spiritual realm.

II. "Wonderful Counselor" or more literally "wonder of a counselor" describes the unique effect of his teaching and counsel. It was teaching not from what he had learned from others but out of his own being. It was teaching with authority.

III. "The mighty God" stresses Jesus' victory over his enemies. His might and power are unmatched by any human or superhuman powers.

IV. "The everlasting Father." As John attempted in the opening verse of his gospel, so Isaiah gives an affirmation of the pre-existent, eternal nature, and oneness of God. He has and demonstrates constant, enduring, and endless care of his people.

V. "The Prince of Peace" describes the provider of a lifestyle. Where Christ rules, there is peace. The condition of yielding to the Prince of Peace gives us a foretaste of what it will be like when Christ reigns over all.—W. Thomas Baddley.

SUNDAY: DECEMBER NINETEENTH

MORNING SERVICE

Topic: What Can We Learn from the Shepherds? (Advent)
SCRIPTURE: Luke 2:8–17.

I. *Simple people.* (a) How interesting that God's angels announced Jesus' birth to sheep tenders in the fields. Wouldn't it have seemed more logical to choose the influential or the famous in high places and plush surroundings? Wouldn't the announcement have received more attention if shared from the lips of society's stars instead of from those near the bottom of the social and economic ladders?

(b) If not to society's best, wouldn't the announcement have been better aimed at religion's best? The shepherds didn't qualify in this respect, at least not in the eyes of men. Their occupation kept them from observing the traditions surrounding the ceremonial laws. Jewish leaders looked down on them as crass and unorthodox.

(c) Perhaps God's choice of these shepherds should remind us that he does not always see men as we do. He loves the poor as much as those in the middle class, the common as much as the famous, and the religious failure as much as the spiritual leader.

II. *Great joy.* The traditional wishes of the season—"Merry Christmas" and "Happy Holidays"—seem hollow compared to the angel's greeting: "I bring you good tidings of great joy" (v. 10). Beautiful cards and bountiful gifts do not bring this joy, but Jesus does. In him we "rejoice with joy unspeakable and full of glory" (I Pet. 1:8). The world's observance of Christmas is most often characterized by unsatisfied longings and unsavory diversions. The Christian has a reason and knows the best way to celebrate.

III. *Quick obedience.* (a) How did the shepherds react to the angels' message? They discussed it briefly: "Let us now go," they decided, and "they came with haste" to Bethlehem (vv. 15–16).

(b) God wants more than new knowledge when he reveals himself to people. No matter how much we know, it's not enough until we do what's right with what we know. Holding it in our heads will not substitute for expressing it with our lives. We, like the shepherds, should act quickly upon what we learn from God.

IV. *Eager testimony.* (a) When the shepherds found what the angels had described, "they made known abroad the saying which was told them concerning the child" (v. 17).

(b) The first Christmas was marked by sharing the fact of Christ's coming and the reason for it, and so has it been through the ages. Even today much of the world pauses to top trees with stars, to bake angel-shaped cookies, and to arrange nativity scenes on mantels and tabletops. May we who know him best do all we can to guarantee that such traditions remain meaningful. May God help us to share by our words why Jesus came and to show by our lives what Jesus does.—Mark A. Taylor in *The Lookout.*

Illustrations

TIME AND ETERNITY.   A baby was born in a stable in Bethlehem. The word was made flesh. Christmas is a time when we think of two worlds coming together. God's world and man's world touch. We speak of the incarnation—God becoming man. We feel the touching of time and eternity. Heaven and earth are joined in a special union. We celebrate the meeting. The everyday and the eternal come together. In the Eucharist God dwells in me and I in him as a thin wafer of bread touches my lips. Confusion and joys and problems are seen in perspective. Land and sea are joined. Life is is at its fullest.—Peter C. Robinson in *The Living Church.*

IF I HAD BEEN THERE.   "If I had only been there! How quick I would have been to help the baby! I would have washed his linen. How happy I would have been to go with the shepherd to see the Lord lying in the manger!" Yes, you would! You say that because you know how great Christ is, but if you had been there at the time you would have done no better that the people of Bethlehem. Childish and silly thoughts are these! Why don't you do it now? You have Christ in your neighbor. You ought to serve him, for what you do to your neighbor you do to the Lord Christ himself.—Martin Luther.

LAWS AGAINST CHRISTMAS.   In 1659 the General Court of Massachusetts enacted a law providing "a fine of five shillings for every offense if a body be found observing, by abstinence from work, by celebrating or attending a religious service . . . such a day as Christmas Day." England had enacted similar laws about the same time. They were repealed in 1662. The Massachusetts law was not repealed until 1681.

Sermon Suggestion

CHRISTMAS: A REKINDLING OF HUMAN LOVE. Text: II Cor. 13:11. (1) Christmas is a time to get intouch with our feelings. (2) Christmas is a time of spiritual renewal.

(3) Christmas is a celebration steeped in sentiment filled with warm recollections and memories of Christmases past. (4) Christmas is a time which confronts us with the Christ event—the story of God's love and the drama of redemption. (5) Christmas is a time for the rekindling of love in human hearts in order to realize our true humanity.—Kenneth L. McCoy.

Worship Aids

CALL TO WORSHIP. "Behold, I bring you good tidings of great joy, which shall be to all people. For unto you is born this day in the city of David a Savior, which is Christ the Lord. Glory to God in the highest, and on earth peace, good will toward men." Luke 2:10–11, 14.

INVOCATION. O Father of infinite love, whom even the heavens could not contain, our hearts beat quickly with joy as we behold thee coming into the world incarnate at Bethlehem. Reveal thyself to us in all thy glorious majesty and holiness as we kneel at the manger of thy Son.

OFFERTORY SENTENCE. "When they were come into the house, they saw the young child with Mary his mother, and fell down, and worshiped him. And they presented unto him gifts; gold, and frankincense, and myrrh." Matt. 2:11.

OFFERTORY PRAYER. Our Lord Jesus Christ, whose birthday has become a season of benevolence and giving, bless these our gifts which we offer in thankfulness for thyself, God's unspeakably precious gift.

PRAYER. O God our Father, we thank thee for Christmas. For gifts given and gifts received, for family gatherings in which those who are separated gather together for a time, and for letters from those from whom we have not heard for a long time, we give thee thanks, O God.

For the spirit of goodwill which is all through the land, for this time when men remember, if only for a little, that it is more blessed to give than to receive, and for this time when men find happiness in bringing happiness to others, we give thee thanks, O God.

O God, our Father, bless those for whom there is little joy at Christmas time.

Bless those who are aged and alone and who have no one left to remember them.

Bless those who have lost dear ones and who at Christmas time are very conscious of the one who is not there.

Bless those who are poor and who are hurt by their poverty, not for their own sakes but for the sake of the gifts they long to give but cannot.

Bless those who are ill and who must spend this time of joy in pain.

Bless those who are far from home and far from friends and who are lonely and homesick among strangers in strange places.

Bless those who feel their loneliness and their loss more keenly in this time of fellowship and joy.

O God our Father, at Christmas time we give thee thanks for thy greatest and thy best gift, Jesus Christ our Lord.

We thank thee that he who is the king of glory entered into a humble home and took our common life upon him that he might make us what he is and that we in him might become thy sons and daughters.

Grant that at this Christmas time Jesus Christ may be born again within the hearts of each one of us.—William Barclay.

EVENING SERVICE

Topic: Returning to Bethlehem (Christmas Eve)

TEXT: Luke 2:15.

I. We desire to go back to that first Christmas Eve in Bethlehem, and in a way, we must. Why?

(a) Because for the personal incarnation of God into our lives, it makes no difference who was at the stable manger that night if you are not there.

(b) It makes no difference what songs the angels sang if you do not hear their proclamation.

(c) It matters little that the shepherds heard the news if you do not hear it.

(d) It is of small consequence that gifts

of gold, frankincense, and myrrh were given if you don't give your dedication, love, and trust.

II. In that spiritual sense, you must be there in Bethlehem, realizing that to you personally is born this night a savior, who is Christ the Lord. He is your very own redeemer, born to wipe out all past sin and guilt. To you is born a savior to inject and inspire your life with new wonder, new love, new meaning, new peace, and new joy. That's why God sent his Son into the world—for you.

III. Much more significant than your going back to Bethlehem is the fact that God in Jesus Christ has come forward to your hometown on this Christmas Eve.

(a) God in Christ is born and alive and loving and wants to break through the noisy, impolite crowds with his word of salvation in all the Bethlehems of our contemporary living.

(b) He wants tourists, beggars, and souvenir hawkers to pause, listen, and respond. He wants today's shepherds and wise men in the form of factory workers, clerks, teachers, students, lawyers, executives, farmers, and business people to stop, listen, and be confronted with his redemption in Christ Jesus. More important than your being there is the truly good news that he is here.

IV. This Christmas Eve feel his presence and see his love reflected in the face of the Christ child. He is here, giving you one more opportunity to turn over your allegiance in new ways and deeper forms to his Son who proceeded from cradle to cross for you and for your salvation. He is here. Rejoice and respond with your worship and works.—John H. Meyer.

SUNDAY: DECEMBER TWENTY-SIXTH

MORNING SERVICE

Topic: The Pioneer of Life

TEXT: Acts 3:15.

I. In his sermon Peter chided his countrymen because they had recently asked for the release of Barabbas, a murderer, and called for the crucifixion of Jesus. He said, "You killed the Prince of life." Moffatt translated the passage: "You killed the Pioneer of life."

(a) The words "prince" and "pioneer" seem to connote almost the exact opposites of living. When we hear the word "prince," we think of that which is established. When we hear the word "pioneer," we think of that which is starting. Prince suggests rich environment, and pioneer suggests rough and rugged surroundings.

(b) Both words fit Jesus of Nazareth. I am not surprised Peter called Jesus the prince of life. He was of the royal line of David according to the gospel genealogy. He was regal in his bearing. He was princely in his power. Also Jesus was a pioneer. He started something so significantly new that we date our calendar from his birth. The hinge of history was on the stable door at Bethlehem.

II. The word "prince" turns our thought to background. The word "pioneer" sets us thinking about foreground. Our day needs to make a better combination of background and foreground.

(a) We can divide any gathering of people into two groups according to their attitude toward background and foreground. On the one hand are those who are so enamored of the past that they close their minds against anything new. On the other hand are those who are so impatient with the past that they run restlessly and sometimes recklessly toward anything new.

(b) We must also think of Christ the pioneer, who leads us forward into the future. There is always danger of getting so attached to the good old days that we fail to see the good that is ahead.

(c) Let us behold Christ the prince to give us perspective on the background of life and Christ the pioneer to give us hope and confidence for the foreground.

III. The word "prince" suggests government, organization; the word "pioneer" suggests personal, individual effort. Think how resourceful the early pioneers were in doing things for themselves. Our day needs a better combination of organized effort and individual effort.

(a) We recognize the need of organization in our complex living. Robert Wicks reminds us that if a fire broke out in the old-fashioned one-room country school house, all that was needed was to cry, "Fire, everybody for himself." But if a fire should break out in one of our large three or four story city school buildings and the cry went up, "Fire, everybody for himself," the result would be panic, chaos, perhaps death. We must be organized if we are to live together.

(1) Religion must be organized if it is to exert influence in reforming the civic life of a community. We need organization if we are to have effective religious education for our youth. We need organization to make our worship of God more personally helpful.

(2) The church is the body of Christ and through it he makes his spirit active in the world. Let us exalt Christ as prince, the head of the church, the vast organization which belts the globe, builds hospitals and schools, beautifies the earth with cathedrals, and enriches life with the noblest music and art.

(b) We must not lessen our emphasis on Christ the pioneer, who encourages personal exploratory experience. The Christian church was founded and grounded in first-hand experiences of God in Christ. And if it loses that, no organizations, however large, can save the vitality of the church. But Christ the pioneer can go forth this very day with you to do something so uniquely personal and interestingly original that religion would come alive to us.

IV. This quickening creative power of Christ the pioneer accounts for the way the RSV translates our text—"the author of life." Christ is the prince of life, as the KJV puts it, for he is royal head to whom we look back and to whom we look up. He is the pioneer of life with whom we march confidently and personally into the future. Christ is the author of life, for a pioneer is one who creates new paths and powers for those who follow him and thus writes new chapters in their lives.—Ralph W. Sockman.

Illustrations

LOST. Vermonters tell of the stranger who got off the road somewhere north of Brattelboro and landed in the wilderness of the Green Mountains in a town like Stratton or Glastenbury. Being now completely lost, the motorist hailed a lumberjack who was hauling logs out of the woods with his team of horses. "How do you get to Burlington from here?" he asked. After long cogitation and several chews on his plug of tobacco, the Vermonter answered, "Stranger, if I were going to Burlington, I wouldn't start from here."—Edward C. Dahl.

ONE WISH. It was on New Year's Eve on the battlefront in Korea. The temperature had plunged to 42° below 0, and 18,000 American marines were preparing to face 100,000 Communist troops. At midnight, they were being served a supper. It consisted of cold beans which had to be eaten out of cans while each soldier stood watch beside armed tanks. That night one newspaper correspondent grew philosophical and asked a huge marine, "If I were God and could give you one thing you'd rather have more than anything else in the world, what would you ask for?" That marine, whose clothing had frozen as stiff as a board, whose beard was encrusted with mud, and whose hands were blue with cold as he ate the beans with a trench knife, said, "I would ask for tomorrow."—Jerry Hayner.

Sermon Suggestions

REACHING BEYOND YESTERDAY. Text: II Cor. 5:17. (1) We have a right to be proud of past achievements. (2) We feel an irresistable temptation to do better. (3) We die when we stop reaching for new heights.—Clarence J. Forsberg.

YOU CAN MASTER LIFE. Text: Phil. 4: 11–13. (1) All people have a capacity for courage. (2) All people have a capacity to handle life's ordinary and less dramatic circumstances. (3) The capacity of acceptance is within the grasp of all people. (4) All people may, like Paul, lay hold on the power of Christ by trusting him and seeking his guidance.—Homer J. R. Elford.

Worship Aids

CALL TO WORSHIP. "Great is the Lord, and greatly to be praised; and his greatness is unsearchable. One generation shall praise thy works to another, and shall declare thy mighty works." Ps. 145:3–4.

INVOCATION. Almighty God, who hast given us minds to know thee, hearts to love thee, and voices to show forth thy praise, we would not know thee if thou hadst not already found us. Help us to know thee with pure minds and to praise thee with a clear voice.

OFFERTORY SENTENCE. "God is not unrighteous to forget your work and labor of love, which ye have showed toward his name, in that ye have ministered to the saints, and do minister." Heb. 6:10.

OFFERTORY PRAYER. Eternal God, give us a vision of thy glory that no sacrifice may seem too great, and strengthen us in every step we take from selfishness to generosity.

PRAYER. Eternal God, in whose keeping are our yesterdays and our tomorrows, we thank thee for the breath of life which has sustained us until this hour, and we pray for wisdom and strength to fill these days with useful service and to face the future unashamed and unafraid. Forgive us for the idle hours we have wasted, the days of fretfulness we have spoiled, the duties we have avoided, and the hearts we have hurt. O God, make us great enough for these great days. Lift us out of our littleness of spirit. Enlarge our horizons and clear our vision to see the true needs of our nation. Widen our sympathies to serve thy whole family throughout the world that faith, hope, and love may dispel doubt and fear and hate. Lengthen our lives by linking them with loved ones gone before us, and lead us in the way everlasting.

EVENING SERVICE

Topic: Burn Those Bridges

TEXT: Luke 17:32.

I. There are certain situations and certain times in life when there is nothing at all to be gained by looking back.

(a) Sometimes it is quite perilous to constantly review and repeatedly rehearse the backward look. There is an urgent need for deliberate forgetfulness. There is a time when wisdom insists that we must forget the past and look resolutely ahead to the future. There comes a point when we have to decisively let go of what was and take a firm hold on the possibilities of what may be.

(b) Some of us, no matter how difficult the struggle may be, will have to burn some bridges that reach back in memory to an unhappy experience, event, or relationship before we can have any possibility of peace of mind or happiness.

II. At the beginning of a new year when many once again go through the generally futile ritual of making resolutions, the new year might be better hailed as a good time to start burning bridges to an old habit.

III. Here is the person who hasn't burned his bridges and still crosses them to live in the remembrance of things past. There are those who would cross those bridges of memory again and again instead of striding boldly into a promising future. If so, how much better it would be to throw away the clippings, destroy the letters, and cast out the photos. Some bridges to the past have to be demolished before we can ever hope to take the high road to the future.

(a) The past can be of service to us. Good memories of days gone by can nourish us. Good souls of our years past can live on in memory and sustain us. Good thoughts from other times can come from the shadows of memory to strengthen us.

Let us cultivate the garden of memory and tend to it well, but let us turn to pulling out the weeds that might otherwise choke that garden and make it barren.

(b) It is well that we should reflect on them and draw from them whatever good they may have to offer. Yet in doing this let us not say, "Oh, if I only could do it over —that decision, that attitude, that relationship, that piece of work." It cannot be done over. Better that we admit this and have done with it. No need is there to go over that too-well traveled bridge. How much wiser it would be to burn it, for at the other side are only the quicksands of vain regret. Remember Lot's wife?

IV. As the new year approaches, take now out of the depths of your mind and soul those failures from the past and those hidden-in-the-heart hurts which you feel you have endured and dig a grave and bury them so deep they can never come to life again. Place a marker over them—"To Be Forgotten Forever."

V. Turn then to the dawn of a new day with new hope, new courage, new tasks to be done, and new opportunities to be faced. Do this as with the words of St. Paul, "Forgetting those things which are behind" and "Reaching forth unto those things which are before."—Charles L. Copenhaver.

SECTION X. Ideas and Suggestions for Pulpit and Parish

FIRST STEPS. Education, not baby sitting, is the purpose of the first steps department of the Sunday school of the Southport Heights Christian Church in Indianapolis, Indiana. Trained leaders introduce newborn babies and toddlers to their first steps toward Christ by emphasizing sharing and caring experiences and individualized lessons with appropriate aids on nature, Jesus, the Bible, and the church.

GOLDEN DOORKNOBS. The First Baptist Church in Clinton, Mississippi, each year presents Golden Doorknob Awards to the person in each age division in the Sunday school who makes the most contacts in behalf of of school attendance.

INTRODUCTIONS. When a family comes forward to join the fellowship, introduce them properly to the congregation. Tell something of their past, their occupations, where they live, their hobbies—tell something about the persons. Just telling their names is not enough.—Knofel Staton.

WHY MEMBER NAMETAGS? (1) It is a matter of etiquette. It is rude to expect only visitors, who already feel conspicuous, to wear nametags and stand out even more.

(2) In thousands of congregations many members do not know the names of all of the other members.

(3) The wearing of nametags by the members suggests this is a congregation that expects visitors and new members.

(4) The use of nametags has been found to be an essential element in congregations of 200 to 300 or more members which seek to become genuine caring, sharing, supportive, and loving fellowships.

(5) The use of nametags enlarges the number of members known by name by members of the nominating committee and thus encourages broadening the base of participation.

(6) The use of nametags helps the newly arrived minister or staff member or guest speaker to learn and remember people's names.

(7) Asking new members to hand out and collect the nametags can be very helpful in facilitating the assimilation of new members into a congregation.

(8) By providing distinctive nametags for each class, circle, group, or organization reinforces the identity and sense of unity and cohesiveness of individual groups and the group life within a congregation.—Lyle E. Schaller in *The Clergy Journal*.

SOUP-ER BOWL SUNDAY. On Super Bowl Sunday a large bowl was placed at the altar of the Grace United Methodist Church in Savannah, Georgia, so that worshipers might make contributions to help alleviate the suffering of persons experiencing hunger throughout the world.

225

SUNDAY DISCUSSION.   At the 9 A.M. service on Sunday at the First Christian Church in Hollywood, Florida, there is prayer, meditation, hymn singing, communion, but no sermon. Instead worshipers participate in an open forum in which ideas and opinions are exchanged with the pastor as moderator. The 11 A.M. service follows the traditional worship pattern.

CLINIC.   At an evangelism clinic held at the First Cumberland Presbyterian Church in Chattanooga, Tennessee, participants received training in such areas as visiting evangelism, follow-up evangelism, and sponsor evangelism—visiting people, sharing the doctrines and programs of the church, and helping new members meet the congregation and become active in the work of the church.

SWEETHEART FELLOWSHIP.   Every woman is every man's sweetheart at the First Christian Church in Atlanta, Georgia, when the men prepare and serve a Valentine's Day dinner for the ladies.

SUNDAY NIGHTERS.   Members of the Prospect United Methodist Church in Covington, Georgia, during a spring attendance campaign, wore buttons that proclaim "I'm a Sunday Nighter" and signed up friends, neighbors, and relatives on fish-shaped cards which were hooked together. Sunday school classes competed to see which could get the longest string of fish signed up to attend Sunday night services.

ILLUSTRATED SERMONS.   A talented mother at the Bethel Reformed Church in Harvey, Illinois, gathers the children to a side of the sanctuary and transforms the pastor's sermon into stick figures, easily understood symbols, and simpler words. The various sheets are then taped to the altar rail so the sequence is readily followed.

BIBLE GROUPS.   The Cass Community United Methodist Church in Detroit, Michigan, surrounded by housing projects, apartment buildings, and multiple family dwellings, sponsors weekly Bible study groups in eight of the complexes.

LENTEN REMINDERS.   A folder distributed by the Westover Hills United Methodist Church in Richmond, Virginia, provided guidelines for determining what gift should be put in the collection box on each day in Lent. Among them the following:

The Salvation Army states that tonight there will be about 1,000 persons in Richmond with no place to sleep. If you have a place to sleep tonight, give 25¢.

Over fifty percent of the population of Pakistan is too poor to buy food, even if it is available. Contribute today one percent of your last major bill at the grocery store.

This prayer was prayed by a newly literate Christian returning to his homeland in Costa Rica: "I am going home to many who cannot read. So, Lord, make me to be a Bible so that those who do not read the Book may read it in me." Contribute 5¢ for each time you have read from the Bible during the last seven days. If your contribution is less than 15¢, please read Prov. 8:22–35.

Leprosy is still one of the major diseases in India. A woman in her late seventies walked a round trip of twenty-five miles to visit her five grandchildren in a leprosy village. Contribute 25¢ for each vehicle owned by you or your family. You may deduct that amount for each person you know with leprosy.

FOOD-ENERGY SAVERS.   During Lent the members of the First United Methodist Church in Brighton, Michigan, became food-energy savers. They prepared nutritional and meatless meals, engaged in fasting for a purpose, and each Sunday turned in the money thus saved for world hunger relief. A display in the narthex dealt with the nutritional value of grain foods. On Sundays the fasters deposited their money in hollowed-out loaves of bread near the display.

HOME COMMUNION.   During Lent the pastor and two elders of the Whitehaven Cumberland Presbyterian Church in

Memphis, Tennessee, hold communion services in members' homes and thereby recall the upper room experience of Jesus and his disciples.

LENTEN SACKS.   Some of the women in the First Christian Church in Stinnett, Texas, made small cloth bags out of scrap material and closed with a yarn drawstring at the top. During Lent these tiny fabric sacks were mailed with the newsletter to each family. An accompanying letter said: "The enclosed cloth bag is provided for your Easter offering. Between now and Easter we suggest that you keep the bag on the dining room table and encourage all family members to place a coin in it each day. By Easter you will have at least thirty coins—the amount paid to Judas to betray Jesus. But instead of being used for betrayal, they will be used to show the love of Jesus in the world. We ask you to bring your coins to church on Easter."—Herb Miller in *The Disciple.*

CHANCEL THEMES.   The altar committee of Shepherd of the Lakes Lutheran Church in Walled Lake, Michigan, establishes a worship mood for the various seasons. Themes have included a Lenten focus on the cross and a crown of thorns wall hanging and for Easter a life-sized empty tomb against the chancel wall.

THE WAY OF THE CROSS.   Seven separate, continuous scenes depicting the last week in Jesus' life are portrayed at night during Holy Week on the lawn of the Beechwood Baptist Church in Louisville, Kentucky. More than 150 church members participate as actors and assistants. Each scene has its own lighting and sound system.

TREASURE HUNT.   Sunday school students at the Bristol United Methodist Church in Flint, Michigan, celebrated Palm Sunday with a Holy Week treasure hunt. Participants were divided into teams which followed stenciled footprints to different classrooms where various events were represented.

The triumphal entry into Jerusalem was depicted with palm fronds and the singing of hosannas. Coins represented the money changers in the temple. Judas' betrayal was remembered by thirty pieces of silver. The Last Supper, where communion was taken, was symbolized with bread sticks.

At Gethsemane the students prayed with Jesus. His trial was represented by shouts of an angry crowd, the robe and crowd of thorns, and the symbolic washing of hands, Pilate's action in disclaiming responsibility for Jesus' death. The crucifixion scene featured a cross, a nail, and the pungent fragrance of wine and vinegar.

Each child entering the empty tomb received a flower to celebrate Jesus' victory over death.—*Michigan Christian Advocate.*

SYMBOL.   Vials containing caterpillars are distributed to families in the St. Paul Lutheran Church in Funkstown, Maryland, at a proper time so that parishioners may watch butterflies emerge during the Easter weekend.

Easter decorations at the St. Andrew Lutheran Church in Muncy, Pennsylvania, include large butterflies that are suspended from the ceiling of the sanctuary.

Seven hundred hand-made butterflies were distributed at the Easter services of the Old Stone United Methodist Church in Meadville, Pennsylvania. The three stages of the butterfly's life were interpreted as corresponding to the stages in the Christian's life. The larva represents man's condition on earth. The chrysalis in its cocoon—seemingly lifeless—is a symbol of Jesus in the grave. The butterfly, bursting forth in beauty, symbolizes eternal life.

EASTER WALK.   Following Easter morning worship, the pastors, the adult, youth, and handbell choirs, and members of the congregation of the First United Methodist Church in Hampton, Virginia, participate in an Easter walk from the church to a nearby mall where they proclaim the Easter message in song and word.

HOME HOSPITALITY.   Emulating the practice recorded in Acts 2 in which one of the first things done by converts was to eat together, families in the Wesley United Methodist Church in Alexandria, Virginia, invite other families of the church to have a meal in their homes on Pentecost.

LOVE IN ACTION.   Members of the Grace United Methodist Church in Manassas, Virginia, designated May as Love-in-Action Month. Weekly expressions of love were writing letters of appreciation to others, making phone calls that show appreciation, doing kind deeds for one another, and making visits to church members not previously visited.

VBS FOR TEENS.   The Sherman Church of God in Norton, Ohio, holds an evening vacation Bible school for teens. Starting at 6 P.M., the week-long school includes singing, prayer, a Bible lesson, and guest speakers or tours that are usually keyed to the lesson.

PAINT JOB.   Is the problem not only that the church needs painting but also that there are no funds for the job? Perhaps the Port Wallis United Church in Dartmouth, Nova Scotia, has an answer. Volunteers of all ages did scraping and painting, and sponsors for each worker made donations.

DEACON AT THE DOOR.   So that the comments and suggestions made to the pastor by worshipers as they leave church on Sunday may not be forgotten or neglected, the pastor of the Deep Creek United Methodist Church in Virginia has a deacon at his elbow who takes notes on those people to visit, things to do, and ideas to explore.

CELEBRATING.   At four special services at the Cradock United Methodist Church in Portsmouth, Virginia, the theme of "Celebrating the Church" was emphasized by speakers whose topics were "Celebrating Grace," "Celebrating Fellowship," "Celebrating the Family," and "Celebrating the Spirit."

LABOR SUNDAY.   Suggestions for observing Labor Sunday and emphasizing the concern of the church for what the day represents: (1) wear work clothes to church, (2) display symbols of work instruments in church, (3) share work experiences with fellow church members, (4) hold special programs showing the history of labor in the United States including changes in age, sex, and industrial makeup, and (5) create understanding through dialogue between representatives of labor and management.—Lemuel C. Carter.

ARTS FESTIVAL.   During a week in the fall the First United Methodist Church in Grand Rapids, Michigan, sponsors a religious arts festival that features religious paintings, sculpture, weavings, pottery, and banners by western Michigan artists.

WORLD COMMUNION.   The observance of World Communion Sunday in the Presbyterian Church in LaPorte, Colorado, began at sundown on Saturday—about the time communion was being served in Japan—with a vesper service followed by an international potluck dinner. At 9 P.M. a vigil of world communion began and continued throughout the night. As it became 11 A.M. in various countries around the world, moving from east to west, the worshipers focused on a particular country by singing appropriate songs, eating snacks representative of the country, and discussing such relative issues as human rights, economic justice, disarmament, and poverty. At 6:45 A.M. on Sunday a service of morning prayers was followed by a South American breakfast and Holy Communion at 11.

THANK YOU SUNDAY.   The Church of Christ in Delta, Ohio, held a Thank You Sunday. Members were asked to put their expressions of appreciation for those who had been kind or had rendered service, often unheralded, to the church in a box at the back of the sanctuary. The names of those receiving notes were read during the morning service, and those people came forward to receive the notes.

DIAL-A-CONCERN.   Members of the First Cumberland Presbyterian Church in Austin, Texas, may dial the church each day and hear a three-minute recorded message that includes a word of affirmation, a brief prayer, information about people, programs, and events, and sometimes a chuckle.

LIFE LINE.   A telephone answering device at the Christian Church in Catlin, Illinois, provides a six-minute, compact Bible study, which is changed daily and is available day and night. Those using the service, called Life Line, are encouraged to have a Bible, pencil, and paper at hand when they call.

SWAT PROGRAM.   Soul Winning Action Team, a ministry for youth at the Barbe Baptist Church in Franklin, Kentucky, promotes and encourages commitment to Christ and his word, to the Christian lifestyle, to the program of the local church, and to an awareness of the joyful life in Christ.

COUPON CLIPPING.   Should coupon clipping be limited to readers of newspapers and magazines? No was the conclusion of the leaders of the Foundry United Methodist Church in Virginia Beach, Virginia, where at a worship service the parishioners were given a page of coupons and were encouraged to sign the ones they felt they could support during the follow-

ing week. The coupons were then taken to the chancel rail in an act of commitment. Coupons included promises to engage in daily Bible reading, visiting, tithing, praying for the church, peace, and those in need, and accepting leadership roles in the church.

MISSIONS EMPHASIS.   *Church of God Evangel* offers two ideas for missions support that have been used in churches. (1) A tithe of the tithe calls for the giving of ten percent of the church surplus at the end of each month to missions. (2) Developing the operational budget so that all offerings on the fifth Sunday of five-Sunday months are set aside for missions. Fifth Sunday preaching focuses on missionary themes.

SUMMER CHRISTMAS.   Christmas in August with tinsel, bells, carols, Christmas lights, and choke cherries substituting for holly was the way the congregation at Pioneer Log Church in Sand Lake, Ontario, wished their summer residents the best wishes of the festive season.

FAMILY TREE.   Each family in the Hopewell United Methodist Church in Dry Fork, Virginia, was asked to make, purchase, or donate an ornament to be placed on the family Christmas tree at the church each year.

SECTION XI. A Little Treasury of Illustrations

STANDING ALONE. A pine forest grew for years without suffering damage from storms. A timber company cut all the trees from a two hundred foot strip through a section of the forest. A magnificent pine tree was left exposed on the west side. It had stood for over thirty years surrounded by the other trees. Few pines are as straight and perfectly formed. It was a beautiful pine tree, but it now lay on the ground. It had withstood many storms surrounded by the other trees. After its neighbors were removed, it fell when the first rains softened the ground and the winds blew. It could not stand alone.—K. G. Durham.

TIME AND TIME AGAIN. A. J. Cronin, while living in Scotland at a time he was trying to regain his health and seeing if he could become a writer, threw into the fire the manuscript of what was to have been his first novel. He was utterly discouraged. In his dejected mood he walked out into a field and began visiting with an old Scottish farmer. As he told the man what he had done there was silence for a time, and then he stopped his digging of the bog long enough to say: "No doubt you're the one that's right, Doctor, and I'm the one that's wrong, but my father ditched this bog all his days and never made a pasture. I've dug it all my days, and I've never made a pasture. But pasture or no pasture, I cannot help but dig. For my father knew and I know that if you only dig long enough, a pasture can be made here." That brief statement, emphasized by the

farmer's spade stuck sharply into the bog, put a new resolve in Cronin's heart and launched him onto his great career as a writer.

MISSING THE TRAIN. In a play by Lord Dunsay the first act begins with a man just missing his train. As he arrives at the station, the gates close in his face. This seems to touch off a whole series of incidents which make his life a failure, and he is always thinking, "If only I had arrived one second earlier." Then he is given a chance to go back and change one event in his past, and naturally he chooses to go back and arrive on time for that train. Life starts over for him from that point, and the circumstances are changed. But it turns out to be just as much a failure as before, and the playwright is saying that our destinies lie not so much in the external events as they do in our own inner character.

CONFUSED PURPOSE. Joel owned one of the finest young sheep in his country. His lamb had won many awards, and Joel was an object of his neighbor's envy. Because of their jealousy, the neighbors decided to take Joel's lamb from him by force. Joel saw them coming and realized their intention. Quickly he took the lamb into his house, bolted the door, loaded his rifle, and began shooting. He first fired from the east window, then crossed the room and fired from the west window, and then returned to the east window. Joel continued this action, crossing the room, back and forth, back and forth. But each time he tripped over the lamb. Finally he became so exasperated at his difficult defense that he opened the door, kicked the lamb outside, and went on fighting his enemies.—John H. Townsend.

IN GOD WE TRUST.   Following the Civil War, Salmon P. Chase, Secretary of the Treasury, received appeals from many people to honor God in some suitable manner on our coins. He instructed the director of the mint to come up with a motto which expressed that dependence on God and to print it on our coins. Several different mottos were tried before the phrase, "In God We Trust," gained wide favor in 1864. When the eagle and double eagle of new design appeared in 1907, the motto was omitted, and there was a great outcry. In response to public sentiment, Congress passed an Act on May 18, 1908, requiring the motto to appear on all coins issued thereafter.—Brian L. Harbour.

TAKING THE RISK.   Who can save a child from a burning house without taking the risk of being hurt by the flames? Who can listen to a story of loneliness and despair without taking the risk of experiencing similar pains in his own heart and even losing his precious peace of mind? Who can take away suffering without entering it?—Henri Nouwen.

ALL IN THE NAME.   John Henry Jowett during a holiday season went to the countryside for a rest. The famous minister was visiting in a quiet village chapel and took a seat almost unnoticed in the little congregation. When the time approached for the beginning of the service, the deacons consulted anxiously and decided to ask the stranger if he would lead the service. Jowett said that he would try. He preached a sermon with which he was familiar. It was one he had preached at his own church, Carr's Lane, one of the great churches of England. The village congregation was strangely unresponsive. After the service the deacons expressed formal thanks to him for getting them out of their difficulty.

Later in the week one of the newspapers announced that Jowett of Birmingham was enjoying a holiday in that particular community. On Friday a deputation of the village church asked the minister if he would preach on the following Sunday. Greatly surprised at this invitation, Jowett answered, "But I preached for you last Sunday." "Oh, yes, we know that now, but we did not then know that you were Jowett of Carr's Lane."—G. Ray Jordan.

PRODIGAL PARENT.   One cold winter day a man came to my study and asked if his name was still on the church membership roll. I searched the record and found that ten years before his name had been placed on the inactive list. He sat quietly for a time and then said with a note of pathos: "More than ten years ago!" Then he poured out his story, telling what he had been doing during those many years, the work he had done, the money he had made, and the way he had spent it. Then he said: "I suppose you read of that liquor store robbery which took place downtown the other night. They found out who did it. My son was one of the gang." As he wept, he said: "For over ten years I let my boy see me forgetting God and the church. For ten years I let him see me work in the fields on Sunday the same as any other day. For ten years he smelled liquor on my breath every time I came home from town. For ten years I've been showing him that I believed that life is simply what you can get out of it, and it doesn't matter too much how you get it. For ten years I let him grow up without knowing the things which would have kept him out of this scrape. He's not a bad boy, but I'm a poor father."—Homer J. R. Elford.

GOD AND OUR NEED.   Christian prayer is not telling God what to do. It is rather telling him what we think we need. In the last resort Christian prayer has always left it to God's own wisdom to decide what precisely he is to do about our need.—John Baillie.

DANGER.   The greatest danger facing this country is the danger of moral lassitude, liberty turned to license, rights demanded and duties shirked, the moral sense deteriorating, the traditions and standards of the nation weakened, the spiritual forces within it losing ground.—Robert J. McCracken.

WHO'S KNOCKING?   An old fellow who was living alone began refusing to admit people to his house, though several attempted to see him. A knock would come at the door, and the old gentleman would go to the door and peer at the glass pane in the door to see who was calling. "No! I am not going to allow a man with an ugly old face like that in my house." He would turn and leave the door unanswered. The next time a knock came, he would go, look, and turn away grumbling, "If they want to see me they are going to have to shave off those whiskers" or "If a person wants to call on a fellow, he ought to at least wear decent clothes, not rags."

After so many were turned away, someone called the old man's daughter, fearing that her father's failing mind had snapped. She came, and he told her the kind of people who had knocked at the door. She was confused because she had known the people and they were not at all like her father had described them. She asked him to come to the door with her and then realized that the poor old fellow had not seen anyone who came to call but only himself each time reflected in the pane of glass in the door.—James Westbrook.

WHERE IS GOD?   Years ago a woman died in New York City. When her will was read, it was discovered that she had left her not inconsiderable estate simply "To God." Legal requirements had to be fulfilled. So to settle the estate and fulfill the requirements, a case was filed naming God as a party thereto. A legal summons was duly issued, and the court went through the motions of trying to serve it. The final report stated, "After due and diligent search, God cannot be found in New York City."—Hoover Rupert.

GOD'S IDEA.   Music is God's idea. Scripture tells us that he is surrounded by heavenly music and that choirs will sing throughout eternity. We are told that the heavens declare the glory of God. In the book of Job we read that at the dawn of creation the morning stars sang together. We might tend to dismiss this last idea as imagery and poetic language, except that scientists have found that each star emits a radio signal that identifies it from all other stars.—Barbara Joyce Bush in *The P. E. O. Record.*

UNFINISHED.   Michelangelo was one of the world's greatest artists. Many people find his statues very interesting because quite a number of them he left unfinished on purpose. In Florence, Italy, one of his statues depicts a man. The man's arms and legs are protruding out of a massive block of granite, but the rest of the man is left largely unfinished—his head, his back, and so on. There were quite a number of other statues that Michelangelo left in exactly the same condition—unfinished. He did this deliberately because he wanted to convey a message to his viewers. Like the statues, all human beings are basically unfinished products.—David G. Maze.

BEYOND SCIENCE.   A friend recalls that in the ninth grade his teacher explained the "big bang" theory of earth's formation. A condensation of the sun caused an explosion which resulted in the emergence of earth and other planets. After class, the disturbed teenager inquired how he could believe that along with the account of Genesis he had studied in Sunday school. The wise teacher said thoughtfully, "Who created the sun?" What wisdom, to realize that one can adhere to the teachings of modern science and have faith in God also!—Bevel Jones.

NEED AND RESPONSIBILITY.   If it is every man's need to be loved, it is the Christian's responsibility to love him as he is. If it is every man's need to be controlled by law, it is the Christian's responsibility to provide an understanding of God's law in today's world. If it is every man's need to grow with freedom, it is the Christian's responsibility to see that the possibility of this growth is made actual in today's society for everyone. If it is every man's need to see the wonder of God's world and to respond in awe to God's holiness, it is the Christian's responsibility to bring him into the life of the church, where he may "seek the Lord where he may be found."—Randolph Crump Miller.

INNER SPACE. Before man controls outer space, he needs to learn to control the space that lies immediately under his hat. Man has been seeking to control outer space, but he has not yet learned how to control himself. He needs to learn to control inner space before he can control outer space. He needs to learn to control his own heart before he controls the heart of the universe. He needs to learn how to get along with his fellow men before he tries to get along with potential men on other planets.—Harold E. Buell.

HUB OF LIFE. A professor illustrated the Christian life by drawing on the chalkboard a wagon wheel with its spokes and rough-hewn hub. "This wheel," he said, "represents your life. The spokes are the varied interests you have." Then he named the spokes—business, home, recreation, pleasure, politics, the church, and other concerns. Then he said: "The hub of the wheel is most important, for the spokes are tied into the hub and the hub touches each spoke. Without the hub, the spokes have no meaning. The question is, what constitutes the hub of life, the one thing about which all else revolves?"—Harleigh M. Rosenberger.

HIDDEN TREASURE. An old lady in Scotland was so poor that the community had to support her, even though her son had come to America and had become very wealthy. "Why doesn't John help his mother?" the neighbors often whispered.

One day a neighbor suggested that her son would surely help her if he knew of her need. Mother-like, she defended her son: "Oh, John is so thoughtful, but he needs all his money. He's a good boy. See, he writes to me every week, the nicest letters. And in every letter he sends a picture. They are strange pictures." "Did you save them?" asked the neighbor. "Oh, sure," replied the mother, as she reached for her Bible. "I save all his letters and put the pictures in the good book."

Between the leaves of the Bible the visitor found hundreds of United States bank notes, more than enough to keep the old mother in comfort. She had a treasure, but she did not know it.—Arthur Tonne.

DOUBLE SHOCK. Norman Cousins was waiting at a railroad station in Stamford, Connecticut. Several other persons, including some men in uniform, were also present, waiting for the express to take them to New York. Suddenly the door to the waiting room flew open, and a woman, screaming hysterically, burst into the room. A rugged-looking man pursued her. The woman screamed that the man was trying to kill her and asked the people to help her. The woman then grabbed Cousins, and he tried to put her behind him, away from the man. The man tried to knock Cousins out of the way, grabbed the woman's wrist, and began pulling her through the doorway. Cousins tried to free her and was able to hold on to her long enough for the man to realize that he could not take her with him. He then grabbed her purse ran off into the night. They called the police and began to minister to the woman who was still moaning and had suffered a cut eye. Cousins said that he looked around the room, and except for three or four persons who were trying to help, the rest of the people seemed unconcerned. Cousins wrote, "I am not sure which was greater, the shock of the attack that had just occurred or the shock caused by the apparent detachment and unconcern of the other people, especially the men in uniform."—Charles E. Ferrell.

STEWARDSHIP OF LIFE. The criticism and reshaping of economic relations and institutions is a fundamentally moral task in which Christians should be actively involved. Economy, rightly understood, is the God-given stewardship of life. In Christ the people of God are freed and enabled, individually and corporately, to participate in the quest for greater economic justice and the achievement of the conditions of human well-being.—Lutheran Church in America.

ENLARGEMENT. The night sky does something to the star gazer. It does us creative good to see Orion driving his hunting dogs across the zenith. It enlarges the self to know great art, to have studied great architecture, to have felt the spell of epic herosims, to have swung to the rhythms of Homer's strophes, to have shaken to the passion of Roland or Romeo or Francis of Assisi, to have wrestled with Kant's categorical imperatives, to have heard the roll of Drake's drums, to have been borne on the music stream of Beethoven's symphonies, to engrave the prologue of John's Gospel on the heart, to have said the sonorous affirmations of the Nicene Creed.—Phillips Endicott Osgood.

SALESMAN. Bishop William A. Quayle was a passenger on a railroad coach which was otherwise occupied by a number of salesmen. The conductor approached him and, thinking that he too was a salesman, asked, "What do you sell?" Quayle smiled and said, "Horizons!"—James R. Webb.

WHOSOEVER WILL. A man had a strange dream. In heaven he saw a huge arch through which all the redeemed of the ages were entering. On it was written, "The elect of God." Then he looked at the arch from earth's side. Over that side were the words, "Whosoever will may come."—R. C. Foster.

THE COMING OF CHRIST. Rome was a flea market of borrowed gods and conquered peoples, a bargain basement on two floors, earth and heaven, heavy wheels without spokes, eyes sunk in fat, sodomy, double chins, illiterate emperors, fish fed on the flesh of learned slaves. There were more people in the world than there have ever been since, all crammed into the passages of the Coliseum, and all wretched. And then, into this tasteless heap of gold and marble, he came, light and clothed in an aura, emphatically human, deliberately provincial, Galilean, and at that moment

gods and nations ceased to be and man came into being.—Boris Pasternak.

MASTER OF MEN. Jesus asks from me my all, yet he gives himself to me utterly. He is the most knowable man who ever lived, yet no one has ever explained him. He asserts his authority at every turn, yet he withdraws from the applauding crowds. He raised from the dead, yet he deliberately chooses death. He has power such as none has ever had before or since, yet he ever knocks and waits and listens before he passes the low lintel of human life awaiting the true bow of the heart, the full allegiance of the will, and concerned that no violence to our mental processes is ever demanded of us. He died two thousand years ago, yet to thousands he is a greater reality than their dearest friend, without whom joy would pass away from life and leave it cold and bleak and dead. —Leslie D. Weatherhead.

TEACHING MODEL. The Latin term for education is *erudire*. This means that what is raw (*rudis*) must be given form and be shaped to become truly human. In the Greco-Roman world education was indeed the art of making out of the raw material of children fit soldiers, responsible citizens, respectable fathers, or whatever other educational ideal predominated. The Hebrew key term for education is *jasar* which means to flog, to discipline, and to instruct. Both in the Greco-Roman and the Jewish society children were thus considered as objects of education, and mature adulthood was the aim. Jesus put a child in the midst of his disciples who aspired to be great. He reversed pedagogy, and the child became his teaching model for the quarreling adults.—Hans-Ruedi Weber.

DESERT PLACES. The fathers of the church were not afraid to go out into the desert because they had richness in their hearts. But we, with richness all around us, are afraid because the desert is in our hearts.—Franz Kafka.

RUSTY CANS. In the book by Astrid Lindgren, Pippi Longstocking is a delightful little girl who always overcomes. Everything in life becomes an opportunity for her. As a "thing" finder, she happened on an old rusty can. She exclaimed that that was her lucky day. Asked what good an old can was, she replied that it could be used for a number of things. It could be a can for cookies to go into. Or it might be a can that cookies didn't go into. It turned out to be a helmet, and she decided that was just what she needed.

We need to become more like the delightful Pippi. When the rusted cans of life come our way, we need to figure out how they can be useful to us. Only when we look at every experience as an opportunity, can we be persons who overcome.— Dathene Stanley in *The Secret Place.*

A LAYMAN CONFESSES.   The church dare not evade its obligation to proclaim God's judgment over all human activity, even as it proclaims his mercy and forgiveness. The role of prophet is active, often disruptive and always painful, and it is thoroughly unpleasant to those on the receiving end of the preaching. I know this, because if the church today were to do its full duty, I would be among those called to repent. As an employer I can see I should have moved more swiftly during the last thirty years in respect to equal treatment of blacks, women, and the nationals of other countries. I should have been prodded to accept responsibility for helping solve the worst problems in the communities in which we operate. The church should have reminded me in convincing terms that my right to make a profit could not be asserted at a cost to the quality of life anywhere else.—J. Irwin Miller.

CHANGE.   An old man was asked if he believed that his baptism as an infant had truly changed his life. His reply was in two parts. First, he said, he believed that in baptism more is begun than is effected. However, he went on: "I give thanks for my baptism, for without it my life would have been very different. I believe that, as selfish and as stubborn as I have been, were it not for the presence of Christ I would have been insufferably worse."— Edward W. Jones.

FROM WITHIN.   God's intercourse with us is not an authority which crushes us into worms but a love which respects and safeguards our personalities, and the same must be the law of our intercourse with one another, as individuals and as nations. He knocks at the door of our lives, and we can let him in, but the latch is on our side. It is from within human personality that he seeks to help us through prophet and saint and sage, supremely through the expression of his character in Jesus Christ, and through all the ages by the whisper of his Spirit in our hearts, and it is through our own personalities that the response which admits his love and life must be made.— W. C. Braitwaite.

PASS IT ON.   If what you have gained from your religion is something that you could possibly hold to yourself without wanting to impart it to other people, then it is not God's best gift in the gospel and it is not salvation. The fact that you are not passing it on proves that you haven't got it. If you have got it, it will make you pass it on because of what it is.—William Temple.

CONTRADICTION.   All Christians must be in the ministry, whatever their occupation, because a non-witnessing follower of Christ is a contradiction in terms.—Elton Trueblood.

QUERY.   George Docherty entertained a friend, a Scottish minister who had never been to the United States before. After seeing some of the sky-scraping, air-conditioned buildings that dot the skyline of every large city in this country, after visiting several electronically-equipped medical complexes, and after viewing Kennedy Space Center, his friend turned to Dr. Docherty and asked: "How does a preacher say to the people of the United States, 'You cannot save yourself'?"— John Thompson.

WHAT THE SAMARITAN DID.   Christian love is not something vague and general. Christian love is specific and practical. It is not love of an idea or principle. It is love of people, not people in general, but individuals one by one. The good Samaritan did not go home and form a committee or write a letter to the local newspaper or call one of the organized charities. He changed his own plans, interrupted his journey, and used his own resources to put his love into action right then. Perhaps we may think that an act of this kind is a little thing, but such an act as this is contagious and spreads with the speed of light. —Gerald Kennedy.

EPITAPH.   Not far from New Delhi on a simple black stone are the words of Gandhi. The epitaph reads, "My prayer for my country is that India will be so strong that she will give herself for the world: a man for his family, a family for a village, a village for a district, a district for the country, the country for the world."

TAKING TIME.   Thornton Wilder in *Our Town* gives us a poignant slice of life, tracing the childhood, youth, courtship, marriage, and life of a young girl. She has such trouble accepting her death that she is allowed, given dramatic license, to return to any day of her life that she chooses, but she is counseled by experienced elders not to choose any day that is very important. She chooses her fourteenth birthday to relive. There is her mother in the kitchen, so busy doing for her, baking the cake, planning the party, and rushing around, that their love is submerged in the haste of it all. "Listen to me! Look at me and see me! Let's really take time to know and to touch one another! This time is too precious to waste living just on the surface of life!" But her mother doesn't hear, and the day is over, and she returns to the narrator to report to him: "They just don't understand. None of us understands, do we, until it's too late?"—James D. Righter in *Virginia Advocate*.

NOT A MISTAKE.   It's never a mistake to tell a man how interesting he is, to say "I don't know" if you really don't, to take the time and trouble to put another person at ease, to ask the advice of an expert, to listen attentively to what another person is saying, to take good advice and to withhold offering your own until asked.—*The War Cry.*

PLAYING IT SAFE.   The sin of this generation of Christians may be that we play it safe. We are the one-talent person whose sin was not that he was lazy but that he was afraid. He was fearful of losing what he had. There are times in the life of every Christian when he must go for broke. Just as we have deodorized the faith, so we have taken the risk out of it.—W. Stanley Mooneyham.

MODERN MAN.   If he is in a tight spot, he borrows money on the furniture. If he is low, he lights a cigarette. If he is lonely, he goes to a movie. If he is maladjusted, he goes to a psychiatrist. If he has a headache, he takes an aspirin. All from the outside in. The Christian remedy is from the inside out.—E. Stanley Jones.

TOO BUSY.   Julia Ward Howe was talking to Charles Sumner, the distinguished senator from Massachusetts. She asked him to interest himself in the case of a person who needed help. The senator answered, "Julia, I've become so busy I can no longer concern myself with individuals." "Charles," she replied, "that's remarkable. Even God hasn't reached that stage yet."—*The Presbyterian Outlook.*

WORSHIP FEELINGS.   The sign on the front of a church in Indianapolis reads: "Join us for worship. You will feel better for it!" It is far from obvious that worship will make one feel better. To be sure, in a very ultimate sense, surrendering oneself to God in thankful trust will make one be better. But along the way to being better the Christian is sure to go through times of feeling worse. Repentance, after all, involves a painful loss of self, an abandonment of false securities, and the travail of new birth. It is also true with respect to what happens on Sunday mornings. Woe to you when they say it feels so good.— Richard John Neuhaus.

WONDER. Olive Schreiner, when a young child, read for the first time the words of Jesus. She ran to her mother crying: "Mummy, Mummy, isn't it wonderful? Now we can all live like this."

ADVICE. Charlie Brown says to Lucy, "I've never felt so low in my life. I just don't belong anywhere. I just don't fit in anywhere. I just don't know what I am going to do." Lucy says: "Have you thought of looking at life this way, Charlie Brown? Life is a deck of cards, and we are all just part of the deck. Some of us are aces, some are 10s, or 9s or 5s or 4s. We can't all be face cards, can we, Charlie Brown? We can't all be kings and queens." "No, I guess we can't," he says. "Look at it this way, Charlie Brown," she says. "Maybe you are the two of clubs." "I doubt it," says Charlie Brown. "Even the two of clubs takes a trick now and then!"

WORSHIP. Worship loosely defined means those religious exercises in which we engage as a part of the community that remembers Jesus. The New Testament word is *ekklesia* which means simply assembly. The assembling of the people of God was essential to their life. They assembled for the purpose of worship. This was in the tradition of the Old Testament where the assembling of the people of God was fundamental to the very understanding of their identity. When we think of the assembly of the community of those who remember Jesus, we inevitably think in terms of times, places, rites, and ceremonies. We think of a building. We think of appointments within a sanctuary—a baptismal font, a communion table, a pulpit, an organ with the pipes prominently displayed where people can count them. We think of vestments and of a cross. All these are symbols and indirect means of communication. They are efforts to manifest that which is beyond manifestation, to represent that which cannot be finally represented, to express that which is ultimately inexpressible, and to communicate that which is incommunicable.—Kenneth G. Phifer.

FAITH-LIFT. A pastor was saying how much the members of the congregation appreciated the planting of a few attractive flowers on the church lawn. One woman put it this way: "The whole place looks like it has had a face-lift!" It also sounds like a faith-lift.—*The War Cry.*

ATTAINING LOVE. There are many who want me to tell them of secret ways of becoming perfect, and I can only tell them that the whole secret is a hearty love of God and the only way of attaining that love is by loving. Just as you learn to speak by speaking, to run by running, and to work by working, so do you learn to love God and man by loving. Begin as a mere apprentice and the very power of love will lead you to become a master of the art.—Frances of Sales.

CARING. A boy, carrying a basket of eggs in the street, tripped on the curbstone, dropped the basket, and smashed the eggs. People gathered round, as people do. One said, "What a pity!" Another said: "Poor little chap! I hope he won't get a whipping." Another said: "I am sorry he is crying. Let's comfort him." Then one man stepped out of the crowd, put his hand in his pocket, and said, "I care half-a-crown." Turning to the man next to him, he said, "How much do you care?" He replied, "I care a shilling."—Leslie D. Weatherhead.

PASSION FOR SOULS. We are Christlike just in proportion as we possess a passion for souls. It has often been said that we cannot keep Jesus unless we give him away. Spiritual life is like electricity. No current passes through unless the wire is connected at the sending end as well as at the receiving end.—Frank Laubach.

EXPLANATION. A little boy was asked by his Sunday School teacher to draw some scene out of the nativity account in the Bible. He took his crayons in hand and drew an airplane with a lady, a man, and a little child in the back of the plane and another man in the front. The teacher asked, "What is this?" He replied, "This is

Mary and Joseph and the baby Jesus on the flight into Egypt!" "But who is the man in the front of the plane?" queried the teacher. "Oh," he said, "that is Pontius the Pilate."—James R. Webb.

HOLY FIRE.   Join the great company of those who make the barren places of life fruitful with kindness. Carry a vision of heaven in your hearts, and you shall make your home, your college, and the world correspond to that vision. Your success and happiness lie in you. External conditions are the accidents of life, its outer trappings. The great, enduring realities are love and service. Joy is the holy fire that keeps our purpose warm and our intelligence aglow. Resolve to keep happy, and your joy and you shall form an invincible host against difficulty.—Helen Keller.

JUDGMENT.   I do not believe that we human beings can erect a kingdom of God on this earth and transform our world into a paradise. Or that we might be able to produce a new human being through a change of the social structure. To me it is much more certain that man has the fall in his past and cannot escape its sphere of influence. Even if he were to break away to other galaxies, he would take himself and his questionableness along.—Helmut Thielicke.

COMMENT IN 1889.   America is now sauntering through her resources and through the mazes of her politics with easy nonchalance; but presently there will come a time when she will be surprised to find herself grown old—a country crowded, strained, perplexed—when she will be obliged to fall back upon her conservatism, obliged to pull herself together, adopt a new regimen of life, husband her resources, concentrate her strength, steady her methods, sober her views, restrict her vagaries, trust her best, not average, members.—Woodrow Wilson.

LIVING BY HOPE.   The hoping person is fully aware of the harshness and losses of life. In order to hope, one must have had experience of fearing, doubting, or de-

spairing. Hope is generated out of a tragic sense of life. It is painfully realistic about life and the obstacles to fulfillment, within and without. The Christian believer cannot simply focus attention on the positive in life, since there is a cross at the heart of Christian faith preceding any resurrection. For the devout Jew, there is the remembrance of the painful exile, out of which deliverance comes. Unless a person passes through a "valley of the shadow of death," can genuine hope be born? With this understanding we can appreciate anew St. Paul's insistence that everyone lives by hope. Hope is the sense of possibility. In despair and trouble, it is the sense of a way out and a destiny that is going somewhere, even if not to the specific place one had in mind.—Roy W. Fairchild from Finding Hope Again (Harper & Row).

INVITATION.   God comes to us in Jesus Christ to invite us to set aside all lesser loyalties and to center our life and faith on him. God in Jesus Christ stands over against all the lesser gods we worship and invites us to such faithful worship of him so as to know that life which is life indeed. Jesus stands for the person we can become and promises us God's help to become that person and to do the deeds of Christian love and justice.—L. Wilson Kilgore.

ONE DAY AT A TIME.   A lady met with a serious accident which necessitated a painful surgical operation and many months of confinement in bed. When the physician had finished his work and was taking his leave, the patient asked, "Doctor, how long shall I have to lie here helpless?" "Oh, only one day at a time" was the cheery answer. And the poor sufferer was not only comforted for the moment but many times during the succeeding weary weeks did the thought, "only one day at a time," come back with its quieting influence.—Marjorie W. Smith in the P.E.O. Record.

SOURCE OF REFRESHMENT.   Michael Steinberg reports a revealing episode in Haydn's life. It seems that when he was seventy a choral society in the little town of Bergen on the Baltic isle of Rugen had performed his oratorio, *The Creation*, and had written to thank him for the joy his music had brought to them. Haydn wrote in reply: "You give me welcome assurance —and this is the greatest comfort in my declining years. Often as I struggled with obstacles of every kind opposed to my works—often as my physical and mental powers sank, and I had difficulty in keeping to my chosen course—an inner voice whispered to me: 'There are so few happy and contented men here below—on every hand care and sorrow pursue them—perhaps your work may some day be a source from which men laden with anxieties and burdened with affairs may derive a few moments of rest and refreshment.' This, then, was a powerful motive to persevere, this the reason why I can even now look back with profound satisfaction on what I have accomplished in my art."

HIS BAPTISM.   St. Louis IX of France was born in 1215 and became king of France at the age of eleven, under the regency of his mother. For forty years he was an energetic and considerate ruler. So prayerful and self-sacrificing was his life that even Voltaire admitted, "He united the virtues of a king to those of a hero, to those of a man." This Christlike king used to sign himself "Louis de Poissy" (Louis of Poissy)—the city where he was baptized. One day he remarked to a courtier, "In Poissy I received the greatest honor of my life." "Your majesty is mistaken," the courtier objected. "You mean in the city of Rheims." "I am not mistaken," insisted the monarch. "It is true that in Rheims I was consecrated king on earth, but I was made a Christian in Poissy, and there I acquired my right to a throne in heaven." —Arthur Tonne.

CANDLEFLAME.   We walk by faith, but let us remember what faith is for. That little candleflame, lighted at the altar of the Most High, was given us that, guarding it from the wailing winds of doubt and the shuddering earthquakes of pain, we might hold its flickering light close to the ground where we must daily walk—not to hold aloft in a vain attempt to peer into things too high for us, lest from the darkness between the stars we hear the mocking laughter of God.—Kenneth J. Foreman.

CONTROLLING ANGER.   A man was raging against a Quaker who quietly bore his ill-temper. Afterward the man felt ashamed of himself and asked the Quaker how he was able to manage such self-control. The Quaker replied: "Friend, I will tell thee. I was naturally hot and violent. I found it imprudent. I observed that people in anger speak loudly. I made it a rule not to allow my voice to go above a certain level, and by careful observance I have, by the blessing of God, mastered my natural temper."—Bernard Brunsting.

LEGEND.   There is a legend about a bird which sings just once in its life more sweetly than any other creature on the face of the earth. From the moment it leaves the nest, it searches for a thorn tree, and does not rest until it has found one. Then, singing among the savage branches, it impales itself upon the longest, sharpest spine. And, dying, it rises above its own agony to outcarol the lark and the nightingale. One superlative song, existence the price. But the whole world stills to listen, and God in his heaven smiles. For the best is only bought at great pain . . . or so says the legend.—Colleen McCullough in *The Thornbirds.*

CITIZEN POLITICIANS.   If religious values are to be considered in collective decision-making, persons of religious faith must do whatever is necessary to assure their consideration. Religiously sensitive persons must become conscientious citizen-politicians if there are to be satisfactory and effective solutions to the public policy problems that confront every generation.—James I. Spainhower.

CRITICISM.   The Tang emperor, Li-Shih-Min, founder of the dynasty, was once infuriated by a censor, Tai Tsung, who insisted on contradicting him in front of the court. When he told his wife that he would never be master in his own empire as long as this critic drew breath, his empress withdrew to her dressing room and later returned in ceremonial robes. "I have heard," she said, "that an enlightened emperor finds courageous censors. You have just admitted that you have such a one. I have robed myself in your honor."—Edward G. Bolland in *Pastoral Life.*

FRUITION.   While Jesus is the focus of the biblical hope, he is not the conclusion of that hope. The Bible suggests that the kingdom of promise which begins in him will reach some further culmination in the mercy of God. That is why Jesus taught his disciples to pray, "Thy kingdom come." So we hope that the justice and mercy we have known in Jesus may reach their full fruition in God's own time and in God's own way. And we remember that God's ways are often surprising. We wait to be astonished by that kingdom which may come as oddly as Christ came in Bethlehem.—David Bartlett in *The American Baptist.*

GREATNESS.   The church is made great not by soft seats and subdued light but by wise and courageous leadership both in the pulpit and in the pew. She is made great not by sweet tones of the organ but by gentle yet strong personalities that somehow reflect Christ. Not by tall towers with their chimes and bells but by the lofty vision of the tall-souled people is the church made great. The church becomes great not by a big budget but by big hearts in big people who love and serve. Not by a large membership but by God's presence and direction.—*The Anglican Digest.*

SPELLED OUT.   What about the main thing in life, all its riddles? If you want, I'll spell it out for you right now. Do not pursue what is illusory—property and position: All that is gained at the expense of your nerves decade after decade and is confiscated in one fell night. Live with a steady superiority over life. Don't be afraid of misfortune and do not yearn after happiness. Our envy of others devours us most of all. Rub your eyes and purify your heart; and prize above all else in the world those who love you and wish you well.—Aleksandr Solzhenitsyn.

BECAUSE OF JESUS.   Jesus said it is better to give than to receive, better to love than to be loved, better to suffer wrongs than to seek revenge, better to be poor and humble than to be rich and proud, and better to die trusting in the ultimate vindication of God's righteousness than to live with a craven compromise. Jesus can be worshiped, loved, admired, or hated. But he cannot easily be ignored. After twenty centuries his radically unselfish lifestyle remains a challenge to which each one of us, sooner or later, must respond in some way. Because he reminds us of that challenge, Christmas can never become entirely pagan, however hard our culture works to make it so.—Louis Cassels.

WHAT MAKES A HYMN "GOOD"?   (1) Good hymns are God-centered, not man-centered. (2) Good hymns are theologically sound. (3) Good hymns are doctrinal in content. (4) Good hymns have words of beauty, dignity, reverence, and simplicity. (5) Good hymns display preciseness and finesse of poetic technique and expression. (6) Good hymns turn heavenward.—E. Margaret Clarkson in *Christianity Today.*

NEVERTHELESS.   Faith is always connected with something that I cannot prove and which is nonetheless definitely certain to me. It is also always a belief against something, for example, against the evidence which appears to contradict my faith. In faith there is, to put it biblically, a "nevertheless."—Helmut Thielicke.

BY DISCIPLINE AND EFFORT.   ~~Shortly~~ after I turned eighteen, I learned that an old hero of mine, a famous German scientist, had written a paper claiming that we could get to the moon with rockets. I couldn't wait to get that paper. But when it came, my heart sank. The paper had almost no text to it. It was one long, complicated mathematical equation.

The trouble was, I didn't like math. I'd failed the subject in school. But this is what it took to get a rocket into space. Not romantic stories. Not daydreams but math. When I found that I'd have to learn math if I wanted to put a rocket into space, I learned math. And with it, I eventually got rockets that could probe space too. But first came months and years of hard, unromantic work.

I think prayer is the hardest kind of work, if in work you include the ideas of discipline, regularity, effort, and sacrifice. To be effective, prayer has to be backed up by discipline and effort.—Wernher von Braun.

SACRAMENTAL VIEW.   It is in the sacramental view of the universe, both of its material and of its spiritual elements, that there is given hope of making human both politics and economics and of making effectual both faith and love.—William Temple.

WHAT LOST?   Who can deny that it is well for trains to run on schedule, for meetings to begin promptly, for efficiency to be measured by time studies? By ordering time in abstract modules we have gained the regularity necessary to live with the machines we have created. And we have been rewarded with what we unquestionably consider a higher standard of living. But what have we lost in the process? —Sam Keen.

POSTSCRIPT.   Arthur Gordon tells of that day when his family decided to move from the old family homestead in Georgia. While going through the multitude of things, he came upon a bundle of letters written by his grandmother to members of the family just after the Civil War period. They had been stuck away in an old trunk in the attic.

As he began to read through a few of the letters, Arthur's attention was caught by the unusual way in which his grandmother closed each one with this line, "Have I told you lately what a wonderful person you really are?"

This post–Civil War era was not exactly a time known for its charm, but here was a lady who had the insight and gracious-ness in writing to her family to keep alive her affections by asking, "Have I told you lately what a wonderful person you really are?"—Carl J. Sanders.

HE WOULDN'T CHANGE.   Some years ago there was a newspaper report about a man in England named Arthur Arch. He had just turned 95. But the newsworthy thing about Arthur Arch was that for forty-two years he had been precisely twenty minutes late for any meeting or appointment he had. Not that he was not prompt. He was precisely prompt. However, he was always twenty minutes late. He reported that as a result he had been fired a half-dozen times for tardiness. He had missed a great many trains. When asked to explain why he was always twenty minutes late, he said: "It's all very simple. In 1922 the clocks were changed twenty minutes. I never accepted this. Nobody was going to take twenty minutes off my life. I have just always kept my watch at the old time— twenty minutes late." He vowed that he was never going to change his clocks to be in step with the world. "I am going to die twenty minutes late to show them I was right!"—Hoover Rupert.

WHAT IS SIN?   Sin is leaving home without caring, cutting yourself off from the cradle of your existence. Sin is trying to live as though you had no home, no God, no one but yourself to be responsible to or for.—Theodore P. Ferris.

TRUST.   Trust in yourself and you are doomed to disappointment, trust in your friends and they will die and leave you, trust in money and you may have it taken from you, trust in reputation and some slanderous tongue may blast it, but trust in God and you are never to be confounded in time or eternity.—Dwight L. Moody.

ONE MAN'S SIN.   A man living in a village in Scotland once wore a strange coat to church. The front of the coat was completely covered with patches, large and small and of various sizes and colors. On the back of the coat was only one tiny, almost inconspicuous patch. His friends

wait to question him about the
ll," he responded, "the patches
at of the coat represent the sins
of my neighbors. As you can see, they
come in various sizes, shapes, and colors
and are quite numerous." "But what
about the patch on the back?" asked someone. "Oh," he replied, "that's my sin. As
you can see, it is quite small, and I can't
even see it when I have the coat on."—
John Wade.

KEY TO MEANING. A living experience
of God is the crowning knowledge attaina-
ble to a human mind. Each one of us needs
the redemptive power of religion for his
own sake, for on the tiny stage of the
human soul all the vast world tragedy of
good and evil is re-enacted. In the best
social order that is conceivable man will
still smolder with lust and ambition and be
lashed by hate and jealousy as with the
whip of a slave driver. No material comfort
and plenty can satisfy the restless soul in
us and give us peace with ourselves. All
who have made test of it agree that religion alone holds the key to the ultimate
meaning of life, and each of us must find
his way into the inner mysteries alone.—
Walter Rauschenbusch.

GRATITUDE. It is recorded of the Pilgrims in Plymouth that "at noon men stag-
gered by reason of faintness for want of
food, yet ere night, by the good providence and blessing of God, we have enjoyed such a plenty as though the windows
of heaven had been opened to us." Harry
C. Kennet said that Elder Brewster, sitting
down to a meal of clams and a cup of cold
water, looked up to heaven and returned
thanks "for the abundance of the sea and
for the treasures hid in the sand." In spite
of their troubles and difficulties, the Pilgrims worked, prayed, and built homes in
a new world.—David A. MacLennan.

TIMING. If you will not fight for the
right when you can easily win without
bloodshed and if you will not fight when
your victory will be sure and not too
costly, you may come to the moment when
you will have to fight with all odds against
you and only a precarious chance of survival. There may even be a worse case.
You may have to fight when there is no
hope for victory because it is better to perish than to live as slaves.—Winston
Churchill.

WHOLENESS. The fingers that weaved
the rainbow into a scarf and wrapped it
around the shoulders of the dying storm,
the fingers that painted the lily-bell and
threw out the planets, the fingers that
were dipped in the mighty sea of eternity
and shook out this old planet, making the
ocean to drop and the rivers to stream—
the same fingers can take hold on these
tangled lives and can make them whole
again.—Gypsy Smith.

COUNTLESS PROBLEMS. The problems
of taking ourselves too seriously are
countless. Afraid to fail, we no longer risk.
Afraid that someone will see behind our
image, we no longer share. Afraid that we
will appear to need help, we can no longer
be vulnerable. Afraid to appear not religious enough to some, we can no longer
confess. We withdraw into a petty world
consumed with emptiness and fear, covered with a thick shell, worshiping an im-
potent God. The tragic result of taking
ourselves too seriously is that in our fear
of becoming childlike, in our fear of
becoming a fool for Christ, and in our fear
of being seen as we are, we discover all too
late that it is impossible to be fully human
and fully alive.—LaVon Koerner.

VIRTUE. To be able everywhere one
goes to carry five things into practice constitutes virtue. They are courtesy, magnanimity, sincerity, earnestness, and kindness. With courtesy you avoid insult. With
magnanimity you win all. With sincerity
men will trust you. With earnestness you
will have success. With kindness you will
be fit to command others.—Confucius.

FORGIVEN. A man was converted in a
revival meeting. The next morning a
friend who had heard of his high adventure met him and said, "Jim, I understand
you were converted last night." "Yes,"

said Jim, "I was converted." "Well," continued his friend, "I suppose that now you will pay me that twenty-five dollars you owe me." "No," said Jim, "the Lord forgave me of that along with my other sins."

ORDINARY EGG.   It may be hard for an egg to turn into a bird. It would be a jolly sight harder for it to learn to fly while remaining an egg. We're like eggs at present. And you can't go on indefinitely being just an ordinary, decent egg. We must be hatched or go bad.—C. S. Lewis.

UNWORTHY.   In a museum in Vienna is the piano which Beethoven used during his days of creativity. One day a brash young American girl sat down at the piano and began playing a bit of jazz on it. After a while she turned to the attendant and asked him if any famous pianists had ever visited the museum and seen the piano. The man answered that the world-famous pianist Paderewski had once seen the fine instrument. "Oh," said the girl, "he must have played something beautiful on it." "On the contrary," replied the attendant, "Paderewski did not feel worthy of touching it."—Charles E. Ferrell.

AN ANCIENT TALE.   A rabbi traveling in dangerous countryside with a donkey, a lamp, and a hen to provide eggs, uncomplainingly bowed to God's will when the donkey bolted, the lamp blew out, and the hen died. In the morning he discovered that marauding soldiers had passed within yards and would certainly have killed him if the donkey had brayed, the light betrayed his presence, or the hen clucked.—C. Tyson Jarrell.

GIFT OF CARING.   Every human being has a great yet often unknown gift to care, to be compassionate, to become present to the other, to listen, to hear and to receive. If that gift would be set free and made available, miracles could take place. Those who can sit in silence with their fellowman, not knowing what to say but knowing that they should be there, can bring new life in a dying heart.—Henri Nouwen.

ENIGMA AND CHALLENGE.   To the speculative mind, the world is an enigma. To the religious mind, the world is a challenge. Speculation does not precede faith. Worship of God precedes affirmation of his realness. We praise before we prove. We respond before we question.—Abraham J. Heschel.

COUNSEL.   The young bride-to-be was highly nervous at the rehearsal. She seemed so confused that she was unable even to practice the service. So the clergyman called her into his study. The minister said to her: "I know you're anxious and tomorrow is going to be scary and emotional, but I have a favorite formula which will carry you through the ceremony.

"When you enter the church and the procession begins, you will be walking down the same aisle that you have walked down many times before. There is nothing strange or different about those few yards. Just think of all the Sundays you have gone down them to find your seat in the pew. Concentrate on that *aisle.*

"When you are about halfway down, you will look up and you will see the altar before which you and your family have worshiped many years. Concentrate on that *altar.*

"Then when you're two-thirds of the way down, you will see the one to whom you will pledge your love and with whom you will spend the rest of your life. Concentrate on *him.* "

The girl seemed a little calmer when she left the study. The practice service went well. And by next afternoon, when the wedding march began, she seemed completely composed. Except for one small thing. As she was slowly walking down the church, the people in each pew she passed began chuckling. You see, they overheard her muttering: "Aisle. Altar. Him! Aisle. Altar. Him! I'll alter him!"—Roger O. Douglas.

GIFT OF GRACE.   It is true that what is an unspeakable gift of God for the lonely individual is easily disregarded and trodden underfoot by those who have the gift every day. It is easily forgotten that the fellowship of Christian brethren is a gift of grace, a gift of the kingdom of God that any day may be taken from us, that the time that still separates us from utter loneliness may be brief indeed. Therefore, let him who until now has had the privilege of living a common Christian life with other Christians praise God's grace from the bottom of his heart. Let him thank God on his knees and declare, "It is grace, nothing but grace, that we are allowed to live in community with Christian brethren."—Dietrich Bonhoeffer.

LOVING.   He had been walking for an hour, and his journey was only half completed. The snow was deep, and the church was still far away. Stopping to rest in a doorway, a stranger asked, "Where are you going, son?" "Going to Dr. Moody's church," replied the boy. The stranger asked, "Why do you walk past all these other churches to go to his church?" "Because they really know how to love a fellow down there," shouted the child.—Larry Kennedy.

CUE.   An eight-year-old boy was rather shy. His parents were very pleased when he was asked to announce the principals of the nativity in the school Christmas pageant. The father was so elated that he went out and bought him the finest suit he could find. To give his son some assurance, the father pinned the names of the characters of the nativity on the inside of the son's new coat. When the characters of the Christmas pageant appeared, the boy announced: "That is Jesus in the manger, Mary is nearby, and Joseph is standing next to her. The three men are er-er—" He could not remember, so he took a quick look on the inside of his coat and blurted out: "Hart, Schaffner, and Marx!"—John Thompson.

DAILY RECKONING.   If you had a bank that credited your account each morning with $86,400, that carried over no balance from day to day, and allowed you to keep no cash in your account, and every evening cancelled whatever part of the amount you had failed to use during the day, what would you do? Draw out every cent, of course!

Well, you have such a bank, and its name is "Time." Every morning it credits you with 86,400 seconds. Every night it rules off, as lost, whatever of this you have failed to invest to good purpose. It carries over no balances. It allows no overdrafts. Each day it opens a new account with you. Each night it burns the records of the day. If you fail to use the day's deposits, the loss is yours. There is no going back. There is no drawing against tomorrow. You must live in the present—on today's deposits. Invest it so as to get from it the utmost in health, happiness, and success. —Ken Sopher.

WORK TO BE DONE.   Open your eyes and look for some man or some work for the sake of men which needs a little time, a little friendship, a little sympathy, a little sociability, or a little human toil. Perhaps it is a lonely person or an embittered person or an invalid or some unfortunate inefficient to whom you can be something. —Albert Schweitzer.

BOOK LEARNING.   John Wesley had a conflict with a pious fellow who didn't have much use for education. The man wrote a letter to Wesley, saying, "The Lord has directed me to write to you that, while you know Greek and Hebrew, he can do without your book learning." Wesley replied: "Your letter received. I wish to say that while the Lord does not direct me to tell you, yet I wish to say to you on my own responsibility that the Lord does not need your ignorance either."—Charles E. Ferrell.

ONE MAN'S EFFORT.   Art Buchwald wrote about a man who singlehandedly tried to save New York City. The two of them were riding in a cab. When they got out, Buchwald's friend paid the cabbie and said: "Thanks for the ride. You did a superb job of driving." The cabdriver looked at him in a suspicious way and said, "What are you, some kind of wise guy?"

Buchwald asked his friend why he did that, and the reply was, "I'm trying to bring back love into New York City." He explained his mission: "Suppose that cabdriver had twenty fares. That means because I was nice to him he is now going to be nice to twenty other people. And those people in turn are going to be nice to clerks and waiters and employees and maybe even their own families."

Buchwald was skeptical. He asked, "Does it work?" The man replied, "Nothing is lost if it doesn't."

They continued down the street, the man being kind to people as they walked. Finally Buchwald said, "You just winked at a very plain-looking woman." "I know," the man replied, "and if she's a schoolteacher, her class will be in for a fantastic day."

GOSPEL AND FAITH.   The gospel and faith belong together inseparably. Therefore we may not speak of faith as something which could exist apart from the gospel. Faith is not a state of the soul which man must have or that by its aid he may receive the gospel. It is the gospel which is primary and creates faith and awakens it in us. When one hears the gospel and is conquered by it, that is faith. Faith is not prior to the gospel and independent of it. It arises only through one's meeting with the gospel.—Anders Nygren.

AN ASTRONAUT'S FAITH.   I tell people that God has a plan for them. I say that if God controls the universe with such infinite precision, controlling all the motions of the planets and stars, this is the working out of a perfect plan for outer space. I believe that God has the perfect plan for inner space, the spirit of man. This plan was manifest when he sent his Christ to die for us, to forgive our sins, and to show us he has a plan for our lives.—James B. Irwin.

THE FRUIT OF THE SPIRIT.   The fruit of the Spirit is an affectionate, lovable disposition, a radiant spirit and a cheerful temper, a tranquil mind and a quiet manner, a forebearing patience in provoking circumstances and with trying people, a sym-

pathetic insight and tactful helpfulness, generous judgment and a big-souled charity, loyalty and reliableness under all circumstances, humility that forgets self in the joy of others. In all things self-mastered and self-controlled.—Arthur W. Pink.

UPDATING.   A man went to an old friend to ask for a loan of some money. He offered no collateral, and he didn't want to be charged any interest. The friend expressed the fact that he didn't think their friendship was close enough to justify such a claim on it, and so he refused to make the loan.

"But, John," the man said, "how can you say that to me? We grew up together. I helped you make it through school. I even saved you from drowning once. I helped you get started in business. I persuaded my cousin to marry your sister. I can't believe that you'd say that we are not close enough for you to make me a loan."

"Oh," replied John, "I remember when you did all of that. What bothers me is what have you done for me lately?"—Jerry Hayner.

COMPELLING MISSION.   When Tolstoy finished his great novel, *War and Peace*, he was utterly exhausted. On it he had completely given his creative powers. He spent sleepless nights and was threatened with a severe nervous breakdown. One day a friend, walking with him along a country road, laid his hand on his arm and took him to task. "You are a man of means, a Russian count, a wealthy landowner with servants at your beck and call. Your future is secure. Why must you write books and drive yourself to the verge of insanity?" Tolstoy did not answer for two minutes. Then he stopped in the middle of the road and answered: "I am the slave of an inner compulsion. I have a consuming fire in my bones. I have to write or else go mad." Without a similar sense of an all-consuming and compelling mission we can achieve but very little either in art or in life.—Ernest Edward Smith.

LEADERSHIP.   General Eisenhower used to demonstrate the art of leadership with a simple piece of string. He'd put it on a table and say: "Pull it and it'll follow wherever you wish. Push it and it will go nowhere at all. It's just that way when it comes to leading people."

READING THE BIBLE.   I have endeavored to read the scriptures as though no one had read them before me, and I am as much on my guard against reading them today through my views yesterday as I am against being influenced by any foreign name, authority, or system whatever.—Alexander Campbell.

COMMITTED PEOPLE.   Little bands of committed men and women have an impact on history out of all proportion to their numbers or apparent abilities. In the main they are usually recruited from the least promising ranks of society. They are not noble or wealthy or well educated or particulary talented. All they have to offer is themselves, but that is more than others give to anything. For when a handful of wholly committed human beings give themselves fully to a great cause or faith, they are virtually irresistible. They cut through the partial and fleeting commitments of the rest of society like a buzz saw through peanut brittle.—Dean M. Kelley.

MADE WILLING.   F. B. Meyer once struggled with self-surrender and complete commitment to Christ, wanting to fully yield to Christ in discipleship and yet holding to a personal reservation which he was still unwilling to relinquish, and in the agony of the desperate conflict raging in his soul finally cried out, "Lord, I am not willing to surrender everything, but I am willing to be made willing."

PLANNING.   An architect was under cross-examination. "Are you a builder?" "No," replied the man, "I am an architect." The lawyer responded, "They are the same." "No," answered the architect. "An architect conceives the plan, and the builder is the carpenter." "Perhaps," said the lawyer, "you can inform the court who was the architect of the Tower of Babel?" The architect said, "There was no architect, sir, and hence the confusion."—George Lewis McGlothin.

FLICKERING CANDLE.   In Solzhenitsyn's play, Candle in the Wind, written in 1960, the plot centers in the work of scientists in the field of cybernetics. The protagonist of the play, Alex, is not sure it is real wisdom to tamper mechanically with the human personality, concerned that the artificially-induced state of happiness will dehumanize the patient. In one of the dialogues between Alex and the self-confident director of the cybernetics laboratory, Alex comments, "You once said you feel like a relay runner—that you would be proud to pass on the baton of Great Physics to the 21st Century. Well, I'd like to help pass on to the next century one particular baton, the flickering candle of our soul." The candle in the wind is the life of the soul, and Solzhenitsyn is observing that this candle has all but flickered out in our world today.—John Thompson.

FATHERS AND SONS.   A little boy asked his father, "Do fathers always know more than sons?" The father said, "Yes." The next question: "Daddy, who invented the steam engine?" The father said, "James Watt." Then the son came back, "But why didn't James Watt's father invent it?"—Gregory Bateson.

"PEANUTS" INSIGHT.   Linus was reading in the Bible one day and said: "I really enjoy reading Paul's letters. It's like opening someone else's mail."

PREEMINENCE.   There are a good many things God will put up with in the human heart, but there is one thing he will not put up with—a second place. He who offers him a second place offers him no place at all.—John Ruskin.

COMMUNICATING.   Giles Gilbert Scott, an English architect, designed the Liverpool Cathedral and the street telephone booth used throughout Britain. Both the cathedral and the telephone booth are for communication—God with man, man with God, man with man. When we are in fellowship with God, we can be in fellowship with our brothers and sisters. These fellowships, vertical and horizontal, can begin in the morning and make the day to come a great day.—Bramwell Tripp.

BEGINNING AGAIN.   An American visitor went to the studios of the English artist Burne-Jones. This woman had done considerable painting and was convinced that she had quite a talent. Burne-Jones endured looking at samples of her work and listening to her talk. At length he asked if she cared to look at some of his paintings before she left. The woman graciously agreed. He took her farther into his studio where many pictures were displayed. She was perceptive enough to know true art when she saw it and was hushed into silence. When bidding her farewell Burne-Jones said in a kindly voice, "And now, my dear, what to you mean to do with your art?" She lowered her head and replied quietly, "I mean to begin again."—John H. Townsend.

GRATITUDE.   On the roof of a church in Werden, Germany, one can see the stone carving of a lamb. There is a story behind that stone. A man was working on the roof of this church when his safety rope broke and he pitched headlong into the churchyard below. The yard was cluttered with huge stones. But the man was not hurt seriously. Between two of the blocks a lamb was nibbling grass. The man fell on the lamb, crushing it to death, and breaking what would have been a fatal fall. In gratitude that workman carved a lamb out of a stone and placed it on the roof. It was a gracious way of expressing his thanks to the dumb animal that had unknowingly saved his life.—Arthur Tonne.

GUIDANCE.   A friend of mine was getting off a train in the Cleveland terminal, and a young man got off in front of him, carrying a suitcase in one hand and a cane in the other. The man walked awkwardly as he felt his way with the cane. "May I help you carry your suitcase?" my friend asked.

"No, thanks, I don't need any help with the suitcase" came the reply. "But if you wish you may guide me up these stairs so I won't run into anyone. I am blind and I have a new set of artificial legs. But I've got to learn to make my own way, you know."

When they got to the top of the stairs, my friend took the young man rather firmly by the arm to guide him through the crowd entering the terminal. But the blind man stopped at once and spoke quietly: "No, don't take possession of me. Just guide me, please. Put your hand on my shoulder. That's all I need."—William L. Stidger.

UNDER ARREST.   During a period of fierce opposition to organized religion in Soviet Russia, the secret police raided a humble home where they knew a Christian group met for study and worship. After identifying the offenders, the officer in charge announced that there were seven under arrest. "No," corrected an aged Christian, "there are not seven but eight." Annoyed, the officer counted again. "Seven is all I find," he said. "Who is the eighth?" "Jesus our Lord" came the response.

WHAT GOD ASKS.   One often hears people say, "If I were President of the United States, if I were General of the Army, if I were Admiral of the Fleet, if I were Secretary of State, then I would do thus and so." But you are not, and in all probability you never will be. God only asks us to do the best we can with what we have where we are. He judges us not by our achievements but by our honest efforts; not by how near we are to the top of the mountain but by the direction which we are facing. The blunt fact is we could all be better than we are and do better than we do. We were meant to fly like eagles, and we have no right to act like sparrows. No one will ever be able to say, "I have done everything I possibly could."—Joseph R. Sizoo.

BIDING THEIR TIME. Miss Perkins was a little old lady who lived by herself in a large house on a busy street very near the center of the city. She dressed in old-fashioned clothing and seemed a social anachronism in both her appearance and manner. How she manicured her garden! Especially in autumn she must have raked the fallen leaves several times a day. One thought that she sat near the window and watched them fall and then rushed out to catch them before they defiled her precious lawn. A group of doctors bought the adjacent property with a view to erecting a large medical arts building and having next to it a sizable parking lot. Miss Perkins's house stood squarely in the middle of this. Would she sell? She would not, for any price. In this house she had been born and in this house she intended to die. So the doctors did not argue. They put the building on one side of her and the parking lot on the other, knowing that nature would take care of the situation and that after Miss Perkins's death they could name their own price and tear the house down.

Many people feel exactly that way about the church—an old-fashioned institution to be humored and tolerated because it is on its way out anyway. Before long it can be torn down completely to make way for a medical building, a scientific laboratory, a social agency, or even a broadcasting studio. These things, after all, perform the church's function more effectively. These things make religion unnecessary.—Leonard Griffith.

WHOM TO HONOR. There was a saint who was a renowned preacher. But it was this renown which troubled him no end and caused him grief, for it tempted him to think well of himself and to consider that perhaps it was his own wisdom he was speaking and not that of the holy teachings. Thus whenever he would be praised after having preached a fine sermon, he would grow angry and turn his face away.

On one such occasion, after having delivered an especially impressive message, a number of people began to laud him for his wonderful words. Able to hear no more but controlling his anger, he said to them, "Be silent and listen to what I have to say.

"In a small, out-of-the-way Russian town there lived a mayor whose life was as ordinary and uneventful as the life of any other mayor of a small out-of-the-way Russian town. Imagine his astonishment one day, when out of the clear blue sky there walked into his humble office the Czar of all the Russians. He was beside himself with excitement. He did not know what to do first. He bowed and scraped and bowed again. He kissed the boots of the Czar, arranged the room, and prepared the best chair for him to rest on.

" 'No,' said the Czar, 'I don't want all this attention. Everywhere I go people put on a show, abandon their daily tasks, dress in their finery, and act their best. For once in my life I want to see my people as they really are, without preparation or affectation. Come, disguise me as a peasant, and we shall visit the town.'

"The mayor, taken aback by the strange request but obedient to the Czar's every wish, found a proper disguise and made the Czar over into a peasant. Still unsure, he went to get the Czar's carriage. 'No, it is your carriage we shall ride in.' He offered the Czar his seat. 'No, you sit in your accustomed seat, and I shall sit at your feet.' And so they traveled slowly through the village, stopping at every corner and viewing the life of the people. Wherever they went, the people, seeing the mayor seated in his official place in the official carriage, bowed low, greeting him with the highest respect and honor.

"Imagine how the mayor felt," concluded the preacher, "when he saw the people saluting him, honoring him, praising him—and ignoring the Czar!"—Samuel H. Dresner.

OBSERVATION. A boy from the Middle West who had never before seen the ocean made a trip to the West Coast. As he looked out across the vast Pacific, he stood quietly. "Well," asked a friend, "what do you think of it?" "It's wonderful," replied the boy, "but I hate to see all that water out there doing nothing."—Wallace Fridy.

AN OLD LEGEND.   Reprobus, a giant of vast stature, was in search of a man stronger than his royal self. Neither could Reprobus serve the devil for the devil feared the cross. By the aid of a hermit he decided to serve the cross. Finding that he had little gift for fasting and prayer, he devoted himself to a work of charity. On his broad shoulders he offered to carry travelers across a bridgeless river. One day a child asked to be carried across the stream. Halfway to the other shore, Reprobus felt his gigantic back straining under what was an unbearable weight, yet he reached shore with his burden. He said to the child, "If I had carried the whole world on my back, it could not have weighed as much as you." "Do not be surprised," the child replied, "for you have carried on your back the world and him who created it." Thus Reprobus became St. Christopher, the Christ-bearer.—Kendig Brubaker Cully.

AZTEC LEGEND.   The beautiful gardens of earth were inhabited by gods and goddesses who had only one regret—their lovely world was dark. Being gods, they determined to do something about it. Two deities were selected to sacrifice themselves so that the world might be illuminated. One god was rich and proud, and the other was poor and humble. Their Mexican names are difficult to pronounce, even more difficult to remember. The first was Tecuziztecatl, and the second was Nanaoatzin.

On top of a tremendous, five-storied pyramid which still stands near Mexico City—larger than the largest pyramid in Egypt—a great fire was kindled. To this fire the rich, young god Tecuziztecatl brought precious offerings of gorgeous feathers and jewels. But he lacked the courage to leap into the fire himself. Four times he failed. The world remained dark.

Then the poor god Nanaoatzin with his humble gifts came resolutely forward and in one swift jump reached the heart of the sacrificial flames. Immediately the sun appeared, a vast red ball of fire and light. Tecuziztecatl was so ashamed that he too sprang into the fire, and immediately the pale white moon appeared.—Stewart W. Herman.

RENEWAL.   I had the privilege of spending two days with Albert Schweitzer at his hospital in Lambaréné. It was a wonderful experience to follow him about during the day and join the staff for dinner in the evening. Schweitzer was eighty-four years old then, and he was active from morning until night. He climbed the hills, as agile as a goat, and he kept his eye on everything from the repairing of a boat to the performing of an operation. At night he was tired, and he looked tired. He ate without much conversation. Then he walked across the floor to the piano, and he walked like a weary man. We sang a hymn together, and he returned to his place. After the Lord's Prayer, he opened the Bible and read from the scriptures. Then, behold, a kind of miracle! The weariness dropped away, the eyes sparkled, the face was alight with the excitement of a child. The Bible seemed to have renewed his youth like the eagle's.—Gerald Kennedy.

TWO HEADS.   Sir William Wilberforce, elected to the English Parliament in 1780 and converted to Christ four years later, made the cause of slavery and its abolition in the British Empire his life's concern. After years of fighting this cancer of his country, now an old man, he won the battle. Parliament met one evening to outlaw the traffic in slaves. His good friend, the younger Pitt, addressing Parliament that night, closed with these words, "Tonight I am thinking of two heads and two pillows. One is the head of Napoleon, tossing feverishly on his pillow on the island of St. Helena, after having left a trail of blood from Jena to Waterloo. The other is the man whose life's work we are met to honor. If I were to choose, I would not choose the head of Napoleon. I would choose the head of him who will rest tonight, after our vote is taken, on the pillow of Wilberforce."—Alvin N. Rogness.

EVALUATION.   As the years pass, the world's esteem for Abraham Lincoln has grown steadily until Lincoln has become the most universally loved American of all time. But we easily forget that during his administration as President of the United States he was the object of constant attack. President Lincoln could read, almost any day he cared to take the trouble, scoffing criticisms of his appearance and his grammar, malicious attacks upon his character, or shockingly intemperate and hateful denunciations of his conduct in office. Less than a year before Lincoln was assassinated, shortly after his renomination as candidate for re-election and Andrew Johnson's nomination as vice-presidential candidate, the *New York World* published this evaluation of Lincoln and his political partner: "The age of statesmen is gone, the age of rail-splitters and tailors, of buffoons, boors and fanatics, has succeeded. In a crisis of the most appalling magnitude, the country is asked to consider the claims of two ignorant, boorish, third-rate backwoods lawyers, for the hightest stations in the government. God save the Republic!"—Harold E. Kohn.

STOREHOUSE. Louis Binstock wrote of a man, financially secure, with position and prestige, who confessed to his rabbi that he had nothing for which to live. He would not take "the same, old-time bunk —'Have faith in the Lord'—and presto! all your troubles are over, and life is beautiful forever afterward." The rabbi insisted that the man help himself by using the great storehouse of spiritual power God has placed within every soul. He told the old Chinese story of the little fish who had heard that without water no living creature could survive. The little fish swam frantically from pond to river to ocean in search of water, until a wise old fish convinced him he had been in water since the day he was born. The little fish began the long swim home and said, "I had water all the time, and I didn't know it."

SERENITY. There was a day, some three hundred years ago in Edinburgh, when the June sunshine poured into the condemned cell of a prison where James Guthrie, knight of Christ's covenant, was lying. His servant, James Cowie, was with him; and remembering as he awoke that this was to be the day of his dear master's execution, their last day on earth together, he began to weep, as even brave men have wept at the hour of final parting. His weeping aroused his master. "Come, come," said Guthrie gently, "no more of this!" Then pointing to the dancing sunbeams, he went on. "This is the day which the Lord hath made; we will rejoice and be glad in it." This is the strong, ineffable serenity of the man who has committed his soul to Christ, the resurrection and the life. For he, the vanquisher of death, is able to keep it secure in that decisive hour. —James S. Stewart.

LAMENT. Two English soldiers fought in the wars of Queen Anne, the one a petty officer and the other a private sentinel. They had been close friends for years but had quarreled over a love affair and had become bitter enemies. The officer then so misused his authority as to persecute the sentinel and fret him almost to the point of madness. This went on for months. One day, having a name for valor in the field, they were both selected to share in a desperate attack which was unsuccessful. In the retreat which followed the officer was struck down by a shot in the thigh, and as his old comrade rushed past him he cried, "Oh, Valentine, will you leave me here to perish?" Valentine, himself injured, immediately returned and in the midst of heavy fire bore his wounded enemy to what looked like a place of safety. As he reached it he was hit by a chance ball and fell dead under his burden. The officer, forgetting his wound, rose up and, tearing his hair and throwing himself on the bleeeding body, cried, "Ah, Valentine, was it for me, who have so barbarously used thee, that thou hast died?" —Hugh Miller.

DEPTH OF LOVE. J. R. P. Sclater told of a sculpture representing Christ and Mary Magdalene which he had seen during a holiday in Italy. Mary is often portrayed by painters and sculptors as a beautiful young girl, the victim of her own beauty and the lusts of men. This artist had expressed a different conception. He had represented her as a vice-ridden old hag, rotten with disease of body and spirit, and yet he had succeeded in imprinting on the ravaged face a dawning wonder and hope in the recognition that even for her Christ had a welcome and an ambition. The love of Christ went out unswervingly not only to the pitiful, sodden wreckage of humanity but also toward those who were actively malignant and venomous, who hated him and crucified him. "Father, forgive them; for they know not what they do." That cry from the cross is the measure of the depth of the love of Christ. It means that there is no depth of iniquity into which men and women may fall but there is a deeper depth of love waiting to receive them into its purifying embrace.—A. C. Craig.

ILLUMINATION.   Maude Royden had a friend who one troubled day said to her such a lovely thing that she remembered it and was helped by it all the rest of her life. It did so such for her that she was constantly sharing it with other people in distress. Long after she repeated it to the very friend who had first said it. The friend replied: "What a perfectly lovely thing to say. Who said it?" "You did," replied Miss Royden. "Oh, no," the friend answered, "it is a beautiful thing to say, but I never said it!"

That woman, illumined by fellowship with God, unconsciously became light to another's darkness. Distressed by a friend's need, she said what her illumined mind perceived, then forgot it. It seemed the natural thing to say—as natural as a remark about the weather or a bit of counsel out of rich experience. It was the natural thing to say, but it would not have been natural unless her mind had been naturalized to the situation by the grace of God. She had become so at home with the divine perspectives that, when she uttered them, they made no special impression on her. Later, when her own utterance was repeated to her, she did not recognize it as her own. That is the illumination of the saints. They are luminous without knowing it because they keep company with the great Luminary.—Albert E. Day.

FRUITFUL INFORMATION.   Phillip Guedella was writing the biography of the Duke of Wellington, and among the things which he had examined carefully was a packet of receipted bills—a "fruitful source of information," he calls it. Guedella said this: "Show me how a man spends his money, and you will show me what kind of a man he is."

PARABLE.   Hugh Price Hughes arrived in the city by train one cold, snowy morning. As he got off the train, the station was like many railroad stations with the crowds and the redcaps, save that in spite of the snow and the cold, everybody was barefooted. They wore no shoes. When he went into the station, it was the same. He could hardly contain his curiosity, but he walked on to take a cab. Again he noted that the cab driver was barefooted. "Pardon me," he said to the driver, "I was just wondering why you don't wear shoes. Don't you believe in shoes?" "Sure we do," said the driver. "Of course we believe in shoes." "Why don't you wear them then?" asked the man. "Ah, that's the question," said the driver. "Why don't we wear shoes? Why don't we?"

The man went on to the hotel. There it was the same. The clerk, the bellboys, everybody was barefooted. He went into the coffee shop, sat down at the table opposite a nice-looking fellow. But he couldn't help noting that the man was barefooted. "Pardon me, sir," he said, "I see you aren't wearing shoes. I wonder why? Don't you know about shoes?" "Of course I know about shoes," said the man. "Then why don't you wear them?" "Ah, that's the question," said the man. "Why don't we? Why don't we?"

After breakfast he walked out on the street in the snow. There again everybody was barefooted. At a red light he turned to a stranger and said, "Sir, I note that everybody in this town is barefooted. I wonder if you don't know about shoes. They would protect your feet from the cold, and they would give you many benefits." "We know about shoes," said the stranger. "Do you see that great building across the street with its tower? That's one of our great shoe-manufacturing establishments. We're very proud of it, and once a week great crowds of people gather to hear the man in charge over there tell them about shoes and how wonderful they are and what they can mean to man." "Then," asked the stranger, "why don't you wear shoes?"

ONE AT A TIME.   A parrot was the special pet of a certain hunting club, and its cage hung between the main dining room and one of the lounge rooms. As persons passed by, the parrot would say over and over the only words it knew: "One at a time, gentlemen, one at a time." There came a day when he escaped from his cage and wandered into the surrounding woods. Some of the members organized a searching party, and they found him just in time for he had blundered into a hornet's nest and they were stinging him. But the old parrot, in the midst of it all, was saying the only words he knew, "One at a time, gentlemen, one at a time!"—Robert E. Goodrich, Jr.

IN HIS STEPS.   Archibald Rutledge wrote of the widow of a black preacher who was always doing something for the poor and who seemed to rear all the orphans and illegitimate children in the community. He was so impressed by the quality of her life that he built her an immaculate little home in his own backyard. He completely equipped it with new furniture and moved her in. To his horror the first thing she did was to invite into her new, shining home the most disreputable woman in the county. "How," he remonstrated, "could you have invited that creature into your pretty new home?" The soft answer was "Jesus would."

ORIENTAL FABLE.   A man said to his neighbor, "I would like to borrow your rope." The neighbor answered: "I am sorry, but I am using my rope. I am tying up a heap of sand." And the man said to the neighbor, "You can't tie up sand with a rope." "Oh, yes," said the neighbor,

"you can do almost anything with a rope if you don't want to lend it."

HEALING.   I was preaching in a series of revival services. One morning a lady phoned, asking to see me. She seemed in distress, but I could not possibly free any time for her until after the service that night. I promised to talk with her then. When I did meet her, she was smiling and so happy that she seemed to bubble over.

I asked, "Are you sure you're the lady who phoned me this morning?"

She said, "Yes, but I don't need your help now, so I won't keep you."

I said, "Lady, when a person has changed as completely as you have, I want to know what happened." So we sat down in the front pew of the church, and she told me her story.

Her husband had died suddenly, leaving no money nor insurance for the support of his wife and their four children. He did have a small electrical-supply business. In the business was a man the husband had trained for six years, and the woman felt she could carry on the business with that man's help. She had one competitor in that community, and he tried to buy her out, offering only a fraction of what her business was worth. When she wouldn't sell, he became angry and told her he would force her out of business. He cut prices and did everything he could against her, yet she held on. Then one day the man her husband had trained told her he was quitting. He was going to work for the competitor, who had offered him more money than the woman could pay.

She carried on by herself as best she could, but it was a struggle. Sometimes her children did not have enough to eat. Worse was the hatred she had in her heart against the man who had hurt her. Hate is poison for both our souls and our bodies and she knew that, yet she could not seem to do anything about it.

It was in that situation she had phoned me that morning. That night she arranged for a neighbor to sit with her children, and she came to church to talk with me about it after the service.

My sermon that night was on the cross. I talked about how, through imagination and memory, we can actually see back across the years. In detail I described Christ's praying in Gethsemane, the coming of the soldiers, the betraying kiss of one he had trusted, and his trials before Herod and Pilate. I told about his humiliation before that mob as they stripped off his clothes, how they drove in the nails, hung him up to die, and then spat on him, mocked and ridiculed him.

I took about forty-five minutes to describe that picture as vividly as I could. Then I said: "Listen! He is about to speak!" We strained our ears and across the centuries his voice came clear and strong, saying, "Father, forgive them." Then I invited those present to come to the altar and pray.

The woman told me that, as she knelt, the only thing she could think of was the man she hated so. She found herself praying for him. She prayed the prayer the Master prayed, and she felt cleansed and whole again. She told me how she had no fear of the future. When Christ comes into our hearts, we can love even as he loved.
—Charles L. Allen.

EVERYTHING IN READINESS.   An estate was expertly tended by a caretaker. Every tree was trimmed, the grass cut, and stately beds of flowers were in bloom. Yet not a soul was around to take in the beauty except the caretaker. A visitor asked, "When was the owner last here?"

"Twelve years ago."

"Then from whom do you get your instructions?"

"From his agent living in Milan."

"But does he ever visit the estate to inspect it?"

"No."

"And yet you keep it trim as if he would come tomorrow?"

The gardener interrupted to say, "As if he were going to come today, sir."—Reuben K. Youngdahl.

WHITE HOUSE VISITOR.   An old druggist from Springfield, Illinois, made the journey to Washington for no other purpose than to see Abraham Lincoln and tell him a few yarns. It had been Mr. Lincoln's habit to stop in at the drug store from time to time to exchange stories with the quaint old man, and one day the druggist discovered that he usually did it when he was on the eve of a difficult law case or when he had some special load on his mind.

The old apothecary was under no delusions as to his own skill as a politician, and he had no requests to make of the President nor suggestions as to how the war was to be conducted. But he did have some good stories that were designed to relieve anxiety, and armed with a mind full of fun and good cheer he presented himself at the White House and was given a cordial welcome.

Late that night, when the dinner was done and all the guests were gone, Mr. Lincoln and Uncle Billy found themselves a quiet place. Then the President said, "Billy, what did you come to Washington for?"

"Just to see you, Mr. Lincoln," the old druggist replied. "Just to see you and tell you some yarns."

"Didn't you want a post office or anything?" the President persisted.

"No, sir, I just wanted to be with you for a little while."

And with that the President bowed his head for a moment, and lifting his eyes, infinitely sad, he began to unload his heart. For an hour he poured into the ear of the man he could trust all the pain and grief of his soul. No one knows what the Union may owe to the humble man who assumed a stewardship over another man's grief in the hour of his testing.—Roy L. Smith.

ADORATION.   There is a spot some 2,000 feet above Darjeeling, India, where a visit before daybreak, if the weather is favorable, may bring you the slow emergence of the whole Himalaya range from Kanchenjunga to Mt. Everest. To look at that immaculate, glittering sweep of white radiance is to have something happen in you. You do not want to climb the range, to photograph it, to paint it, to survey it, to quarry it, to mine it, or to own it. Your one longing is to be left in quiet before it to marvel that anything on this earth could be so wonderful. Adoration is something like that. There is an ancient Hindu prayer that says only, "Wonderful, wonderful, wonderful."—Douglas V. Steere.

EXPRESSING SYMPATHY.   My first pastorate after graduation was a rural congregation in Ontario, Canada, in an area composed of descendants of Northern Ireland settlers who were hard-working, devout, and frugal.

One of the village physicians was Dr. Ferguson, a bluff-speaking, able, and active man of over sixty years, who had a large practice covering a wide territory and responded to both day and night calls.

One bitterly cold and snowy night the doctor was called to a remote part of the county where a poor farmer's wife was in birth pains. Despite a long day's work, he set out in his cutter in the darkness over the poor roads on his mission of mercy. The birth was a complicated one, and just before the break of day the mother, in giving a life to the world, died. The husband was distraught, and it was with a heavy heart that Dr. Ferguson drove back to the village.

Tired and sad, he hitched his team to a post and entered the main store where a group of men were gathered around the big stove. He stamped the snow from his feet, unbelted his fur coat, and told the story of the tragedy of the practically destitute farmer, newly widowed, and with a new-born babe to care for. Voices were raised in sympathy. "What a pity!" was repeated over and over by the members of the group. The doctor's eyes traveled around the faces of the vocal sympathizers. Suddenly he whipped off his old fur cap and said, "Boys, how much is your sympathy worth?"—James W. Clarke.

SECURITY.   Linus, sitting with his beloved blanket in one hand and his thumb in his mouth, is suddenly attacked by Snoopy, the unpredictable dog, who latches on to the blanket and heads out the door with Linus hanging on for dear life. Snoopy does everything to get the blanket away: he jumps on Linus, trips him, and pulls for all he is worth. Finally, battered and worn, Linus reappears at the door.

"Are you crazy?" says common-sense Lucy. "It's cold outside. You could catch pneumonia rolling around out there in the snow." To which Linus replies wearily, "The struggle for security knows no season."

UNFORTUNATE BELIEVER.   The Danish poet Jorgenson tells of a conversation between an atheist and a devout Christian.

"You are fortunate in being a believer," the atheist said.

"You are quite mistaken, sir. One is not at all fortunate when one is a believer. It is the greatest misfortune that can happen to you to become a Christian. You are fortunate who do not believe in anything. You can order your life as you please and at the same time keep your good conscience. We have received the gift of faith and the responsibility it entails, and it often weighs so heavily upon us that we nearly faint under it, as under the burden of a cross."—Elmer S. Freeman.

CAUSE AND CRAFT.   When Abraham Lincoln was killed, his body was taken to Springfield by way of the large cities in the East. Usually the funeral procession went from the railroad station to the city hall, where the body would lay in state and the people would come to express their sorrow and respect. As the hearse was moving slowly through the streets of New York City which were lined with thousands of people, a big, husky woodsman pressed forward through the crowd to see it. He jostled a few people and stepped on the feet of a man who cried out angrily, "Don't walk on my feet!" The big fellow was instantly apologetic and said, "Excuse me, sir, but I must see the coffin." "Why must you?" asked the man. "Two of my brothers died in the same cause he did," replied the woodsman sadly. "Besides," he said proudly, "he was one of my craft and I could never go back to the woods without seeing and blessing his coffin." The crowd parted and let him through.—Gerald Kennedy.

SUNDAY MEETING.   Edward Shillito tells of a group of young men who were looking for a time to call a meeting of a committee to plan a tennis tournament. The hour of eleven on Sunday morning was suggested, and all but one agreed.

"Sorry, but I can't make it. I'm going to church," he said.

A dead silence fell. Then one said, "Do people do such things still?"

Another added, "Perhaps you might tell us why you go to church."

"I go to look for God."

SUBMISSION AND COOPERATION. A man who loves violin music has the means to buy a very fine violin. He purchases the very finest radio obtainable and builds up a library of great musical scores. He is able to take any piece that is announced on the radio and put it on his music stand so that he can play along with the orchestra. The announcer says that the Philadelphia Orchestra is going to play Beethoven's Seventh Symphony. The man in his home puts that symphony on his stand and tunes his violin with what he hears coming from the orchestra.

The music that comes from the radio we might call foreordained. The orchestra is going to follow the score just as Beethoven wrote it. The man in his living room starts to scratch away at the first violin part. He misses beats, he loses his place and finds it again, he breaks a string and stops to fix it. The music goes on and on. He finds the place again and plays on, after his fashion, to the end of the symphony.

The announcer names the next work that is to be played, and the fiddler puts that score on his rack. He finds pleasure in scraping his fiddle along with the violins in the great orchestras. Their music is determined in advance. What he must do is to learn to play in their tempo and in their key. He must follow the score as it was written in advance. If he decides that he wants to play "Yankee Doodle" when the orchestra is in the midst of a Brahms number, there will be dissonance and discord in the man's house but not in the Academy of Music.

After some years of this, the man may turn out to be a creditable violin player. He may have learned to submit himself to the scores that are written and to follow the programs as played. Harmony and joy come from this submission and this cooperation.

The plan of God is rolling toward us, unfolding day by day, as he had planned it before the foundation of the world. The score of God's plan is set forth in the Bible. In the measure that I learn it, submit myself to it, and seek to live in accordance with all that is therein set forth, I shall find myself in joy and in harmony with God and his plans. Prayer is learning to play the same tune that the eternal plan of God calls for and to do that which is in harmony with the will of the eternal composer and the author of all that is of true harmony in life and living.—Donald Grey Barnhouse.

LIGHT AND DARKNESS. Gabriel Marcel spoke of his conversion to the Christian faith. "I can in no sense boast of having arrived," he said. "All I can say is that some parts of me have struggled up into the light, but much of me remains in the darkness." The sinner is he who persists and even rejoices in remaining in the darkness; the saint is he who gladly rejoices in the light of Christ and places himself daily, hourly, where that light can shine upon him and transfigure him.—W. B. J. Martin.

GOD'S PLENTY. A hospital chaplain tells of finding a patient who was completely discouraged. Spiritual dejection was added to physical weakness.

"I have no faith," the patient lamented.

"Even when you cannot have faith in God," the chaplain said, "remember that he has faith in you."

The patient looked up, startled. This was a new idea; it had a new force. It turned her around. Now instead of focusing on her lack, she was thinking of God's plenty.—Elmer S. Freeman.

THE CAVE PEOPLE. A group of people lived in a large cave. No one could recall how long they had lived there because their earliest memories were of the cave. Life in the cave was really not too bad. It was rather dark and it could be damp and uncomfortable, but it was secure. Each person in the cave knew that, when he awoke from sleep, the cave would still be there. If one could get used to the dampness and the darkness, living in the cave could be a tolerable experience. At least it was better than going out into the light.

The light was at one end of the cave, and if a person came near it, his eyes would burn and ache. The people concluded that whatever was beyond the light was dangerous and hostile. This was confirmed in their minds by the fact that the few people who over the years had ventured into the light had never returned.

Once a person came from the light, entered the cave, and invited people to leave the cave. He told them that at first the light would hurt their eyes and that the outside world was bigger and more complicated than the cave. He also told them they would be immediately tempted to return to the security of the cave. However, if they could live in the light for a while, they would find a world of beauty. They would find a world in which people were honest with their feelings and a world in which truth was valued. They would find a world in which people could love more fully because they could see themselves more clearly. Although this new world was bigger and more complicated, the people who lived in it would not trade it for the darkness of the cave, even though the cave was more secure.

So the man invited the cave people into this new world of light.

Some stayed in the darkness; some came into the light. The decision, in the final analysis, depended upon how much they wanted to find the real world.—Kent D. Moorehead.

THINGS OF VALUE. We have been taught that we ought not to put too much stock in things. Jesus said, "A man's life does not consist in the abundance of his possessions." By that he meant that a man's life should not be spent in the accumulation of washing machines, automobiles, and gadgets. Life means more than the acquisition of money. But things can be very precious to us and mean a great deal to us if they are the right things and if we think of them in the right way. That is because we cherish them not for the sake of the things themselves but for the spiritual values they hold for us.—Curtis Beach.

STONY PATH. "The road is too rough," I said. "Dear Lord, there are stones that hurt me so." And he said: "Dear child, I understand. I walked it long ago." "But there's a cool green path," I said. "Let me walk there for a time." "No, child," he gently assured me, "the green road does not climb." "My burden," I said, "is far too great. How can I bear it so?" "My child," said he, "I remember its weight. I carried my cross, you know." "But," I said, "I wish there were friends with me who would make my way their own." "Ah, yes," he said, "Gethsemane was hard to face alone." And so I climbed the stony path, content at last to know that, where my Master had not gone, I would not have to go. And strangely, then, I found new friends, the burden grew less sore as I remembered—long ago he went that way before.—Leona Bays Gater.

ABSOLUTES. A friend, who had spoken to a group of students in England on the claims of the Christian gospel, was questioned by one who objected violently to his defense of Christian absolutes.

"Everything," he said, "is relative. No absolutes whatever exist or could exist."

"Are you sure?" asked my friend.

"Yes! I'm sure!"

"Are you absolutely sure?"

Silence!

Most of us begin to realize that nothing can be relative unless there is some absolute over against which we can say it is relative and that mankind must have and will find absolutes to which we can be vitally related.—David H. C. Read.

HOLDING THE COLORS. A college boy named Jerome Davis with a regiment of Wisconsin infantry was under fire for the first time during the Civil War. The regiment was ordered to advance and hold a certain ridge. Davis, the color sergeant, later to become a Congregational missionary to Japan, marched as ordered until he gained the ridge. Crouching behind a stump, he looked back. The regiment wasn't there.

As he looked down the slope, Davis saw the ragged line wavering and threatening to break as bullets whined and men fell. But Sergeant Davis held his ground. In a few minutes an orderly came forward, crawling on his stomach. When he was near enough, he shouted, "Sergeant Davis, bring the colors back." Davis shouted his reply: "The colors are where they belong. Bring up the regiment." This they did and won the battle.—Harold Blake Walker.

HOMING INSTINCT.   Students of natural history know of the wonderful instinct of direction displayed by birds and beasts and fish. It's sometimes called the homing instinct. Cats and dogs often find their way back across wide stretches of unknown country. Pigeons fly directly to their homes hundreds of miles away. Swallows and other migrant birds take a confident aerial journey between destinations that are thousands of miles apart. Salmon return to spawn in the rivers of their birth. Young eels steer their way through a wide, heaving ocean to hereditary waters which they have never seen. Nothing in all nature is more wonderful than this amazing instinct of the lower creation for home.—Henry S. Date.

CASUAL OBSERVERS.   The White Star Lines' *Titanic* sailed from Southampton, England, one happy day. It was a luxury liner which was to put all others to shame. It was furnished exquisitely and was reported to be unsinkable.

Fanfare was the mood of the day when 2,223 people set sail. On board were the rich and the poor. About midnight on April 15, 1912, 1,600 miles northeast of New York City, the crew sighted an iceberg—the terror of navigation experts. However, this ship was not to fear icebergs. Nothing could sink it. It was 882.5 feet long and had a gross tonage of 46,328.

A great party was in progress as the iceberg was sighted. A plaque on the bar, not officially placed by the company but by some individual, read: "There is no God."

Buoyed by the strength of these thoughts, many people gathered on an upper deck at midnight to observe the iceberg. At the same time a compartment below struck the huge monster. The sound was heard and the shock was felt, but no one feared. They casually observed this monster which was eating away at that which held their lives in balance.

The ship began to list. Panic set in, and 1,517 people lost their lives in the icy waters of the North Atlantic. The ship *Carpathia* rescued 706 persons in lifeboats and from the water.

A neighboring ship sighted the flares sent up for help, but crewmen, under the assumption that no trouble could come to the ship, thought the flares were small rockets used in gala festivities. From a distance of a few miles, this other ship observed in the darkness what it considered to be a party but what became the greatest sea tragedy known to man at that time.—Merle A. Johnson, Jr.

INTOLERABLE CONDITIONS.   Henry Clay Dean, in the latter part of the last century, decided that he could no longer live in his home state. He wrote to a friend: "The black Republicans have come into power in Iowa: they enacted the nefarious prohibition law, there was hanging gone; now they are drifting into Universalism, and there is hell gone. I will not live in a state that does not believe in whiskey, hanging, and hell."

ROAD PATROL.   Suppose the good Samaritan came upon the wounded man and took him to the inn and cared for him. Then came the next day, and he found another man in the same condition and dealt with his wounds in the same way. Suppose that, on the next day and on the next, he met wounded travelers at the same place beside the same road and that he helped and cared for each of them. Suppose this went on for weeks. Would we not think that there was something deficient in his faith and love if he never thought to ask who was patrolling that road against bandits?—William Miller.

WORLD WITHOUT LOVE.   In J. D. Salinger's story, "A Perfect Day for Banana Fish," Seymour, the chief character, has had some kind of nervous breakdown while serving in the armed forces. When he returns to civilian life, he finds it difficult to adjust to reality. He lives with his wife, but his wife doesn't seem to understand him. At least this is the impression she gives to Seymour. He has no close friends, and even his relatives hold him at arm's length.

One day he wanders to the beach and meets a young girl. The girl accepts him, and while they search for banana fish, she admires his knowledge and his ability. Soon the girl has to go home, and Seymour has to return to the adult world. Suddenly he cannot face it. His wife is waiting for him, but somehow she isn't a wife any more—she is a stranger. So he quietly picks up a gun and kills himself.

There are no villains in this sad little story. Nobody persecutes Seymour. No one is trying to make his life miserable. His wife doesn't leave him, and as far as we know, she isn't a nagger. The tragedy of Seymour is simply that no one understands him and no one accepts him as he is. Seymour's world is a world without love, so he shoots himself.—W. C. Tupling.

LOVE LETTER.   A young girl had a very poor reputation in the orphanage where she lived. Nothing she did was right. Everything seemed calculated to annoy not only her teachers and supervisors but the other children as well. One day her roommate told the matron that she had seen Ruth place notes in the branches of a tree that stood in the yard. The matron was delighted, for here was her opportunity to be rid of the troublesome girl. She rushed out to the tree, found the note, and read it. Then she hung her head and silently passed the paper to her assistant. The girl had simply written: "To whoever finds this, I love you."—Theodor Reik.

LIGHTED CANDLES.   During the nineteenth century in England, it became quite commonplace for teenage boys to run away from the mill towns and go to sea. It was the only escape from the factory that seemed to present itself to these young persons, and they took the opportunity frequently and in great numbers. And it became something of a custom for their mothers to put lighted candles in the windows at night so that, if and when the boys came home, there would always be a shining symbol of welcome. In some mill towns, window after window would gleam into the night a mother's hope. And, of course, word of sea disasters would come occasionally, or rumors of battle, or reports of great storms. Often parents would not hear of their son for years and years but still light would burn bravely in spite of despair, in spite of doubt, in spite of all possibility that anything would ever come of this hope.—David A. Edman.

NOTHING.   A rabbi, a cantor, and a humble synagogue cleaner are preparing for the day of Atonement. The rabbi beat his breast and said: "I am nothing. I am nothing." The cantor beat his breast and said: "I am nothing. I am nothing." The cleaner beat his breast and said: "I am nothing. I am nothing." And the rabbi said to the cantor, "Look who thinks he's nothing."—Alan Paton.

AGONY.   I heard a man say: "I spent twenty years trying to come to terms with my doubts. Then one day it dawned on me that I had better come to terms with my faith. Now I have passed from the agony of questions I cannot answer into the agony of answers I cannot escape. And it's a great relief."—David Roberts.

REACTIONS.   Lord Byron and Sir Walter Scott were both lame. Byron was embittered by his lameness; he brooded on it until he loathed it; he never entered a public place but his mind reverted to it. He was so obsessed with it that much of the color and zest of existence were lost to him. Scott never complained or spoke one bitter word about his disability, not even to his dearest friends. It is not surprising that on one occasion Sir Walter should have received a letter from Byron with this sentence in it: "Ah, Scott, I would give all my fame to have your happiness."

WHY? Franz Kafka wrote a story, *The Trial*, that is really a parable, about a respectable banker, Joseph K, who one morning is arrested by mysterious persons for no apparent reason. This unreasonable event awakens Joseph K to ask for the first time in his life, "Why?"

The very raising of the question of meaning to life is the beginning to its answer. "As long as man struggles only with the problems of his everyday existence—food, work, health, and sex—he is not very much above the animals; he begins to be a man only when he starts to wonder what life is all about."

EXPERIENCE. George Fox grasped the idea that Christian experience could be couched in the present tense. He was able to arouse men and women in a remarkable way by the direct question: What canst thou say? He discovered the power which always emerges when men move over from speculation to experience and when they provide a verification of the reality of what they experience by the only evidence which is convincing—the evidence of changed lives.—Elton Trueblood.

PRIORITIES. A missionary was confronted by a very sick baby, held in his Indian mother's arms.

"This child is very, very ill," the missionary said, after a careful inspection, "but if you take him right now to the mission hospital ten miles away, they can probably save his life."

"But if I do that, who will take care of my buffalo?" asked the mother.

"Well," replied the missionary, "which is more important—your buffalo or your baby?"

"Oh, my buffalo, of course" was the unexpected reply. "I'll have another baby in a year or two anyway, but a new buffalo would cost 150 rupees and I never could afford that."—David M. Stowe.

PURPOSE. Paul Harrison, one of the great medical missionaries, chose Arabia for his work. It was one of the toughest spots he could choose, and he did it deliberately. Out of that experience came a great witness to Christ and the church.

As a young medical student at Harvard's Peter Bent Brigham Hospital, Harrison showed unusual brilliance. Dr. Harvey Cushing, head of the Department of Surgery, wrote to him and invited him to join his staff. This meant a chance to continue medical research with a great surgeon. Dr. Cushing had said to him, "You have it in you to go to the top." Harrison never hesitated. He wrote back: "Dear Dr. Cushing, I thank you for the great honor you have done me in inviting me to work under you. There is nothing I should like to do more if I were free. But years ago I determined to use my medical knowledge, such as it is, on a mission field. That is still my purpose."—Daniel Walker.

NUMBERING THE YEARS. We number our years from the birth of our Lord. The Jew numbers his years from the creation of the world according to Jewish tradition. The Roman numbered his years from the legendary founding of Rome by Romulus and Remus. On Roman buildings you find the initials A. U. C., followed by a date. The initials stand for *ab urbe condita*, "from the founding of the city." The Greek numbered his years from the first Olympic games. What the temple sacrifice was to the devout Jew, what the triumph of a victorious general was to the martial Roman, the Olympic games were to the sport-loving Greek.—Frank Halliday Ferris.

WORSHIP. Worship is the truest exercise in and expression of believing. The worship of God is that human activity which, above all else, moves away from the worshiper, beyond the worshiping community, even beyond humanity itself, to him. Is not formal worship, some ask, an irrelevant waste of time? Perhaps it can be so construed. For candles and flowers are as irrelevant as the song of birds, hymn and chant are as nonutilitarian as a lover's kiss, and prayers and litanies are just words—cheap as children's smiles. And yet that is the whole point of it—that we who are poor bring to God who lacks nothing that which costs us nothing to bring but which expresses to him our faith and devotion and, before the world, our dependence.—D. T. Niles.

SIGHT.   General William Booth, founder of the Salvation Army, when told that he was permanently blind, asked his son Bramwell, "You mean that I am blind?"

"I fear that we must contemplate that," his son answered.

"I shall never see your face again?" asked the general.

"No," said Bramwell, "probably not in this world."

"Bramwell," said the general, "I have done what I could for God and for the people with my eyes. Now I shall do what I can for God and for the people without my eyes."—Harold Begbie.

CASK OF SELF.   From the superintendent of the insane asylum in Ibsen's *Peer Gynt* comes this response to a question asked of him: "Besides themselves? Oh no, you're wrong. It's here that men are most themselves—themselves and nothing but themselves. Sailing with the outspread sails of self. Each shuts himself in a cask of self—the cask stopped with a bung of self and seasoned in a well of self. None has a tear for other's woes or cares what anyone thinks."

SONG.   Some years ago, E. Stanley Jones preached in Latin America at a public meeting sponsored by a Roman Catholic, a theosophist, and an atheist. In her introduction, the Roman Catholic lady said: "You may be surprised that this meeting is sponsored by such a diverse trio, but the reason is this: Stanley Jones has a song in his heart, and Latin America dearly loves music."

LIVING HIGH.   James A. Knight says that, when he was visiting in Bergen, Norway, the guide told him of a family who lived on a small farm located on the top of a mountain outside of Bergen. The rough country and the height made it impossible to use horses, and a two-hour walk was required to reach the farm on top of the mountain from the point where transportation stopped. But the family was independent. They made essentially everything they needed. The mother would sometimes knit as she climbed up and down the mountain. An American, after he had seen how hard this life was, asked the mother, "Does it pay to live here and put up with all of this?" She replied without a moment's hesitation, "Life itself is pay enough."

PILATE'S QUESTION.   It would be interesting to know the inflection of voice with which Pilate's question was uttered. Was it scorn, as Francis Bacon supposed in his comment: " 'What is truth?' said jesting Pilate and would not stay for an answer"? Or was it, as another interpreter has suggested, "the cynicism of a disillusioned man of the world"? Or was there in Pilate's voice at least an undertone of plaintive wondering and of wistful hope: "Is it possible that here, in this Jewish teacher of such majestic, commanding presence, there is light on life's central, unsolved enigma?" Or was there in Pilate's voice a self-contradictory combination of derision and wondering, of cynicism and hope with which the man of the world of every age, whether sophisticate or statesman, responds to this baffling enigma—to this man who is truth? Pilate uttered the world's poignant, ever-insistent, ever-thwarted question: "What is truth?" He puts it to One whom Christian faith declares not simply to know the truth but himself to be, in some profound, mysterious sense, the truth which sets men free. —Henry P. Van Dusen.

BEYOND THE HORIZON.   All of us have heard about William James and Henry James, two brilliant brothers, but what of their sister Alice? She could lay claim to prominence in her own right. An invalid from her eighteenth year to the year of her early death at forty, she knew all about handicaps, but you would never know that she had been bedridden as you read through her journal. Her biographer comments: "She never accepted the horizons of invalidism."—Francis B. Sayre, Jr.

WORDS.   The meaning of words is determined by the ideas behind them and a person's reaction to them. P.W. Bridgeman wrote, "The true meaning of a word is to be found by observing what a man does with it, not by what he says about it." The definition of a word is more than more words about a word. The value of a dollar bill is determined not by the words that are written on a bit of paper but on the integrity of the government behind it. If the government becomes irresponsible, the dollar bill is worthless. Words are empty if the ideas which have created them cease to be valid. They may become dangerous shibboleths.

All this is especially true and relevant in the area of religion. We make a great deal of the Book. Our religion is Bible centered. Our ethics, our language, and our theology all come out of the Book. The Bible is full of words; indeed, to be exact, it contains 773,692 words, but all too often the words are meaningless. We read them as Hamlet read when Polonius asked him, "What readest thou, my Lord?" And Hamlet replied, "Words, words, words." When you lose sight of the ideas behind the words, they become meaningless and a dangerous fetish.—Joseph R. Sizoo.

COURAGE REGAINED.   There was a period in Martin Luther's life when he was forced into retirement. In order to stay alive and continue the fight, he had to hide and stay quiet. But the idleness robbed him of his courage. "Would that we might live no longer," he wrote to his friend Melancthon. "Our God had deserted us." But a little later, when he could come out of hiding and throw himself into the center of the struggle again, his courage came back, and he wrote that mightly hymn of the Reformation: "A mightly fortress is our God, a bulwark never failing."

SOMETHING NEW.   When Emily Brontë was eight years old, her clergyman father took her for a walk out across the moors from their little village of Haworth. He tried to tell her of the wonders of creation and growth and asked, "What is here which was not here a hundred years ago?" And Emily answered, "Me."

BREACHED WALL.   The building of the great wall of China was a tremendous enterprise of gigantic proportions, involving the labor of hundreds of thousands of workers. It was the largest and strongest wall of history, a mightly safeguard against invasion. Yet it was breached three times by the enemy within a few years after its completion not because the wall itself gave away but because the gate-keepers were bribed.

PERMANENT GOOD.   Georges Clemenceau, as a young man, went to visit England. After he got back to France, he said that he had met two great men in England. One of them was an English parson, Samuel Barnett, who had become the warden of Toynbee Hall, the first settlement house in the East End of London. In her biography of her husband, his wife said of Barnett that all kinds of persons used to come down to the East End from London's West End with large blueprint plans for the redemption of those dreary slums, but they never really accomplished anything. She said that her husband concluded that the only permanent good ever done in East London was done by those who were willing to take time and trouble with individuals and that this conviction was his own rule of life.—Willard L. Sperry.

NO VISION.   The father of President Woodrow Wilson was a clergyman whose spiritual gifts and discernment were widely known. God made of him one of his choicest vessels. One day Dr. Wilson was in the company of some fellow pastors who were talking to one another somewhat glibly about their visions. He sat in troubled silence through it all. Finally, one of his colleagues made bold to ask him: "Dr. Wilson, haven't you had some great word from God? Haven't you experienced some ecstatic vision of God in Christ?" The beloved pastor let his eyes wander slowly around the circle from face to face, and then, settling his serene gaze on the countenance of the questioner, said: "No, none to speak of. None to speak of."—Frederick E. Reinartz.

LINCOLN. Millions there are who take him as a personal treasure. He had something they would like to see spread everywhere over the earth. We can't find words to say exactly what it was, but he had it. It's there in the light and shadow of his personality.—Carl Sandburg.

MEANS AND ENDS. An English bishop, preaching before a society made up of the country's top-ranking scientists, facetiously threw out the suggestion that it might not be a bad thing if all science lecture rooms and laboratories were closed for twenty years so that man's moral and spiritual development might have a chance to catch up with his scientific knowledge. By the very suggestion he brought down on himself an avalanche of ridicule and abuse. He must have known in advance what would happen. I suppose he said what he did not with any expectation that his proposal would be acted upon but to secure publicity for a perfectly sound contention, namely, that ingenuity about means must be matched by wisdom about ends, that moral sense should not lag behind technical skill, and that for every advance in man's scientific knowledge there ought to be a corresponding advance in his moral character.—James McCracken.

DEAD ISSUE. Henry Ward Beecher was on a walk with his dog when a woodchuck ran across the road and down a hole. The dog dashed over to the hole and barked madly. Every time they went down the road afterwards, the dog ran to the hole and barked. He did not realize it was now a dead issue.

INDEX OF CONTRIBUTORS

SERMON TITLE INDEX

(Children's stories and sermons are identified cs; sermon suggestions ss)

SCRIPTURAL INDEX

INDEX OF PRAYERS

INDEX OF MATERIALS USEFUL AS CHILDREN'S STORIES
AND SERMONS NOT INCLUDED IN SECTION VIII

INDEX OF MATERIALS USEFUL FOR SMALL GROUPS

INDEX OF SPECIAL DAYS AND SEASONS

TOPICAL INDEX